LEADERSHIP & MANAGEMENT
IN THE IRISH HEALTH SERVICE

D1348051

LEADERSHIP & MANAGEMENT IN THE IRISH HEALTH SERVICE

Edited by Anne-Marie Brady

Gill & Macmillan

Gill & Macmillan Ltd
Hume Avenue
Park West
Dublin 12
with associated companies throughout the world
www.gillmacmillan.ie

© Anne-Marie Brady 2010
978 07171 46130

Index compiled by Cover to Cover
Print origination in Ireland by O'K Graphic Design, Dublin
Printed by GraphyCems, Spain

The paper used in this book is made from the wood pulp of managed forests. For every tree felled, at least one tree is planted, thereby renewing natural resources.

A CIP catalogue record for this book is available from the British Library.

For permission to reproduce copyright material the publishers gratefully acknowledge the following:

Becoming a Master Manager: A Competing Values Approach, 4th Edition by Robert E. Quinn *et al.* © 2007. Reproduced with permission of John Wiley & Sons, Inc.; *Organizational Culture and Leadership: A Dynamic View* by Edgar H. Schein © 1985. Reproduced with permission of John Wiley & Sons Inc.; *Exploring Corporate Strategy: Text and Cases, 8th Edition*, Gerry Johnson, Kevan Scholes and Richard Whittington, Financial Times/Prentice Hall. Reproduced with permission of Pearson Education © 2008; *The Character of a Corporation, 2nd Edition* by Rob Goffee & Garreth Jones. Reproduced with permission of Profile Books © 2003; 'The knowledge, skill and ability requirements for teamwork: Implications for human resource management' by Michael J. Stevens & Michael A. Campion (1994) *Journal of Management* 20(2), 503–530. Reproduced with permission of Sage Publications © 1994.

The publisher has made every effort to trace all copyright holders, but if any have been inadvertently overlooked we would be pleased to make the necessary arrangement at the first opportunity.

Contents

Contributors

EDITOR AND CONTRIBUTING AUTHOR

Anne-Marie Brady BSN MS PGDipCHSE PGDipStats RGN RNT

Anne-Marie Brady has been involved in undergraduate and postgraduate education since 2000 and has been employed as lecturer in Trinity College Dublin since 2002. She completed a Masters in Nursing at Northeastern University Boston, Massachusetts in 1999, a Postgraduate Diploma in Clinical Health Sciences Education in 2001 and a Postgraduate Diploma in Statistics in 2009. Her particular area of research and teaching interest is health care leadership and management. She has considerable international nursing experience, having worked in the United Kingdom, the United States of America and the Irish Republic, and has developed a unique understanding of the importance of leadership and management skills in health service employees. She is near completion of a PhD and is currently a Health Research Board Fellow in the area of health services management.

CONTRIBUTING AUTHORS

Dr Michelle Butler MSc PhD RGN RM

Michelle Butler has been involved in teaching and research in health services management for a number of years. Her research interests include the professional development of midwifery, midwifery competence and education, health care policy and planning, health service management, research methodology, assessment and evaluation. She has published extensively in the field of health care management in Ireland.

Anne Carrigy MSc RGN

Anne Carrigy has recently taken up the post of National Director of Serious Incidents at the HSE. She was previously Director of Nursing and Head of Corporate Affairs. Elected to An Bord Altranais by the nursing profession in October 2002, she was subsequently elected President by the Board in January 2003. She has been a member of the Medical Council since 2007 and was appointed to the Implementation Steering Group for the Commission on Patient Safety in 2009.

Dr Elizabeth Curtis MEd PhD RGN

Elizabeth Curtis is a lecturer in nursing in the School of Nursing and Midwifery, Trinity College Dublin. She received her PhD and MEd degrees from the School of Education, Trinity College. She has taught management and research methods to both undergraduate and postgraduate students for a number of years and has developed several MSc nursing programmes. She has many years' experience in supervising postgraduate student research projects in a number of disciplines, including education. Her research interests are diverse and include health service management – particularly in the areas of job satisfaction, leadership, change management – and neurosciences nursing. She is currently engaged in a number of research projects, including a study on job satisfaction among public health nurses.

Breda Doyle MSc HDipQuality RGN

Breda Doyle qualified as a Registered General Nurse in 1994, specialising in nursing in spinal cord injuries. She undertook the Diploma in Health Services Management in 1998, a Higher Diploma in Quality and Healthcare in 2005 and completed an MSc in Quality and Safety in 2008. She has been working as Quality and Accreditation Manager at the Mater Misericordiae University Hospital since 2003. She is currently working as project co-lead on the Patient Safety Commission Implementation Project Team in the Department of Health and Children.

Sandra Fleming MSc RGN RPN RMHN RNT

Sandra Fleming has been involved in nurse education since 1988. She was awarded an MSc in Education and Training Management from Dublin City University in 1998 and has been employed as a lecturer in nursing in the School of Nursing and Midwifery, Trinity College Dublin since January 2001. She has extensive experience in developing and teaching undergraduate and postgraduate nurse education programmes. She lectures in her research interest areas: intellectual disability nursing, curriculum design and development and the theory and practice of clinical health science education.

Phil Halligan BNS MSc RGN RNT FFNRCSI

Phil Halligan is currently a lecturer in the School of Nursing and Midwifery and Health Systems, University College Dublin. She lectures in health service management, leadership and quality improvement and is responsible for curriculum development in this area at undergraduate and postgraduate level. She is Director of the MSc in Applied Health Management and MSc in Nursing and involved in research relating to this area. She has extensive experience overseas and in Ireland and is currently pursuing a PhD in the area of leadership in clinical practice.

Eilísh Hardiman BSc MBA PGDipN RGN

Eilísh Hardiman is the CEO of the project to design and build the new children's hospital. She was previously Deputy CEO/Operations Manager of St James's Hospital, the largest academic teaching hospital in Ireland. She has over 15 years of experience in health care management and has been awarded an MBA from the Smurfit School of Business, University College Dublin. She is working at the forefront of health care in Ireland and is able to offer a unique perspective on leading change.

Paula Hicks MSc

Paula Hicks is currently employed as a researcher and project manager in the Centre for Health Informatics at Trinity College Dublin. She has for a number of years been involved in teaching health informatics at undergraduate and postgraduate levels to a range of health care and computer technology professionals. She has also been involved in a number of health informatics projects. The current focus of her research is developing virtual communities for children in hospital, and the culmination of this work has led to two key developments: Áit Eile (Another World), which provides a range of services for hospitalised children; and Solas, a more customised system for young people with cancer. In recent years she has contributed to the development of a health informatics curriculum for health care professionals and has published in this area.

Marie Kehoe BScN MScN RGN CPHQ

Marie Kehoe is currently employed as the Area General Manager, Quality and Risk for the HSE South and has the lead for the Quality Function in the national Office of Quality and Risk. She worked for 18 years in the United States, initially as a staff nurse on a medical-surgical unit and then moving into the field of quality improvement. She returned to Ireland and joined the HSE in 2002. Marie holds a BSc in Nursing and a MScN degree specialising in Community Health. Marie is also qualified as a Certified Professional in Healthcare Quality (CPHQ). She is Past President of the Irish Society for Quality and Safety in Healthcare (ISQSH). While in the States, Marie worked extensively in the development and implementation of integrated care pathways (ICPs) and has founded a network for individuals who are in the process of working with ICPs in Ireland – the Irish Care Pathway Network (ICPN), which has gained over 70 members since its inception in late 2006.

Anne-Marie Malone BSc MBA RGN RSCN RMN RNT

Anne-Marie Malone is a lecturer in nursing in the School of Nursing and Midwifery, Trinity College Dublin. She trained in general and children's nursing as well as midwifery prior to gaining clinical experience nationally and internationally. She has been teaching general nursing since 1995. Her research interests are in the areas of nursing and health service management. She is involved in developing and teaching courses on health care management at both graduate and undergraduate levels.

Dr Catherine Mc Cabe BSc MSc PhD RGN RNT

Catherine Mc Cabe has been involved in developing and teaching undergraduate and postgraduate nursing programmes since 1996 following completion of a BSc in Nursing Studies at University College Dublin. In January 2001 she was awarded an MSc in Nursing by the University of Manchester and in February 2002 joined Trinity College Dublin's School of Nursing and Midwifery as a lecturer. In 2009 she completed her PhD and is currently the Director of Teaching and Learning (Undergraduate) at the School of Nursing and Midwifery, Trinity College Dublin.

Her particular area of interest is communication and its role in delivering high-quality patient care, professional growth and developing health care services in a collaborative and transformational way. She has published widely on this topic in nursing.

Sharon Morrow BSc (Hons) MBA RGN

Sharon Morrow is Business Manager of SAMs directorate in St James's Hospital, Dublin, the largest academic teaching hospital in Ireland. She undertook an MBA at the Smurfit School of Business, University College Dublin and is currently pursuing an MSc in Medical Ethics and Law. She lectures in financial management in health care at both undergraduate and postgraduate levels.

Sile O'Donnell BA MBS(HRM) FCIPD

Sile O'Donnell is employed as Assistant National Director of Human Resources (Organisation Design and Development) in the Health Service Executive in Ireland. She has published in the area of health service management and HRM and also lectures in HRM at the Smurfit School of Business, University College Dublin. She has developed a unique and informed perspective on the area of health resource management and is working at the forefront of the transformation process in the HSE.

Acknowledgments

I would like to take this opportunity to thank all of the contributors to the book for their commitment and efforts in making this book a reality. I would like to thank Harry and my children, Sarah, Luke, Ella and Mia, for their patience during the months of preparation. I would also to thank my friend Susanna for her immense practical and caring support in recent years. Finally, I would also like to thank my Mum, Mary, for her consistent interest and pride in whatever I pursue.

Anne-Marie Brady

Introduction

nternationally, governments are concerned with efficiency and effectiveness within the health services. The provision of health care is a critical issue for most countries due to changing demographical profiles and consumer expectations in a time of unprecedented advancement and proliferation of medical technology. Developments in the Irish health services have focused the attention of health care policy makers on the issues of clinical leadership and management. Recent health policy reports such as the 2001 health care strategy (DoHC 2001), *Action Plan for People Management* (DoHC 2002) and the Health Service Executive's *Transformation Programme 2007–2010* (HSE 2007) have emphasised the importance of strength in this area and have influenced the inclusion of a leadership and management component in all undergraduate and postgraduate health professional courses in Ireland.

The Irish health care system is complex and largely influenced by the historical events that have shaped its development. Disproportionate attention has been placed on the acute sector, with the result that continuing care and community services are not sufficiently developed to effectively respond to the demand for service. The Irish health service is facing challenging times as the reform agenda gathers momentum (DoHC 2003). A core function of professional work in health care is co-ordination of care, so developing leadership and management skills in practice that can respond to the requirements for patient-centred care is essential. Professionals who work in the health service are required to understand the context of change and to develop the necessary skills to respond effectively to the change process.

The impetus for this book comes from the experience of teaching undergraduate and postgraduate health professional students and the realisation of the need for a comprehensive textbook on healthcare leadership and management that is informed by the unique elements of the Irish health service. The book attempts to provide a broad overview of the issues in Irish health care management. It aims to provide a practical understanding of the service, examines the major activity areas of health care management and reviews some of the contemporary developments in this area. It is designed to provide an in-depth and analytical understanding of the health services and health policy in Ireland. This book draws extensively on national and international literature in health care management. The contributors have been selected for their particular expertise and experience of both leadership and management delivery/education in the Irish health service.

The book is presented in four sections that are designed to guide the reader to reach an understanding of the context and the key leadership and management issues of the health system in which they work. It is anticipated that the material will assist the reader in developing the skills to make an effective contribution to the management function of the health service.

Part One: The Health Care Environment

It is important for health care professionals to understand the context of the health care system in which they work, so Chapter 1 provides an overview of the structure, functioning and governance of Irish health care system, in addition to highlighting some contemporary debates around health service provision. Chapter 2 considers the policy and economic forces that impact on health care staff in their everyday work and seeks to illustrate how care delivery decisions are impacted on by the policy and economic developments in the health system at large.

Part Two: Fundamentals of Service Provision

The concept of leadership and effective management, and its potential to inspire the delivery of high-quality care, is explored in Chapter 3, which provides a comprehensive insight into some contemporary theories in this area and how they may apply to working in Irish health care. The historical, political and social influences on the organisational culture of health care are considered in Chapter 4. Delegation has become an critical component of health care professional work in modern health systems and Chapter 5 seeks to get to grips with the fundamentals of safely providing care through others. Financial management is examined in Chapter 6, with an effort to evaluate how health care professionals can contribute to enhancing budgetary performance. Human resource policies and personnel management are discussed in Chapter 7.

Part Three: Developing Professionals in the Health Service

Suitably motivated individuals using effective communication skills working in teams are key components in the day-to-day provision of a high-quality health service. Concepts of motivation, communication, conflict resolution and teamwork are all considered in the three chapters in this section.

Part Four: Developing the Health Service

The final section of the book is devoted to the broader issues associated with the development of the Irish health service. Strategies to overcome resistance and lead change are discussed in Chapter 11. A variety of quality improvement initiatives in health care are considered in Chapter 12: one in particular – care pathways – is given detailed attention in Chapter 13. Finally, Chapter 14 provides a comprehensive overview of the world of informatics in modern health care and an insight into key developments in this area in the Irish health service.

In addition to the traditional text, chapter objectives, summary and references, a series of **reflective questions** are included at the end of each chapter to prompt further discussion in both the classroom and the work setting. **Case studies** are employed where appropriate to enable the reader to engage with the content of the text from a service provider/user perspective. Each chapter directs the reader to **additional sources of information**, such as further reading, professional organisations and online resources.

The primary readership for this textbook is postgraduate students undertaking third-level health services courses in the Irish Republic. The book should be of interest to all students undertaking health service degrees and courses in which clinical leadership is an element of professional performance. It should also benefit undergraduate health service students whose education programmes include leadership and management-related requirements. It will be of interest to all students undertaking health service professional degrees who wish to understand the health service that will shape their future careers, and it will appeal to health care managers with an interest in current leadership and management issues in health care.

REFERENCES

DoHC (Department of Health and Children) (2001), *Quality and Fairness: A Health System for You*. Dublin: Stationery Office.
— (2002), *Action Plan for People Management*. Dublin: Stationery Office.
— (2003), *Health Service Reform Programme*. Dublin: Stationery Office.
HSE (Health Service Executive) (2007) *Transformation Programme 2007–2010*. Available at http://www.hse.ie/eng/Publications/corporate/ transformation. html, accessed 1 October 2009.

The Health Care Environment

1
Structure of the Irish Health Service

Anne-Marie Brady & Sile O'Donnell

OBJECTIVES
- To provide a brief comparative analysis of health systems structures within other jurisdictions.
- To provide a broad overview of the role and structures of government and relevant departments in relation to health care.
- To provide a broad overview of the structure of the Irish health sector and the interrelationships between the main bodies and agencies.
- To provide a brief outline of the governance arrangements within the main health sector organisations.
- To provide an outline of key developments in relation to the ongoing restructuring of the health services.

INTRODUCTION

In many OECD countries the public sector assumes a dominant role in the structure and financing of health care, and determining an appropriate level of spending on health is an ongoing dilemma for governments. There are similarities across the OECD in relation to difficulties in ensuring access to health care and value for money; however, the challenges are manifested differently. In Ireland, health is heavily funded by the state and, as in other countries, there is a constant tension between the desire to provide a first world health system and the need to restrain costs and manage resources. Internationally, the provision of health care is an important political issue as countries respond to demographic changes, transformed consumer expectation and the proliferation in recent years of medical technology and capacity. The expectations of consumer organisations and individuals can conflict with attempts by government to change structures or limit medical expenditure in the interest of community need. The population of Ireland is 4,239,848 and it is estimated to rise to 4,900,000 by 2025 (DoHC 2007). Ireland's total fertility rate (a measure of the average number of children per woman) is, at 1.88, currently the second highest in Europe, the European average being 1.44 (OECD 2009). Therefore Ireland currently has a very young population and a significant increase in the ratio of older persons in the population is projected in the coming decades.

There are significant differences between countries as to how health care is funded, structured and delivered, and considerable differences in the percentage of gross domestic product (GDP) devoted to health care. The critical structural difficulties faced by the Irish health service are a number of decades in the making, with an over-reliance on acute services, under-investment in community care and infrastructure contributing to fragmentation of care and inappropriate usage of acute services. These issues are all considered in this chapter, which seeks to illuminate the structure and governance of the Irish health service.

TYPES OF HEALTH CARE

In examining the structure of the Irish health system it is necessary to consider the types of health care that are provided in any health system.

Primary care: normally community based, primary care usually represents the first point of contact or access for individuals to health service providers. This type of care encompasses a wide range of health professionals including general practitioners, nurses, midwives, dentists, pharmacists, physiotherapists, occupational therapists and social workers. Primary care includes a myriad of activities: individual needs may include medical assessment, diagnosis, therapy, nursing, midwifery, health education, counselling and social services.

Secondary or tertiary care is focused on acute care services, maternity and specialist services and is primarily hospital based.

Chronic care involves all the ongoing care provided in long-term residential settings and homes. In the Irish health care structure, it encompasses social and continuing health care, for example day and long-term residential care services for care groups such as intellectual disability, psychiatry and older persons.

HEALTH SYSTEMS – AN OVERVIEW

There are a variety of health systems approaches. The organisational structure of a health system will, in the main, be determined by the funding structure that underpins it. This can create challenges, for example where the creation of an integrated primary care service structure to deliver multi-faceted services to patients and service users is developed within a care group-funded structure. Health care systems can be classified according to their funding arrangements, and they may lie anywhere on a continuum from free market with little or no government input to a government monopoly system funded by taxation (Blank & Burau 2004). Along this continuum are three models that represent aspects of health service provision in many countries.

Private insurance model: This system is defined by the absence of state involvement in the provision of service. It is derived from the assumption that the funding and provision of care is better left to market forces and is best represented by the United States and Switzerland, which are primarily private insurance models. Private health insurance is also significant in Germany and duplicates the universal access public provision in Australia, Italy, Spain and Ireland.

Social insurance model: The organisation of this model varies considerably across countries and may include social or state insurance. It is usually defined by universal coverage enabled through health insurance funded by a combination of individual and government contributions. Examples are Germany, the Netherlands and Japan.

National health service: This model is defined by universal coverage funded by general taxation, best represented by the United Kingdom and New Zealand. It is often free at the point of use. It is reliant on budget finance and draws upon a number of salaried and private contractors to provide services. This system is good for ensuring access but can weakly incentivise improvements in efficiency.

All the systems described above may include elements of direct payment or co-payments by the user.

Figure 1.1: Types of health system by provision and funding

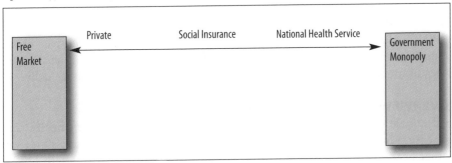

Source: Blank & Burau (2004)

DEVELOPMENT OF THE IRISH SYSTEM

The Irish health care system has developed in an ad hoc fashion over the last decades and is somewhat difficult to categorise as it is a mixed system of funding and provision structures. The system is an eclectic mix of elements of the private and the national health service models described above. Services are delivered through a combination of private, public and voluntary organisations and the system has been criticised for being fragmented.

The framework for the structure, governance and finance of the Irish health system is defined by a series of Health Acts 1947, 1970 and 2004. Before 1 January 2005, health care was governed, organised and delivered through the regional health boards, which were in the main organised and structured according to population size. The initial structure, laid down in the Health Act of 1970, formed the basis for the eight health boards and gave centralised responsibility for the running of the health services to the Department of Health. As the population of the east of the country grew, due to decreasing emigration and increasing migration from the rest of the country, the Eastern Health Board was renamed East Regional Health Authority (ERHA), which comprised three separate regions. (The current structure has been influenced by the local politics of the old health board arrangements.) Access to services was determined by income, with a portion of the population deemed eligible for GP, hospital and prescription services that were free at point of service. GP services for eligible individuals was administered through the General Medical Scheme (GMS), which provided a capitation system for the provision of GP services to those citizens below a certain income threshold. The remainder of the population had to pay for GP and prescription services.

Under the health board system, services in Ireland were delivered through a complex set of organisations that spanned the statutory and voluntary sectors. The major criticism levelled at the health boards was related to their persistent budgetary over-runs and the negative effect of local politics on integrated health planning and appropriate resource usage. The Brennan (DoHC 2003a) and Prospectus (DoHC 2003b) reports identified the lack of accountability and fragmentation within the structures of the Irish health system. The Health Service Reform Programme (DoHC 2003c) and the Health Act (Government of Ireland 2004) heralded a major reorganisation of the structure of health care delivery in Ireland; and, indeed, the system has undergone significant change in recent years, in particular with the establishment of the Health Service Executive (HSE). Ongoing reforms recently announced are focused on reorganising health care organisational structures to achieve a more integrated model of service delivery.

OVERVIEW OF THE IRISH HEALTH SYSTEM

All OECD countries have some element of public finance in their health care provision but the Irish health care system has features which distinguish it from other health care systems. In a study of the Irish 'health basket', Smith (2009) explains that the structures that define entitlement in this country are complex and that the cost of access to primary care is higher than in other systems. It is estimated that 29 per cent of the population have medical cards and a further 75,589 people have GP visit cards (HSE 2007a). The Irish health system determines entitlement according to income: two main category classifications are used (see Table 1.1). The acute care sector is heavily funded by general taxation, as is Category I medical card provision. The system has been classified as a universal access and a socialised model, due to its provision of health care free at point of service to Category I (medical card) patents. As of 1 January 2009 the automatic entitlement to a medical card for the over-70s has been substituted with a means test system.

Table 1.1: Entitlement/access to care

Access to health care	Category I	Category II
GP care	100%	0
Prescriptions	100%	Excess above €120 per month
Public hospital in-patient	100%	€75 per night up to maximum €750 per annum
Public hospital outpatient	100%	100%
A&E attendance (referred by GP)	100%	100%

In the Irish health system, access to primary care services is, for the majority of people, determined by ability to pay (a notable exception being public health nurse (PHN) services) and is reliant on out-of-pocket payment for GP visits privately and co-payment of up to a €100 per month for drugs under the Drugs Payment Scheme. The potential avenue to access health care by bypassing the GP system and attending A&E directly is obstructed by the statutory requirement to pay a €100 attendance charge in the event of self-referral. This charge does not apply if the patient has a letter of referral from a general practitioner. Out-of-pocket charges also apply to in-patient stays; Irish Category II patients pay €75 per night to an annual maximum of €750. A unique element of Irish health care, and one that contrasts greatly with other countries, is the mix of private and public patients within publicly funded organisations receiving different standards of care. Ireland does provide universal access to specialist services, as hospital outpatient visits are free at point of service. However, this service may be provided by a non-consultant hospital doctor in training and therefore the standard of care can differ considerably from that enjoyed by patients who are able to attend privately.

The percentage of Irish citizens who feel it necessary to supplement or duplicate the universal access supposedly already provided in the public sector is of interest, and it is estimated that 50 per cent of the Irish adult population have private health insurance. In some way it could be said that the country already operates a social insurance model, given the percentage of the population who deem it necessary to pay for duplicate cover for acute services. The structures that have evolved and underpin the system conspire to favour private patients over public and there has been considerable objection to the propensity of the system to advantage one over the other. Two waiting lists are in operation within public hospitals, with the result that private patients can access specialist care and services ahead of those most in need (Burke 2009; Wren 2003; Tussing & Wren 2006). Health expenses over €125 per annum are, with some exceptions, eligible for tax relief at the marginal rate of 20 per cent.

It is broadly understood that all OECD countries, with the exception of Mexico, Turkey and the United States, have achieved universal or near-universal health coverage (Docteur & Oxley 2003). In Ireland a large percentage (estimated to be about 78 per cent) of health expenditure comes from central government and the system has been described as a universal access system. Indeed, the structure of the system provides free acute and primary care service at point of access to Category I medical card holders. The majority of the population (approximately 70 per cent) who are described as Category II are also entitled to free access at point of service to specialist care in the acute sector. In contrast, access to primary care through GP services is determined by ability to pay: therefore the Irish system is not a complete system of universal access. As Ireland operates a gatekeeper structure, in which referral from a GP is required for access to specialist care in the acute sector, it follows that even access to specialist services is to some extent determined by ability to pay. A patient may access specialist services through the A&E system, but they will be required to pay €100 at point of service unless they have paid and received referral from a GP.

The public health service employs 111,062 people in total and comprises a complex set of organisational and professional structure, which would require considerable analysis. For the purposes of this book, two professions will be briefly considered: the medical and nursing professions.

Ireland has a lower number of physicians per capita than most European countries.There are fewer physicians in Ireland than in other OECD countries: Ireland has 3.03 per 1,000, compared to an OECD average of 3.1; and there are reports of fewer specialists in certain areas.

Figure 1.2: Practising physicians: density per 1,000 population (2007)

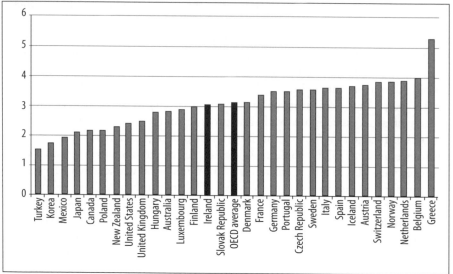

Source: OECD (2009)

The number of consultants in the country has increased but is falling short of demand, a result in some part of the process of cost containment since 2004. Prior to the establishment of the HSE the appointment of hospital consultants was determined by Comhairle na nOspidéal, an organisation upon which consultants had a majority representation (Burke 2009), and there was evidence of inadequate numbers even prior to 2004. The ESRI (2009) report on the impact of demographic change on the demand for and delivery of health care in Ireland suggests that a significant increase in the number of doctors will be needed to meet the growing demands of the Irish population. Access to specialist care can be obstructed due to a shortage of consultants in specialities such as neurology, rheumatology and dermatology.

The unique elements of the Irish consultant's contract enabled individuals to operate as salaried employees in the public service and also charge 'fee for service' for private work. The defining characteristic of consultant-led care in the Irish health structure is its reliance on junior doctors (who have varying levels of competence and experience, depending on their stage of education) to work long hours. The consultant contract in Ireland has been criticised for the relatively short number of hours that constitute the public commitment, enabling the individual to exercise their own discretion and judgment as to how much, if any, of their contracted hours are spent delivering care to public patients. While the system does result in adequate remuneration for individual junior doctors who work long hours, it does mean that there is a considerable overtime wages burden on the Irish taxpayer, which in terms of quality of patient outcomes does not always represent the best value for money.

There has been considerable comment in the Irish health literature of how the system incentivises consultants and organisations to favour private patients in terms of access and level of quality in service delivery. Burke (2009) argues strongly that there is apartheid in Irish health care and advances the argument that this two-tier system has been an insidious and habitual element of Irish health policy in recent decades. The Hanly Report (DoHC 2003d) sought to limit the practice of consultant-led care where care is delivered across a number of smaller hospitals by junior doctors at different stages in their training. The European Working Time Directive (DoHC 2004) has been a driving force in the move to increase the number and availability of consultants working in the public service. Traditionally only a small number of Irish consultants worked exclusively with public patients and they were usually found in specialities such as paediatrics, gerontology and psychiatry, where opportunities and incentivisation to operate a two-tier system are of course, while by no means absent, not as prevalent.

The recent increase in the consultant remuneration package has been referred to in some sectors as a 'sweetheart deal'. The purpose of the renegotiated contract is apparently to afford greater access to consultant-delivered care and improve access to specialist care. At the time of writing it is not clear if the new contract will deliver on the consultant-delivered care desired in the public health service. It is questionable whether the recently negotiated remuneration rates are sustainable and it remains to be seen how effective plans to limit the amount of private activity undertaken will be, given that it is such a well-established custom and practice in the Irish health service. Wren (2004) argued that more modest salary levels would enable the recruitment of more specialists. Indeed, basic economics would suggest that limiting the monopoly that underpins specialist care could also enable a reduction in salary costs. Under the terms of the renegotiated contract the HSE is making some effort to police the cap of 20 per cent of time spent with private patients. There is some scepticism as to how effective we have been to date in monitoring the 80/20 mix in care delivery which had always been an inherent element of the contract prior to renegotiations. It remains to be seen what nature of sanction will be possible if a consultant should be found to be non-compliant with the cap. Burke argues that the revised consultant contract continues to incentivise private work within the public system and that it 'reinforces rather than deconstructs the two-tier system of care' (Burke 2009:17). Indeed, increasing the number of consultant posts may enhance career pathway and expectations for indigenous Irish-educated doctors and may disincentivise these groups from patterns of emigration seen thus far. This may provide better value for taxpayer investment in the education of doctors and provide the culturally attuned medical workforce desired by the public.

Figure 1.3: Practising nurses: density per 1,000 population (2007)

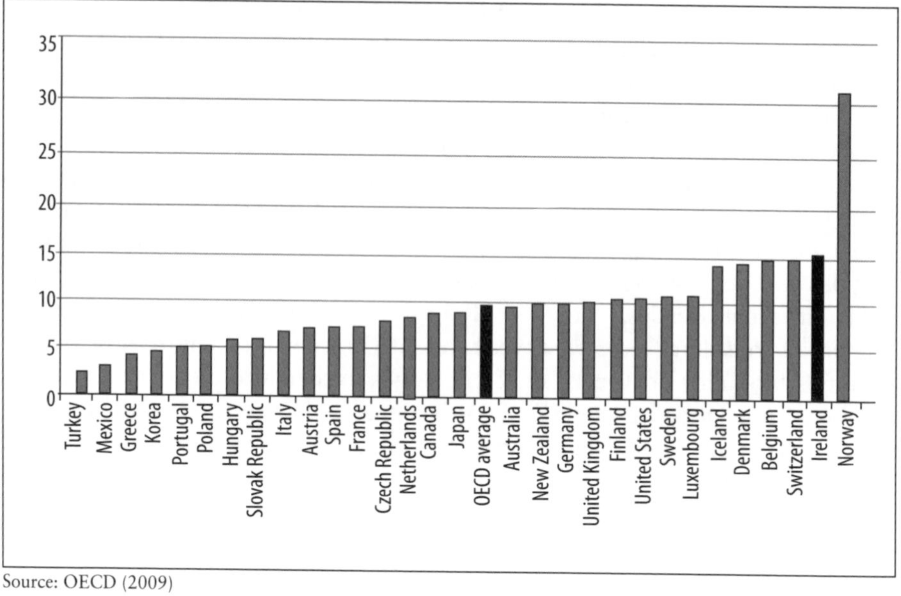

Source: OECD (2009)

The number of practising nurses in 2007 was 15.5 per 1,000, a proportion significantly higher than the OECD average of 9.56 (see Figure 1.3).

However, efforts to ensure comparability across OECD countries have limitations. Variations in skill mix and the low proportion of assistive personnel in the service are not taken into account. The numbers recorded in some countries may reflect whole-time equivalents rather than head counts registered (as recorded by An Bord Altranais). Many of the countries to which Ireland is compared in terms of numbers of nurses operate generic education courses, where numbers working in the various disciplines of psychiatry, general, learning disability are not recorded as they are here. Many Irish nurses are recorded on more than one part of the register, and in some countries midwives are not counted in nursing numbers. The numbers do not reflect whole-time equivalents engaged in the system and in Ireland up to 40 per cent of Irish nurses are working part-time. Therefore this relatively high nurse density may not be regarded as a full picture of the number of Irish nurses engaged in the health system.

HEALTH – THE BLACK HOLE

There is a negative public perception of Irish health care services (Burke 2009) and negative commentary in relation to health was even evidenced with an off-the-cuff remark of one prominent politician describing the Department of Health as 'Angola'. Politically health is viewed as a poisoned chalice in some sectors, and sometimes described as a 'black hole'(Wren 2004). The Euro Health Consumer

Index (EHCI) findings (Health Consumer Powerhouse 2009) suggest a 'domestic marketing problem in Ireland'. Even though Ireland has moved up two places in the EHCI since 2008 and now ranks 13th out of 33 European countries, the findings of the patient organisation survey give a less positive picture than the official data (Health Consumer Powerhouse 2009). The Netherlands was the best performing country, with a total score of 875 out of a possible 1,000 points, followed by Denmark (819) and Iceland (811). Ireland generally performed well, with a score of 711, ahead of the United Kingdom and Italy; however, it scored poorly in the area of e-health. Ireland scored top marks in four of seven health outcome measures: infant deaths per 1,000; cancer five-year survival; preventable years of life lost per 100,000 in the 0–69 age group; and percentage of diabetic population of patients with HbA1c (the amount of glycated haemoglobin in your blood) levels above seven.

There is undoubtedly a public relations issue in relation to trust in the health service, no doubt fuelled by the myriad of scandals in relation to standards of care in recent years. Wren (2004) rejects the interpretation of Irish health spending as a 'black hole', arguing that Ireland's expenditure on health in the early 2000s could not deliver the anticipated outcomes, given the level of capital deficiencies that had been the norm in previous years. There has indeed been a marked increase in capital spending on health care; however, it must be examined in the context of the underspend that occurred from the 1970s to the 1990s. The effect of reduced spending on health, particularly through the 1980s and in the early 1990s, is still felt in Ireland at a time when other OECD countries are increasing their spending on health (Wren 2004).

Health spending
Total health spending accounted for 7.6 per cent of gross domestic product (GDP), lower than the OECD average of 8.9 (see Figure 1.4).

Figure 1.4: Health expenditure as % of GDP (2007)

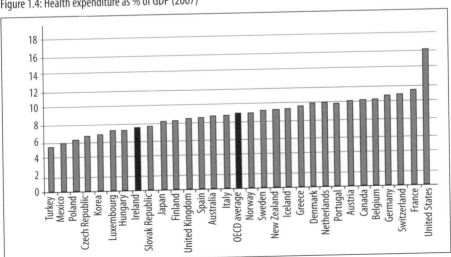

Source: OECD (2009)

The USA spends the most on health, with 16 per cent of GDP allocated to health, followed by France (11 per cent) and Switzerland (10.8 per cent). Germany, Belgium and Austria also devoted in excess of 10 per cent. In terms of health spending per capita, Ireland is above the OECD average (€2,984) at €3,424, but we do rank significantly lower than some other European countries that spend in excess of €4,000 (see Figure 1.5).

Figure 1.5: Total expenditure on health per capita, US$ purchasing power parity

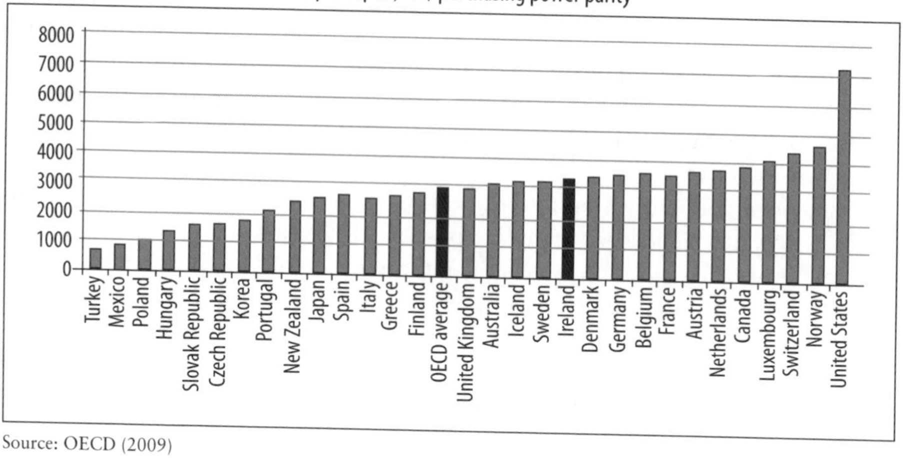

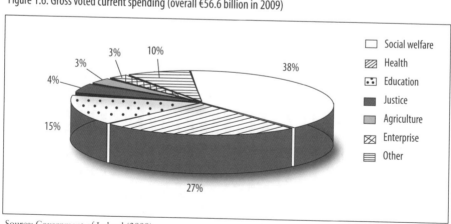

Source: OECD (2009)

The number of acute beds in Ireland in 2007 was 2.7 per 1,000, below the OECD average of 3.8 per 1,000. Worldwide, the number of beds has fallen due to shorter lengths of stay. Health estimates for 2009 record health spending in Ireland as 27 per cent of total gross expenditure, and the total funding for 2009 is estimated to be €14.79 billion.

Figure 1.6: Gross voted current spending (overall €56.6 billion in 2009)

Source: Government of Ireland (2009)

Forty-five per cent of all health care spending is in the acute care sector, 20 per cent on community health services, general practitioner services and pharmaceuticals, and seven per cent on mental health services. The remaining 28 per cent is spent on a range of services that may be broadly described as social care.

Figure 1.7: Health service expenditure

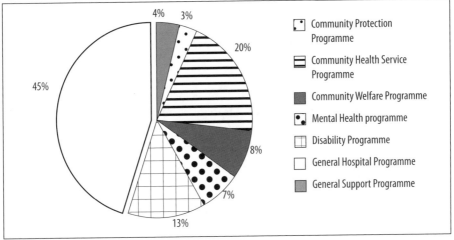

Source: DoHC (2007)

Comparison with health systems internationally is complicated by the eclectic nature of the Irish health system and by the differences in the way different countries conform to the System of Health Accounts (SHA) introduced by the OECD in 2000. The estimate of health spending also necessitates an estimate of private spending on health. Private expenditure includes the purchase of health care service by insurance companies; out-of-pocket expenses by individuals for primary care; and expenditure on private hospitals and diagnostic facilities. Tussing and Wren (2006) explain that a significant portion of spending in health care actually funds social programmes. The OECD definition excludes the bulk of spending under the Community Welfare Programme, which funds services ranging from home help to contributions to patients in private nursing homes, and the Disability Programme, which funds residential care and home care for people with intellectual and physical disabilities.

DEPARTMENT OF HEALTH AND CHILDREN
The Department of Health and Children has responsibility for the overall organisational, legislative, policy and financial accountability framework of the health sector (see the organisation chart in Appendix 5 following this chapter). It has a statutory responsibility to support the minister in the formulation and evaluation of policies for the health services. It also has a role in the strategic planning of health services. This is carried out in conjunction with the Health

Service Executive, voluntary service providers, government departments and other key stakeholders. Its core objectives are to support the minister and the government by:

- advising on the strategic development of the health system including policy and legislation – its strategy statement sets out the high-level objectives of the department, and it takes account of the priorities of government
- supporting their parliamentary, statutory and international functions
- evaluating the performance of the health and social services
- working with other sectors, such as education, to enhance people's health and well-being.

In accordance with the Public Service Management Act 1997, each government department is required to prepare a strategy statement every three years. (See www.dohc.ie for copies of strategy statements, including the 2008–2010 strategy statement.) The Department of Finance also plays an important role in relation to health care policy making and expenditure in terms of pay determination, allocation of expenditure and vote control (see www.finance.gov.ie for further information).

In addition to the Minister for Health and Children, there are four ministers of state attached to the Department of Health and Children:

- Children and Youth Affairs
- Disability and Mental Health
- Health Promotion and Food Safety
- Older People.

HEALTH SERVICE EXECUTIVE (HSE)

The HSE incorporates the former health boards and a number of former organisations and agencies including the Health Service Employers' Agency, the Office for Health Management and Comhairle na nOspidéal.

> The establishment of the HSE represents the beginning of the largest programme of change ever undertaken in the Irish public service. Prior to this our health care services were delivered through a range of different agencies, each of which was independently answerable to the Department of Health and Children. It was a complex structure that made it difficult to provide nationally consistent health services.
>
> (HSE 2008a)

The HSE, which was established under the Health Act 2004, is the largest organisation in the state, employing over 111,000 whole-time equivalent staff, with an annual budget of €14.9 billion. The Health Act 2004 states that the objective of the HSE is to efficiently use the resources available to it in order to provide services that improve, promote and protect the health and welfare of the public. Health and personal social services are delivered to the population living in the Republic of Ireland directly by the HSE and through the many voluntary hospitals and agencies that are funded by it. These will be described later in this chapter.

Prior to the establishment of the HSE, health and social personal services were planned and delivered through ten health boards (established under the Health Act 1970) and the Eastern Regional Health Authority (established under the ERHA Act 2000), and the agencies and hospitals that they funded. The health boards were accountable to the Department of Health and Children, and each health board had a board of elected and nominated representatives to whom it was also accountable. The HSE replaced the ten health boards and the Eastern Regional Health Authority in 2005, and a number of other agencies, including Comhairle na nOspidéal, the Health Service Employers Agency and the Office for Health Management, were also transferred to the HSE.

Under the Health Act 2004, the HSE is obliged to fulfil a number of requirements in relation to the planning and delivery of services. It must produce a corporate plan every three years and an annual service plan and submit these to the Minister for Health and Children for approval, who in turn submits them to the Houses of the Oireachtas for approval. The HSE delivers services directly and through the funding of voluntary agencies and hospitals. It enters into arrangements with these hospitals and agencies and provides direct funding for the delivery of agreed amounts of services through annual service level agreements. Community, residential and rehabilitative training services are also provided by a large number of voluntary organisations that receive grant aid from the HSE, as provided for under the Act. Since its establishment there has been a considerable reorganisation of the administrative structure of the HSE.

Governance

The role and functions of the board of the HSE, which are set out in detail in the Health Act 2004, are significant. Section 12 (1) of the Act defines the board of the HSE as 'the governing body of the Executive with authority in the name of the Executive, to perform the functions of the Executive'. The board has responsibility under the Act to appoint a CEO, under the terms of the Public Service Management (Recruitment and Appointments) Act 2004. The board comprises 11 members and the CEO of the HSE (see Sections 11 to 16 of the Health Act 2004 for further information).

The respective roles and responsibilities of the board and CEO are also made clear in the Health Act 2004. Section 18 of the Act states that the function of the CEO of the HSE is to 'carry on and manage and control generally the business and administration of the Executive . . . and perform any other functions assigned to him/her under the Health Act or as delegated by the Board. S/he is responsible to the board for the performance of his/her functions and the implementation of the Board's policies.' The significance of this role, which marks a change from the role of the CEO in the previous health board structure, is highlighted in Section 20 of the Health Act, which states that 'the CEO is the Accountable Officer in relation to the Appropriation Accounts of the Executive for the purposes of the Comptroller and Auditor Generals Acts 1866 to 1998'. Prior to the establishment of the HSE, the role of accounting officer for the health vote lay with the secretary general of the Department of Health and Children. The appointment of the CEO as the designated accounting officer means that the postholder is ultimately responsible for the spending of public monies.

While further reform of the service delivery structures was initiated in October 2009, when the HSE was established in 2005 its structures were divided into three service delivery units: the Population Health Directorate; the Primary, Community and Continuing Care (PCCC) Directorate; and the National Hospitals Office (NHO). The structures also comprised core National Support Directorates including Human Resources, Finance, Estates and shared services. A Regional Forum was also established in each of the four administrative areas of the HSE, which are described below. These forums, which comprise representatives from city and county councils, make representations to the HSE on the health and personal social services in their area.

The structure of the HSE in mid-2009 was as follows.

Population Health, whose function is to promote and protect the health of the entire population.

Primary, Community and Continuing Care, responsible for delivery of health and personal social services in the community and other settings. These services include primary care, mental health, disability, child, youth and family, services for the elderly, community hospitals, continuing care services and social inclusion services. PCCC is divided into four administrative areas as follows:

- HSE Dublin Mid-Leinster – 28.7 per cent of the population
- HSE South – 25.5 per cent of the population
- HSE West – 23.9 per cent of the population
- HSE Dublin North-East – 21.9 per cent of the population.

The National Hospitals Office (NHO) is responsible for delivering acute hospital and ambulance services throughout the country through a structure of eight hospital networks. The hospital network manager in each network is accountable for the planning and delivery of services within agreed targets in the hospitals in their area. Service delivery is planned and agreed annually through service level agreements between the eight hospital network managers and the NHO and through agreements with individual public statutory and voluntary hospitals, for example in relation to national specialities (including heart, lung and liver transplants, bone marrow transplants, spinal injuries, paediatric cardiac services and medical genetics). The service level agreement process and how it differs according to the type of hospital involved is discussed in the next section.

Hospitals

Broadly speaking, there are three types of hospital in Ireland.

Statutory public hospitals are owned and funded by the HSE. (Prior to the establishment of the HSE, these hospitals were funded by the health boards.) These hospitals agree business plans with hospital network managers in order to receive funding. (See Appendix 3 at the end of this chapter.)

Voluntary public hospitals are funded through service level agreements made with the NHO as provided for in the Health Act 2004. Some voluntary public hospitals are owned by private bodies, such as religious orders. Other voluntary public hospitals are incorporated by charter or statute and are often run by boards appointed by the Minister for Health and Children. Prior to the establishment of the HSE, voluntary hospitals in the eastern region (Dublin, Kildare, Wicklow) received funding through the making of 'service arrangements' with the Eastern Regional Health Authority, while voluntary hospitals in all other counties made arrangements and received their funding directly from the Department of Health and Children.

Private hospitals. These independent hospitals can operate as for-profit or non-profit. These are a number of arrangements in place to increase the number of beds in order to alleviate some of the bed congestion caused by the private–public mix and a number of plans to increase the number of co-located hospitals in the sector. The system of co-location of private hospitals has been a central element of the political agenda advanced by the current administration and has been quite controversial.

Hospitals can also be categorised as acute general hospitals, single specialism hospitals (for example Cappagh Hospital, the Eye and Ear Hospital) or acute specialist hospitals (e.g. paediatric, maternity). They can also be further classified as providing secondary and/or tertiary (national) services.

A range of initiatives are under way within the NHO to improve services for patients, efficiency and effectiveness, including the development of a new national children's hospital, the National Cancer Control Programme, and the development of clinical directorates and clinical networks.

Primary, Community and Continuing Care services

Primary care is the first point of contact that people have with the health and personal social services. Traditionally much of primary care services are delivered through general practitioner services. GPs operate as private and independent contractors, remunerated by capitated amounts for Category I patients or fee for service arrangements for Category II patients. GPs have a distinct role within the system as they act as a gatekeeper to specialist services. The approach to the award of GMS practices and the ability of GPs to practise independently has resulted in an ad hoc development of primary care services in the country. It has also contributed to duplication and small GP practices with insufficient investment in technology and infrastructure to support the needs of a modern health care system. In fact many GPs are geographically isolated and removed from the other members of the multidisciplinary team in the community. *Primary Care: A New*

Direction (DoHC 2001) set out a new direction for primary care as the central focus for the delivery of health and personal social services in Ireland. The strategy proposes a model of primary care team working, with teams providing services to a population of between 4,000 and 10,000. It is intended that the further development of primary care services will allow hospitals to concentrate on those who need more complex interventions in the hospital sector.

Members of primary care teams include GPs, nurses/midwives, health care assistants, home helps, physiotherapists, occupational therapists, social workers and administrative staff. A wider primary care network of other primary care professionals such as speech and language therapists, community pharmacists, dieticians, community welfare officers, dentists, chiropodists and psychologists is being developed to provide services for the enrolled population of each primary care team, which is between approximately 30,000 and 50,000. The HSE 2009 Service Plan sets an objective of having 210 primary care teams in place. It is making some efforts to increase the number of primary care centres in the country, although in reality many in urban areas are actually private enterprises. Because of the reductions that must, in line with government policy, be made to current workforce levels, the main focus of the reconfiguration of PCCC services and resources is on the redeployment of staff and the redefinition of existing roles and job descriptions.

PCCC services cover a wide range of areas, including:

- primary care services, including general practitioner services (which are privately provided by self-employed GPs)
- public health nursing
- community paramedic services
- speech and language services, etc.
- mental health services
- child care services
- disability services
- social inclusion services
- elderly/nursing home services
- dental services.

In addition to the direct provision of these services, there is also a range of voluntary agencies that provide services in these areas, for example in the area of physical, sensory and intellectual disabilities (see Appendix 2 to this chapter for a list of the main agencies).

In accordance with the Health Act 2004, PCCC enters into service arrangements with certain voluntary organisations, whose income is above a stipulated amount. The process of developing service agreements takes place at both national and local level, a reflection of the structures in many of the organisations concerned. It also provides funding to a large number of other voluntary organisations across the country. Details of these organisations can be found on the Department of Health and Children website.

RESTRUCTURING THE HEALTH SERVICES

There have been criticisms as to the success of the reformed structures. Burke (2009) argues that despite the attempt of the 2004 Health Act to clarify the distinct functions of the HSE and the Department of Health and Children, their roles remain blurred. The minister is accountable for national pay negotiations in relation to public service pay, conditions of service and superannuation. The Department of Health and Children (2009a) is also responsible for workforce planning and long-term strategic planning such as cancer control. 'The Minister for Health and Children is accountable for developing and articulating government policy on health and personal social service, and for the overall performance of health service' (DoHC 2008).

There are a total of 475 whole-time equivalent staff in the Department of Health and Children. There is concern about duplication of work between the Department and the HSE. The secretary general of the Department, in his address to the Dáil Public Accounts Committee (DoHC 2009b), reported that its main activities now incorporate parliamentary work, preparing legislation and statutory documents and representing the interests of the country to international organisations such as the WHO, OECD and other health organisations. The Department is linked to the Health Information and Quality Authority (HIQA), the Irish Medicine Board, the Irish Blood Transfusion Service, the Food Safety Authority, the Health Research Board, the National Treatment Fund and the various professional regulatory bodies.

The HSE's Transformation Programme 2007–2010 (HSE 2007b) was launched in late 2007. The programme was prepared following consultation with staff and other key stakeholders. It sets out a vision for the HSE in which 'everybody will have easy access to high quality care and services that they have confidence in and that staff are proud to provide'. It also sets out a core mission for the HSE: 'to enable people live healthier and more fulfilled lives'. More effective integration of hospital and community services was identified as one of the organisation's priorities when the HSE launched the Transformation Programme. In 2008 the HSE developed this priority further through the establishment of an Integrated Services Programme, the objective of which is to ensure that patients and service users can access and receive seamless services, regardless of their location.

The key objectives of the programme were to:

- empower front-line clinicians, other clinical staff and managers to make effective local decisions
- reduce the distance between local service providers and the leadership of the HSE
- ensure strong local accountability and adherence to robust national planning processes
- support high-quality clinical and business decisions
- support consistent management of performance, quality and outcomes.

Work continues in relation to the restructuring of the HSE to enable the achievement of these objectives. The most recent developments include: the creation of a National Directorate for Quality and Clinical Care; and the merging of the Primary, Community and Continuing Care Directorate and the National Hospitals Office into one National Directorate for Integration:

> An integrated health and social care model develops services with the service user at the centre of services. Patient and clients in an integrated system are more likely to receive the type and quality of care they need, when they need it in the most appropriate setting and from the most appropriate health professional.

(HSE 2008b:17)

Figure 1.8 HSE regional operating units

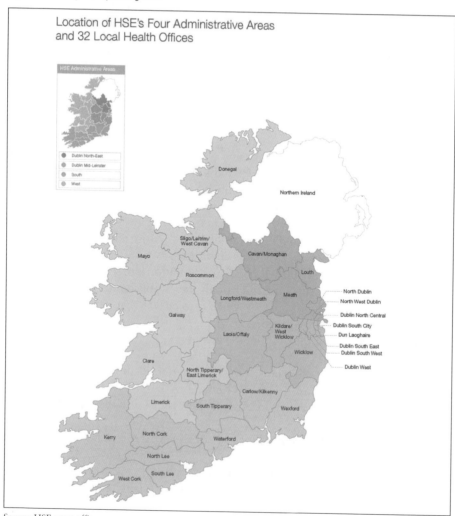

Work is under way to integrate the former Population Health Directorate into the Clinical Care and Quality Directorate and regional operating units. While various options were proposed during the restructuring programme regarding the creation of regions, as at October 2009 it is proposed that four regional operating units based on the existing administrative structures would be established, with a significant strengthening of integration and accountability (see Appendix 4 to this chapter for the new HSE organisation chart).

It is proposed to recruit four regional heads to have full accountability and responsibility for the delivery of all PCCC and hospital services in their region, within an overall national framework of objectives and policies. There will be four care groups nationally for services for children and families, older people, disabilities and mental health. Proposals to reconfigure local health offices and hospital networks to support this model are currently being developed.

OTHER BODIES

There are a number of agencies that are funded directly from the Department of Health and Children's vote allocation, including the National Treatment Purchase Fund, the Crisis Pregnancy Agency, the National Cancer Screening Service, the Mental Health Commission, the Health Information and Quality Authority and the Health Research Board (see Appendix 1 following this chapter). There is a Programme for Rationalisation of Agencies in the Health Sector, as outlined in Appendix 2. The Health Information and Quality Authority (HIQA) was established in 2007 as part of the ongoing reform of the health services. HIQA is an independent authority that reports to the Minister for Health and Children, and it has a broad range of powers and functions. It was set up to drive quality, safety, accountability and best use of resources in health and social care services, and its core functions are as follows:

- developing health information systems
- promoting and implementing quality assurance programmes
- overseeing accreditation
- developing health technology assessment
- reviewing and reporting on selected services.

CONCLUSION

The chapter has drawn attention to the structural and governance provision in the Irish health system. As illustrated in this chapter, the Irish health system is not easily classified as it has a mix of funding sources which define the structure and organisation of health care delivery. Ireland has embarked upon a wide-ranging series of reforms in recent years to advance the structure and governance arrangements that underpin the delivery of health care. Reforms in the public service have advocated stronger governance with devolution of authority and responsibility.

Since its establishment there has been considerable reorganisation of the administrative structure of the HSE. The National Hospitals Office and the Primary Community and Continuing Care Directorate have recently merged into the Integrated Services Directorate. It is anticipated that its regional sections will be required to operate performance contracts in relation to clinical quality, service volumes and service improvement.

The aspiration to achieve consultant-delivered care in the Irish health system has yet to be achieved. There are quarters which advocate a further restructuring of Irish health care so that universal access can be extended to primary care funded by a system of social insurance. A multitude of government reports underpinned the reform agenda that commenced in 2005; however, the under-investment in community care structures has been a major obstacle to streamlining and reorganising care delivery structures. The success of the health strategy is dependent on advances in the social care provision for older people and people with disability in the community. The coming years will be an interesting period in health care, with considerable changes to the structure of the Irish health service under way, which will no doubt require significant time to bed down.

REFLECTIVE EXERCISES

1   The HSE is currently developing structures to enable and empower the delivery of integrated care at regional and local levels. What do you see as the main challenges and critical success factors in relation to the delivery of integrated care?

2   Discuss how the functions of the Department of Health and Children and the HSE within the current health care structure influence your area of work.

3   The private/public mix is a distinguishing feature of the Irish health system. Discuss how this phenomenon compares internationally and its advantages and disadvantages for both health providers and consumers.

4   Conduct a SWOT analysis of the health care sector. What are the key challenges and how will they impact on the delivery of health care services? What are the opportunities and how might they best be maximised?

ADDITIONAL RESOURCES

An Bord Altranais: www.aba.ie

Capital Investment for Health. Case Studies from Europe, http://pr4. netatlantic.com/t/1694353/2924751/103024/0/

Department of Health and Children: www.dohc.ie

FÁS (2009) *Quantitative Tool for Workforce Planning in Health Care* (Report by the Skills and Labour Market Research Unit), http://www. forfas.ie/media/egfsn090617_healthcare_report.pdf

Financing Health Care in the European Union: Challenges and Policy Responses, http://pr4.netatlantic.com/t/1694353/2924751/103025/0/

Health Service Executive: www.hse.ie

Health Service Reform: www.healthreform.ie
Institute for Innovation and Improvement: http://www.institute.nhs.uk/
Leadership Qualities Framework, http://www.nhsleadershipqualities.nhs.uk/
Medical Council: www.medicalcouncil.ie
OECD Health Data 2009: http://www.oecd.org
OECD (2008) *Public Management Reviews – Ireland: Towards an Integrated Public Service* http://www.oecd.org/document/31/0,3343,en_2649_33735_40529119_1_1_1_1,00.htm

APPENDIX 1: BODIES UNDER THE AEGIS OF THE DEPARTMENT OF HEALTH AND CHILDREN

Adoption Board
An Bord Altranais
Children Acts Advisory Board
Crisis Pregnancy Agency
Dental Council
Food Safety Authority of Ireland
Food Safety Promotion Board
Health and Social Care Professional Council
Health Information and Quality Authority
Health Insurance Authority
Health Research Board
Health Service Executive
Institute of Public Health
Irish Blood Transfusion Service
Irish Medicines Board
Medical Council
Mental Health Commission
National Cancer Registry Board
National Cancer Screening Service Board
National Council on Ageing and Older People
National Council for the Professional Development of Nursing and Midwifery
National Haemophilia Council
National Paediatric Hospital Development Board
National Social Work Qualifications Board
National Treatment Purchase Fund
Office for Tobacco Control
Opticians Board
Pharmaceutical Society of Ireland
Poisons Council
Postgraduate Medical and Dental Board
Pre-Hospital Emergency Care Council
Voluntary Health Insurance Board
Women's Health Council

APPENDIX 2: PROGRAMME FOR THE RATIONALISATION OF AGENCIES IN THE HEALTH SECTOR

Agency	Rationalisation Measure	Timeframe
National Council on Ageing and Older People	Integrate into the Office for Older People, Department of Health and Children	Merged 1 September 2009
Children Acts Advisory Board	Integrate into the Office of the Minister for Children and Youth Affairs, Department of Health and Children	1 January 2010
Women's Health Council	Integrate into the Department of Health and Children	2009
National Cancer Screening Service and National Cancer Registry Board	Integrate into the HSE	Target date 2010
Crisis Pregnancy Agency	Integrate into the HSE	1 January 2010
Drug Treatment Centre	Integrate into the HSE	1 January 2010
National Social Work Qualifications Board, Pre-Hospital Emergency Care Council and Opticians Board	Integrate into the Health and Social Care Professionals Council where functions are appropriate	Not possible to indicate accurate merge date but no sooner than 1 January 2011
Postgraduate Medical and Dental Board	Integrate with the HSE/Medical Council	Merged in January 2009
National Council for the Professional Development of Nursing and Midwifery	Integrate with the HSE/Bord Altranais	Bill to be published 2009
Food Safety Authority of Ireland, Irish Medicines Board and Office of Tobacco Control	Amalgamate into a new Public Health and Medicines Safety Authority, to be created	Target date 1 January 2011

Source: DOHC (2009a)

APPENDIX 3: PUBLIC HOSPITALS

Bantry General Hospital
Beaumont Hospital
Cappagh National Orthopaedic Hospital
Cavan/Monaghan Hospital Group
Children's University Hospital, Temple Street
Connolly Hospital, Blanchardstown
Coombe Women's Hospital
Cork University Hospital
Cork University Maternity Hospital

Galway University Hospitals
Kerry General Hospital
Letterkenny General Hospital
Lourdes Orthopaedic Hospital, Kilcreene
Louth County Hospital, Dundalk
Mallow General Hospital
Mater Misericordiae University Hospital
Mayo General Hospital
Mercy University Hospital, Cork
Mid Western Regional Hospital, Dooradoyle
Mid Western Regional Hospital, Ennis
Mid Western Regional Hospital, Nenagh
Mid Western Regional Maternity Hospital Limerick
Mid Western Regional Orthopaedic Hospital Croom
Midland Regional Hospital Mullingar
Midland Regional Hospital Portlaoise
Midland Regional Hospital Tullamore
Naas General Hospital
National Maternity Hospital, Holles Street
Our Lady of Lourdes Hospital, Drogheda
Our Lady's Children's Hospital Crumlin
Our Lady's Hospital, Navan
Portiuncula Hospital, Ballinasloe
Roscommon County Hospital
Rotunda Hospital
Royal Victoria Eye and Ear Hospital, Dublin
Sligo General Hospital
South Infirmary–Victoria Hospital, Cork
South Tipperary General Hospital
St Colmcille's Hospital, Loughlinstown
St James's Hospital
St John's Hospital Limerick
St Luke's General Hospital Kilkenny
St Luke's Hospital, Rathgar (Cancer Services)
St Mary's Orthopaedic Hospital, Cork
St Michael's, Dun Laoghaire
St Vincent's University Hospital, Elm Park
Tallaght Hospital
Waterford Regional Hospital
Wexford General Hospital

Source www.hse.ie (last updated 26 January 2009)

APPENDIX 4: HSE ORGANISATION CHART

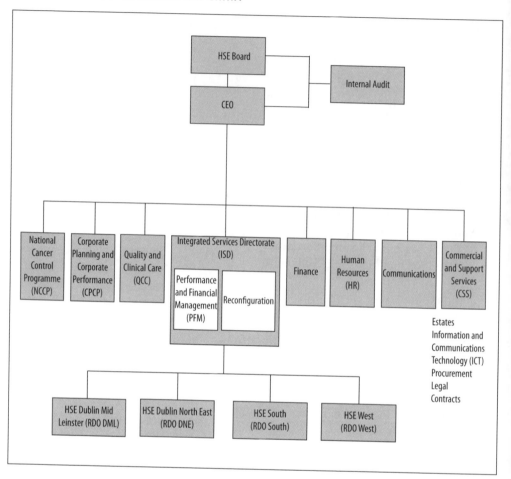

APPENDIX 5: DEPARTMENT OF HEALTH AND CHILDREN ORGANISATION CHART*

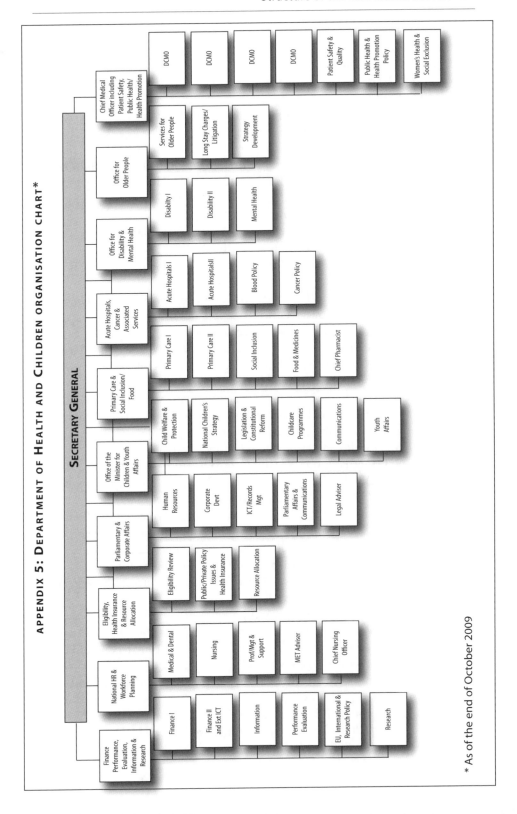

SECRETARY GENERAL

Finance Performance, Evaluation, Information & Research
- Finance I
- Finance II and Ext ICT
- Information
- Performance Evaluation
- EU, International & Research Policy
- Research

National HR & Workforce Planning
- Medical & Dental
- Nursing
- Prof/Mgt & Support
- MET Adviser
- Chief Nursing Officer

Eligibility, Health Insurance & Resource Allocation
- Eligibility Review
- Public/Private Policy Issues & Health Insurance
- Resource Allocation

Parliamentary & Corporate Affairs
- Human Resources
- Corporate Devt
- ICT/Records Mgt
- Parliamentary Affairs & Communications
- Legal Adviser

Office of the Minister for Children & Youth Affairs
- Child Welfare & Protection
- National Children's Strategy
- Legislation & Constitutional Reform
- Childcare Programmes
- Communications
- Youth Affairs

Primary Care & Social Inclusion/ Food
- Primary Care I
- Primary Care II
- Social Inclusion
- Food & Medicines
- Chief Pharmacist

Acute Hospitals, Cancer & Associated Services
- Acute Hospitals I
- Acute Hospitals II
- Blood Policy
- Cancer Policy

Office for Disability & Mental Health
- Disabilty I
- Disability II
- Mental Health

Office for Older People
- Services for Older People
- Long Stay Charges/ Litigation
- Strategy Development

Chief Medical Officer including Patient Safety, Public Health/ Health Promotion
- DCMO
- DCMO
- DCMO
- DCMO
- Patient Safety & Quality
- Public Health & Health Promotion Policy
- Women's Health & Social Exclusion

* As of the end of October 2009

REFERENCES

Blank, R. H. and Burau, V. (2004) *Comparative Health Policy*. Hampshire: Palgrave Macmillan.

Burke, S. (2009) *Irish Apartheid: Healthcare Inequality in Ireland*. Dublin: New Island.

DoHC (Department of Health and Children) (2001) *Quality and Fairness: A Health System for You*. Dublin: Stationery Office.

— (2001) *Primary Care: A New Direction*, Dublin: Stationery Office.

— (2003a) *Report of the Commission on Financial Management and Control Systems in the Health Service* (Brennan Report). Dublin: Stationery Office.

— (2003b) *Audit of Structures and Functions in the Health Systems* (Prospectus Report). Dublin: Stationery Office.

— (2003c) *The Health Service Reform Programme*. Available at http://www.healthreform.ie, accessed 10 October 2009.

— (2003d) *Report of the National Task Force on Medical Staffing* (Hanly Report). Dublin: Stationery Office.

— (2004) *Guidance on the Implementation of the European Working Time Directive*. Dublin: Stationery Office.

— (2007) *Health Trends*. Dublin: Stationery Office.

— (2008) *Corporate Business Plan*. Available at http://www. lenus.ie/hse/bitstream /10147/65206/1/corpbusplan2008.pdf, accessed 10 October 2009.

— (2009a), *Annual Report 2008*. Dublin: Stationery Office.

— (2009b) Opening statement by Mr Michael Scanlan, Secretary General of the Department of Health and Children at the meeting of the Dáil Committee of Public Accounts, 7 May 2009. Available at www.dohc.ie/ press/speeches/2009/20090514.html, accessed on 10 October 2009.

Docteur, E. and Oxley, H. (2003) *Health Care Systems: Lessons from the Reform Experience* (OECD Working Paper). Available at http://www.oecd.org/dataoecd/5/53/22364122.pdf, accessed 10 October 2009.

ESRI (Economic and Social Research Institute) (2009) *Projecting the Impact of Demographic Change on the Demand for and Delivery of Healthcare in Ireland*. Available at www.esri.ie, accessed 23 October 2009.

Government of Ireland (2004) Health Act. Dublin: Stationery Office.

— (2006) *Towards 2016 – Ten Year Framework Social Partnership Agreement 2006–2015*. Dublin: Stationery Office.

— (2009) *Budget Estimates*. Dublin: Stationery Office.

Health Consumer Powerhouse (2009) *Euro Health Consumer Index*. Available at http://www.healthpowerhouse.com/files/Index%20matrix%20EHIVI%202009.pdf, accessed 10 October 2009.

HSE (Health Services Executive) (2007a) *Annual Report and Financial Statement*. Dublin: HSE.

— (2007b) *Transformation Programme 2007–2010*. Dublin: HSE

— (2008a) *Towards 2016 Review and Transitional Agreement*. Dublin: HSE.

— (2008b) *Corporate Plan 2008*. Dublin: HSE.

— (2009) *National Service Plan*. Dublin: HSE.

OECD (2009) *OECD Health Data 2009 – Frequently Requested Data*. Available at http://www.oecd.org/document/16/0,3343,en_2649_34631_2085200_1_1_1_1,00.html, accessed 10 October 2009.

Smith, S. (2009) 'The Irish health basket: a basket of care?', *European Journal of Health Economics* online, 5 August.

Task Force on the Public Service (2008) *Transforming Public Services – Citizen Centred – Performance Focused*, Department of the Taoiseach. Dublin: Stationery Office.

Tussing, A. Dale and Wren, M.-A. (2006) *How Ireland Cares*. Dublin: New Island.

Wren, M.-A. (2003) *Unhealthy State: Anatomy of a Sick Society*. Dublin: New Island.

— (2004) 'Health spending and the black hole', *Quarterly Economic Commentary*.

2
Health Policy and Economics
Michelle Butler

OBJECTIVES
- To provide an overview of health policy and economics.
- To provide an overview of the way in which health services in Ireland are financed.
- To situate the Irish health system in relation to health systems found in other countries.
- To identify trends in expenditure in Ireland and related economic factors.
- To examine the public/private mix in Ireland.
- To examine economic influences in health care.
- To identify issues of access and eligibility.
- To review recent health care reforms.

INTRODUCTION

Health policy is 'agreement or consensus on issues to be addressed in order to achieve a desired result or change' and 'agreement on goals and objectives, the priorities between these objectives and the main policy directions for achieving them' (Ritsatakis *et al.* 2000:1). Johnson-Lans (2006:3) suggests that health economics is about value, 'more specifically, with maximising well-being in a world where choices must be made about the allocation of scarce resources'. Health policy can be linked very closely with health economics, where policy makers are concerned with how best to provide for the health care needs of the population in a time of burgeoning costs and ever-tightening fiscal constraints. Trade-offs may be required between equity, access, universal coverage, freedom of choice and cost containment (Weale 1988). Over time health systems become shaped by the cumulative effects of decisions made by policy makers. This chapter will examine how health care in Ireland is funded and will explore the impact of policy and economic developments in the health system at large on the delivery of care received by the individual.

HEALTH POLICY

The purpose of health policy is to 'to clearly define measurable and obtainable objectives that can guide changes in health care delivery that will effectively and efficiently produce a healthy society by improving the health of individuals' (Lancaster 1999:319). Health policy is inherently political in nature, involving multiple, diverse stakeholders, who very often may have very different, and sometimes competing, priorities and expectations. Weiss (1987:47) suggests that health care programmes themselves are 'the creatures of political decisions. They [are] proposed, defined, debated, enacted, and funded through political processes, and in implementation they remain subject to [political] pressures – both supportive and hostile.'

Policy is a cyclical process, and the policy cycle involves the identification of a problem or agenda setting, policy formulation, policy implementation and policy evaluation. Policy evaluation provides the information required to begin the cycle once again and this part of the cycle is often referred to as *closing the loop*. For further details of the policy process see Milstead (2004).

Over recent years those involved in health policy decisions have become concerned with economics in health care provision. Dobrow *et al.* (2004:207) suggest there has been greater recognition of and attention to 'the classic economic dilemma between the scarcity of resources and our potentially unlimited wants, raising difficult resource allocation, rationing and priority setting questions'. Even in Ireland's recent unprecedented period of economic growth, a cautious approach was promoted to funding health care, emphasising the need to demonstrate real returns for any increases in investment in health care (McCreevy 2003).

THE IRISH HEALTH SYSTEM
The Organisation for Economic Co-operation and Development (OECD 1997:116) described the Irish health system as a unique structure, comprised of a 'mixture of a universal health service, free at the point of consumption and a fee-based private system where individuals have to subscribe to insurance if they wish to be covered for medical expenses'. This 'mixture' relates both to the provision and to the funding of health services and the relationships between funders, providers and end users of health care. The Irish health system was also described as a social assistance model by the OECD (1992) in its comparative analysis of health care across countries, on the basis that the poorest one-third of the population are entitled to free services at the point of delivery (Wiley 2005). Wiley (2005) suggests that the Irish health system has evolved into the current 'mixed' system of provision and funding by drawing on a number of models. In 2006, 78 per cent of Irish health care expenditure came from public funding and the remainder through private funding (OECD 2008).

The World Health Organisation (WHO 2000:xi) describes a health system as 'comprising all the organizations, institutions and resources that are devoted to producing health actions. A health action is defined as any effort, whether in personal health care, public health services or through intersectoral initiatives, whose primary purpose is to improve health.' In the Irish context the health system includes a range of public and private providers, providing a range of hospital and community curative, preventive and diagnostic services, funded by general taxation, private health insurance and direct payments. The Irish health system, rather uniquely, also includes an element of personal social services which in 2005 accounted for just over eight per cent of non-capital publicly funded health expenditure (using data from CSO (2008b)).

Eligibility for health care

In Ireland, approximately one-third of the population are eligible for Category I ('medical card') cover on the basis of means testing, particular health needs and participation in approved government training and employment schemes (Nolan 2008). Providers of care for patients with Category I eligibility are reimbursed by the Primary Care Re-imbursement Service (PCRS – previously the GMS (Payments) Board). The remainder of the population (Category II) must pay the full costs of family doctor consultations, all prescribed medications (costs in excess of €120 per month can from 1 January 2010 be reclaimed through the Drug Payment Scheme), and certain direct payments for hospital care (€66 for those attending for outpatient services, €100 for patients attending the emergency department without referral from a GP, and daily charges of €75 for in-patient care up to a maximum of €750 per annum (Department of Finance 2008)). Although Category I eligibility could be interpreted as the provision of cover for those most marginalised in Irish society, access to health care needs also to be considered separately from eligibility as access is determined by factors other than ability to pay. The proportion of the population covered by category/eligibility has fallen from 40 per cent in 1977 (O'Dowd 2007). Also, approximately 27 per cent of the Irish population have neither Category I eligibility nor private health insurance (CSO 2008a). This includes those who sit just above the means testing thresholds but who are on incomes well below the average industrial wage (see Nolan 2008).

Resourcing health care

In Ireland, resources for public health care are generated primarily through general taxation. Tax-financed systems are progressive, so long as the taxation system itself is progressive (i.e. tax liability is proportional to income, and those earning more make a greater contribution). However, in Ireland health care competes with other public services for a share of the resources generated through taxation. In the Irish context, 29 per cent of the €52.8bn of public spending (gross voted current spending) in 2008 was allocated to health. This was second only to social welfare (32 per cent). Almost €14bn was allocated to health care for 2009 (see Table 2.1). While this relatively high allocation to health care suggests health care is high on the agenda of government, this system of income generation for health care exposes the health system to changes in the economy which reduce the availability of public resources. Even in a stable economy, this system exposes health care financing to the relative value attached to health care and other public services by society, or more specifically, by the value attached to health care by individuals and groups with power within society.

Table 2.1: Voted expenditure for health care 2009 (€000)

Current expenditure	
Health Service Executive	12,149,325
Department of Health and Children	506,943
Capital expenditure	
Health Service Executive	20,450
Department of Health and Children	581,720
Total	**13,258,438**

Source: Department of Finance: Government Estimates 2009

One way to avoid this competition is to ring-fence health care funding. This happens in health systems funded through the social insurance model, which is common in several European countries. In the social insurance model, insured persons pay a regular contribution based on income or wealth, and not on the cost of the services they are likely to use. Health care is purchased on behalf of insured persons from public and/or private providers. Access to care is based on clinical need, not ability to pay. Participation is usually mandatory and contributions are paid by employees and employers. The size of pools varies from system to system and since social health insurance is separate from taxation and other publicly mandated systems, the income from contributions must cover the fees paid for the services to which members are entitled. Schemes may receive government subsidies and generally contributions for unemployed, disabled and elderly persons are collected from designated pension, sickness or unemployment funds or from taxation (Normand *et al.* 2006).

A third general approach to health care funding is the private finance system. Here health care is seen as a private commodity subject to market mechanisms, and individual choice of provider is a primary concern. Resources are raised individually and paid directly by users or through private health insurance. The most often cited example of a private finance system is the health system in the United States. Although Medicare and Medicaid provide cover for older Americans and those defined by each state to be poor, health care is seen as a private matter and individuals purchase care directly from private providers.

Several features of a private finance system are to be found in the Irish health system. The private health care sector in Ireland, also referred to as the 'independent sector', is mainly comprised of GPs, but the number of private hospitals and clinics has grown considerably over recent years (O'Dowd 2007). In addition, a number of new services have been introduced by the private sector, perhaps most notably the provision of emergency department services (although these are usually available only during business hours). In addition, private beds are provided in public hospitals, with the proportion of public to private beds set at approximately 80:20. The growth in private providers is mirrored by a growth in private health insurance from 17 per cent in 1977 to 50 per cent in 2005

(O'Dowd 2007). In 2007, 49 per cent of the population had voluntary health insurance (CSO 2008a) provided by four private health insurance companies.

Voluntary health insurance was first introduced in Ireland in the 1950s with legislation (the Voluntary Health Insurance Act 1957) to provide for the establishment of the Voluntary Health Insurance Board. This was to enable those who were not eligible for public hospital services, or who wished to avail of private or semi-private care, to make arrangements to cover the costs of private health care. The Health Insurance Act was passed in 1994 to open up the private insurance market in light of an emerging single European market. Premiums are linked to the range and levels of services available to subscribers from a range of public and private providers. Health insurance subscriptions are tax-deductible at the standard rate of tax and any health expenditure not reimbursed through the health insurance provider can be claimed against tax at the marginal rate (Wiley 2005).

Mossialos and Dixon (2002) suggest that health systems in which private health insurance is widespread generate a highly regressive pattern of distribution. In 2006, the US health care system was the most expensive of the 22 OECD countries, costing just over $2 trillion. This equated to 15.3 per cent of gross domestic product (GDP) compared with the OECD average of 8.4 per cent. Despite this, 45 million Americans, as many as 30 per cent in some states, were uninsured (Alakeson 2008). In addition, in private health insurance systems, competition between insurers forces them to adjust the premiums of enrollees according to their relative risk, and individual contributions are linked to illness rather than to income. Such systems are also subject to the problem of adverse selection, where those who voluntarily take out health insurance tend to do so on the basis of known or anticipated need for health care. Thus they tend to cost more to insure than the average person.

Health insurers use various mechanisms to attempt to control adverse selection, such as underwriting, rating premiums according to individual risk, excluding pre-existing conditions from cover, and limiting coverage to members of groups formed for reasons other than to buy insurance coverage (e.g. union members). Insurers may also exclude certain expensive services or treatments or require patients to share the costs of treatment. Kutzin (2001) suggests that strong government involvement is required to regulate such markets to prevent segmentation of the population into different risk pools which would make it increasingly difficult to finance the premiums of people in sicker pools. Insurers may also provide packages which are more likely to appeal to younger, healthier subscribers (e.g. maternity care, health screening), aimed at limiting the risk in the pool.

In Ireland, several mechanisms have been applied to the private health insurance market. These include community rating, open enrolment, lifetime cover, minimum benefit and risk equalisation (Health Insurance Authority 2008). Community rating requires the same premium to be applied to all individuals regardless of personal characteristics. While premiums are related to the benefits available, the level of risk that a consumer poses does not affect the premium paid.

This is a mechanism to pool the health risks of the population; and revenues saved from healthy members cover the costs of sicker members.

Open enrolment requires all applicants to be accepted regardless of their risk status. Lifetime cover guarantees consumers the right to renew their policies regardless of age, risk status or claims history. Minimum benefit is provided for in regulations introduced by the Minister for Health and Children in 1996, which set out the minimum levels of benefit that must be provided by all insurance contracts sold in Ireland that provide cover for in-patient hospital services (Health Insurance Authority 2008).

Risk equalisation aims to protect community rating by ensuring that insurance providers who take on or have a higher proportion of older people (on the basis that they are more costly to insure) are compensated through a levy applied to insurance providers with a lower proportion of older people. In 2005, the Health Insurance Authority (the statutory regulator of health insurance in Ireland) recommended the commencement of the risk equalisation scheme (which had been provided for in the 1994 legislation). One of the providers (BUPA Ireland) took out a challenge to the introduction of risk equalisation in the High Court in May 2005, but the legality of risk equalisation was upheld under both Irish and EU law. However, the Minister for Health and Children (Mary Harney) held off on the introduction of the scheme until the government had started converting VHI (Ireland's largest provider) from a statutory body to a commercial body (Global Insight 2008).

Revenue collection, fund pooling and purchasing health care

The three elements of health care financing identified by Mossialos *et al.* (2002) are revenue collection, fund pooling and purchasing. Revenue collection in a health system funded through general taxation is always associated with prepayment and large pools. Individuals, households and firms pay direct taxes or indirect taxes levied on commodities and transactions. These can be levied at the national, regional or local level. Taxes can be general or earmarked for a specific area of expenditure. Prepayment provides protection against uncertainty and the risk of having to make large out-of-pocket payments, or not having the means to pay out of pocket to access services. However, most health care systems have an element of patient cost-sharing (direct payment), even those with universal coverage ('everyone in the population has access to appropriate promotive, preventive, curative and rehabilitative health care when they need it and at an affordable cost' (WHO 2005:1)). Direct payment may also be used where prepayment (insurance or taxation) is inadequate, to reduce demand, or to ration services. In the Irish health system, out-of-pocket charges apply to Category II patients using hospital services. Some of these direct charges (e.g. emergency department charges) are aimed at discouraging inappropriate use. Although income is generated though direct payments, charges tend to be notional and the income generated tends not to cover the economic cost of the service or treatment.

Risk pooling or fund pooling is the accumulation of prepaid health care revenues and the spreading of risk among the participants through cross-subsidies from low-risk to high-risk individuals. Larger pools will benefit from economies of scale and will require lower contributions to protect against uncertain needs (Kutzin 2001). In private health insurance, funds are pooled between subscribers of the same insurance provider. However, the pool may not be shared equally to the same extent as in social insurance pools. Premiums may be related to an individual's risk and pooling may not be between high-risk and low-risk members unless community rating is applied.

Purchasing is 'the transfer of pooled resources to service providers on behalf of the population for which the funds were pooled' and involves the distribution of the funds pooled between competing claims to meet certain pre-specified goals (Kutzin 2001:180). Traditionally in the Irish health system an incrementalist approach had been adopted to purchasing: health boards received funding based on what had been allocated the previous year with some adjustments for agreed new developments, increases in pay costs, service-specific items relevant to each health board and projected inflation rates. Using Rice and Smith's (2002) paradigm, Wiley (2005) describes the Irish approach to resource allocation as prospective funding based on expected future expenditure using fixed budgets. Wiley (2005) identifies a significant historical dimension which generally underlies the determination of health service budgets in Ireland and the absence of formula-based resource allocation approaches.

However, over recent years there has been a 'conscious move' away from this approach towards the development of 'more systematic decision-making tools' for the allocation of health care resources (Lynch 1998:104). The introduction of case-mix budgeting in acute hospitals is one example of such tools, which aim to link funding more closely to agreed levels of service. The Health (Amendment) (No. 3) Act 1996 provided for the introduction of service planning in the Irish health system. The Act required the eight health boards at the time to enter into an annual cycle of planning, through which they would set out in a service plan the services to be provided over the following year for the funding received by the Department of Health and Children. The legislation set out very specific requirements for health boards in relation to the service planning process and their interaction with the Department of Health and Children. With the subsequent establishment of the Eastern Regional Health Authority (ERHA), provider plans were introduced to clarify funding and service arrangements between the ERHA and hospitals and other agencies providing care to the population in the Eastern Region. With the abolition of the eight health boards and the ERHA and the establishment of the Health Service Executive (HSE) in 2005, service planning continues between the HSE and the Department of Health and Children and between the HSE and agencies providing care on its behalf.

TRENDS IN HEALTH EXPENDITURE IN IRELAND

Current expenditure on health care in Ireland is 8.9 per cent of gross domestic product (GDP) (OECD 2008). However, measuring health expenditure as a proportion of GDP has its limitations where there are sudden fluctuations in growth. This can be seen in the Irish context. In the recession of the early 1980s, when growth was less than two per cent (Fitz Gerald and Kearney, 2000) health expenditure as a proportion of GDP was 7.72 per cent. In contrast, in the late 1990s when growth in GDP was about 10 per cent, health care expenditure was about 6.5 per cent. However, in 1980, expenditure on health care was €890.10m, whereas in 1995 it was €2.9bn. A more stable comparative measure of expenditure is expenditure per capita. Total expenditure (public and private) on health care in Ireland in 2006 was US$3,082 per capita. This is just above the OECD average of US$2,824. Health care expenditure in the United States is the highest of all OECD countries whether measured as a proportion of GDP (15.3 per cent) or expenditure per capita (US$6,714).

Ireland experienced an unprecedented period of economic growth between 1995 and 2007, peaking at more than 10 per cent in 1997 and 1999 (ESRI 2008). Public expenditure on health care has changed dramatically over the last twenty years, primarily related to dramatic changes in economic growth. In the mid-1980s, when Ireland experienced negative growth in GDP, this resulted in contraction in public investment in health care and significant retrenchment in health services. The impact of the period of retrenchment in the 1980s is still to be found today, particularly in relation to bed capacity. Savings during this time of contraction were found mainly by reducing hospital expenditure. Between 1980 and 1988 expenditure on hospital services declined by 15 per cent, comprising: a reduction in acute hospital beds by 20 per cent; a reduction in average length of stay of 19 per cent; a 25 per cent reduction in hospital bed days; and a five per cent reduction in discharges from acute hospitals (Wiley and Fetter 1990). In 2007 Ireland had 20 per cent fewer hospital beds per capita than the OECD average and it is estimated that there were 1,118 too few beds in the system (PA Consulting 2007).

In contrast, health expenditure (in constant terms) increased by 23 per cent between 1990 and 1996, and by 86 per cent between 1996 and 2002 (Wiley 2005). However, the recent period of economic growth was short-lived: in 2009 the Irish economy declined by 7.5 per cent and a further contraction of 1.5 per cent is predicted for 2010 (Department of Finance 2009). In his Pre-Budget Outlook (Department of Finance 2009) the Minister for Finance announced the need to make an adjustment to the budget of €4 billion in 2010 in order to stabilise the budget deficit. This is likely to be reflected in significant cutbacks in all public expenditure.

ECONOMICS AND THE DEVELOPMENT OF IRISH HEALTH POLICY

Prior to 1947 health services in Ireland were financed largely through local taxation, but there was growing concern about the increasing burden being placed on local sources of finance due to increasing costs and a growing range of services; and also about disparities in services provided from county to county (Commission on Health Funding 1989). A White Paper published in 1966 proposed that ultimate responsibility for health service financing should rest with the state and that there should be changes in the administration of the services. A modern health system would require services that would span county boundaries to provide the concentration of population required to support these services (Wiley 1998).

The 1966 White Paper on Health and the Health Act 1970 that followed were the first real attempts to change the service radically since the Poor Relief Act of 1838. They also tried to address one of the main criticisms at the time that there was a two-tier system in place with persons using the dispensary system having no choice of doctor and being separated from private medical patients. This led to the introduction of the General Medical Services (GMS) scheme in 1972. This scheme was administered jointly by the eight health boards, which provided for a choice of doctor and pharmacist for those eligible, based on a means test (O'Hara 1998).

The next key policy document, *Health, the Wider Dimensions*, was published in 1986 (DoH 1986). At the time of the review, the health board system had been in place for some time (and there had been considerable development and expansion of the system in the wake of the 1970 Health Act), and it was considered an opportune time to review the whole approach to health and to consider modifications in health policy required to meet the needs of the 1990s and beyond. There were particular concerns about trends in the utilisation of services and the potential mismatch between demands and resources in the future, and international developments needed to be reflected in national policy. Equity was defined as 'The distribution of available health services over the population on the basis of need and an equitable sharing of the cost of providing such services' (DoH 1986:18) and concern was noted about how access could be guaranteed to the whole community with individuals being required to pay on the basis of their financial means. Equality of health was noted as a concern – that each individual should have the same opportunity to enjoy good health. The document noted the existence in Ireland of clear inequalities based on age and sex groups, socio-economic groups and the need to recognise that these inequalities do exist and to frame policy responses that would promote equality in health based on an analysis of the differences. It also identified that a mix of national and local-level responses would be required. It reported that the traditional view of efficiency in terms of 'squeezing the fat out of the system' was too narrow and that changes in the basic design of the system needed also to be considered. It also highlighted the need for fundamental analysis of the value for money of services and how this could be improved through economic incentives in the system. It stated that a system of a public/private mix had evolved over a long period of time and should be opened up to debate. A range of issues was identified in relation to management and planning, in particular accountability at health board level and the lack of integrated planning due to the programme structure. It identified the need to adopt a new approach to planning and information and financial management that would involve measurement of health needs in local populations and the identification of health goals and a formal planning cycle.

The Commission on Health Funding was established in 1987 in the wake of public concern and dissatisfaction with a range of across-the-board cuts undertaken in response to economic difficulties at the time, which were seen as rather crude and in need of rigorous review. In its report (Commission on Health

Funding 1989) the commission identified a range of weaknesses in the planning, organisation, management and administration of the system which reduced its efficiency, effectiveness and responsiveness. It noted the strong focus on hospital systems and inequities and rationing in the system.

The key theme in *Shaping a Healthier Future*, introduced in 1994 (DoH 1994), was the need to reorientate the Irish health system towards improving the effectiveness of health and personal social services. It proposed that prevention, treatment and care services should be more clearly focused on improvements in health status and quality of life. It highlighted the importance of equity and quality of service, and the need to focus on the provision of a positive outcome rather than on the provision of a level of service.

The latest health strategy, *Quality and Fairness: A Health System for You* (DoHC 2001b), builds on many of the priorities set out in 1994. In terms of resourcing health, it states that the strategy outlines the largest concentrated expansion in services in the history of the Irish health system. Proposals are set out over the full range of services and it is stated that these proposals are the result of detailed research and expert input addressing system-wide as well as programme-specific issues. There is a strong focus on implementation and the document concludes with an implementation plan. The strategy sets out four national goals (see Table 2.2) and six frameworks for change.

Table 2.2: Four national goals set out in the 2001 Irish health strategy

1	Better health for everyone	• Health of the population at centre of public policy. • Promotion of health and well-being intensified. • Health inequalities reduced. • Specific quality of life issues targeted.
2	Fair access	• Eligibility is clearly defined. • Scope of eligibility framework broadened. • Equitable access for all categories of patient.
3	Responsive and appropriate care delivery	• Patient at the centre in planning care delivery. • Appropriate care in the appropriate setting. • The system – capacity to deliver timely and appropriate services.
4	High performance	• Standardised quality systems – best patient care and safety. • Evidence and strategic objectives underpin all planning.

Source: DoHC (2001b)

Key themes in the six frameworks for change are: the need to strengthen primary care and to reform the acute hospital system; the need to target investment using an evidence-based approach and prioritised programmes; and the need for transparent funding systems where funding is linked to service plans, outcomes and incentives for efficiency. Also highlighted are the need to develop approaches to human resource management, the need for organisational reform, the establishment of the Health Information and Quality Authority (HIQA) and the need to invest in and develop information available for planning and organisation. The strategy sets out 121 targets to be achieved over specified timeframes. The 2001 strategy is also underpinned by the primary care strategy, *Primary Care: A New Direction* (DoHC 2001a). Although this was published alongside the *Quality and Fairness* strategy, the primary care sector remains underdeveloped and under-resourced.

Three major reviews of health services have been conducted since the 2001 strategy: the Brennan Report (DoHC 2003a); the Prospectus Report (DoHC 2003b); and the Hanly Report (DoHC 2003c). The key issues identified are summarised in Table 2.3.

The Brennan Report (DoHC 2003a) is the *Report of the Commission on Financial Management and Control Systems in the Health Service*. In its detailed review, the commission noted the absence of any organisation responsible for managing the health service as a unified national system. It also noted that financial management and control systems were not designed to develop cost consciousness among those who make decisions to commit resources and provided no incentives to manage costs effectively; insufficient evaluation and analysis of existing programmes and related expenditure; and inadequate investment in information systems and management development.

The aim of the Prospectus review (DoHC 2003b) was to audit the extent to which the structures and functions of the health system are organised to deliver on the ambitions of the health strategy *Quality and Fairness* (DoHC 2001b). The review found the complex and fragmented structures in the Irish health system an obstacle to achieving improvements. It noted the continued involvement of the Department of Health and Children in operational matters, reducing clarity around organisational accountability, and overlap between specialist agencies and other bodies. It recommended the rationalisation of certain agencies through mainstreaming or merging and the need for standardisation and co-ordination across the system. The review identified particular gaps in relation to governance and accountability and highlighted the need to strengthen service planning and to align resource allocation and planning cycles; the need to strengthen service evaluation; the absence of a consistent focus on the consumer; and the need for a clearer focus on stakeholder participation required at each level of the system.

The Hanly Report (DoHC 2003c) is the *Report of the National Task Force on Medical Staffing*. The task force recommended the development of acute hospital services that are consultant-provided rather than consultant-led and the reconfiguration of acute hospital services to provide patients with access to specialist staff. It also highlighted the need for high volumes of activity in order to maintain consultants' expertise and quality care, and the need to ensure access to appropriate diagnostic and treatment facilities. It recommended the development of integrated hospital networks and supra-regional and national specialist services.

Table 2.3: Summary of issues identified in Irish health policy

Health system	Outcomes
	Equity
	Integration
	Patient focus and stakeholder participation
	Emphasis on acute services
	Capacity and funding
	Decision-making and strategic planning
	Quality systems and information management
	Human resource management
	No one organisation managing a unified health system
	Need to streamline organisations
	Accountability, evaluation and cost-consciousness
	Medical education and training
Hospitals	Configuration of acute hospital services
	Consultant-led rather than consultant-provided
	Shortage of non-consultant hospital doctors (NCHDs)
	Critical mass to sustain consultants and for quality care
Community services	Underdeveloped
	Under-resourced

Source: DoHC (2001b, 2003a, 2003b, 2003c)

CHALLENGES TO HEALTH CARE FINANCING

In a review of health policy across countries, Saltman *et al.* (1999) identify five common key economic challenges facing health policy makers. The first of these is dealing with scarcity. As the resources required to pay for health care become more constrained, pressures on health expenditure increase. Certainly scarcity of resources has been a recurrent theme in Irish health policy. Saltman *et al.* (1999) suggest that this leaves policy makers with two basic options that may also be complementary. One is to move funds from other areas of public sector expenditure or to increase taxation or social insurance contributions. The other option is to control health expenditure by influencing either demand for or supply of health services. In Ireland, a relatively high proportion of public expenditure is allocated to health and this has continued to be the case as economic circumstances change. There has also been a trend to reduce taxation over the last decade or so. However, there are several examples of attempts to reduce demand for and supply of health services. These include the direct payments required of Category II persons who use acute hospital services and GP services, and the use of waiting lists to control numbers seeking elective services. While these direct charges reduce inappropriate use of such health services, they also deter necessary use. Waiting times and overcrowding experienced by patients when they attend for outpatient and emergency department services also act as deterrents to using publicly funded services and provide an incentive to opt for private health care (Tussing & Wren 2006) or to purchase private health insurance.

The second major economic challenge is in relation to funding systems equitably and sustainably and balancing equitable and sustainable funding for services with scarce resources. In Ireland, approximately one-third of the population has Category 1 eligibility, meaning they have full access to all publicly funded health services, on the basis of means testing. While the proportion of the population eligible has remained at approximately one-third, the threshold for access changes over time. For example, the expansion of Category I eligibility to include those over 70 years of age in 2001 (without means testing) came at a time when the government was moving the income-based eligibility line downward by failing to increase it in line with rising incomes, thus taking free medical care away from the poor. Tussing and Wren (2006) estimate that in November 2005, 350,000 lower-income people were not covered by medical cards who would have been covered had coverage remained at its 1996 level. Eligibility does not ensure access to care when it is required and significant differences are reported in the length of time public and private patients wait for elective procedures and to see a consultant (Tussing & Wren 2006). Aside from waiting list times, other factors may limit access to services for those eligible to use them, such as the geographical location of services, the availability of services outside normal business hours, waiting times and the acceptability of services. Differences are also reported in the level of service received between public and private patients, for example whether they receive consultant-led or consultant-provided care, and in the standard of accommodation (Tussing & Wren 2006). Equity also relates to equality, or the opportunity that each individual in society has to reach their full potential in relation to health. Significant inequalities in health have been noted in Ireland, including differences between occupational groups; those less well off or marginalised having poorer health outcomes; geographical differences and particular geographical hot spots; and significant differences in healthy lifestyles between socio-economic groups (CMO 1999). Differences have also been noted in relation to gender and urban–rural locations (Balinda & Wilde 2001).

The third challenge is to allocate resources effectively, and Saltman *et al.* (1999) identify instruments such as contracting that have been developed in countries to provide stronger links between funding and the achievement of policy objectives. There are several examples of such approaches in Ireland over recent years. These include the development of service planning, which links funding with the services to be provided by the HSE and service providers over the coming year, and case-mix budgeting which aims to link acute hospital funding to activity levels based on diagnosis-related group (DRG).

The fourth key challenge is to deliver care efficiently. Difficulties here relate to inefficiency at the micro level, poor co-ordination among providers, lack of incentives for efficient service provision, lack of adequate information on the cost and quality of services, inadequate management of capital resources and the quality of services. Several of these issues have been identified in recent reviews of health services in Ireland.

The fifth key challenge is to implement change. Saltman *et al.* (1999:13) suggest that 'Reform failures have little to do with the relative merits of the reform programme but rather reflect inadequate understanding of the process of reform implementation and the management of change.' They report that policy implementation is influenced by a range of contextual factors and the implementation process is directly affected by the system of government and the distribution of authority as well as the way in which the process itself is conducted. The pace of implementation – whether to go for a 'big bang' or incrementalist approach – and the involvement of stakeholders are seen as key determinants of policy change. The development of the latest Irish health strategy (DoHC 2001b) involved nationwide consultation with key stakeholders. In addition, the strategy itself included an implementation plan and the 121 targets included are reasonably specific and time-bound. Regular reviews of progress have been undertaken over the eight years since the strategy was first launched. In addition, corporate and service plans produced by the HSE reflect the targets set out and the progress made year on year towards achieving the objectives. There is no doubt that the approach adopted was a 'big-bang' approach and the health system in 2010 is considerably different from that in 2001. However, further bedding down of the reforms is required before the full effects of the reforms can be evaluated fully.

CONCLUSIONS

Several economic concerns have influenced the development of health policy in Ireland since the 1960s. These include the availability of resources in the light of increasing demands and changing population demographics. There has also been significant concern about the lack of transparency in relation to financing health services and the need to adopt more systematic and analytical approaches to planning. The service planning process and case-mix funding provide a stronger link between funding provided and the services provided. However, further developments are required to more closely match services to the assessed needs of the population as a whole and the different groups within the population. Issues such as cost containment, equity, efficiency, effectiveness and accountability prevail despite a range of policy statements over the years highlighting the need to address these concerns. Examples of specific experiences and concerns continue to feature regularly in the Irish news media. The Irish health system has undergone a sustained and progressive programme of reform since the Health Act 1970, which has been renewed regularly through subsequent health strategies. However, the most recent wave of reforms has involved a major restructuring of the health system itself. Although these reforms are based on wide consultation and expert reviews, it will take some time for the reforms to become properly established and for their effects to impact on health outcomes. In addition, the sudden downturn in the economy will prove to be an additional challenge to the reform programme itself.

REFLECTIVE EXERCISES

1   In your own experiences as a health care provider, manager, patient, relation
    or citizen, how does economics affect health services in Ireland?

2   How equitable is the Irish health system?

3   What are the options available to health policy makers in Ireland to increase
    investment in health care?

4   Would a social insurance model be more appropriate for the Irish health
    system?

REFERENCES

Alakeson, V. (2008) 'America's health choices', *British Medical Journal* 27 (337):
    720–2.

Balinda, K. and Wilde, J. (2001) *Inequalities in Mortality: A Report on All-Ireland
    Mortality Data*. Dublin: Institute of Public Health in Ireland.

CMO (1999) *Annual Report of the Chief Medical Officer*. Dublin: Department
    of Health and Children.

Commission on Health Funding (1989) *Report of the Commission on Health
    Funding*. Dublin: Government Publications.

CSO (Central Statistics Office) (2008a) *Health Status and Health Service
    Utilisation: Quarterly National Household Survey, Quarter 3 2007*. Dublin:
    Central Statistics Office.

— (2008b). *Principal Statistics: Estimated Non-Capital Health Expenditure by
    Programme*. Dublin: Central Statistics Office.

Department of Finance (2008). *Summary of 2009 Budget Measures – Policy
    Changes*. Available at http://www.budget.gov.ie/2009/budgetsummary09
    .html#_Toc211585097, accessed 17 December 2008.

— (2009) *Pre-Budget Outlook*. Statement issued on 12 November 2009 by the
    Minister for Finance, Mr Brian Lenihan TD. Available at
    http://www.finance.gov.ie/viewdoc.asp?DocID=6080, accessed 16 November
    2009.

Dobrow, M., Goel, V. and Upshur, R. (2004) 'Evidence-based health policy:
    context and utilisation', *Social Science and Medicine* 58: 207–17.

DoH (Department of Health) (1986) *Health, the Wider Dimensions: A
    Consultative Statement on Health Policy*. Dublin: Stationery Office.

— (1994) *Shaping a Healthier Future*. Dublin: Stationery Office.

DoHC (Department of Health and Children) (2001a) *Primary Care: A New
    Direction*. Dublin: Stationery Office.

— (2001b) *Quality and Fairness: A Health System for You*. Dublin: Stationery
    Office.

— (2003a) *Report of the Commission on Financial Management and Control
    Systems in the Health Service* (Brennan Report). Dublin: Stationery Office.

— (2003b) *Audit of Structures and Functions in the Health System* (Prospectus
    Report). Dublin: Stationery Office.

— (2003c) *Report of the National Task Force on Medical Staffing* (Hanly Report). Dublin: Stationery Office.

ESRI (Economic and Social Research Institute) (2008). *Irish Economy: Current Trends*. Available at http://www.esri.ie/irish_economy/, accessed 17 December 2008.

Fitz Gerald, J. and Kearney, I. (2000) *Convergence in Living Standards in Ireland: The Role of the New Economy?* Dublin: Economic and Social Research Institute.

Global Insight (2008) 'BUPA calls for government intervention as Irish High Court rejects challenge to risk equalisation scheme'. Available at http://www.globalinsight.com/SDA/SDADetail7608.htm, accessed 1 December 2008.

Health Insurance Authority (2008) *Risk Equalisation: Updated Guide to the Risk Equalisation Scheme, 2003 as prescribed in Statutory Instruments No. 261 of 2003, No. 710 of 2003, No. 334 of 2005 and No. 220 of 2007*. Available at http:// www.hia.ie/sec3_reports/Updated%20Guide%20to%20Risk%20 Equalisation%20Scheme.pdf, accessed 11 December 2008.

Johnson-Lans, S. (2006) *A Health Economics Primer*. USA: Addison Wesley.

Kutzin, J. (2001) 'A descriptive framework for country-level analysis of health care financing arrangements', *Health Policy* 56: 171–204.

Lancaster, J. (1999) *Nursing Issues in Leading and Managing Change*. St. Louis: Mosby Inc.

Lynch, F. (1998) 'Health funding and expenditure in Ireland' in McAuliffe, E. and Joyce, L. (eds), *A Healthier Future? Managing Healthcare in Ireland*. Dublin: Institute of Public Administration.

McCreevy, C. (2003) Launch of Health Reform Programme, comments by Charlie McCreevy TD, Minister for Finance (18 June). Available at http://www.finance.gov.ie/viewdoc.asp?DocID=168&CatID=1&StartDate=01 +January+2003&m= , accessed 11 December 2008.

Milstead, J. (2004) *Health Policy and Politics: A Nurse's Guide*. USA: Jones & Bartlett Publishers.

Mossialos, E. and Dixon, A. (2002) 'Funding health care in Europe: the options' in Mossialos, E., Dixon, A., Figueras, J. and Kutzin, J. (eds), *Funding Health Care: Options for Europe*. Buckingham: Open University Press.

Mossialos, E., Dixon, A., Figueras, J. and Kutzin, J. (eds) (2002), *Funding Health Care: Options for Europe*. Buckingham: Open University Press.

Nolan, A. (2008) 'Evaluating the impact of eligibility for free care on the use of general practitioner (GP) services: a difference-in-difference matching approach', *Social Science and Medicine*, 67: 1164–72.

Normand, C., Thomas, S. and Smith, S. (2006) *Social Health Insurance: Options for Ireland*. Dublin: Adelaide Society.

O'Dowd, T. (2007). 'The private sector in healthcare: contributing to service but not to research', *Irish Journal of Medical Science* 176: 261–5.

OECD (Organisation for Economic Co-operation and Development) (1992) *The Reform of Health Care – A Comparative Analysis of Seven OECD Countries.* Paris: OECD.

— (1997) *OECD Economic Surveys: Ireland.* Paris: OECD.

— (2008) *OECD Health Data 2008: How Does Ireland Compare?* Paris: OECD.

O'Hara, T. (1998) 'Current structure of the Irish healthcare system – setting the context' in Leahy, A. and Wiley, M. (eds), *The Irish Health System in the 21st Century.* Dublin: Oak Tree Press.

PA Consulting (2007) *Acute Hospital Bed Capacity Review: A Preferred Health System in Ireland to 2020.* London: PA Consulting Group.

Rice, N. and Smith, P. (2002). 'Strategic resource allocation and funding decisions' in Mossialos, E., Dixon, A., Figueras, J. and Kutzin, J. (eds), *Funding Health Care in Europe: The Options.* Buckingham: Open University Press.

Ritsatakis, A., Barnes, R., Dekker, E. *et al.* (2000) *Exploring Health Policy Development in Europe.* WHO Regional Publications.

Saltman, R., Figueras, J. and Sakellardies, C. (1999) *Critical Challenges for Health Care Reform in Europe.* Buckingham: Open University Press.

Tussing, A. and Wren, M. (2006). *How Ireland Cares: The Case for Health Care Reform.* Dublin: New Island.

Weale, A. E. (1988) *Cost and Choice in Health Care.* London: King's Fund.

Weiss, C. (1987) 'Where politics and evaluation research meet' in Palumbo, D. (ed.), *The Politics of Program Evaluation.* Newbury Park: Sage.

WHO (World Health Organisation) (2000) *The World Health Report 2000: Health Systems, Improving Performance.* Geneva: WHO.

— (2005) *Achieving Universal Health Coverage: Developing the Health Financing System.* Geneva: WHO, Department of Health Systems Financing.

Wiley, M. (1998) 'Health, housing and social welfare' in Kennedy, K. (ed.), *From Feast to Famine: Economic and Social Change in Ireland 1847–1997.* Dublin: Institute of Public Administration.

— (2005) 'The Irish health system: developments in strategy, structure, funding and delivery since 1980', *Health Economics* 14: S169–86.

Wiley, M. and Fetter, R. (1990). *Measuring Activity and Costs in Irish Hospitals: A Study of Hospital Case Mix.* Dublin: Economic and Social Research Institute.

Fundamentals of Service Provision

3
Leadership and Management Principles

Phil Halligan

OBJECTIVES
- To critically discuss the work context of leaders and managers.
- To critically discuss the nature of leadership and management in health care.
- To review the historical development of leadership and management theories.
- To critically evaluate the concepts of leadership and management.
- To examine how relevant the theories of leadership and management are to the context of health care.

INTRODUCTION

In the contemporary media, the principles of leadership and management in the Irish health service are often debated, as leadership has become viewed as a panacea for all ills in the context of rapid social change. While the focus on leadership is essential for moving the health agenda forward, there has been little consensus regarding what counts as leadership, why leadership is needed and how leadership relates to the health care context. Conversely, management is viewed as a mundane activity, with many agreeing that the health service is over 'managed' and under 'led'. The principles of leadership and management appear to be poorly understood by clinicians, particularly in terms of their application and in regard to why clinicians need to be competent in both leadership and management in order to deliver patient care effectively. This chapter has two aims: to clarify your understanding of leadership and management; and to challenge the assumptions you may have in regard to these principles. Thus, it will enable you to think critically about what you have observed about leadership and management in clinical practice and to appraise what has been written about leadership and management in the health care context. In addition, current theories of management and leadership in the context of health care will be examined in order to enable you to develop a deeper understanding of the principles and competencies that managers must possess in order to manage and lead in a constantly changing environment. Therefore, it is important to discuss the work context of leaders and managers.

This chapter is aimed primarily at health care providers who operate at the front line of services in managing care provided to patients. In this chapter, the multidisciplinary team which, for example, consists of medical, nursing, and allied health professionals will be referred to as 'clinicians' and health facilities will be referred to as health care organisations (HCOs).

THE HEALTH CARE CONTEXT

The nature of leadership and management is linked inextricably to the nature of the environment; thus changes at national and governmental levels tend to be felt at the grass roots of clinical practice. Currently, the environment in which clinicians work is in a state of reform. A key feature of this reform involves the devolution of accountability for spending. This means that clinicians, health professionals and general mangers are now held responsible for the financial implications of their clinical and management decisions. The Health Service Executive (HSE) clinical managers are now required to prepare a service plan for the current year. However, many clinicians are restricted from participating in political decisions and have limited ability to influence decisions made in their organisations. According to Tussing and Wren (2006), accountability remains blurred; thus, more clarity is needed on the respective roles of the HSE and the Department of Health and Children.

Currently, the Irish health care system is large in scale and increasing in complexity (DoHC 2003a). Health care organisations are complex social systems, hierarchical and rigid, partly due to the multiple external agencies required to maintain the functioning of the organisation: for example, the government, accreditation agencies, professional organisations, educational institutions, insurance companies, private employers, pharmaceutical companies, researchers, patient advocacy groups and the media. The problem is that the diverse interests of all of these auxiliary agencies simultaneously influence the way the organisations are organised; consequently, the fundamental features of organising, including communication, shared goals and problem solving, are difficult to achieve. Often, organisations representing a single professional group, such as the Irish Nurses and Midwives Organisation (INMO) or the Irish Medical Organisation (IMO) attempt to exert influence on behalf of their members, for example by lobbying for improved regulations and increased funding in order to provide better care for their clients, such as the INO lobbying to reduce patients' waiting times. In addition, health care organisations are characterised by increasing specialisation, for example centres of excellence and increasing interdependence among care providers; these factors may result in further impingement on the capacity of clinicians and managers to communicate effectively. The dynamics of each profession unfolds in multiple hierarchies which shape the organisation's culture, socialisation processes and day-to-day activities (Ramanujam and Rousseau 2006).

The core of the hospital workforce is comprised primarily of professionals, including physicians, nurses, pharmacists, occupational therapists and physiotherapists; each profession has its own governing authorities. In the Irish public health service sector, approximately 101,978 people are employed; thus, health is one of the largest public service employers (DoHC 2001). The distribution of professional staff employed in the health service from 1997 to 2006 is presented in Figure 3.1. A large proportion of the staff are employed on a short-term basis or contract; thus, for these individuals, building a capacity to work together is difficult as they have limited organisational ties and few shared experiences. Furthermore, the linkages across hierarchical levels and functioning divisions are weak; therefore staff may serve different missions and interact with various constituencies (Ramanujam & Rousseau 2006). In particular, physicians often provide services to several hospitals, thereby weakening their attachment to one organisation.

Figure 3.1: Distribution of staff in the Irish health service

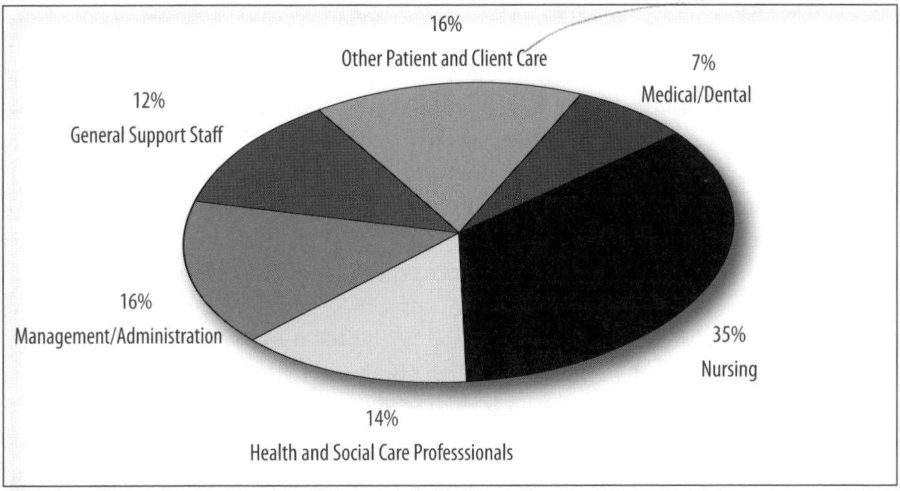

Source: DoHC (2008)

Today, patients and their families are now better informed than ever before. Many consumers can access information via the internet from agencies such as Cochrane Collaboration and the National Institute for Health and Clinical Excellence (NICE). Although guidelines to best practice are provided on many medical conditions, they may have negative implications for the financial health of HCOs. The primary aim of providing this information is to increase research-based awareness of these conditions, but it results in many clinicians facing dilemmas about the cost of certain treatments and finding the resources and skills necessary to provide them. Patients' support and advocacy groups have also grown and have become increasingly active in lobbying governments for quality care. Consequently, professionals and managers are under greater pressure to seek new ways of improving the quality of care and to evaluate the outcomes of care based on international best practice.

The use of services is also steadily increasing as a result of the changing demographic pattern that has emerged due to increases in longevity, chronic illness, immigration, patient expectations and inequalities. In Ireland, population projections for the next 20 years indicate that the population will increase and that the largest proportion of the population will consist of older people. Furthermore, the 'two-tier' element of hospital treatment, whereby public patients do not have the same access to elective treatment as do private patients, has increased the discontent that clinicians have to face daily.

In this section, the context of Irish health care has been examined and the many challenges faced by health care managers and leaders in the contemporary health care system have been presented. The following sections will examine the concepts of leadership and management; why they are important, and why they are significant in health care.

LEADERSHIP

There is much confusion regarding what leadership is, who the leaders are, and what purpose leaders serve in the health care system. In the last decade, the emphasis on leadership in the health care system has resulted in the design of numerous development programmes to enhance the leaders' ability to deliver care. For example, the three-day   Leading an Empowered Organisation (LEO) programme was designed for health care professionals from all disciplines with all levels of expertise.

In times of uncertainty and turbulence, there is always a call for leadership. When problems emerge the question on everyone's lips is, 'Where are the leaders to sort them out?' Leadership may be one of the most examined, most observed and least understood phenomena on earth (Burns 1978). Everyone assumes that they are an expert on leadership and believes that leadership is something 'out there' that belongs to a few privileged people or is someone else's responsibility. In health care, leadership is mainly thought of as someone in a senior management position in the hospital or at the top of their professional hierarchy. Although many professionals occupy senior positions, they often fail to lead. It is assumed that leadership is achievable without any preparation and that skills can be obtained adequately in standard 'line management' courses. An additional problem is that health care professionals tend to be insular and parochial in that they concentrate on their own clinical domain and, therefore, do not seek to influence the broader social-political factors that impinge on health for all, for example poverty, homelessness and unemployment.

Stogdill (1974) has highlighted the fact that there are almost as many definitions of leadership as there are people who have tried to define leadership. Although leadership can viewed from many perspectives, the most common views are that leadership is derived from: a *personality perspective*, whereby the leader has a combination of special traits that enables him/her to accomplish tasks; a *group process perspective*, whereby the leader has a centre-stage role and embodies the will of the group; the perspective of *an instrument of goal attainment*, who helps leaders achieve their goals and ensures that their needs are met; and a *skills perspective*, which stresses the capabilities that make effective leadership possible.

Northouse (2004) contends that the following components are central to leadership: it is a *process*, involving *influence*, occurs within a *group* context and involves *goal* attainment. Leadership can be complementary to management and involves influencing across, up and down within the organisation and externally to the organisation. It is about working with people to maximise their potential as individuals and team players in order to create a positive, healthy work environment. In addition, leadership demands and challenges you to know yourself and have a good awareness of your qualities as an individual and a leader. Northouse's (2004:3) definition reflects these essential components: 'leadership is a process whereby an individual influences a group of individuals to achieve a common goal'.

In addition, further confusion exists between the concepts of leadership and clinical leadership. According to Millward and Bryan (2005), leadership is about behaviour, setting direction, opening up possibilities, helping people to achieve, and communicating. In contrast, they claim that clinical leadership is about facilitating evidence-based practice and improved patient outcomes through local care. The analysis and discourse of clinical leadership is the most 'poorly developed, reflecting perhaps a lack of investment in clinical practice and the lack of recognizable clinical leaders' (Antrobus 1997:45).

Effective leadership is viewed as being of significant importance as it is a key ingredient in the reform of the Irish health service. The Irish government (DoHC 2001) has stated that clear leadership, consistent effort and wide collaboration are essential elements in implementing system reforms. Within the health service, the concept of leadership is emphasised throughout many documents on reform (Commission on Nursing 1998; DoHC 2001, 2003a, 2003b). The most recent Irish health strategy (DoHC 2001), which has established a vision of a health care system, states that what is required is:

> A health system that supports and empowers you, your family and community to achieve your full health potential. A health system that is there when you need it, that is fair, and that you can trust. A health system that encourages you to have your say, listens to you, and ensures that your views are taken into account.
>
> (DoHC 2001:8)

The health strategy's vision of reform states that an effective, positive and potent force for change within is one which offers significant opportunities for future clinicians to engage fully in leadership.

Traditional leadership theories

Leadership theories were developed and popularised during times of great change. Many leadership theories focus on the leader, the relationship between the leader and the subordinate/follower or the situation/environment in which the leader has to operate. Figure 3.2 gives an overview of the evolution of leadership theories.

Figure 3.2: Evolution of the major theories of leadership

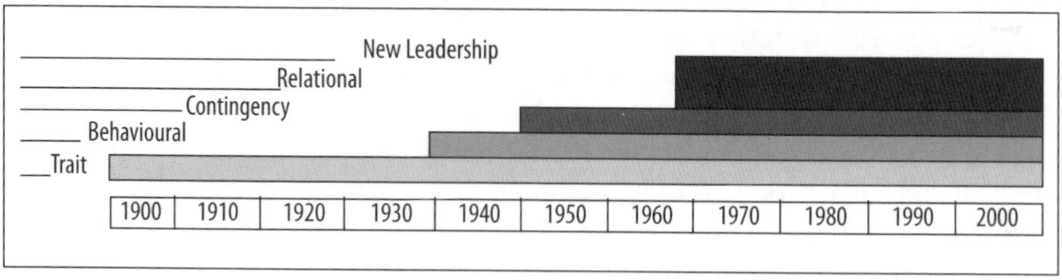

	1900	1910	1920	1930	1940	1950	1960	1970	1980	1990	2000

New Leadership
Relational
Contingency
Behavioural
Trait

Trait Theory

The 'Great Man Theory', one of the first leadership approaches, proposed that leaders are born with certain traits and natural abilities of power and influence. In the 1920s, researchers began to examine the question of whether leaders have specific traits, such as intelligence, height, charisma, that differentiate them from nonleaders and contribute to their success. It was hypothesised that if traits could be identified leaders could be predicted. However, in general, research indicated that a weak relationship exists between personal traits and leader success. In viewing leadership as a trait, the focus is solely on the leader and leadership is conceptualised as a set of innate properties possessed by certain people. The selection of personnel is often built on dubious criteria, for example a potential leader may be 'talent spotted' by the hierarchy and encouraged to go for promotion, which reinforces the myth that leaders are born and not made.

In 1948, Stogdill reviewed the literature in order to determine what traits had been found to be consistent with effective leadership and, in doing so, revealed a number of traits, including intelligence, initiative, honesty, interpersonal skills, and self confidence; more importantly, however, it was found that particular traits were often relative to the situation. Intelligence was the trait that most often emerged in studies (Kotter 1990). In Judge, Colbert and Ilies's (2004) meta-analysis study, they also found that intelligence and leadership were significantly associated with each other.

Although the picture of personal qualities for leadership is still not complete or agreed, an implication of these findings is that organisations should concern themselves with the selection of leaders rather than with the development of leaders (Grint 2001). The strength of the trait perspective of leadership is that it is intuitively appealing, has a large research base, has offered an in-depth understanding of the leader component in the leadership process and has provided benchmarks against which individuals can evaluate their personal leadership attributes (Northouse 2004). However, the trait approach does not delimit a definite list of leadership traits, nor does it link traits with organisations or employee outcomes, and it does not take the impact of situations into account. The trait approach ignores the environmental influences on the leader's personality and vice versa. Although traits continue to be of interest to researchers, the emphasis has now shifted to the emotional intelligence component of the leader.

Behavioural theory

When it became clear that researchers were not able to identify a specific set of traits, the focus of attention shifted to examining what leaders *do* rather than who leaders *are*. Behavioural theorists propose the idea that a good leader is anyone who adopts the appropriate behaviour. Thus, the focus of research changed from a factor that one possesses to an activity that an individual engages in, which suggests that leadership can be learned. The research that emerged after this shift in focus attempted to determine the specific dimensions of leader behaviour and the ways in which the behaviour of effective leaders differs from that of ineffective ones. The Leader Behaviour Description Questionnaire (LBQD) instrument, developed by researchers at the Ohio State Research Centre, which was administered to hundreds of employees, resulted in two categories of leader behaviour types: *consideration* and *initiating structure*. Consideration refers to the extent to which a leader is sensitive to the followers' feelings and problems and establishes mutual trust; in contrast, initiating structure pertains to the extent to which a leader directs task to be completed, works people hard, plans and provides explicit working schedules. Today, these leader behaviour types continue to be used in assessing leadership behaviours.

At the University of Michigan, research took a slightly different approach in which the behaviour of effective and ineffective supervisors were compared; this research produced two types of leadership behaviour, which correspond to the Ohio State dimensions: *employee-centred* and *job-centred*. However, unlike the Ohio State categories, the Michigan researchers viewed the leadership behaviour categories as distinct from each other. Building on the work of Ohio State and Michigan studies, Blake and Mouton (1964, 1978, 1985) developed a theory known as the Leadership Grid, in which leaders are rated on a scale of one to nine according to two criteria: *concern for people* and *concern for production*. The aforementioned theories assume that a leader adopts a general leadership style, but in contrast, a more recent leadership theory, the Leader-member Exchange Theory (LMX) developed by Graen (2004), explores the specific relationship between a leader and each individual group member. The LMX theory is based on the idea that a unique relationship develops between a leader and each of his/her subordinates, which determines how the leader behaves towards the member and how the member responds to the leader. Thus, leadership became viewed as a series of dyads or two-person interactions. Proponents of LMX theory examine the question of why leaders have more influence over and a greater impact on some members than others and focus on the concept of exchange – what each party gives to and receives from the other. 'Rich' dyads are those in which there is a high level of giving and receiving by both partners, while 'poor' dyads are those in which there is very little give and take between dyadic partners.

Contingency theory

In contingency theory, developed by Fiedler (1967), the effective contextual and situational variables influencing leadership behaviours were examined. Fiedler proposed that leaders can improve their leadership effectiveness by analysing their situation and tailoring their behaviour to it. Contingency theory is based on two forms of leadership behaviour: *relationship-motivated* and *task-motivated*. This model suggests that a model of contingent leadership can be constructed by using the 'Least Preferred Co-worker' (LPC) instrument, which involves asking each worker who s/he least likes to work with. The results of this research indicate that task-orientated leaders perform best in situations where there is either high or low control, whereas relationship-motivated leaders work best in situations where such polar extremes do not exist. Thus, in extreme uncertainty or extreme certainty situations, task-motivated leaders are more successful than relationship-motivated leaders (Grint 2001). Contingency theories, also known as situational theories, emphasise that leadership does not occur within a vacuum, separated from the various elements of the group or organisational situation. In the contingency or situational approach, both the essence of the individual and the context are knowable and critical; the context of the organisation environment determines the specific kind of leadership behaviour (Grint 2001). According to Grint, a particular problem is that the environment is constantly turbulent, as in HCOs; thus, what is appropriate today may be inappropriate tomorrow. A weakness of the contingency model is that it ignores the attributes of the subordinates and does not measure the leader's preferences for co-workers; however, Grint (2001) has raised the question of whether we are absolutely certain that we can measure the 'situation' with any degree of accuracy. Furthermore, contingency theories do not explain *how* leadership styles vary in terms of organisational level or at the top executive level (Zaccaro and Klimoski 2001; Gill 2006) and they do not explain how leaders can change either their style or the situation (Nicholson 2001). Furthermore, contingency theories do not explain the leadership processes of acquiring and interpreting the meaning of information, social networking and strategic decision making (Fleishman *et al.* 1991).

Path-goal theory

Another well-known and often-cited contingency approach to leadership is the 'Path-Goal Theory', developed by House (1971). House proposed that leaders change their behaviour to match the situation and that the leader's responsibility is to increase the subordinates' motivation to attain personal and organisational goals. The leader is able to increase the subordinates' motivation in one of two ways: by clarifying the rewards that are available to the subordinates by working with them in order to help them identify and to learn the behaviours that will result in successful task accomplishment and organisational rewards; or by increasing the rewards that the subordinates value and desire by talking to them in order to learn which rewards, such as a pay increase or promotion, are important to them. The path-goal theory involves four categories of leader behaviours which every leader is able to adopt, depending on the situation: *supportive*, *directive*, *achievement-oriented* and *participative styles*. Supportive leadership resembles consideration or people-oriented leadership, described earlier, in which concern is shown for the subordinates' well-being and personal needs. The leader is open, friendly and approachable and creates a team climate in which all persons are treated as equals. In directive leadership, subordinates are informed of what they are supposed to do – this is similar to initiating structure or task-oriented leadership. The leader's behaviour includes planning, making schedules, setting performance goals and behaviour standards and stressing adherence to rules and regulations. Participative leadership involves consulting with subordinates about decisions, which may include asking for opinions and suggestions, encouraging participation in decision making and setting up meetings with subordinates in the workplace. In achievement-orientated leadership, clear and challenging goals for subordinates are established and high-quality performance and improvement over current performance are emphasised. The leaders inspire confidence in subordinates and assist them in learning how to achieve high goals. In the path-goal theory, four important situational contingencies are necessary: 1) the personal characteristics of group members (e.g. ability, skills, needs and motivations); 2) the work environment, including the degree of task structure (formal job descriptions and work procedures); 3) the nature of the formal authority system (the amount of legitimate power used by leaders and the extent to which policies and rules constrain employees' behaviour); and 4) the work group itself (the educational level of the employees and the quality of relationships between them).

Relational theory

In the late 1970s researchers began to investigate how leaders and followers interact and influence each other. Relational theorists view leadership as a relational process that engages all participants and enables each person to contribute to achieving the vision, in contrast to perspectives that view leadership as something that a leader does to someone (Daft 2005). The most notable leadership categories in relational theory are servant, transactional and transformational leadership theories.

Servant leadership

Servant leadership theory was developed by Greenleaf (1977). Greenleaf asserts that servant leaders transcend self-interest in order to serve the needs of others, to help others grow and develop and to provide the opportunity for others to gain materially and emotionally. In organisations the top priority of servant leaders is to attend to the needs of others, including employees, customers, shareholders and the general public. The servant leadership model is based on four basic precepts: put service before self-interest; listen first to affirm others; inspire trust by being trustworthy; and nourish others in order to help them become whole (Daft 2005). Servant leadership brings out the best in one's followers and requires that leaders rely on one-to-one communication in order to understand the abilities, needs, desires, goals and potential of the followers (Linden *et al.* 2008). In emphasising personal integrity and the forming of strong, long-term relationships with employees, the servant leadership model resembles the transformational leadership concepts of idealised influence and intellectual stimulation (Linden *et al.* 2008). However, Stone *et al.* (2004) argue that a difference between these approaches is that servant leadership focuses on that which is best for the followers, while transformational leadership emphasises the vision of the organisation. To date, servant leadership has been discussed almost entirely within the American context (Farling *et al.* 1999) and there is little empirical evidence concerning the applicability of servant leadership across cultures (Hale & Fields 2007). Thus, the question arises whether servant leadership is a North American concept with limited utility. Recent studies have begun to test the servant leadership model, using evidence produced from 1999 to 2004, including the work of Farling *et al.*, (1999), Page and Wong (2000), Russell and Stone (2002), and Sendjaya and Santora (2002) and the development of instruments by Laub (1999), Page and Wong (2000), and Sendjaya and Santora (2002). In the health care literature, servant leadership is often advocated as an appropriate model of leadership to follow. The attraction of the servant leadership model may be due to the health professional's desire of wanting to serve and contrasts sharply with approaches in which one wants first and foremost to be a leader.

Transactional and transformational leadership

In transactional leadership, an exchange or transaction occurs between leaders and followers. The leader recognises the followers' needs and desires and then clarifies how those needs and desires will be satisfied in exchange for the follower meeting specified objectives. In other words, followers receive rewards for job performance. Transactional leaders focus on the present context and excel at keeping the organisation running smoothly and efficiently; they are particularly good at traditional management functions such as planning and budgeting. Transactional leaders maintain stability within the organisation rather than promoting change, and these skills are important for all leaders.

In contrast, transformational leadership is characterised by the ability to bring about significant change, whereby leaders do more than interact with subordinates or followers. Transformational leaders stimulate followers to transcend their own interests for the greater good of the group, organisation or society. According to Bass and Avolio's (1994) 'model of transformation', leaders tend to use one of the following approaches: *individualised consideration* (listening; identifying personal concerns, needs and abilities; delegating by way of development; feedback and coaching), *intellectual stimulation* (questioning the status quo, challenging their thinking, encouraging imagination and creativity), *inspirational motivation* (clear vision, treating threats and problems as opportunities to learn) and *idealised influence* (expressing confidence in vision, displaying a sense of purpose, determination, trust and persistence) (Gill 2006). Transformational leaders have the ability to produce change in the organisation's vision, strategy and culture by focusing on intangible qualities such as vision, shared values and ideas in order to build relationships. Thus, transformational leaders have the potential to create change in followers and in organisations. The most effective leaders exhibit both the transactional and transformational leadership patterns, tend to use consultative, participative, delegative and directive styles to a significant extent and are more active and flexible in their leadership behaviour (Gill 2006). However, Bass and Avolio's model is not without its shortcomings, as issues regarding the validity of its factor structure have been highlighted by Den Hartog and Koopman (1997) and Hinkin and Tracey (1999), and low discriminant validity among the scales has been noted by Avolio *et al.* (1999). In addition, very little attention has been given to vision, which Deetz *et al.* (2000) have identified as the key difference between a leader and a manager. The generalisability of the model across hierarchical levels in organisations has also been questioned (Bryman 1996); and Edwards and Gill (2003) and Oshagbemi and Gill (2004) have found that transformational leadership has been displayed more at higher levels, while Bass (1997) states that it occurs at all levels.

Kouzes and Posner's five practices of exemplary leadership

Kouzes and Posner's (1987) model, one of the best-known models of transformational leadership and the most widely used instrument in the health care literature, was developed from an analysis of personal best cases and is now known as the Five Practices of Exemplary Leadership:

1   Model the Way
2   Inspire a Shared Vision
3   Challenge the Process
4   Enable Others to Act
5   Encourage the Heart.

From their analysis, Kouzes and Posner developed the 'Leadership Practices Inventory' (LPI), which attempts to provide a 360° perspective on the leadership practices that they uncovered. The LPI is today one of the most widely used leadership assessment instruments.

Situational leadership

Situational leadership, developed by Hersey and Blanchard in the late 1980s, is a model, not a theory. It proposes that there is not a best way to influence people. The leadership style a person should use with individuals or groups depends on the followers' readiness level. According to Hersey *et al.* (1988), people tend to be at various levels of readiness, depending on the task that they are asked to do. Ability and willingness are the major components of readiness. No one style is effective in all situations; the appropriateness and effectiveness of a style depends on the situation. Hersey and Blanchard propose four styles of situational leadership. In Style 1 (S1), leadership is characterised by above average amounts of task behaviour and below average amounts of relationship behaviour. In contrast, Style 2 (S2) consists of above average amounts of task and relationship behaviour, while in Style 3 (S3) there are above average amounts of relationship behaviour and below average amounts of task behaviour, and in Style 4 (S4) there are below average amounts of both relationship behaviour and task behaviour. The readiness concept pertains to specific situations and not to a total sense of readiness.

MANAGEMENT

While the concept of management can be traced back to 3000 BC, the study of management is a relatively new field. Management is viewed as a business and human organisation activity and, put simply, refers to getting people together to accomplish desired goals. Thus, management can be considered an art in that it involves getting things done through people. The person or people who perform the act(s) of management are referred to as managers. In all organisations management tends to operate at three levels: top, middle and front line. How a person operates as a manager tends to be very individualistic. On the basis of extensive literature reviews and discussions with health care managers, one is led to believe that management is something that one dislikes, and that managers are often viewed as 'out of touch' with what is happening. The contemporary changes occurring in the Irish economy challenge health care managers to be prudent in terms of reducing costs and meeting the demands for services while simultaneously providing a culture of safety and well-being.

A general lack of management skills in employees can be detrimental to any organisation; however, in health care organisations the importance of management cannot be over-emphasised. As far back as the Briggs Report (1972), good care has been equated with good management. The consequences of poor management include poor decision-making, frustrated employees, lower productivity, higher incidence of medical errors and high turnover, sick leave and absenteeism among employees, all of which, ultimately, have an impact on patient care. Supervisors and managers must have vocational and technical knowledge about their specialised field of operation in the organisation and knowledge about management functions and principles. The work component of all jobs rests on two pillars of work: technical and management.

A brief description of the progression of the main schools of management thought now follows. One of the first management theories, the classical perspective, emerged during the nineteenth century and encompasses three areas: scientific management; bureaucratic organisations; and administrative principles.

The classical perspective

Among the most notable theorists on the study of management practices during the nineteenth century were Frederick Taylor (1856–1916), Henri Fayol (1841–1925) and Max Weber (1864–1920).

Frederick Taylor: scientific management

Frederick Taylor, now known as the father of scientific management, was a young engineer who, frustrated with the lack of improvements in labour productivity, suggested that the problems lay in poor management practices. His experiences as an apprentice, a foreman and then a chief engineer gave Taylor first-hand knowledge of the workings of the organisation and the ability to see opportunities for improving the quality of management (Koontz & Weihrich 1988). Taylor proposed that precise procedures developed from studying individual situations replace decisions based on rules of thumb and tradition. The basic principles of scientific management are that standard methods for performing each job are developed; employees who have the appropriate abilities for each job are selected, trained in standard methods and supported by planning their work, eliminating interruptions and providing incentives for increased output. However, Taylor did not take a number of factors into account, including the social context of work, the higher needs of employees and variance between individuals, but tended to view employees as uninformed and ignored their ideas and suggestions (Daft 2003).

Henri Fayol: administrative principles

Henri Fayol, a French engineer, focused on the organisation as a whole entity. On his journey to the top of the company, Fayol documented his own management experiences and, in doing so, produced 14 management principles which he later reduced to four: unity of command; division of work; unity of direction; and scalar chain. Fayol proposed that these principles could be applied to every organisation and identified five basic functions of management: planning, organising, commanding, co-ordinating and controlling. These functions are now used in almost all managerial job descriptions; they provide the foundation of textbooks on management principles that are used today; and they apply to political, religious, military and other undertakings (Koontz & Weihrich 1988). It is important to note that Fayol's principles were based on his own experience in industry and he emphasised that the principles should be treated as flexible. However, Fayol believed that there is a better way, other than by experience, to learn to manage: by developing a body of knowledge that can be taught (Wren *et al.* 2002). In contrast to Taylor's supervisory position, Fayol used a bottom-up approach.

Max Weber: bureaucracy theory

The word 'bureaucracy' introduced by Max Weber proposed the idea that organisations that are based on rational authority are more efficient and more adaptable to change. He believed that hierarchy, authority and bureaucracy lie at the foundation of all social organisations (Koontz & Weihrich 1988). Weber also argued that using rational authority would mean that employee selection would be based on competence rather than 'whom you know'. The central tenets of bureaucratic organisations are that labour is divided along clear lines of authority and responsibility, positions are organised in a hierarchy of authority, all personnel are selected on the basis of their qualifications, all administrative decisions are recorded in writing, management is separate from the ownership of the organisation, and managers are subject to rules and procedures in order to ensure reliable and predictable behaviour.

The behavioural approaches

The second management approach, known as the humanistic perspective on management, emphasises the importance of understanding humans in the workplace and has two elements: the human relations movement, and the human resources perspective.

The human relations movement

A series of experimental studies on worker production were conducted at an electrical company in Chicago, Illinois, circa 1924, in an effort to increase productivity; these studies are referred to as the Hawthorne studies. The studies were conducted over a six-year period and involved four experimental and three control groups. Professors Elton Mayo and F. J. Roethlisberger determined the effect of illumination and other conditions upon workers and their productivity. Modifying rest breaks, shortening length of workday and varying incentives pay systems did not explain any changes in productivity, but social factors did: these included morale, satisfactory interrelationships between members of a work group and effective management (motivation, leading and communicating). However, it is important to note that the Hawthorne studies had numerous flaws that may have affected the results: for example, the participants received a pay increase for participating; they may have felt important; and their behaviour changed due to being observed (the Hawthorne effect). Despite the flaws of the Hawthorne studies, this research demonstrated the treating employees well will result in better outcomes or performance.

The human resources perspective

The human resources perspective combines prescriptions for the design of job tasks with theories of motivation and proposes that jobs should be designed to avoid dehumanising and demeaning situations for employees and to allow employees to develop their full potential. Abraham Maslow, a psychologist, proposed in 1943 a hierarchy of needs: physiological needs; safety needs; love needs; esteem needs; and the need for self-actualisation. However, this is not a simple classification system: individuals may order their needs differently by placing some needs before others. Although it has been popular due to its intuitive appeal, Maslow's theory has been controversial among researchers. Porter (1961) found that managers higher up the organisation placed a greater emphasis on self-actualisation needs, and Wahba and Bridewell's (1976) review of research findings revealed that there was no clear evidence that human needs are classified into five categories: they proposed two – those of deficiency and growth needs. They also found that many individuals do not move from lower to higher needs and that higher-level needs can influence behaviour even when some lower-level needs are unfulfilled.

Maslow's ideas about motivation influenced the thinking of Douglas McGregor (1906–1964), also a psychologist, who formulated two managerial assumptions about people (Theory X and Theory Y). Managers who subscribe to Theory X believe that most people dislike responsibility, therefore they must be coerced, directed and threatened with punishment in order to get them to perform. In contrast, Theory Y assumes that people enjoy work and seek responsibility, are self-directed and self-controlling. According to McGregor, Theory Y is, for guiding management thinking, a more realistic view of workers. However, McGregor's concept was meant to be provocative, not research-based, inviting managers to reflect on how their assumptions about people affect their behaviour towards employees (Bloisi *et al.* 2007).

Knowledge of an employee's motivation is essential to understanding the direction that person's behaviour is likely to take. The way behaviour is directed is key to performance. Many of the motivation theories have been researched in the United States and therefore emphasise an individual perspective. In many cultures, the group is the centre of attention and in many organisations individuals work as a team, as in HCOs. Furthermore, many members of the team may be from different countries, placing a greater challenge on managers to motivate employees, and this calls for managers to be better prepared to provide the means necessary to influence staff motivation.

The systems approach

Recently, attention has focused on analysing organisations as 'systems' (Mullins 2005). A system is a set of interrelated parts that functions as a whole in order to achieve a common purpose (Daft 2005). Systems theory pertains to the study of the nature of complex systems in the natural world, in society and in science and proposes that the parts are interrelated and that the whole is greater than the sum of its parts. The emphasis within systems theory shifts from the parts to the organisation of the parts, and recognises that the interactions between the parts are a dynamic process. In systems theory, the total work organisation, the interrelationships of structure and behaviour and the range of variables within the organisation are of particular interest (Mullins 2005). A system consists of five components: inputs, transformation process, outputs, feedback and the environment. An organisation can be either a closed or an open system, but it is important to note that systems are rarely ever either fully open or closed, but are open to some influences while being closed to others. A closed system exists in isolation from its surrounding environment and is often used to refer to a theoretical scenario where perfect closure is an assumption. However, in practice there are only varying degrees of closure; no system can be completely closed. In contrast, an open system interacts continuously with its environment and the basic characteristics are environment, input, throughput and output.

So far in this chapter the concepts of leadership and management have been separated out for clarity; however, differences and similarities between leadership and management are not always evident in practice. The following sections will examine the duality of leadership and management; and how they relate to the context of health care.

THE DUALITY OF LEADERSHIP AND MANAGEMENT

Many scholars mistakenly view leadership and management as synonymous, while others view managers and leaders as different or complementary. It is often difficult to distinguish between the terms 'leadership' and 'management' as many of the roles within the health care organisation require managers to lead and expect leaders to manage. A discussion on the relationship between management and leadership is now presented.

Leadership versus management

The concept of leadership can be traced back to Aristotle (384–322 BC), while management, as a concept, emerged early in the twentieth century. Although most of the literature presents the terms leadership and management as an 'either–or' choice, it is generally accepted that the functions of leaders and managers differ conceptually, and these functional differences are not universally defined (Kotterman 2006). Furthermore, the dichotomy of leadership and management does not adequately capture the realities of leadership and management (Yamasaki 1999); for example, some authors argue that leadership requires more complex skills than management and that management is a role of leadership (Gardner 1990).

The main difference noted between leadership and management is that their function, purpose and focus are very different. The primary function of management is to provide order and consistency, whereas the main function of leadership is to produce change and movement. Northouse (2004) concurs with Kotter (1990), in stating that management seeks order and stability while leadership seeks change. In addition, the major activities of management are played out differently from those of leadership. According to Manthey (1990), a manager guides, directs, and motivates, while a leader empowers others; therefore every manager should be a leader. Yukl (1998:5) argues that you should 'view leading and managing as distinct processes but not . . . view leaders and managers as different people', and Yukl and Lepsinger (2005) take this view one step further, stating that you should assume that each role requires a different type of person. Zaleznik (1977) contends that while managers are reactive and prefer to work with people to solve problems but have no emotional attachment to the individuals, leaders are emotionally active, involved and change the way people think about what is possible. In contrast, Daft (2005) argues that managers and leaders are not inherently different types of people; managers have the abilities and qualities needed to be effective leaders. Leadership cannot replace management; it is a role that should be in addition to that of management.

Yukl (1998) acknowledges that clear differences exist between management and leadership, but claims that there is also considerable overlap. While management relationships are based on formal authority, whereby people accept that a manager can tell a subordinate what to do at work, leadership is based on personal influence and the followers are empowered to make many decisions. Leadership aims to pull, rather than push, people towards goals. A manager's power comes from his/her position of authority, whereas in leadership power may come from the personal character of the leader. Therefore, leadership does not require that one holds a formal position and many people in authority do not provide leadership. The differing source of power is one of the key distinctions between management and leadership.

For management and leadership two different outcomes are created. Management is focused on short-term results and on meeting stakeholders' expectations; in contrast, leaders create change through their integrity and, due to their long-term focus, help the organisation to thrive over the long haul. Alimo-Metcalfe and Alban-Metcalfe (2004) agree that management is about targets, creating strategic plans, monitoring standards, gathering and analysing data, while leadership is about behaving in a way that will increase the followers' motivation and other outcomes, including job satisfaction, self-esteem, commitment and self-efficacy. According to these authors, leadership gets to 'the bits that management can't reach'; they argue that leadership without management is an abrogation of responsibility. Zaleznik (1992) views management more negatively, as reactive, impersonal, lacking in empathy, punishing, coercive, and control orientated; managers tend to adopt impersonal attitudes towards goals. In contrast, Zaleznik (2004) views leaders as being active, visionary, open-minded, working from high-risk positions, intuitive and empathetic; leaders prefer to work with individuals but recognise that organisations need both managers and leaders in order to succeed.

Similarly, Bennis and Nanus (1985) maintain that there is a significant difference between management and leadership and argue that to manage means to accomplish activities and master routines, while to lead means to influence others and to create visions for change. In other words, 'managers are people who do things right and leaders are people who do the right thing' (Bennis & Nanus 1985:21). However, this perspective tends to portray managers and their actions as ineffective (Yamasaki 1999). McCrimmon (2006) argues that the whole movement to differentiate leaders from managers along personality lines has failed miserably and that the truth is that both leaders and managers can be inspiring; they just have a different focus.

While many authors highlight the differences between leadership and management, there is also considerable overlap. For example, both managing and leading can be carried out by the same person, but an appropriate balance is required to do so. While too much emphasis on managing can discourage risk-taking and create bureaucracy, on the other hand too much emphasis on leadership can disrupt order and create change that is impractical (Yukl & Lepsinger 2005).

Kotter (1990) states that the importance of leading and managing depends, in part, on the situation. The bigger the organisation becomes, the more the need for management increases, while the more dynamic and uncertain the external environment becomes, the more the importance of leadership increases (Yukl & Lepsinger 2005). Leadership within complex organisations, as described by Kotter (1990), establishes direction by creating a vision and strategies for producing change, by aligning people through communicating the direction, creating coalitions that understand the vision and are committed to its achievement, and by motivating and inspiring followers by keeping people in the right direction, despite barriers to change, by appealing to their very basic human needs, values and emotions. Bass (1990) states that sometimes leaders manage and sometimes managers lead. This does not mean that management is never associated with change nor that leadership is never associated with order. Leadership, by itself, is not able to keep an operation on time and on budget year after year and management, by itself, is not able to create significant useful change. Although many managers possess the abilities and qualities needed to be effective leaders, leadership cannot replace management; leadership should be in addition to management (Rost 1993; Zaleznik 1992; Daft 2005). McCrimmon (2006) states that in modern organisations, populated by intelligent knowledge workers, managers need to be good coaches, nurturers and developers of people in order to get the best return out of such talent. If organisations are to prosper they need the processes of both leadership and management. When there is sufficient management and insufficient leadership, this can lead to poor performance (Kotter 1990). According to Yamasaki (1999), competency in leadership and in management is required as managers are important and efficient but leaders are effective. Any combination, other than strong management and strong leadership, has the potential to produce highly unsatisfactory results. However, Kotter's (1990) research revealed that few people were able to carry out both roles effectively.

Gardner (1990), who takes a different angle, states that the most visionary leader is faced with decisions that every manager faces, for example how to allocate resources or when to trust someone with an assignment. According to Gardner, there are two categories: leaders and leaders/managers. The managers in the second category are those persons who would be described as leaders in the first category. The six differences between the two categories identified by Gardner are presented in Table 3.1. Gardner notes that managers are linked tightly to an organisation, while a leader may not be affiliated with an organisation, for example Florence Nightingale and Ghandi.

Table 3.1: Differences between leaders and leaders/managers

Leaders think longer term.
Leaders link the unit they are in charge of to the greater realities.
Leaders reach and influence followers beyond their jurisdictions, beyond boundaries.
Leaders put heavy emphasis on the intangibles of vision, values and motivation and understand intuitively the non-rational and unconscious elements in leader–constituent interaction.
Leaders have political skill to cope with the conflicting requirements of multiple constituencies.
Leaders think in terms of renewal.

Source: Gardner (1990)

RELEVANCE OF LEADERSHIP AND MANAGEMENT PRINCIPLES IN HEALTH CARE

Overall, the principles of leadership and management have contributed significantly to the heath care literature, but the question remains regarding the extent to which they are appropriate to the health care context. Leadership theory does not always fit comfortably within the clinical setting, in particular, nor in the health care system as a whole (Firth-Cozens & Mowbray 2001). Much of the management and leadership research was conducted in the United States, where the health care system is vastly different from the Irish system, and does not address the issue of cultural contexts. However, the literature does suggest that these theories are transferable to many contexts, including health care, but their transferability raises many issues. For example, patients differ from the traditional customer in that they are often in a state of crisis, are most likely to be compromised physically, mentally and psychologically, and their lives may be endangered. Health care services are delivered rapidly and across various organisation boundaries (McCallin 2003). Furthermore, Shortell and Kaluzny (2006) suggest that there are significant differences between HCOs and industrial organisations:

- Defining and measuring output is more difficult.
- The work involved is more variable and complex.
- More of the work is of an emergency and non-deferrable nature.
- The work permits little tolerance for ambiguity or error.
- The work activities are highly interdependent.
- The work involves a high degree of specialisation.
- Organisations are highly professionalised and loyalty is often given to the profession rather than the organisation.
- Dual lines of authority exist that create problems of co-ordination and accountability and confusion of roles.

While each organisation may be different, if not unique (Shortell & Kaluzny 2006), many of the above characteristics are evident in many hospitals. It is particularly challenging for managers when professionals have to depend on each other to provide services and involve values on a daily basis.

Leadership and management theories have been tested primarily in the disciplines of behavioural psychology, business and military studies: very few have been tested in the health care service. Health care organisations are 'disconnected hierarchies' with an inverted power structure in which people at the bottom have greater influence over day-to-day decision-making than those at the top (Ham 2003), but much of the empirical research in general and in health care has focused on upper management and leaders. Further research is required that examines the extent to which these theories of leadership and management are appropriate to health care and how they contribute to improved employee and organisational outcomes. Robinson (2007:2), in a television interview, compared corporate and health care organisations and stated that:

The Health Service is very protected, so you can take your time, you don't have to change, it's all very casual and very, very different; much, much slower than it would have been in almost even the worst run commercial organisations. Often what is missing is a sense of leadership, a sense of we're all in this together, being able to get people excited about being part of something, which is after all, one of the most important things you can do. I think that no matter what discipline or no matter what area you're looking at, the people who really know the answers are the ones who face the problems right down at the sharp end. They know what the issues are, and they know how to solve them.

Ham (2003) concurs with Robinson's perspective, and notes that although health care organisations have a large degree of control, within these organisations the ability to influence decision-making is more constrained than it is in other organisations. According to Ham, health professionals are unwilling to make changes unless they can see benefits for their patients and their own practice. Others argue that leadership must be exercised at all levels, in all settings (Crisp 2000), and that managers should negotiate rather than impose policies and recognise that their principal role is to support staff while persuading the staff to acknowledge the need to increase their accountability (Olsen & Neale 2005). Olson and Neale also state that clinical leadership is needed at all levels and have highlighted the fact that time spent on management often leaves senior personnel with too little time to provide the leadership required to maintain the standards of clinical care.

CONCLUSION

There is a vast literature on leadership and management, representing a hundred years of research. The leadership and management literature has been dominated by the 'style' concept, which is based on the assumption that leader behaviour is either task- or person-oriented, authoritarian or democratic and that an effective leader is one who is democratic and is able to deploy either a task- or a person-oriented style in order to suit the particular situation. However, little has been written on explaining why this particular approach makes a leader effective or on how effective leadership is possible (Breakwell & Millward 1997). Recent work in HCOs has been dominated by the concept of transformation leadership as one that emphasises the importance of interpersonal and influential skills. However, many of theories have not been tested in health care organisations and the focus is often on managerial leadership or supervisory management. It is difficult, then, to know what makes effective leadership or management possible in a hierarchical organisation with a traditional governance structure such as HCOs.

Commonly, leadership is confused with management, but it is well established that there may well be some overlap in practical terms. Some authors argue that, at any level, anyone can be a leader, without necessarily being formally accredited with this role. For the proper functioning of organisations, management is just as important as leadership and both functions are needed if organisations are to prosper and succeed. Most of the literature present an 'either–or' view of management and leadership, viewing managing and leading as mutually exclusive roles, but this has implications for promoting people to fill vacancies and selecting people for promotion. However, the existing theories of management and leadership do not provide a clear explanation of how the roles of management and leadership are interrelated and how they jointly affect outcomes.

The nature of the health care organisation has been shown to have different demands from those of other organisations, such as industrial or commercial organisations. Managers from all disciplines face on a daily basis challenges for which they are ill prepared. Many managers are caught in a vicious crossfire of competing demands and must balance the provision of compassionate care with a business model of cost and containment. The relevance of traditional theories of management and leadership has been questioned in the area of health care. Many assume that they are readily transferable to any context and this is an area where research is badly needed.

Finally, organisations will continue to change and evolve, but managers and leaders must respond to the changes by drawing on both the managers' leading and their managing competencies. It is essential that they recognise the appropriateness of leadership and management theories to their context and the demands of the nature of their work in a constantly changing environment.

REFLECTIVE EXERCISES

Undoubtedly, theories of leadership and management help us to understand the complexity of management in health care organisations. Think about the following questions.

1 What is the practical value of the theories of leadership and management in health care?
2 To what extent are the theories of leadership and management able to help managers solve the many problems that they encounter daily?
3 Is it possible for health care providers to be leaders as well as managers?
4 What are the main differences between leaders and managers?
5 What is the optimal ratio required for both leaders and managers in a health care organisation?

ADDITIONAL RESOURCES

Further reading

Bass, B. (1990) *Leadership and Performance Beyond Expectations*. New York: Free Press.

Greenleaf, R. (1977) *Servant Leadership*. New York: Paulist Press.

Grint, K. (1997) *Leadership: Classical, Contemporary and Critical Approaches*. Oxford: Oxford University Press.

Professional organisations

Association of Occupational Therapists in Ireland: www.aoti.ie
Dental Council of Ireland: www.dentalcouncil.ie
Department of Health and Children: www.dohc.ie
Health Services Executive: www.hse.ie
Hospital Pharmacists Association of Ireland: www.hpai.ie
Irish Institute of Radiography: www.iir.ie
Irish Nursing Board: www.aba.ie
Irish Nutrition and Dietetic Institute: www.indi.ie
Irish Society of Chartered Physiotherapists: www.iscp.ie
Medical Council of Ireland: www.irishmedicalcouncil.ie
National Social Work Qualifications Board: www.nswqb.ie
Pharmaceutical Society of Ireland: www.pharmaceuticalsociety.ie

Online resources

National Council for the Professional Development of Nursing and Midwifery: www.ncnm.ie.
Office for Health Management: www.hseland.ie/index.html.
World Health Organisation (WHO): www.who.int/management/wp10.pdf

Information about the following courses is available from the HSE website (https://elearning.hseland.ie/tohm/tohm2005/svmCourseDetail_New.asp?moduleId=8&LMS=2):
Change Management Coaching Communication with Consideration
Excellence in Service Finance Management
HSE Records Management Personal Development Planning
Learning About the Mental Health Act 2001
Project Leadership
Project Management Self Development
Stress Management
Team Leadership
Team Participation
Time Management.

REFERENCES

Alimo-Metcalfe, B. and Alban-Metcalfe, J. (2004) 'The myths and morality of leadership in the NHS', *Clinician in Management* 12: 49–53.
Antrobus, S. (1997) *Nursing Leadership in Context: A Discussion Document.* London: Royal College of Nursing.
Avolio, B., Bass, B. and Jung, D. (1999) 'Reexamining the components of transformational and transactional leadership using the multifactor leadership questionnaire', *Journal of Occupational and Organizational Psychology* 72: 441–62.

Bass, B. (1990) *Bass and Stogdill's Handbook of Leadership: Theory, Research, and Managerial Application*. New York: Free Press.

— (1997) 'Does the transactional-transformational leadership paradigm transcend organizational and national boundaries?', *American Psychologist* 52: 130–9.

Bass, B. and Avolio, B. (1994) *Improving Organizational Effectiveness through Transformational Leadership*. Thousand Oaks: Sage.

Bennis, W. and Nanus, B. (1985) *Leaders: The Strategies for Taking Charge*. New York: Anchor Books.

Blake, R. and Mouton, J. (1964) *The Managerial Grid*. Houston, TX: Gulf.

— (1978) *The New Managerial Grid*. Houston, TX: Gulf.

— (1985) *The Managerial Grid III*. Houston, TX: Gulf.

Bloisi, W., Cook, C. and Hunsaker, P. (2007) *Management and Organisational Behaviour* (2nd edn), New York: McGraw Hill.

Breakwell, G. M. and Millward, L. J. (1997) 'Leadership under stress', report for DERA, in Millward, L. and Bryan, K. (2005) 'Clinical leadership in health care: a position statement', *Leadership in Health Services* 18: xiii–xxv.

Briggs Report (1972) *Report of the Committee on Nursing* (Cmnd 5115), London: HMSO.

Bryman, A. (1996) 'Leadership in organisations' in Clegg S., Hardy, C. and Nord, W. (1996) *Handbook of Organizational Studies*. London: Sage.

Burns, J. M. (1978) *Leadership*. New York: Harper & Row.

Commission on Nursing (1998) *Report of The Commission on Nursing: A Blueprint for the Future*. Dublin: Statistics Office.

Crisp, A. (2000) 'Leadership: improving the quality of patient care', *Journal of Nursing Management* 14: 43–5.

Daft, R. (2003) *Management*. Ohio: Thomson South-Western.

— (2005) *The Leadership Experience*. Ohio: Thomson South-Western.

Deetz, S., Tracy, S. and Simpson, J. (2000) *Leading Organisations through Transition*. Thousand Oaks, CA: Sage.

Den Hartog, D. and Koopman, P. (1997) 'Transactional versus transformational leadership: an analysis of the MLQ', *Journal of Occupational and Organizational Psychology* 70: 19–34.

DoHC (Department of Health and Children) (2001) *Quality and Fairness: A Health System for You*. Dublin: Stationery Office.

— (2003a) *Audit of Structures and Functions in the Health System* (Prospectus Report). Dublin: Stationery Office.

— (2003b) *The Health Service Reform Programme*. Dublin: Stationery Office.

— (2008) http://www.dohc.ie/statistics/key_trends/health_service_employment, accessed 10 November 2008.

Edwards, G. and Gill, R. (2003) 'Hierarchical level as a moderator of leadership behaviour: a 360-degree investigation', paper presented at the Annual Occupational Psychology Conference, Bournemouth, UK, 8–10 January, in Gill, R. (2006) *Theory and Practice of Leadership*. London: Sage.

Farling, M. L., Stone, A. G. and Winston, B. E. (1999) 'Servant leadership: setting the stage for empirical research', *Journal of Leadership Studies* 6: 1–2, 49–72.

Fiedler, F. (1967) *A Theory of Leadership Effectiveness*. New York: McGraw Hill.

Firth-Cozens, J. and Mowbray, D. (2001) 'Leadership and quality of care', *Quality in Health Care* 10: (suppl. 11), ii 3–7.

Fleishman, E. Mumford, M. Zaccaro, S. Levin, K. Korotkin, A. and Hein, M. (1991) 'Taxonomic efforts in the description of leader behavior: a synthesis and functional interpretation', *Leadership Quarterly* 2(4): 245–87.

Gardner, H. (1990) *On Leadership*. New York: Free Press.

Gill, R. (2006) *Theory and Practice of Leadership*. London: Sage.

Graen, G. (2004) *New Frontiers of Leadership*. USA: Information Age.

Greenleaf, R. (1977) *Servant Leadership: A Journey into the Nature of Legitimate Power and Greatness*. New York: Paulist Press.

Grint, K. (2001) *Leadership: Classical, Contemporary, and Critical Approaches*. Oxford: Oxford University Press.

Hale, J. and Fields, D. (2007) 'Exploring servant leadership across cultures: a study of followers in Ghana and the USA', *Leadership* 3: 397.

Ham, C. (2003) 'Improving the performance of health services: the role of clinical leadership', *The Lancet* 361: 1978–80.

Hersey, P., Blanchard, K. and Johnson, D. (1988) 'Management of organizational behaviour' in *Leading Human Resources*. Englewood Cliffs, NJ: Prentice Hall.

Hinkin, T. and Tracey, J. (1999) 'The relevance of charisma for transformational leadership in stable organisations', *Journal of Organizational Change Management*, 12: 105–19.

House, R. J. (1971) 'A path-goal theory of leadership effectiveness', *Administrative Science Quarterly* 7: 323–52.

Judge, T. Colbert, A. and Ilies, R. (2004) 'Intelligence and leadership: a quantitative review and test of theoretical propositions', *Journal of Applied Psychology* 87: 542–52.

Koontz, H. and Weihrich, H. (1988) *Management* (9th edn). New York: McGraw-Hill.

Kotter, J. P. (1990) *A Force for Change: How Leadership Differs From Management*. New York: Free Press.

Kotterman, J. (2006) 'Leadership versus management: what's the difference?', *Journal for Quality and Participation*, Summer.

Kouzes, J. and Posner, B. (1987) *Leadership: The Challenge*. San Francisco: Jossey-Bass.

Laub, J. (1999) 'Assessing the servant organization: development of the Servant Organizational Leadership Assessment (SOLA) instrument', Dissertation Abstracts International, UMI no. 9921922, in Joseph, E. and Winston, B. (2005) *Leadership and Organization Development Journal* 26: 6–22.

Linden, R., Wayne, S., Zhao, H. and Henderson, D. (2008) 'Servant leadership: development of a multidimensional measure and multi-level assessment', *Leadership Quarterly* 19: 161–77.

Manthey, M. (1990) 'The nurse manager as leader', *Nursing Management* 21(6): 18–19.

McCallin, A. (2003) 'Interdisciplinary team leadership: a revisionist approach for an old problem?' *Journal of Nursing Management* 11: 364–71.

McCrimmon, M. (2006) *Zaleznik and Kotter on Leadership* (online), http://www.leadersdirect.com/Zaleznik%20and%20Kotter%20on%20Leadership, accessed 6 May 2008.

Millward, L. and Bryan, K. (2005) 'Clinical leadership in health care: a position statement', *Leadership in Health Services* 18: xiii–xxv.

Mullins, L. (2005) *Management and Organizational Behaviour*. Essex: Pearson Education.

Nicholson, N. (2001) 'Gene politics and the natural selection of leaders', *Leaders to Leaders* 20: 46–52.

Northouse, P. (2004) *Leadership Theory and Practice*. Thousand Oaks: Sage.

Olsen, S. and Neale, G. (2005) 'Clinical leadership in the provision of hospital care', *British Medical Journal* 330: 1219–20.

Oshagbemi, T. and Gill, R. (2004) 'Differences in leadership styles and behaviour across hierarchical levels in UK organizations', *Leadership and Organization Development Journal* 25: 93–106.

Page, D. and Wong, T. P. (2000) 'A conceptual framework for measuring servant leadership' in Adjibolosoo, S. (ed.) *The Human Factor in Shaping the Course of History and Development*, Lanham, MD: University Press of America.

Porter, L. (1961) 'A study of perceived need satisfaction in bottom and middle management jobs', *Journal of Applied Psychology* 45: 1–10.

Ramanujam, R. and Rousseau, D. (2006) 'The challenges are organizational not just clinical', *Journal of Organizational Behavior* 27: 811–27.

Robinson, G. (2007) *Can Gerry Robinson Fix the NHS?* London: BBC, http://www.open2.net/nhs/has_gerry_fixed_the_nhs.html, accessed 28 February 2007.

Rost, J. (1993) *Leadership for the Twenty-First Century*. Westport, CT: Praeger.

Russell, R. and Stone, A. (2002) 'A review of servant leadership attributes: developing a practical model', *Leadership and Organization Development Journal* 22: 76–84.

Sendjaya, S. and Santora, J. (2002) 'Servant leadership: its origin, development and application to organisations', *Journal of Leadership and Organizational Studies*, 9(2): 57–65.

Shortell, S. and Kaluzny, A. (2006) *Health Care Management, Organization Design and Behavior*. New York: Thomson Delmar.

Stogdill, R. M. (1974) *Handbook of Leadership*. New York: Free Press.

Stone, G., Russell, R. and Patterson, K. (2004) 'Transformational versus servant leadership: a difference in leader focus', *Leadership and Organization Development Journal* 25: 349–61.

Tussing, A. D. and Wren, M. A. (2006) *How Ireland Cares: The Case for Health Care Reform*. Dublin: New Island.

Wahba, M. and Bridewell, L. (1976) 'Maslow reconsidered: a review of research on the need hierarchy theory', *Organisational Behaviour and Human Performance* 15: 212–40.

Wren, D., Bedeian, A. and Breeze, J. (2002) 'The foundations of Henri Fayol's administrative theory', *Management Decision* 40(9): 906–18.

Yamasaki, E. (1999) 'Understanding managerial leadership as more than an oxymoron', *New Directions for Community Colleges* 105: 67–73.

Yukl, G. (1998) *Leadership in Organizations*. New Jersey: Prentice Hall.

Yukl, G. and Lepsinger, R. (2005) 'Why integrating the leading and managing roles is essential for organizational effectiveness', *Organizational Dynamics* 34(4): 361–76.

Zaccaro, S. and Klimoski, R. (2001) *The Nature of Organizational Leadership*. San Francisco: Jossey-Bass.

Zaleznik, A. (1977) 'Managers and leaders: are they different?' *Harvard Business Review*, May/June: 55:67–78.

— (1992) 'Managers and leaders: are they different?' *Harvard Business Review*, March/April: 126–35.

— (2004) 'Managers and leaders: are they different?' *Harvard Business Review*, January: 74–81.

4
Organisational Culture

Anne-Marie Malone

OBJECTIVES

- To define organisational culture.
- To compare and contrast the different theories on organisational culture.
- To explore how organisational culture impacts on organisational performance in health care.
- To indentify what is unique about the context and culture of Irish health care organisations.
- To discuss how organisational culture can be measured.
- To discuss leadership challenges in managing and changing organisational culture.

INTRODUCTION

Organisational culture is a complex, multifaceted phenomenon. Boddy (2005) describes organisational culture as something that can be sensed and observed when people have been exposed to a few different groups, departments or organisations. This, he suggests, can be achieved from observing how people work, presence or absence of rules, communication strategies, behaviour and management styles. Handy (1993:191), comments that culture cannot be precisely defined as it is 'perceived, something felt'. Organisational culture has been identified as impacting on organisation performance and effectiveness; human resource management, including recruitment, retention and performance; innovation and entrepreneurship; restructuring and change. It is influenced by factors both internal and external to the organisation, including the organisation's history and leadership in the formative stages of organisational development, technology, organisational strategy and its people (Handy 1993). Culture can be described as having four functions in the organisation (Nelson & Quick 2006). These are: providing a sense of identity to the organisation and increasing commitment; helping employees make sense of the organisation; reinforcing the values of the organisation; and shaping behaviour by reinforcing norms in an organisation. Schein (2004:3) comments that 'the forces that are created in social and organisational situations that derive from culture are powerful'.

The culture of the Irish health care system is complex and evolving, as it is currently undergoing significant restructuring and reform. It is a health care system that is endeavouring to respond to societal and cultural changes including an increase in the population, changing demographics, increased demand, changing service users, developments in medical care and significant medical inflation during a national and international economic crisis. This system serves a population where there is universal health care coverage, but also where there is a unique private–public mix in health care funding, which results in different levels of access to health care for different groups within the population (Smith 2009). It is also one where health care delivery is focused on the acute hospital sector, where the primary health care system is poorly developed, and care is frequently described as fragmented across the continuum. Accordingly, health care has become a prominent political issue, attracting much negative media attention, most specifically in relation to systems failures.

WHAT IS ORGANISATIONAL CULTURE?

Organisational culture is a complex, multifaceted phenomenon. Accordingly, there are a plethora of definitions in the literature (Scott-Findlay & Estabrooks 2006). These definitions are also impacted on by the disciplinary perspective on organisational culture that the writers have adopted. Cameron (2008) highlights that most writers adopt the sociological perspective on organisational culture, which is that organisational culture is an attribute of organisations, rather than the anthropological perspective, which is that culture is something an organisation is.

In one of the earlier definitions of organisational culture, Porter (1985:24) sees organisational culture as 'that difficult to define set of norms and attitudes that help shape an organisation'. Schein's (1992:12) widely cited definition focuses on assumptions and describes culture as:

> A pattern of shared basic assumptions that the group learned as it solved its problems of external adaptation and internal integration, that has worked well enough to be considered valid, and therefore, to be taught to new members as the correct way to perceive, think, and feel in relation to those problems.

Hofstede (2004:41) describes culture as 'the collective programming of the mind which distinguishes the members of one organisation from another'. Schein's (2004:1) later definition of culture further develops his earlier perspective, to encompass the perspective of culture as interactive and developmental, stating that it is '. . . both a dynamic phenomenon that surrounds us at all times, being constantly enacted and created by our interactions with others and shaped by leadership behaviours, and a set of structures, routines, rules, and norms that guide and constrain behaviour'.

Huber (2006:206) sees culture as being less tangible and comments that culture is like 'a fog in that it blankets everything, is subtle, and forms an invisible cloud that is so powerful it may obscure vision'. Marquis and Huston (2009:279) include the concepts of symbols, interactions and beliefs, defining organisational culture as '. . . a system of symbols and interactions unique to each organisation. It is the ways of thinking, behaving, and believing that members of a unit have in common.'

Despite the plethora of definitions in the literature, there are commonalities among the definitions, which include those of values, beliefs, symbols, assumptions and norms (Table 4.1). Parkin (2009) infers that the specific adoption and enactment of the concepts inherent in the culture of any organisation is how organisations perpetuate their cultures as they guide recruitment, leadership, values and behaviours.

Table 4.1: Concepts inherent in culture

Values	Deeply held ideas or feelings that discern between acceptable and unacceptable beliefs and norms of behaviour and are implied through conduct (Boddy 2005; Parkin 2009).
Beliefs	The assumptions that employees hold about the organisation and what works in that particular organisation (Boddy 2005).
Symbols	'Symbols are objects, events, acts or people that create meaning over and above their functional purpose' (Johnson *et al.* 2008:199).
Assumptions	'. . . deeply held beliefs that guide behaviour and tell members how to perceive and think about things' (Nelson & Quick 2006:536). They may be conscious or unconscious.
Norms	These are expectations of behaviour and conduct and provide guidance about issues such as dress code and attendance at meetings (Boddy 2005; Parkin 2009).

THEORETICAL PERSPECTIVES ON ORGANISATIONAL CULTURE

A variety of frameworks, models and typologies have been developed in the endeavour to further explain the concept of organisational culture. Linstead (2009:163) comments that 'these typologies are necessarily crude and general, but may nevertheless have value in broadly characterising organisations'. Such models also serve to guide research and theory generation (Hatch 1993).

Schein (1985, 1992, 1999, 2004) analyses culture from the perspective of levels (Figure 4.1), with the term 'levels' referring to 'the degree to which the cultural phenomena [are] visible to the observer' (Schein 1992:16). The first and most visible level of artefacts represents what is immediately visible to the observer. This includes the physical environment, its products, published values, work processes, dress codes and communication strategies (Schein 1992). However, Schein (1999:16) cautions that an observer will not know 'what this all means', and therefore suggests talking to insiders to explore what he describes as the next level of culture, which is espoused values.

Figure 4.1: Levels of culture and their interaction

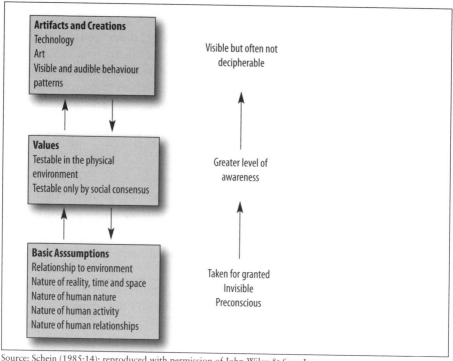

Source: Schein (1985:14); reproduced with permission of John Wiley & Sons Inc.

Schein (1992) identifies that shared values are those which develop when a group is either newly formed or in an established group who are faced with a new problem. First, a solution to a problem is identified and if it is successful, it starts what Schein (1992) describes as a process of cogitative transformation, and then becomes a shared value or belief, and then a shared assumption which is not questioned. Espoused values are those which are not based on prior learning; they identify what people say they will do in a situation but do not reflect what they actually will do in situations where they should be implemented. Schein (1985) states that there must be discernment between those values that are congruent with underlying assumptions and those which are not. This will highlight areas of unexplained behaviour. However, it is necessary to then move to the third level: that of basic assumptions. Schein (1992:22) states that, 'Culture as a basic set of assumptions defines for us what to pay attention to, what things mean, how to react emotionally to what is going on, and what actions to take in various kinds of situations.' Basic assumptions emerge when problem-solving strategies become reality to the point that any other course of action is unthinkable. Changing such assumptions creates significant anxiety, and Schein (1992:22) adds that this is where culture 'has its ultimate power'. He concludes that it is imperative to understand basic assumptions in order to interpret the other levels of culture. Schein (1985) also suggests that this level of understanding leads to a deeper level of cultural awareness which enables leaders and change agents to identify what changes can be made in an organisation.

Johnson (1992) describes the cultural web which '. . . shows the behavioural, physical and symbolic manifestations of a culture that inform and are informed by the taken-for-granted assumptions or paradigm'. It is a process of cultural mapping which explores elements of organisational culture. Johnson *et al.* (2008) also state that the cultural web can be utilised to explore culture within four frames of reference: national; organisational field; functional or divisional level; and organisational level.

Brooks (2006) suggests that different subcultures in health care could use the cultural web to identify the differences in their respective cultures and gain greater understanding and insight from other perspectives. The elements of the web are described as follows:

- *Paradigm:* The paradigm is the central component of the cultural web. It identifies the assumptions and beliefs which are the collective experience applied to a situation. These assumptions and beliefs impact on strategic management and direction of the organisation.
- *Routines and rituals:* Routines are the manner in which work is done. They may be established for many years and reflect core beliefs. Key rituals must be emphasised and others may not. They may be so deeply entrenched that they are difficult to change. Some may be emphasised by continuing education. Brooks (2006) cites patient consultations as an example, and board meetings as an example from a managerial perspective. Other manifestations of routines might be focusing on process rather than outcomes and not celebrating success (Johnson *et al.* 2008).
- *Control systems* identify what is monitored and controlled in the organisation and to what extent each individual element is controlled or monitored. These controls can be historical or related to current strategies, and may be related to either rewards or punishment. Control systems may pertain to funding or to quality of service (Johnson *et al.* 2008).
- *Organisational structures* may be bureaucratic or flat, formal or informal, centralised or devolved. Also, they may emphasise collaboration, fragmentation or competition (Johnson *et al.* 2008).
- *Power structures* may demonstrate how power is distributed in the organisation. The most powerful people or groups in the organisation are most likely to hold the core assumptions of the organisation. Power may also facilitate or hinder change (Johnson *et al.* 2008).
- *Symbols* are denoted through people, objects, events or acts. Symbols may have significant status. They may also signify aspects of the strategy (Johnson *et al.* 2008).
- *Stories* may reflect core beliefs. They may also communicate aspects of the culture, including what is acceptable and unacceptable in the organisation, what constitutes success and failure. They can be a powerful means of communicating what is important in an organisation.

Collectively, these aspects of culture inform the paradigm, which is the fundamental assumptions in the organisation.

Figure 4.2: The cultural web of an organisation

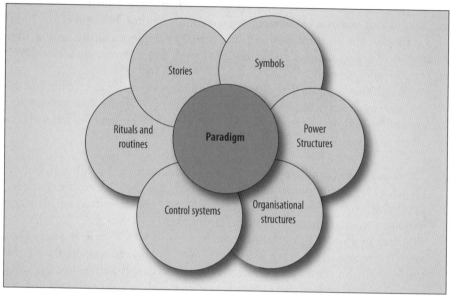

Source: Johnson *et al.* (2008:198); reproduced by permission of Pearson Education Ltd

Figure 4.3: The power culture

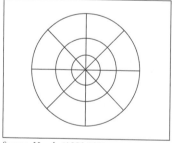

Source: Handy (1993:183)

Handy (1993) describes four varieties of organisation culture, which, he notes, follow on from Harrison's (1972) work. These are the power culture, the role culture, the task culture and the person culture (Handy 1993). The first of these cultures, the power culture (Figure 4.3) is depicted by a web, with the Greek god Zeus as its patron. Power and power over resources is maintained from the centre, with managers being politically minded, but also risk takers. There are few rules and procedures, and it is the end rather than the means that is important. Accordingly, this type of culture is also considered to be adaptable. Networks and friendships are integral to this type of culture and finding the right people is considered pivotal to the success of the organisation.

The second type of culture Handy identifies is the role culture (Figure 4.4), which he depicts as a Greek temple, with Apollo as its patron. This type of culture may also be considered to be bureaucratic, with the pediment representing senior management, who co-ordinate the work of the pillars, which represent the organisation's functions or specialities. Position is the major source of power. There are many rules and procedures. This culture offers predictability and suits employees who want to do their job 'to a standard' (Handy 1993:186) but does not encourage developing employees' capabilities, and may not suit the ambitious unless they can move to the pediment. The role culture functions well in a stable environment, but is slow to change in response to changing environments. This type of culture is seen in organisations such as the civil service, or a monopoly or oligopoly.

Figure 4.4: The role culture

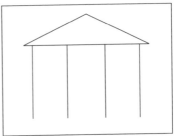

Source: Handy (1993:185)

Figure 4.5: The task culture

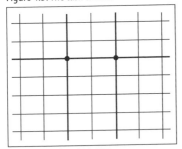

Source: Handy (1993:187)

The third type of culture is the task culture (Figure 4.5). It is represented by a net, and whilst it has no specific deity is best represented by the warrior goddess Athena and Odysseus, the champion of the commando leader. This type of culture is a team culture which is job- or project-orientated, with the emphasis on getting the job done. Work is done in groups which are formed for specific reasons. Expert power is important but Handy (1993) states that personal power and position power also have an influence. This type of culture is flexible and adaptable and can react quickly to changing markets, but tends not to develop specific expertise or economies of scale. When the environment is favourable these cultures flourish, but when resources are limited it frequently changes to a role or power culture. This culture can be found in general management consultancies and account groups of advertising agencies.

The fourth type of culture that Handy delineates is the person culture (Figure 4.6), which he describes as a cluster with the god Dionysus, whom Handy describes as the first existentialist, as its patron. The organisation exists for the individual to achieve their own objectives, rather than for the overriding objectives of the organisation. Examples include barristers' chambers and architects' partnerships. This culture may also exist within a role culture, and the example Handy gives of this is a university professor, who does what is necessary to maintain his position in the organisation but then can pursue his own career within the organisation. Power is usually expert power. Handy also comments that individuals with this orientation, including hospital consultants, may not be easy to manage due to the dynamics between expert, resource and position power. He also comments that the variety in organisational

Figure 4.6: The person culture

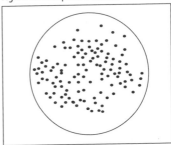

Source: Handy (1993:190)

cultures is correct, on the basis that cultures are influenced by many factors. These he cites as the history of the organisation, technology, the people in the organisation, the size of the organisation, the organisational strategy and the environment. Therefore, he asserts, they differ; and difficulties in organisations arise as a consequence of incongruence between culture and structure relative to the environment.

These theories of organisational culture assist in putting a structure on a complex concept that is difficult to articulate. The cultural web (Johnson *et al.* 2008) identifies dimensions of organisation culture; Handy's (1993) varieties of culture pertain to organisational structure, power and leadership; while Schein (1985, 1992, 1999, 2004) addresses levels of culture. They offer a variety of perspectives which can facilitate the first step in describing and analysing an organisational culture to identify what the culture is, and how it may need to change to facilitate the strategic process.

WHY CONCERN OURSELVES WITH ORGANISATIONAL CULTURE?

Organisational culture impacts on all facets of organisations, most specifically corporate strategy, leadership, organisational performance, human resource management and quality of patient care.

Culture and strategy

Allio (2006:8) highlights the challenges that organisational cultures create in strategic management, stating that 'Strategists continue to struggle with the implications of culture – and the constraints it places on strategy and implementation.' Culture has been identified as the main determinant of strategy. Johnson *et al.* (2008) emphasise that it can be very difficult to change strategy outside the existing culture, with managers and leaders often choosing to engage in incremental change, rather than adopting a new strategy. They highlight that culture can drive strategy to the extent that it eventually results in strategic drift. Braithwaite (2006) explored the impact of the clinical directorate systems in two observational studies. They found that despite this new clinical arrangement, old structuring behaviour continued. The clinical directorate did not appear to have the impact of breaking down barriers between professional groups to promote teamwork. The dynamics between nursing and doctors were fundamentally unchanged, but engaged in from a different perspective. This restructuring did not result in a cultural change. The authors conclude that such changes in organisational restructuring did not produce the anticipated change between professional sub-cultures. As identified by Johnson *et al.* (2008), it was difficult to change the strategy outside the existing culture. Carney (2006) conducted a survey of professional and non-professional middle managers to explore the relationship between organisational culture and strategic involvement among middle managers and also to ascertain how organisational culture influenced strategic involvement in this group. Her findings indicate that strong cultures indicated strategic involvement. For middle managers this is important as middle manager involvement in the strategic process has ramifications for strategic implementation. In her study of directors of nursing, Carney (2004) identified that the structure of the organisation led to middle managers not being involved in strategic development. This impeded them in their roles with lower-level managers, and impacted negatively on quality of care as a consequence of a lack of operational knowledge. Therefore, the structure and strategic process in the organisation impacted on middle managers being able to fulfil their roles from many perspectives.

Culture and leadership

Schein (2004) asserts that values and assumptions emerge as a consequence of leadership. Linstead (2009) delineate the leadership behaviours that shape the culture of an organisation (Table 4.2). This, he asserts can be reinforced or undermined within the context of the structure and culture of the organisation. Studies have demonstrated the linkage between leadership and culture in health care.

Table 4.2: Culture and leadership

Leadership behaviours that shape the culture of the organisation	Organisational factors that reinforce or undermine leadership behaviours
• What they pay attention to and notice. • Their reaction to problems and crises. • Role modelling, coaching, mentoring and teaching. • Their criteria for selection, reward, promotion and sanction. • Influence on organisational structure and policy.	• Mechanism of control in the organisation. • Organisational structure. • Organisational systems. • Formal statements.

Source: Linstead (2009:166–7)

Shirey (2009) conducted a qualitative descriptive study to ascertain the relationship between authentic leadership, organisational culture and healthy work environments, utilising a stress and coping lens. Nurse managers were recruited from three US acute care hospitals, and they completed a demographic questionnaire. The findings indicated that there were differences between the organisational cultures reported, with some being seen in a positive light and others in a negative light. Those who worked in a positive environment demonstrated greater personal satisfaction in their role, and where they had significant support in their leadership roles were more likely to be able to support their own staff to enhance not only the work environment but also patient outcomes. Those who worked in a negative environment demonstrated that they found it more difficult to create a healthy work environment as they were fighting the organisational culture.

Culture and organisational performance

Organisational culture has been identified as a key ingredient in successful organisations, especially in those that are recognised leaders in their industries (Cameron 2008). Quinn *et al.* (2007) and Swayne *et al.* (2008) have adapted Porter's (1985) concept of the value chain and also assert that organisational culture is one of three support activities which contribute to the effectiveness and efficacy of an organisation.

Shortall *et al.* (1991) suggest that patient care outcomes can be related to three separate factors: the skill of the health care professional/s, the functioning of health care teams and the structure and processes in the organisation in which care is provided. These researchers hypothesised that an appropriate culture and leadership in intensive care units would be related to more effective patient care. With regard to culture, best and worst managerial practices were identified. One example of a best practice was a pro-nursing administration and a strong commitment to customer service. The best-performing sites incorporated managerial practices including a team satisfaction-orientated culture, strong leadership, open and timely communication and effective co-ordination. These findings suggest a relationship between the organisational culture and effectiveness.

Alternatively, Alvesson (2002) cautions that there are relatively few systematic empirical studies demonstrating evidence of linkage between organisational culture and effectiveness. Some research findings from health care would concur with this perspective. Bosch *et al.* (2008) researched the associations between restructured health care, including multidisciplinary teamwork, team climate and different types of organisational culture, and quality of care for patients with diabetes in small office-based general practices. A cross-sectional analysis of 83 health care professionals, 30 primary practices and 711 patients was undertaken, utilising two self-report measures. These were the Team Climate Inventory (to measure team climate) and the Competing Values Framework (to measure organisational culture). The researchers concluded that although they did find some significant associations between high-quality diabetes care and organisational culture in primary care, these relationships were marginal. They suggested that their research findings 'contribute to the discussion about the legitimacy of the widespread idea that aspects of redesigning care such as teamwork and culture can contribute to quality of care' (Bosch *et al.* 2008:180).

Culture and change

Culture can have considerable impact on innovation and change in organisations.

Morgan and Obgonna (2008) researched the impact of subcultural dynamics of three professional groups on management-led organisational change initiatives. The specific changes pertained to clinical governance and Trust reconfiguration. The three groups were doctors, nurses and non-clinical managers. Data for this component of the study was collected qualitatively utilising both focus groups and face-to-face interviews within the context of a larger mixed methods study.

The researchers also engaged with participants informally during residential programmes. The findings suggested that there was consensus among the three groups on issues pertaining to the aims and purpose of the health service – individual need for health care – and dissatisfaction with the degree of intervention of external agencies in health care. With regard to the change programme, there were differences between groups. Doctors identified that they felt left out of formal discussions, and also demonstrated concern regarding the direction of new initiatives. Different perspectives within the medical cohort were also identified. In informal discussions with the researchers, some doctors, and especially those in managerial roles, saw the change in a more positive light. Nurses identified more positively with the changes, more specifically that their professional development would be enhanced, and that they would be more empowered to contribute more to patient care. With regard to use of consultants, some nurses demonstrated concern about cost, whereas non-clinical managers perceived it as being necessary. Also, the different groups demonstrated difference in what the researchers call an 'incomplete realisation of certain key values that were promoted by the change programme' (Morgan & Obgonna 2008:56). Nurses generally appeared to be more concerned with teamwork, whereas doctors appeared more individualistic in their approach. A culture of blame was also identified as contributing to differentiation between doctors and nurses. These findings highlight the challenges in managing such change within health care. The researchers suggest, as part of the change process, ascertaining consensus on the super-ordinate goals of change and managing the rest. The authors also comment that the change initiatives appeared to 'surface deep-seated discord and subcultural power interplay between the groups' (Morgan & Obgonna 2008:56).

Culture and human resource management

Human resource management (HRM) is fundamental to organisational success in health care. The human resource (HR) function can be a strategic partner (Lawler 2008) or can be predominately focused on cost containment and administration. Khatri et al. (2006) researched the impact of strategic human resource management in two separate hospitals – a university hospital and a community hospital. They found that in the community hospital the appointment of a new human resource director had changed the culture by transforming HR practices. The findings also demonstrated an appreciation of the linkage between the HR function and improved clinical outcomes. In this study it was demonstrated that the culture of HR practice yielded benefits for the organisation and patients alike.

Culture has also been demonstrated to impact on nurses' quality of work life and on staff retention, etc. Gifford et al. (2002) investigated the relationships between unit organisational culture in seven urban obstetric units situated in five Western American cities and quality of work life measures including organisational commitment, empowerment, job involvement and intent to turnover, utilising the Competing Values Framework and Quality of Work Life

Measures. Their findings suggest that human relations cultural values are positively related to quality of work life measures and negatively related to intent to turnover. These authors suggest that improving quality of working life in the longer term may prove more cost-effective than utilising retention strategies that are primarily financial. Furthermore, they advocate that expenditure utilised in maintaining a control culture might be better employed in changing hospital cultures to create more 'hospitable' cultures for employees (Gifford et al. 2002:22–3). Vandenberghe (1999), in his study of nurses within the Belgian health care industry, demonstrated that person-culture congruence was predictive of nurse recruits staying with their organisation one year after congruence was measured. In conclusion, he suggests that person-culture fit should be considered during the recruitment process to reduce turnover. Handy (1993:191) also states that a fit between the individual's preferred cultural preference and the organisation's 'should lead to a fulfilled psychological contract, to satisfaction at work'.

Culture and quality of care

Patient safety is a critical issue in health care. Brady et al. (2009a) and Brady et al. (2009b) have emphasised the role that culture plays in patient safety. Much research has been conducted in identifying how a culture of organisational safety affects patient safety outcomes. Jain et al. (2006) identified that quality improvements with a cultural component could impact on patient outcomes and reduce costs. These researchers introduced a number of changes including physician-led multidisciplinary rounds, daily discussion on bed availability, and the introduction of sets of evidence-based best practice cultural changes associated with a focus on team decision making. They found that the above changes resulted in a reduction in nosocomial infection in intensive care patients, reduction in adverse events and associated reduction in costs. They identified that communication strategies, including meetings and a new decision-making culture, empowered team members, resulting in positive change. Bellou (2007) explored quantitatively how long-term customer satisfaction could be achieved through organisational culture. The findings indicate that organisational culture significantly impacts on employee customer orientation. Bellou (2007) identifies that this can be achieved though employee involvement practices and facilitative management styles as well as quality assurance mechanisms. She also identifies that this also needs to be incorporated into the vision and goals of the organisation, which would influence such cultural change.

ORGANISATIONAL CULTURE IN HEALTH CARE ORGANISATIONS: WHAT IS DIFFERENT?

Waldman et al. (2003) make a number of assertions about American health care that could be deemed to resonate with experiences of health care beyond the USA. They state that 'The health care industry has achieved an unenviable consensus: nearly everyone is unhappy with it' (Waldman et al. 2003:5). They further clarify that this unhappiness is found among all major stakeholders and pertains to a wide variety of issues including lack of quality control, medical inflation, incidence of adverse events, cost of insurance premiums, lack of access, health care professionals' dissatisfaction with the practice environment and litigation. Health care organisations differ from many other organisations from many perspectives, not only those cited by Waldman *et al.* They are also influenced by national and international developments in both medical care and health care delivery, increased demand for health care arising from changing demographics, changing patterns of ill-health, improved treatment modalities and changes in service users' expectations in an information era. In Ireland, these changes have been paralleled by unprecedented identification of and media reporting of system failures such as the Lourdes Hospital Inquiry (DoHC 2006) and Leas Cross (O'Neill 2006). There has also been the establishment of tribunals and redress schemes, and the establishment of the Clinical Indemnity Scheme based on the concept of enterprise liability (DoHC 2001). There has also been significant restructuring including changes in the role of the Department of Health and Children, the establishment of the Health Service Executive (HSE), the establishment of regional authorities and merging of agencies (DoHC 2003). Both experts and health care professionals have written and published books that heavily criticise the Irish health care system (Doctor X 2007; Wren 2003). All these developments have been the subject of intense political debate and media scrutiny. It is within this context and culture that health care professionals endeavour to deliver care, influenced by how health care is financed and by the structure and systems on which they have varying and often limited impact in influencing broader issues which affect the delivery of optimal care for patients.

Organisational culture in health care organisations has been identified as being different from that in other organisations due to health care organisations' unique managerial and organisational structures (Seren & Baykal 2007). Glouberman and Mintzberg (2001:58) describe hospitals as being 'extraordinarily complicated organisations'. Organisational cultures also differ considerably between health care organisations. Seren and Baykal (2007) aimed to define the relationship between organisational cultures and nurses' and physicians' attitudes towards change in four private hospitals and four public hospitals in Istanbul that had International Organisation for Standardisation accreditation. They found that the dominant culture in private hospitals was a co-operation culture, whilst a power culture was most dominant in public hospitals. The researchers said that they were not surprised by these findings: they stated that an autocratic and bureaucratic managerial approach is often adopted in public organisations, with less teamwork and lower levels of employee participation, satisfaction and development. This, they argued, also impacted on quality issues. They also believed that this differed considerably from private hospitals, where the converse was the case.

Health care organisations have been identified as having strong subcultures. Deal and Kennedy (1982), Handy (1993) and Goffee and Jones (2003) identified that organisations often have different cultures and subcultures. This differs from the perspective of a uniform culture across organisations. However, organisational cultures can also be described as being homogenous at the upper levels of management, created by 'progressive screening, filtering and socialisation' (Waldman *et al.* 2003:6), with subcultures existing in the middle and lower levels in organisations. It is recognised that strong subcultures exist in health care organisations because hospital units tend to be strongly differentiated and consequently develop specific subcultures to sustain their work (Shortall *et al.* 1991). This is compounded by the differing roles of professional groups (Braithwaite 2006). However, Handy (1993) suggests that this differentiation of cultures maximises the effectiveness of certain groups, but is more likely to be successful where there is integration between the differing cultures. He also suggests that single cultures should not prevail and that organisations should try not to have only one culture. Mintzberg and Glouberman (2001) concur with Handy (1993). Their perspective is that differentiation is one of the great strengths of the health care system, but that greater integration is required to address the complexities in managing health care organisations. They advocate that health care systems require cultural change, to a culture where there is co-operation between clinical aspects of care, institutions and the broader systems.

ASSESSING ORGANISATIONAL CULTURE

Assessing the organisational culture is a managerial role (Marquis and Huston 2009). Schein (1992:15) emphasises that 'The bottom line for leaders is that if they do not become conscious of the cultures in which they are embedded, those cultures will manage them.' However, people can be unaware of culture until it is 'challenged or consciously articulated' (Cameron 2008:431). The current data available on health care systems identify that organisational culture in health care organisations is a 'key performance indicator' (Waldman *et al.* 2003:8). These authors further argue that in order to implement change 'fresh thinking and socialisation' are required. However, they highlight that it is essential to read the culture first so as to understand where and how change can be implemented to achieve the desired change.

The process of measuring organisational culture remains challenging as a consequence of its complex, nebulous, multifaceted nature. A variety of approaches incorporating quantitative, qualitative or mixed method approaches have been utilised to achieve this. These approaches have been influenced by the perspective of culture that is taken, which may be sociological or anthropological (Cameron 2008). The sociological approach sees culture as something that can be identified, measured and changed, and that can predict other organisational outcomes, whereas the anthropological approach sees culture as something an organisation is, and that it can therefore be measured independently of any other phenomenon (Cameron 2008).

Quantitative methods have been widely used in researching organisational culture (Scott-Findlay & Estabrooks, 2006). Scott *et al.* (2003) identified a number that were suitable for using in health care organisations. These researchers highlight the challenges in choosing an instrument as each tool is different in terms of conceptual underpinnings, ease of use, scientific properties and the rationale for

Figure 4.7: The competing values framework

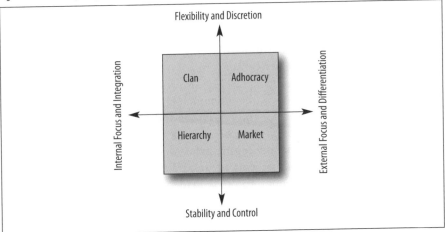

Source: Quinn *et al.* (2007:220); reproduced with permission of John Wiley & Sons Inc.

the research study. The Organisational Culture Assessment Instrument (OCAI) is one example of a quantitative instrument they suggest is suitable for use in health care organisations. This instrument is based on the Competing Values Framework (CVF) (Cameron & Quinn 1999). It endeavours to profile the perceived current organisational culture, and to identify the preferred future culture, based on the organisation's strategy and the current state of the organisation (Quinn *et al.* 2007). The model consists of four quadrants representing four different cultural types, and two dimensions (Figure 4.7). The first quadrant represents the hierarchy culture. This culture is structured, with well-defined policies and regulations, focusing on efficiency, co-ordination and smooth operation. Leadership is cautious and focuses on technical issues. The second quadrant represents the clan culture, where the focus is on people. The culture is friendly and open; leaders are supportive and may be more like mentors and coaches. They encourage teamwork and participation. Success is determined by the internal environment and development of human capital. The third quadrant is the adhocracy culture. This culture is dynamic and entrepreneurial, with leadership being about innovation, risk taking and visioning. It is a future-orientated approach that is focused on rapid growth and resource acquisition. The fourth and final quadrant is the market culture, where the focus is on productivity and results. Leaders are directive and competitive. This culture has an external orientation, and market share and competition are important. The two dimensions in the framework create the four quadrants. The horizontal dimension moves from an internal focus and integration within the organisation to an external focus, differentiation and rivalry. The second dimension relates to stability and control at one extreme and individuality and flexibility at the other. In using this framework to assess organisational culture, scores are calculated based on six content dimensions. The results are discussed and then the OCAI is completed a second time to identify what changes need to be made to the culture to position the organisation where it needs to be (Cameron & Quinn 1999; Quinn *et al.* 2007; Cameron 2008).

This instrument has been used in a number of studies in health care (Gifford *et al.* 2002; Mallak *et al.* 2003). It is, however, a quantitative instrument, although it is advocated that discussion is utilised during the assessment process (Cameron 2008). This type of approach to assessing organisational culture has been criticised by some researchers. Scott *et al.* (2003:928), in their review of quantitative instruments, comment that 'None convincingly addresses those unspoken assumptions that guide attitudes and behaviour and form the stable substrate of culture.' They also suggest that researchers will be frustrated in trying to find one suitable instrument to measure the culture in health care organisations. Ashkanasy *et al.* (2000:145) concur with Scott *et al.* (2003) that the 'exclusive use of quantitative instruments is bound to prove inadequate in many situations'. They advocate what they describe as the 'adjunctive use of qualitative methods as a means to extend the boundaries of the application of quantitative measurement of organisational culture' (Ashkanasy *et al.* 2000:145).

Accordingly, many managers and researchers advocate utilising mixed methods to assess organisational culture. For example, Nelson and Quick (2006:545) advocate the use of triangulation to research organisational culture as it leads to a 'better understanding of the phenomena'. One approach to assessing organisational culture using a mixed method is the 'Double S' cube. Goffee and Jones (2003) advocate utilising their 'Double S' (Figure 4.8) cube, based on the organisational characteristics of sociability and solidarity to assess organisational culture.

Figure 4.8: The Double S cube

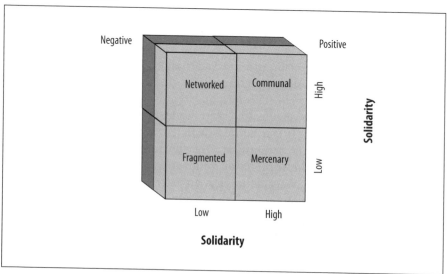

Source: Goffee & Jones (2003:22); reproduced with permission of Profile Books

They use four tests to achieve this, including an observational checklist, a questionnaire, a second questionnaire called 'The Corporate Character Questionnaire' to further analyse the results of the first questionnaire, followed by critical incidence technique. Furthermore, they add that depending on the size and complexity of the organisation, different parts of the organisation, including different teams, may need to be appraised separately (Goffee & Jones 2003). Their approach utilises a sequential mixed method approach and may also have the potential to facilitate the identification of subcultures within an organisation. However, they do not comment on the scientific properties of their approach.

Mallak and Lyth (2009) conducted a case study utilising the CVF and also utilising a Critical Incident Technique (CIT) as the basis for developing an approach to support system integration across decentralised operations in order to provide a seamless care journey for patients. With regard to utilising a mixed methods approach, these researchers highlight how the data from the CIT yielded rich data which could not be elicited by quantitative measures. They acknowledge that this approach is more resource intensive, but rewarded by the quality of data that was elicited to inform the cultural change process. Bosch *et al.* (2008), in their study conducted in a primary care setting using the Team Climate Inventory and the CVF, concur with Mallak and Lyth (2009) and advocate using more complex research designs in future studies, incorporating both quantitative and qualitative methods to gain better insight into organisational concepts. However, Ashkanasy *et al.* (2000:131) counter-argue that multiple methods can be 'complex, expensive and time consuming'. Scott *et al.* (2003) emphasise that the research approach will depend on many factors, including the resources available to the researchers when choosing a methodology.

MANAGING AND CHANGING ORGANISATIONAL CULTURE

Creating a culture to ensure success of the organisation is a leadership role (Marquis & Huston 2009). Organisational cultures may need to change for many reasons, including rapid environmental change, technological change, workforce diversity and mergers and acquisitions (Nelson & Quick 2006). Waldman *et al.* (2003) argue that cultures in health care need to be managed to improve outcomes in health care. They advocate effective strategic planning with dialogue throughout the organisation whilst it is being developed, the development of a consistent vocabulary and conceptual framework between professional and managerial groups and the application of evidence-based improvement to enhance outcomes from both a medical and financial perspective. Scott *et al.* (2003:926) comment that on the surface it appears that such change is easy, but that the 'collective thought processes informing that behaviour at both conscious and unconscious levels' need to be understood. Despite the plethora of theory and research on culture and change, successfully managing organisational change and cultural change remains a significant challenge for managers and leaders. Drucker (1999) emphasises that this is specifically so in traditional institutions such as hospitals because it is a contradiction in terms, as they are designed for continuity.

There are structured models which may guide the process of cultural change (Kotter 1996; Cameron 2008; Alvesson & Sveningsson 2008). They advocate different stages in this process (Table 4.3). Cameron (2008:436) comments that while these steps initiate change in aspects of organisational culture, including values, processes and symbols, they do not ensure that cultural change will occur but 'create a great deal of momentum towards fundamental cultural change'. Alvesson and Sveningsson (2008) also suggest developing the following aspects of the organisation to reflect and promote the new culture: recruitment and selection procedures; socialisation and training programmes; performance appraisal systems; promotion of individuals congruent with the new culture; leadership strategies which reflect the new culture; and use of organisational symbols to reflect the new culture.

Table 4.3 Steps in the cultural change process

Kotter (1996:21)	Cameron (2008:437–40)	Alvesson and Sveningsson (2008:44)
1. Establish a sense of urgency. 2. Create the guiding coalition. 3. Develop a vision and strategy. 4. Communicate the change vision. 5. Empower employees for broad-based action. 6. Generate short-term wins. 7. Consolidate gains and produce more change. 8. Anchor new approaches in the culture.	1. Clarifying meaning. 2. Identifying stories. 3. Determining strategic initiatives. 4. Identifying small wins. 5. Crafting metrics, measures and milestones. 6. Communicating and creating symbols. 7. Developing leadership.	1. Evaluation and determination of strategic direction. 2. Cultural analysis; sketch the desired culture. 3. Analyse the gap between what exists and what is desired. 4. Plan how to develop the culture. 5. Implement the plan. 6. Evaluate the changes and then endeavour to engage in strategies to sustain the cultural change.

Research on managing and changing organisational culture within the context of organisational change has demonstrated difficulties in changing organisational culture even in the context of strategic change. Willcocks (2003) conducted a qualitative longitudinal case study to explore the early experiences of a primary care trust in the United Kingdom. These changes took place to implement policy in the primary care sector. Willcocks highlights the necessity for these organisations to work effectively in order to ensure the overall success of health policy developments. Four themes emerged in the findings: the experience of individual participants and their readiness for change; roles and responsibilities in relation to the primary care group; the process of change and the impact of culture and power structure; and finally the relationships with other organisations in the primary care group network. Willcocks recommends greater support for individuals and greater focus on organisational learning to support the process, development activities to facilitate team building and clarify expectations, and processes to facilitate cultural change, most notably that of questioning. The researcher advocates changes in management and leadership style to manage in a non-hierarchical way and encourage a more participative way of managing. The findings from this study emphasise that many of the steps in the above approaches to managing change, including cultural analysis, creating a guiding coalition, clarification of strategic direction, identifying small wins and anchoring change in the culture, may have facilitated greater understanding of the changes taking place and enhanced organisation effectiveness during the first year.

CONCLUSION

Organisational culture is a complex construct which has been defined in many ways. A number of models have been developed to clarify the concept and also to enable managers and researchers to analyse culture in order to determine what course of action should be taken to move the organisation forward. There is a plethora of research studies that explore the relationship between organisational cultures in health care organisations. Many offer conflicting findings, but there is considerable agreement that organisational culture impacts significantly and when leveraged appropriately can effect changes that can benefit staff and patients alike.

REFLECTIVE EXERCISES

1 Think about your work environment. Using one of the theories of organisational culture, explore what type of culture you work in, what the values are and what some of the underlying assumptions might be.

2 How does leadership in your area of practice contribute to a positive culture? What are the effects of this? Are they positive or negative?

3 How does culture impact on patient care in your area? How could the culture be enhanced to deliver a higher standard of patient care?

REFERENCES

Allio, R. J. (2006) 'Strategic thinking: the ten big ideas', *Strategy and Leadership* 34(4): 4–13.

Alvesson, M. (2002) *Understanding Organizational Culture*. London: Sage.

Alvesson, M. and Sveningsson, S. (2008) *Changing Organizational Culture: Cultural Work in Progress*. London: Routledge.

Ashkanasy, N. M., Broadfoot, L. E. and Falkus, S. (2000) 'Questionnaire measures of organizational culture' in Ashkanasy, N. A., Wilderman, C. P. M. and Peterson, M. F. (eds) (2000) *Handbook of Organizational Culture and Climate*. Thousand Oaks: Sage.

Bellou, V. (2007) 'Achieving long-term customer satisfaction through organizational culture: evidence from the health care sector', *Managing Service Quality* 17(5): 510–22.

Boddy, D. (2005) *Management: An Introduction* (3rd edn). Harlow: Prentice Hall.

Bosch, M., Dijkstra, R., Wensing, M., van der Weijden, T. and Grol, R. (2008) 'Organizational culture, team climate and diabetes care in small office-based practices', *BMC Health Services Research* 8: 180.

Brady, A.-M., Redmond, R., Curtis, E., Fleming, S., Keenan, P., Malone, A.-M. and Sheerin, F. (2009a) 'Adverse events in health care: a literature review', *Journal of Nursing Management* 17: 155–64.

Brady, A.-M., Malone, A.-M. and Fleming, S. (2009b) 'A literature review of the individual and systems factors that contribute to medication errors in nursing practice', *Journal of Nursing Management* 17: 679–97.

Braithwaite, J. (2006) 'An empirical assessment of social structural and cultural change in clinical directorates', *Health Care Analysis* 14: 185–93.

Brooks, C. (2006) 'Working with healthcare professionals', in Walshe, K. and Smith, J. (eds), *Healthcare Management*. Buckingham: Open University Press.

Cameron, K. (2008) 'A process for changing organizational culture' in Cummings, T. G. (ed.) *Handbook of Organizational Development*. Los Angeles: Sage.

Cameron, K. S. and Quinn, R. E. (1999) *Diagnosing and Changing Organizational Culture Based on the Competing Values Framework*. Reading, MA: Addison-Wesley.

Carney, M. (2004) 'Middle manager involvement in strategy development in not-for-profit organizations: the director of nursing perspective – how organizational structure impacts on the role', *Journal of Nursing Management* 12:13–21.

— (2006) 'Understanding organizational culture: the key to successful middle manager strategic involvement in health care delivery?', *Journal of Nursing Management* 14:23–33.

Deal, T. E. and Kennedy, A. A. (1982) *Corporate Cultures: The Rites and Rituals of Corporate Life*. Reading, MA: Addison-Wesley.

Doctor X (2007) *The Bitter Pill*. Ireland: Hodder Headline.

DoHC (Department of Health and Children) (2001) *The Road to Enterprise Liability*, http://www.dohc.ie/press/speeches/2001/20010216a.html, accessed 28 September 2009.

— (2003) *Audit of Structures and Functions in the Health System*. Dublin: Stationery Office.

— (2006) *The Lourdes Hospital Inquiry: An Inquiry into the Peripartum Hysterectomy at Our Lady of Lourdes Hospital Drogheda. The Report of Judge Maureen Clarke S.C.* Dublin: Stationery Office.

Drucker, P. (1999) *Management Challenges for the 21st Century*. Oxford: Butterworth Heinemann.

Gifford, B. D., Zammuto, R. F. and Goodman, E. A. (2002) 'The relationship between hospital unit culture and nurses' quality of work life', *Journal of Healthcare Management* 47(1):13–25.

Glouberman, S. and Mintzberg, H. (2001) 'Managing the care of health and the cure of disease. Part I: differentiation', *Health Care Management Review* 26(1): 56–71.

Goffee, R. and Jones, G. (2003) *The Character of a Corporation* (2nd edn). London: Profile Books.

Handy, C. (1993) *Understanding Organizations* (4th edn). London: Penguin.

Harrison, R. (1972) 'Understanding your organization's character', *Harvard Business Review* 5(3): 119–28.

Hatch, M. J. (1993) 'The dynamics of organizational culture', *Academy of Management Review* 18: 657–93.

Hofstede, G. (2004) 'Cultural constraints in management theories' in De Wit, B. and Meyer, R., *Strategy Process, Content, Context: An International Perspective* (3rd edn). Australia: Thomson.

Huber, D. (2006) *Leadership and Nursing Care Management* (3rd edn). Philadelphia: Saunders Elsevier.

Jain, M., Miller, L., Belt, D., King, D. and Berwick, D. M. (2006) 'Decline in ICCCU adverse events, nosocomial infections and cost through a quality improvement initiative focusing on teamwork and culture change', *Quality and Safety in Healthcare* 15: 235–9.

Johnson, G. (1992) 'Managing strategic change: strategy, culture and action, *Long Range Planning* 25(1): 28–36.

Johnson, G., Scholes, K. and Whittington, R. (2008) *Exploring Corporate Strategy Texts and Cases* (8th edn). Harlow: Prentice Hall.

Khatri, N., Wells, J., McKune, J. and Brewer, M. (2006) 'Strategic human resource management issues in hospitals: a study of a university and a community hospital', *Health Topics: Research and Perspectives on Health Care* 84(4): 9–20.

Kotter, J. P. (1996) *Leading Change*. Boston, MA: Harvard Business School Press.

Lawler, E. E., III (2008) 'Strategic human resource management' in Cummings, T. G. (ed.), *Handbook of Organizational Development*. Los Angeles: Sage.

Linstead, L. (2009) 'Managing culture' in Linstead, S., Fulop, L. and Lilley, S., *Management and Organization: A Critical Text* (2nd edn). London: Palgrave Macmillan.

Mallak, L. A. and Lyth, D. M. (2009) 'Using desired culture analysis to manage decentralized operations', *Engineering Management Journal* 21(2): 27–32.

Mallak, L. A., Lyth, D. M., Olson, S. D., Ulshafer, S. M. and Sardone, F. J. (2003) 'Culture, the built environment and healthcare organizational performance', *Managing Service Quality* 13(1): 27–38.

Marquis, B. and Huston, C. (2009) *Leadership Roles and Management Functions in Nursing: Theory and Application* (6th edn). Philadelphia: Lippincott Williams & Wilkins.

Mintzberg, H. and Glouberman, S. (2001) 'Managing the care of health and the cure of disease. Part II: integration', *Health Care Management Review* 26(1): 72–86.

Morgan, P. I. and Ogbonna, E. (2008) 'Subcultural dynamics in transformation: a multi-perspective study of healthcare professionals', *Human Relations* 61(1): 39–65.

Nelson, D. L. and Quick, J. C. (2006) *Organizational Behaviour: Foundations, Realities and Challenges* (5th edn). Australia: Thomson South Western.

O'Neill, D. (2006) *Leas Cross Review*. Available at http://www.lenus.ie/hse/bitstream/10147/44494/1/8326.pdf, accessed 20 September 2009.

Parkin, P. (2009) *Managing Change in Healthcare Using Action Research*. Los Angeles: Sage.

Porter, M. E. (1985) *Competitive Advantage: Creating and Sustaining Superior Performance*. New York: Free Press.

Quinn, R. E., Faerman, S. R., Thompson, M. P., McGrath, M. R. and St Clair, L. S. (2007) *Becoming an Master Manager: A Competing Values Approach* (4th edn). New Jersey: Wiley.

Schein, E. H. (1985) *Organizational Leadership and Culture: A Dynamic View*. San Francisco: Jossey-Bass.

— (1992) *Organizational Leadership and Culture: A Dynamic View* (2nd edn). San Francisco: Jossey-Bass.

— (1999) *The Corporate Culture Survival Guide*. San Francisco: Jossey-Bass.

— (2004) *Organizational Leadership and Culture: A Dynamic View* (3rd edn). San Francisco: Jossey-Bass.

Scott, S. D. and Pollock, C. (2008) 'The role of nursing unit culture in shaping research utilization behaviours', *Research in Nursing and Health* 31: 298–309.

Scott, T. Mannion, R. Davies, H. and Marshall, M. (2003) 'The quantitative measurement of organizational culture in health care: a review of the available instruments', *Health Services Research* 38(3): 923–45.

Scott-Findlay, S. and Estabrooks, C. A. (2006) 'Mapping the organizational culture in nursing: a literature review', *Journal of Advanced Nursing* 56(5): 498–513.

Seren, S. and Baykal, U. (2007) 'Relationships between change and organizational culture in hospitals', *Journal of Nursing Scholarship* 39(2): 191–7.

Shermont, H. and Krepcio, D. (2006) 'The impact of culture change on nursing retention', *Journal of Nursing Administration* 36(9): 407–15.

Shirey, M. R. (2009) 'Authentic leadership, organizational culture, and healthy work environments', *Critical Care Nursing Quarterly* 32(3): 189–98.

Shortall, S. M., Rousseau, D. M., Gillies, R. R., Devers, K. J. and Simons, T. L. (1991) 'Organizational assessment in intensive care units (ICUs): construct development, reliability, and validity of the ICU nurse–physician questionnaire', *Medical Care* 29(8): 709–26.

Smith, S. (2009) *Equity in Health Care: A View from the Irish Health Care System*. Dublin: Adelaide Hospital Society Health Policy Publications.

Swayne, L. E., Duncan, W. J. and Ginter, P. M. (2008) *Strategic Management of Health Care Organizations* (6th edn). England: Jossey-Bass.

Vandenberghe, C. (1999) 'Organizational culture, person-culture fit, and turnover: a replication in the health care industry', *Journal of Organizational Behaviour* 20: 175–84.

Waldman, J. D., Smith, H. L. and Hood, J. N. (2003) 'Corporate culture: the missing piece of the healthcare puzzle', *Hospital Topics: Research and Perspectives on Healthcare* 81(1): 5–14.

Willcocks, S. (2003) 'Developing the effectiveness of primary care organisations in the UK National Health Service', *Journal of Health Service and Management*. 11117(3): 194–209.

Wren, M. A. (2003) *Unhealthy State: Anatomy of a Sick Society*. Dublin: New Island.

5
Delegation

Anne-Marie Brady

OBJECTIVES
- To differentiate between delegation, allocation, assignment and referral.
- To understand the relationship between delegation, responsibility, authority and accountability.
- To gain insight into the benefits of delegation.
- To determine ways of overcoming obstacles to delegation in practice.
- To develop skills in the process of delegation.

INTRODUCTION

A critical aspect of the reform agenda advanced by the Department of Health and Children (2003) and the Health Service Executive has been concerned with strengthening the governance and accountability arrangements in the health services. The performance of clinical staff is central to the governance agenda and in recent times there has been considerable emphasis on the redirection of education and training of heath care professionals (DoHC 2004, 2006). Reforms of the education of health care professionals have sought to enhance clinical leadership capacity in the services and to ensure that graduates are educated and trained to meet the needs of a modern health system where care is delivered in a multidisciplinary context.

In today's health care environment, clinicians at the front line are responsible for completing more work than they could possibly do themselves and therefore delegation of activities to others (other professionals or health care assistants (HCAs)) is an essential component of everyday work. Indeed, the complexity of modern care delivery means that the diversity of tasks undertaken and delegated by professional staff has increased. Current and emerging care delivery systems rely on some form of 'extender' to the professions, for example much work traditionally carried out by registered nurses (RNs) is now delivered by HCAs, the work of therapists is assisted by assistive practitioners, while emerging pathways for nurses appear to include an extension of the doctor's role. In the last decade advanced nurse practitioner and clinical nurse specialist roles have developed considerably in this country and appear to have incorporated some activities that were previously undertaken by doctors, in addition to providing nursing leadership and advanced expertise. Determining an appropriate level of skill mix is critical to the provision of high-quality service and in any employment site there will be a variety of people with different levels of education, experience and competence who contribute to the delivery of care (Buchan & Calman 2005).

The purpose of this chapter is to explore the issues that arise around delegation and to seek an understanding of its critical components in health care settings. The underlying principles of delegation, including responsibility, authority and accountability, will be discussed. The chapter seeks to illustrate how the delegation process can assist health professionals to delegate more effectively and to illustrate some tools that can assist with the ever-growing nature of modern health care delivery. The benefits of and barriers that may inhibit effective delegation in health care are considered. The health care assistant (HCA) grade in the Irish health service is examined as there has been an effort to advance some uniformity in this role in recent times. Determining why, what, when and how care is delegated is a key concern of professionals practising in the Irish health care services and the questions that should be asked when making such decisions are given close analysis.

WHAT IS DELEGATION?

'Delegation is the process by which responsibility and authority for performing a task is transferred to another individual who accepts that authority and responsibility' (Sullivan & Decker 2005:144). While the authority and responsibility for the completion of tasks is transferred, accountability for the decision to delegate and for the outcome is retained. There is a distinct relationship between delegation and the principles that underpin it: responsibility, authority and accountability. Responsibility may be described as an obligation to complete an activity or task and will held by the **delegator** who is charged with making the decision to delegate. Only those activities within one's sphere of responsibility may be delegated. In the process of delegation complete authority, i.e. the required level of power or influence to undertake a task, is given to the **delegate**. If authority is not delegated, the individual has no power to act and delegation will be ineffective. True delegation implies that the delegate has the authority to do the job, can make independent decisions and is responsible for seeing that the job is done well (Huber 2000). It is necessary to state explicitly that only authority can be delegated, not overall responsibility and accountability. Once a delegation is accepted the delegate shares in the responsibility for the completion of the given task. However, accountability means that the delegator remains answerable not only for the outcome of the task undertaken but also for the decision to delegate. The delegate will be accountable for their own performance in relation to the outcome of the task. To whom they will be accountable will depend on their individual professional and employment status. Health care professionals who are registered with a regulatory body are accountable, as mandated by their code of practice, to their respective professions, ethically to patients and in both criminal and civil law. In addition, health care professionals must also take into account any organisational policies that will have a bearing on decisions they make to delegate. Health care workers who do not hold a professional licence to practise with a regulatory body are also accountable for their performance, although the nature of their accountability will differ, as explained in the section entitled 'Role of the health care assistant'.

The theoretical perspectives that inform delegation can be found in various theories of human motivation and development in work design. The boundaries between activities undertaken as a result of the expansion of health care worker roles and those that result from delegation are sometimes unclear in modern health care. It is to some extent uncharted territory and further effort is necessary to clarify and/or develop guidance on this issue. There is a distinction to be made, depending on the profession, between delegation and other activities that involve the transfer of work to others. For example, in medicine there is a difference between referral and delegation to another professional and in nursing there is a distinction between delegation and allocation or assignment. The General Medical Council (GMC) UK has issued the following guidance on delegation which enables a clear distinction between delegation and referral.

54. Delegation involves asking a colleague to provide treatment or care on your behalf. Although you will not be accountable for the decisions and actions of those to whom you delegate, you will still be responsible for the overall management of the patient, and accountable for your decision to delegate. When you delegate care or treatment you must be satisfied that the person to whom you delegate has the qualifications, experience, knowledge and skills to provide the care or treatment involved. You must always pass on enough information about the patient and the treatment needed.

55. Referral involves transferring some or all of the responsibility for the patient care, usually temporarily and for a particular purpose, such as additional investigation, care or treatment which falls outside of your competence. You must be satisfied that any healthcare professional to whom you refer a patient is accountable to a statutory regulatory body or employed within a managed environment. It they are not, the transfer of care will be regarded as delegation, not referral. This means you remain responsible for the overall management of the patient, and accountable for your decision to delegate.

(General Medical Council 2006:26).

In the nursing profession the distinction between assignment and delegation is important as managers or staff in-charge have legal obligations when allocating work to others. An assignment to another registered nurse will be made based on expectations of the expected competency and ability of a registered nurse. However, in assigning work to junior colleagues or HCAs the transfer or assignment of work also necessitates a delegation decision. In making an assignment of patient care to a subordinate, the registered nurse is required to have an understanding of the skills, knowledge and experience of the delegate so that they can accurately assess whether the assignment falls within their scope of practice. Assignment must take into account the ability of the subordinate to take on the task. It is not anticipated that the nurse making an assignment to another fully competent and experienced nurse is doing anything other than making an allocation of patient care. However, when making an assignment to a new graduate or a nurse who is unfamiliar with a unit, the nurse has a greater responsibility to fully evaluate the abilities and competence of the delegate to take the assignment.

BENEFITS OF DELEGATION IN HEALTH CARE

Demand for accessible, fiscally responsible and high-quality care has resulted in increased examination of care delivery models and professional/assistive roles. The total operating cost of any health care organisation is largely composed of salaries and employment benefits. Models of care delivery determine staff volumes, skill mix and deployment of personnel in health care. The models of care delivery will depend on the type of health care client, the environment in which services are provided, and the training and ability of staff. Unprecedented development in health care structures, global staff shortages and increased demand for fiscal responsibility mean that there is increased reliance on delegation to ensure that care is delivered. Health care professionals are now required to develop skills in managing various types and levels of assistive personnel, which has contributed to increased attention on the issues of delegation that arise in practice. In the past, apprenticeship models of education and hierarchical employment structures were prominent in health care and they relied on task-orientated models of care in which junior staff were assigned to tasks rather than to individual patients, for example doing the medications or dressings. This type of approach relied upon predictability, obedience and rigid control and it is now largely viewed negatively because care was fragmented and most certainly fell short of the patient-centredness aspired to in today's health care environment. Team models of care delivery, now the norm, are dependent on successful teamwork and are highly reliant on effective delegation. These models are more suitable for the multidisciplinary/interdisciplinary team approaches commonly operative in health care, where professionals have reporting to them a number of individuals of various degrees of seniority, experience and responsibility. All are considered essential in the planning and delivery of care, but the leader retains accountability for overall care.

While the involvement of unlicensed personnel in care delivery is an everyday occurrence in health care, such roles are designed to assist, not replace, health care professionals, and caution should be exercised, particularly in professions such as medicine or nursing, in the design and configuration of such roles. 'Role drift' as described by McKenna (2004a), occurs when tasks or work traditionally associated with a profession are shifted, from doctors to nurses or allied health professionals, and from nurses to health care assistants. This development is not exclusive to medicine or nursing and is evidenced in pharmacy, dentistry and other social care professions. There is evidence of concern across the professions in relation to issues of competency and accountability associated with the delegation of care to others (Mackey & Nancarrow 2005; McLaughlin et al. 2000). McKenna (2004b) argues that there is evidence of substitution of RNs and an over-reliance on HCAs in health care, and expresses serious concern for patient safety as growth is unregulated, with insufficient regard to the HCAs' competency and training as they fill the gaps in service. The Leas Cross reports (O'Neill 2006; DoHC 2009) were particularly critical of the deficiencies in nursing skill mix and specialist nursing expertise, inferring that many of the problems in the home arose from inadequacy in the nursing infrastructure. The following recommendation was made:

> The provision of [residential care] should be clarified formally in terms of adequate numbers of adequately trained nursing and health care assistant staff with adequate governance in terms of senior nursing staff. The minimum numbers of nursing staff should be calculated using a modern instrument such as the RCN Assessment tool or the Nursing Needs Assessment tool and at least half of these nursing staff should have the diploma in gerontological nursing. A sufficient number of middle and senior nursing grade staff, relative to the size of the nursing home, will be needed to be added to the calculated total to ensure an adequate infrastructure . . . All health care assistants should have the FETAC training or equivalent. Appropriate acculturation and gerontological training should be provided for all non-national staff [in long-term residential settings].
>
> (DoHC 2009:5)

Concrete evidence is emerging of a positive association between the quality of patient outcomes and the ratio of registered nurses engaged in care delivery (Rafferty *et al.* 2007). Leas Cross is an example of deficiencies in care that can result, even if there is an appearance of adequate numbers of care staff, when the skill mix and ratio of registered nurses is inadequate to respond adequately to patient need.

The health service is growing in complexity and flexibility in relation to by whom, when and where care is delivered. The recent shift in the emphasis of Irish health policy to integrated rather than institutional or community care will only serve to increase the demand for flexibility in care delivery patterns. Overall, the changing practice environment has greatly impacted on the development and number of supportive roles generally and this group of workers plays a crucial role in contemporary health care. There is much greater appreciation of the 24/7 nature of modern health care services, with increased demand for specialist care when and where it is needed. Expanding the role of unlicensed personnel to undertake nursing duties and the expansion of nursing work to include activities previously undertaken by doctors has not been without controversy and there has been disagreement among and across professions as to what is the best approach (Mackey & Nancarrow 2005; McKenna 2004b; McLaughlin *et al.* 2000). The nature and type of tasks to be delegated will be influenced by the jurisdiction. There is no consensus as to what constitutes an expanded role nationally or internationally and practices can vary from hospital to hospital and health region to health region.

Respective professions should determine what, if any, activities may be delegated as they will be accountable for the appropriateness of tasks and whether they are undertaken in accord with established standards of practice. It is not appropriate for health care managers to place undue influence on professionals to delegate where it is unsafe or not in the best interest of the patient. The situational factors must be assessed when determining what may be safely delegated. The main benefit of delegation is to maximise use of the most expensive commodity in any health care budget – human resources. Effective delegation is a process by which specialist care is directed to where it is most appropriately utilised. Delegating tasks to others frees up time to do other things and can positively influence access to services and enable more individuals to receive the appropriate levels of care as required. Effective delegation not only benefits the delegator and saves time but is also an opportunity for delegates to expand their knowledge and skills; it can affect motivation positively, foster commitment, and promote and sustain job interest for individuals.

REGULATORY PERSPECTIVES

Registration is the process by which the state grants permission for suitably qualified individuals to perform certain activities, which if undertaken by a person without registration would be deemed illegal. The purpose of professional registration is to protect the public by identifying the qualifications and educational preparation required to join a particular health care profession and what may done within the scope of practice of the respective professions. The scope of practice for professionals will be determined by the relevant legislation, social policy, and national and local guidelines, in addition to the individual's level of competence. Registered professionals are regulated and accountable to the regulatory body, for example An Bord Altranais for nurses and midwives, the Medical Council for doctors. The regulatory framework for health professionals in this country is commonly referred to as a code of practice and it essentially provides a blueprint of the minimum standard of performance that may be anticipated by a health professional.

Delegation of patient care does fall within the scope of practice of registered health professionals, although formal guidance for health professionals is variable in relation to delegation. The professional body for doctors in this country offers the following guidance for its members:

The medical council considers that doctors have a personal and professional responsibility towards junior colleagues, medical students and other healthcare workers . . . junior doctors should never be asked to perform tasks for which they are not fully competent except under the direct supervision of senior colleagues who can take over should difficulty be encountered. Senior staff must always be willing to undertake troublesome or unpleasant tasks rather than instructing juniors to do so. Delegation of duties to doctors in training of whatever level does not obviate the responsibility of the trainer for the actions taken.

(Medical Council 2004:15).

An Bord Altranais offers the following general guidance in its code of conduct for nurses:

> The nurse shares the responsibility of care with colleagues and must have regard to the workload and pressures on professional colleagues and subordinates and take appropriate action if these are seen to be such as to constitute abuse of the individual practitioner and/or jeopardise safe standards of practice. Each nurse has a continuing responsibility to junior colleagues. He/She is obliged to transmit acquired professional knowledge, skills and attitudes both by word and example. The nurse must not delegate to junior colleagues tasks and responsibly beyond their scope and expertise.
>
> (ABA 2000a).

The Scope of Practice document is more explicit. It states:

> Each registered nurse and midwife is accountable for his/her own practice. The nurse or midwife who is delegating (the delegator) is accountable for the decision to delegate. This means that the delegator is accountable for ensuring that the delegate role/function is appropriate and that support and resources are available to the person to whom the role/function has been delegated. The nurse or midwife (or another person) to whom the particular role/function has been delegated is accountable for carrying out the delegated role/function in an appropriate manner.
>
> (ABA 2000b:9)

Much of the literature on delegation is drawn from the business world and has limited applicability to the health care arena. This subject has garnered more attention in nursing-related publications, probably as a result of the changes in care delivery patterns with changing and emerging role development in the profession. The last decade has seen a marked increase in the use of unlicensed personnel to substitute or augment numbers in the nursing professions in this country. This has been influenced to a large extent by the staffing effects of the change in nursing education from the apprenticeship to the university-based model. Re-emphasis on care in the community, an ageing population and changes to models of care delivery in acute services are just some of the other factors that have impacted on skill mix in nursing. Delegation is an activity in which all health care professionals are engaged to a greater or lesser degree and respective regulatory frameworks should provide guidance as to the appropriateness of delegation.

Nationally and internationally, the codes of practice that relate to the nursing professions address delegation as a prominent issue (NMC 2008; NCSBN 2006; ABA 2000b). In the nursing profession it is accepted that the registered nurse is charged with the assessment of patients' needs, determining what can be delegated and when. There is always provision for the professional to exercise judgment and not to delegate if it is not in the best interest of the patient. Delegation of care can become the 'but for' cause of health care injury and one for which health care professionals may be held accountable in terms of professional negligence. The breach of duty may be not the negligent act of injury through the actions of a subordinate, but the failure to delegate competently (Barter & Furmidge 1994). Inappropriate delegation of tasks or, indeed, insufficient supervision may constitute a breach in the duty of care and has been found to be a cause of negligent injury for which health professionals can be held to account legally, if another reasonable professional would not have made those delegation decisions (Barter & Furmidge 1994).

There are inherent responsibilities for any professional in accepting a delegated task. They must evaluate whether it exceeds their scope of practice, must acknowledge any deficit in competence and are required to provide the appropriate level of feedback to the delegate (ABA 2000b). The *Scope of Professional Practice* for nurses and midwives in the Irish Republic, available online (http://www.nursingboard.ie/en/publications.aspx) is an enabling framework designed to support best practice while affording nurses the opportunity and flexibility to determine what activities are within their sphere of practice (ABA 2000b). This type of document has been prepared by many nursing boards internationally to support nurses in determining what additional delegation they may safely incorporate in their practice in the best interest of patients or clients.

DECIDING WHAT TO DELEGATE

Determining what may be safely and appropriately delegated to another is the first step in any delegation decision. The decision to delegate should be based on a careful analysis of the individual patient's needs. There is a narrow interpretation in health care of the difference between delegating to others and dumping work. Delegation of bits and pieces or things we do not want to do will have a negative effect on staff motivation, particularly if employees perceive that one is only prepared to delegate 'scut work'. The Working in Partnership Programme (WIPP) has developed a guide on delegation for general practice in the UK. This comprehensive instrument highlights some of the key questions that clinical staff should consider in making a decision to delegate a task that has not traditionally been delegated and, indeed, in evaluating the appropriateness of tasks already commonly delegated.

Table 5.1: Delegation guide

Key issues	Things to consider
Before you decide to delegate . . .	
1 Why do you want to delegate?	Has someone asked you to? Will it free you up to do other things? Will it ease your workload? Is there a business case for delegating the work? Does the person asking you to delegate have the authority to do so?

2	Is delegation in the best interest of the patient?	How will patients benefit? What will delegation mean for patients?
3	Assess the task to be delegated.	Ensure the task can be delegated safely. Consider the clinical risk, complexity and predictability of the task. Does the task contain elements of 'professional practice' (assessment, diagnosis, planning and evaluation)?
4	What skills and knowledge are required to undertake the task?	Consider breaking it down, so that you address all elements of the task. Think about communication/interpersonal skills.
5	Do you have the authority to delegate the work?	As the person delegating, are you competent in the task being delegated? Does delegation form part of your role/job description?
6	Who will you delegate the work to?	Do they have the knowledge, skills and competence to undertake the work? Have they competently carried out the task before? Do they feel competent to do the work? If they are not competent, what kind of training and support will they need? Who is responsible for this training?
7	How will the person to whom you are delegating benefit?	Increased confidence? Adds to job interest? Increased motivation?
8	How will delegating impact on their workload? Will they have to delegate some of their work in turn?	Do they have the capacity to take on the new work? What impact might that have on patients? On service delivery?
	Once you have decided to delegate . . .	
9	Discuss the task with the individual concerned.	Do they have any concerns? How will they benefit – what's in it for them? How will it impact on their current workload? Training and supervision? Impact on the rest of the team?
10	Be clear about the task/work to be delegated	Does everyone share the same understanding of what is to be delegated, and the process involved in ensuring the delegation takes place successfully and safely?
11	Ensure all those involved are clear about their accountability ad responsibility.	As the registered professional delegating, what are you accountable /responsible for? Where does the employer's accountability and responsibility lie? What are the accountabilities and responsibilities of the person to whom you are delegating?

12 Develop robust protocols and procedures based on good practice to enable task to be delegated.	Are there systems in place to ensure these are reviewed and updated regularly?
13 Ensure access to appropriate training, education and assessment for person to undertake the task.	Keep a record of this training, education and assessment. Review training needs on a regular basis.
14 Evaluation of delegation.	Did it go to plan? What have been the benefits? If things didn't go to plan, why was that?

Source: WIPP (2007)

PROCESS OF DELEGATION

Delegation in health care is not an exact science and when one is attempting to undertake it there is some element of risk involved. There are number of good principles that should underpin delegation of care, which can minimise or eliminate such risks. These are reasonably well articulated in nursing publications which have applicability across other health care professions. The National Council of State Boards in Nursing (NCSBN) in the United States of America has issued a number of guidance documents on delegation for the nursing profession, and the following is a useful summary of best practice guidance on delegation of care for any health care professional.

Delegation principles

- All decisions of delegation must arise from the fundamental principle of patient safety, health and well-being.
- Regulatory responsibility in relation to delegation should be with the code of practice of the relevant profession.
- Clear principles and guidelines for delegation should be articulated to inform decisions.
- A registered professional should hold ultimate responsibility and accountability for the provision of care in their respective domain.
- Registered professionals should be actively involved and accountable for managerial decisions, practices and policy making related to the delegation of patient care.
- Contemporary health care design does necessitate the use of unlicensed personnel who should assist, not replace, the health professional.
- The work of the health care professions is knowledge-based and cannot be condensed into a list of tasks. Therefore, there must always be provision for specialised education, judgment and discretion while engaged in the process of delegation.
- The assessment, judgment and evaluation aspect of the health professional's role must be preserved.
- Care that is delegated to an unlicensed care worker should not be re-delegated.

- Consumers have a right to health care derived from best practice, so all delegated tasks must be performed to established standards.
- Health care professionals are accountable for the delegation decisions they make.

NCSBN (1995)

The steps taken in successful delegation are often sequential and the whole process has been described as cyclical (Hansten & Jackson 2004). Indeed, all decisions around skill mix and delegation are a continuous process necessitating constant review and evaluation of the needs of the services and the capacity of the individuals engaged in the work. The process is reliant on effective interface between what needs to be done, the delegator, the delegate and the environment (see Figure 5.1). Successful delegation in health care can be achieved by:

- only delegating those tasks for which you have responsibility
- following local policies, job descriptions and professional regulations
- utilising the delegation process.

Figure 5.1: Successful delegation

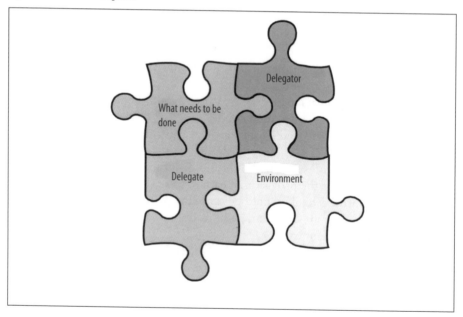

The delegation process is articulated very clearly in the 'Five Rights of Delegation' (NSBCN 1995) (Table 5.2), which provides a resource to enable clinicians to develop competency in this area.

Table 5.2: Five rights of delegation

Right task	The complexity of the task, relevant regulations, the capacity of employees and the level of supervision required are evaluated.
Right circumstances	The process of delegation must take into account the overall circumstances of the practice and work environment.
Right person	The competency and willingness of the person to undertake the task is considered.
Right direction/communication	The direction given should be clear and concise and should include both the expectations and the process of feedback.
Right supervision	The health care professional must be available to provide the appropriate level of supervision required by the delegate.

Adapted from NSCBN (1995)

Right task

The delivery of health care is labour-intensive and the basic aim of delegation is to get work done though other people. There is often more work arising from professional work than can be done by individuals, therefore activities do need to be delegated to support others. The complexity of the task(s), the capacity of employees and the level of supervision required must be carefully evaluated to determine whether an activity is suitable to delegate. It is also necessary to determine whether relevant health care professional practice acts or codes of conduct prohibit the task from being delegated. Health policy and organisational guidelines/procedures must also be taken into account in determining whether a task is suitable to delegate.

Right circumstances

The process of delegation must take into account the overall circumstances of the work and professional environment. It is necessary to evaluate many factors and organisational constraints, such as adequacy of skill mix, staffing and patient acuity, to determine if the delegation is appropriate. Circumstances may be such that a task that is suitable to delegate may be not be so in all instances. Success in delegation is dependent on willingness to engage the participation of others in decision making and to encourage individual initiative as appropriate.

Right person

Delegation occurs when one entrusts another to undertake a specific task that one could have retained. Enabling and empowering subordinates to complete work is key to success in delegation and this necessitates transferring authority, resisting the urge to interfere and allowing the subordinate to operate freely. It is necessary to determine whether the person to whom you are delegating is the right person, with sufficient education, competency or experience to undertake the task(s). In addition, the willingness of the person to undertake the delegated task must be considered. McConnell (1995) suggests the following common sense rules will assist in determining the right person to delegate to. First, only delegate to those you trust, as there is little point in giving additional responsibility to those who are unwilling or unable to take it. Second, delegate to those who are in a position to take additional responsibility and those who actually report to you. A new employee getting to grips with the requirements of the job is not likely to be in the right position for consideration.

Right direction/communication

This refers to the quality of the communication surrounding the process of delegation. The direction given should be clear and concise and should include both the expectations and the process of feedback. This requires attention to detail, with clear delineation of lines of accountability and clarification of arrangements for authority and responsibility.

The process is facilitated by demonstrating confidence in the ability of subordinates and colleagues. McConnell (1995) explains that there are a number of key pieces of information to be communicated to enable a task to be delegated effectively. These include:

- the task to be undertaken
- the expected outcome
- the start time, duration and anticipated completion time
- the procedure for completion of the task
- what is in it for the employee
- the assigned authority.

Right supervision

The supervision of assistive personnel is an expectation of health care professionals operating at both institutional and community health care facilities. Supervision varies and may be direct or indirect, can incorporate direction, guidance, observation, collaborative working or discussion, depending on the situation. It requires judgment and understanding of the practice environment, patient/client need, support worker competency, in addition to the tasks to be undertaken, and may require tolerance for mistakes. The health care professional must be available to provide the appropriate level of supervision required by the delegate as necessary. The level of supervision anticipated during the task and the mechanism by which the outcome may be evaluated are critical elements in the supervision aspect of delegation. A certain level of patience is required to get to grips with what is expected. Employees, by their nature, will need different degrees of supervision. The nature and complexity of the task will differ in magnitude. Any process of delegation should also give consideration to how staff will be rewarded.

The level of supervision required in any episode of delegation will be determined by a number of elements, including:

- level of experience and knowledge
- assessment of competence
- task complexity (is it routine, with predictable outcomes?)
- the health status of the individual
- the practice environment
- availability of support.

ROLE OF THE HEALTH CARE ASSISTANT

Rationalisation in the Irish health services has resulted in increased use of non-licensed personnel in clinical practice. Activities and skills previously within the domain of particular health care professions are regularly delegated to other professions and/or support workers. Health care consumers do have the right to know who is providing their care and that they have the required level of competence to practice. Numerous titles are used to describe the multitude of unlicensed personnel who contribute to care delivery: care assistant, health care assistant, support worker, care staff, nurse's aide and care attendant, to name a few.

The role of the health care assistant (HCA) has to date been ill-defined, with considerable variation across organisations. The level of education and the lack of standardisation in training have considerable implications for health professionals who are making delegation decisions. Recent studies in the Irish Republic have confirmed that the role definition remains obscure, despite the introduction of the health care support certificate course (Keeney *et al.* 2005a, 2005b; McKenna *et al.* 2003). Standardisation of the role is desired (McLaughlin *et al.* 2000) and guidance is required for all health professionals on what and how to delegate so that the HCA role is not abused and patient safety is preserved.

The Commission on Nursing (1998) paved the way for increased use of care assistants and other personnel in the delivery of both nursing and non-nursing care-related activities and recommended that there should be national criteria for entry requirements, education, qualifications and training for this grade of health care worker. Following the commission's work in this area, the report of the Working Group on the Effective Utilisation of Professional Skills of Nurses and Midwives (DoHC 2001) recommended widespread introduction of the grade of health care assistant or maternity health care assistant to the Irish health care team. The report of the High Level Group on Health Care Assistants regarding the implementation of the HCA programme (HSE 2006) recommended that the title of HCA be uniformly adopted in the health service.

Historically there was no minimum educational standard for this grade of worker, although it was generally accepted by employers that a good standard of general education was desirable, and training was delivered after the employee had commenced work (DoHC 2004). As yet training and education of health care assistants in Ireland is not uniformly applied. Much of their education and training has to date been conducted within organisations and has therefore not been standardised. In the HSE, HCAs and their equivalents study for the level 5 Health Care Support certificate of the Further Education and Training Award Council (FETAC) (formerly known as the National Vocational Qualification Award (NVQA)). The curriculum is normally delivered on a part-time basis over six months and incorporates a number of core modules, such as care skills, care support, safety and health at work, communication and work experience, as well as a small number of elective modules which may be suitable for a particular area of health care, for example care of the elderly, maternity care or children's care. Keeney *et al.* (2005a, 2005b) employed multiple methods to access key stakeholders in order to evaluate a pilot of this type of HCA training course in the Irish Republic, using surveys, interviews and direct observation. The course was piloted with 221 health care assistants across a variety of settings and 81 per cent of those undertaking the course graduated successfully. The study found that selection criteria for training varied across sites and recommended that support workers receive a nationally agreed and standardised programme of training (Keeney *et al.* 2005a, 2005b; McKenna *et al.* 2003). The study demonstrated increased knowledge and confidence in participants, with greater understanding of patient-centred care.

In many organisations the HCA qualification is not a prerequisite of employment and therefore many HCAs have no formal training. Much of the communications from the Department of Health and Children (DoHC) and Health Services Executive (HSE) in relation to HCAs suggest that in general it is anticipated that all HCAs will undertake the training; however, the 2006 HSE report does accept that some individuals may not be in a position to do so and that the previous job descriptions will therefore still apply. There are noteworthy advances in standardising the entry and education of individuals employed as HCAs in the Irish Republic. For example, the criteria for 'Standard 24: Training and Supervision of the National Quality Standards for Residential Care Settings for Older People in Ireland' outline that 'newly recruited care staff and those in post less than one year should study FETAC Level 5 awards or their equivalent and long-term care staff have their competency and skills assessed, to ascertain whether they require further training and education' (HIQA 2007). Many of the centres of nursing education that arose from the move to university-based education for nursing have incorporated the training and education of HCAs as one of their core functions, in addition to the ongoing professional education of registered nurses.

Although an HCA qualification does indicate evidence of education and competency to undertake certain tasks, the holder does not have the automatic right to do so, as the decision as to what may be delegated and when will still lie with responsible health care professionals (RCN 2007). The health care assistant role is defined differently in nearly every organisation and the boundaries of the role are interpreted differently throughout the health service. Although the job description is quite generic, its application is still determined locally. In some settings the role is confined to physical care, while in others it may even include assistance with administration of medications. Table 5.3 outlines some of the activities that may be undertaken in this role, although this list is by no means exhaustive.

Table 5.3: HCA activities (depending on area of employment)

Direct clinical care	• Vital signs • Patient hygiene • Patient mobility • Patient nutrition • Reporting any patient information to the relevant professional
Housekeeping	• Turnover of beds • Cleaning/maintenance of equipment
Clerical	• Ordering/managing supplies • Filing/preparing charts
Social care	• Home care assistance • Life support skills • Assistance with medication

An ever-growing portion of care is now delivered by HCAs, but there is limited research available on the role of the HCA in this country (Keeney *et al.* 2005a, 2005b). Health care institutions have responsibility for the orientation, training and supervision of all staff, but HCAs pose unique challenges as there is such variation in their training and job descriptions. This can pose problems for health care professionals who will be required to delegate to individuals whose preparation for the job and nature of training undertaken (if any) is unknown. This is complicated in institutions where the organisational structure does not make explicit the reporting relationship between the HCA and the nurse/health care professional. The DoHC's (2001) report on the effective utilisation of nurses states that, 'Health care assistants engage in both direct patient care and indirect patient care activities following delegation by and under the supervision of a registered nurse or midwife.' In some instances, for example community care, HCAs can report independently of the public health nurses or registered nurses who are charged with supervision and are accountable and responsible for patient outcomes (Begley *et al.* 2004).

The role of health care assistants is not regulated by a professional body, but they are accountable in civil, criminal and employment law for their actions.

Civil law

HCAs are accountable for actions and omissions which they can reasonable foresee could cause harm (for example if an HCA failed to report that they had observed that a patient had fallen).

Criminal law

Any kind of assault on a patient or client can result in an HCA being held to account criminally.

Employment law

All health care organisations are required to screen employees and evaluate performance. Failing to fulfil, or undertaking activities outside of, the HCA job description are all covered under normal employee law.

BARRIERS TO DELEGATION IN HEALTH CARE

There are a number of barriers and obstacles within health care which need to be overcome at an individual and organisational level so that delegation can operate effectively.

Failure to delegate

Delegation has long been accepted as a critical management skill, and considerable attention has been paid to the argument proposing its utility in the work of all professionals. Many of the complaints commonly heard about managers relate to their skills in this area: 'If only he would let me get on with it,' or 'She never delegates anything.' Sometimes clinical staff on the ground can interpret this as an activity that is exclusive to managerial employees. Staff can fail to delegate because they find it difficult to let go of a task they have traditionally undertaken or to trust others to do the job effectively. They may fear the loss of control they perceive in giving away tasks to others or have difficulty in determining what they should do instead. There is fear among health care professionals of an erosion of their role with a shift in boundaries as a result of skill mix changes (McKenna 2004a). The supervisory aspect of delegation may also deter staff from delegating, or they may be uncertain of the responsibilities that accompany such decisions. Under-delegation can also occur when the delegation is attempted but the delegator either withholds the authority or assumes the responsibility for the task. It is also manifested when the delegator fails to communicate effectively, or gives insufficient information or direction. This may be a consequence of insufficient understanding of other health care roles and associated activities.

The failure to delegate is a very common source of frustration for employees and employers and the consequences of ineffective or insufficient delegation in health care are serious. In addition to inefficient use of resources, the failure to delegate can obstruct subordinate development, which can affect skill mix development and staff motivation. A critical reason for delegation failure is the world view of the person who is delegating. An adverse fear of risk is also an obstacle for some, while others may be unaccustomed to delegating, as some health care employment sites make limited use of assistive personnel. Some junior staff do verbalise discomforts in delegating care to support workers they perceive as very experienced. When workload pressures are at their greatest, health care professionals are more likely to resort to delegation. This often leads to protests such as, 'It's faster to do it myself,' or 'It takes longer to explain what I need done than it takes for me to do it.' Great caution should be exercised at such times because effective and appropriate delegation requires conscientious attention and takes time: it does require elements of coaching of another in order to get something done to the standard required. While delegation does take more time in the initial stages the time taken should be interpreted as an investment.

The process of delegation is not without control, as supervisory and evaluative aspects are inherent elements if it is to be done effectively. Clarifying roles, job descriptions, reporting structures and guidelines are all measures that will assist clinical staff in overcoming reluctance to delegate. The Further Education and Training Awards have been introduced to formalise the activity of HCAs and transparency in job descriptions will assist in informing staff of what may be safely and appropriately delegated to others. The inclusion of delegation in the education curriculum, in addition to experiencing positive role modelling in the clinical area, will assist staff in developing the appropriate skills for this aspect of professional work in health care.

Ineffective delegation

There are a number of explanations as to why delegation may be ineffective, most of which can be described in terms of some kind of breakdown in the process of delegation. Over-delegation occurs when there is inappropriate transfer of authority or responsibility and it is usually a consequence of failure to accurately evaluate the task and the competency of the individual to undertake it. Delegation may also be hampered if the authority to undertake the task is not freely given or the expectations are not communicated effectively. Some explanation of the lack of delegation of authority may be found in the failure to define job description responsibilities and duties expected. Cultural differences and language barriers can lead to miscommunication or lack of understanding and may also interfere with the delegation process (Poole *et al.* 1995). If a delegate is not sufficiently culturally attuned or does not understand what they are expected to do, the anticipated outcomes of care will not be achieved.

Reverse delegation occurs when a person of subordinate rank delegates to a person with more authority, for example when a health care assistant delegates putting away supplies or cleaning beds to a staff nurse. Though it is quite possible for the staff nurse to provide assistance, it does mean there is inefficient use of staff nurse resources.

Confidence and belief in oneself is essential to be able to share responsibility with others. Delegation is often seen as an aspect of managerial performance, but it is a skill that is required of all health professionals. Insecurity on the part of the delegate will limit the effectiveness of the delegation. New graduates to the professions have reported insufficient preparation for this aspect of the professional role (Henderson *et al.* 2006; Parsons 1998). The difficulty for many health care professionals, such as nurses, is that their preparatory years are often focused on doing nursing work; and this may not have afforded them the opportunity or preparation for an inherent aspect of modern work practices in health – supervising the work of others. Health care environments are naturally risk-averse as the consequences of mistakes for patient safety are so great. However, this can mean that opportunities to delegate may be lost for fear of failure. It is necessary to maximise the utilisation of all health care roles to meet the need for accessible, high-quality care. Using the delegation process enables appropriate evaluation of risk and anticipated outcomes so that successful delegation is entirely possible.

Delegate resistance

The process of delegation should also be mindful of the motivation of employees in taking on additional tasks. Some employees may fear criticism or making mistakes, or may lack the necessary information or resources to take on additional responsibility. Delegation is likely to fail if the motivation that inspires is one-sided, particularly if the delegator is the only person to gain from it. Employee resistance will be felt directly or indirectly if they do not perceive a gain. Employees who are not offered opportunities of sufficient interest are more likely to lose motivation or become bored. In any organisation it is often the employees who are most valuable who will be most likely to leave when insufficient opportunities to learn are available in the workplace. Efficient delegation requires sensitivity to the needs of staff and the process of delegation. Credit for work is essential in gaining the delegate's trust and co-operation. Tolerance for mistakes with an appropriate level of guidance will contribute to success.

CASE STUDY

The following case study was informed by the findings of the Leas Cross review report. Review the report (http://www.dohc.ie/publications/leas_cross_commission.html) and consider the following information.

A large modern nursing home caring for an older person clientele in an urban location is registered for 111 (93 currently occupied) beds with a very complicated case mix. It has a contract with the HSE, which funds 45 of those beds. The majority of patients are of high dependency and nearly all clients have multiple diagnoses and are on multiple medications. Up to 80 per cent have dementia and/or incontinence at any one time. The Director of Nursing has just been appointed and on the first shift conducts an one-off assessment of dependency levels, which demonstrates the following.

- Light/minimal dependency   8 (9%)
- Medium dependency   31 (33%)
- Heavy dependency   42 (45%
- Maximum dependency   12 (13%)

A review of the rosters for the previous months shows the following staffing and skill-mix patterns.

- **Day shift:** three staff nurses and nine care attendants working 8 a.m.–8 p.m. An additional nine care attendants for the 8 a.m.–2.30 p.m. shift.
- **Day shift ratios:** Staff nurse 3:93. Between 8 a.m. and 2.30 p.m.: all staff 21:93; remainder of day shift: all staff 12:93. At times there are two staff nurses on duty between the hours of 6 p.m. and 8 p.m.
- **Night shift:** two staff nurses and six care attendants working 8 p.m.–8 a.m.
- **Night shift ratios:** Staff nurse 2:93; all staff 8:93.

Very few, if any, of the nursing staff have specialist training in gerontology and by and large the care attendants employed have not completed any formal training. There is no provision for on-site training.

- Discuss the delegation of care activities that occur in this type of long-term residential care setting.
- Discuss how changes in client dependency can have implications for delegation decisions, skill mix and staffing ratios.
- Discuss the implications for all registered health care professionals working in this scenario in the discharge of their responsibilities.
- Discuss the multidisciplinary professional staffing and expertise requirement to deliver the required standard of care in long-term residential care.
- Discuss the contribution of other agencies in ensuring standards of care in this type of facility.
- Discuss the ongoing training and education programme that is needed to support this facility and how it may be accessed and funded.

CONCLUSION

Research on the effect of work design on patient outcomes is just emerging but, given the ever-growing fiscal restraints in health care, delegation of care to others will remain an inherent aspect of professional work into the future. As the Irish health care system continues to evolve, the requirement to delegate in the course of work is not expected to decline. Rightsizing and downsizing are words that are becoming more commonplace in health care, and health care professionals must respond by taking an active role in work redesign and delegation as an effective means of accomplishing high-quality care delivery. Delegation is a mechanism that can facilitate the provision of safe and appropriate care, provided that health care professionals understand and determine the parameters for the appropriate use of extenders to their respective roles. Utilising the delegation process is an effective and practical means of ensuring that delegation decisions taken are safe and in the best interest of patient and clients.

REFLECTIVE QUESTIONS

1 Identify what and when you delegate in your area of work.
2 What are the factors that you consider when deciding what to delegate?
3 Reflect on a time when you have been inappropriately delegated to.
4 Consider how you use the process of delegation in delegating routine activities in the course of your work.
5 If applicable, review the code of conduct for your profession. How is delegation addressed and what guidance does it provide for you?
6 What are the local policies in your place of employment that impact on delegation decisions you make?
7 Identify some activities that you would not delegate. Why?
8 Analyse barriers to delegation in the health care environment.

ADDITIONAL RESOURCES

OECD Health Policy Studies (2008) *The Looming Crisis in the Health Workforce: How can OECD Countries Respond?* – http://www.oecd.org/dataoecd /25/15/41509236.pdf

Royal College of Nursing:
Health Care Assistant Tool Kit – http://www.rcn.org.uk/development/hca_toolkit
Nursing Standard Essential Guide: *Health Care Assistants and Assistant Practitioners: Delegation and Accountability* (2007) – http://www. rcn.org.uk/ _data/assets/pdf_file/0004/198049/HCA_booklet.pdf
Skills for Health (2009) *Developing Skills for Health* – http://www. skillsforhealth. org.uk

REFERENCES

ABA (An Bord Altranais) (2000a) *Code of Professional Conduct for Nurses and Midwives.* Dublin: An Bord Altranais.
— (2000b) *Scope of Professional Practice for Nursing and Midwifery.* Dublin: An Bord Altranais.
Barter, M. and Furmidge, M. L. (1994) 'Unlicensed assistive personnel: issues relating to delegation and supervision', *Journal of Nursing Administration* 24(4): 36–40.
Begley, C., Brady A.-M., Byrne, G., Macgregor, C., Griffiths, C. and Horan, P. (2004) *A Study of the Role and Workload of the Public Health Nurse in the Galway Community Care Area.* Dublin: University of Dublin.
Buchan, J. and Calman, L. (2005) *Skill-mix and Policy Change in the Health Workforce: Nurses in Advanced Roles.* Paris: OECD.

Commission on Nursing (1998) *Report of the Commission on Nursing*. Available at http://www.dohc.ie/publications/report_of_the_commission_on_nursing. html, accessed 9 September 2009.

DoHC (Department of Heath and Children) (2001) *Report on the Effective Utilisation of Professional Skills of Nurses and Midwives*. Available at http://www.dohc.ie/publications/effective_utilisation_of_professional_skills_of _nurses_and_midwives.html, accessed 9 September 2009.

— (2003) *The Health Service Reform Programme*. Available at http://www. healthreform.ie/pdf/hsprog.pdf, accessed 9 September 2009.

— (2004) *Final Report of the Review Group on Health Service Care Staff*. Available at http://www.dohc.ie/publications/health_service_care_staff.html, accessed 9 September 2009.

— (2006) *Preparing Ireland's Doctors to Meet the Health Needs of the 21st Century: Report of the Postgraduate Medical Education and Training Group*. Dublin: Stationery Office.

— (2009) *The Commission of Investigation Leas Cross Nursing Home: Final Report*. Available at http://www.dohc.ie/publications/pdf/leascross.pdf, accessed 9 September 2009.

General Medical Council (UK) (2006) *Good Medical Practice*. Available at http://www.gmc-uk.org/guidance/good_medical_practice/index.asp, accessed 9 September 2009.

Hansten, R. J. and Jackson, M. (2004) *Clinical Delegation Skills* (3rd edn). Sudbury MA: Jones & Bartlett Inc.

Henderson, D., Sealover, P., Sharrer, V., Fusner, S., Jones, S., Sweet, S. and Blake, T. (2006) 'Nursing EDGE: Evaluating Delegation Guidelines in Education', *International Journal of Nursing Education Scholarship* 3:(1), Article 15.

HIQA (Health Information Quality Authority) (2007) *National Quality Standards for Residential Care Settings for the Older Person*. Available at http://www. hse.ie/eng/Publications/services/Older/HIQA_National_Quality_Standards_fo r_Residential_Care_for_Older_People.pdf, accessed 9 September 2009.

HSE (Health Service Executive) (2006) *Report of the High Level Group on Health Care Assistants Regarding the Implementation of the Health Care Assistants Programme*. Available at http://www.hseea.ie/Publications/ 06.01.31.Report%20of%20High%20Level%20Group.%20Final%20Report .pdf, accessed 25 September 2009.

Huber, D. (2000) *Leadership and Nursing Care Management* (3rd edn). New York: Elsevier.

Keeney, S., Hasson, F. and McKenna, H. P. (2005a) 'Health care assistants' experiences and perceptions of participating in a training course', *Learning in Health and Social Care* 4(2): 78–88.

— (2005b) 'Health care assistants: the views of managers of health care agencies on training and employment', *Journal of Nursing Management* 13: 83–92.

Mackey, H. and Nancarrow, S. (2005) 'Assistant practitioners: issues of accountability, delegation and competencies', *International Journal of Therapeutic Rehabilitation* 12(8): 831–8.

McConnell, C. R. (1995) 'Delegation versus empowerment: what, how, and is there a difference?' *Health Care Supervisor* 14(1): 69–79.

McKenna, H. P. (2004a) 'Role drift to unlicensed assistants: risks to quality and safety', *Quality and Safety in Health Care* 13: 410–11.

— (2004b) 'Patient safety and quality of care: the role of the health care assistant', *Journal of Nursing Management* 14: 452–9.

McKenna, H. P., Keeney, S. and Hasson, F. (2003) *Evaluation of the Irish Pilot Programme for the Education of Health Care Assistants*. Dublin: Department of Health amd Children.

McLaughlin, F. E., Barter, M., Thomas, S., Rix, G., Coulter, M and Chadderton, H. (2000) 'Perceptions of registered nurses working with assistive personnel in the United Kingdom and United States', *International Journal of Nursing Practice* 6(1): 46–57.

Medical Council (2004) *A Guide to Ethical Conduct and Behaviour* (6th edn). Dublin: IMO.

NCSBN (National Council of State Boards in Nursing) (1995) *Delegation Concepts and Decision-making Process: National Council Position Paper*. Available at http://www.ncsbn.org/files/publications/positions/delegate.asp, accessed 8 September 2009.

— (2006) *Joint Statement on Delegation: American Nurses Association (ANA) and National Council of State Boards in Nursing (NCSBN)*. Available at https://www.ncsbn.org/1056.htm, accessed 9 September 2009.

NMC (Nursing and Midwifery Council) (2008) *Advice on Delegation for Registered Nurses and Midwives*. Available at http://www.nmc-uk.org/aArticle.aspx?ArticleID=2766, accessed 9 September 2009.

O'Neill, D. (2006) *Leas Cross Review*. Available at http://www.hse.ie/eng/Publications/services/Older/Leas_Cross_Report_.pdf, accessed 9 September 2009.

Parsons, J. C. (1998) 'Delegation skills and nurse job satisfaction', *Nursing Economics* 16(1): 18–26.

Poole, V. L., Davidhizar, R. E. and Giger, J. N. (1995) 'Delegating to a transcultural team', *Nursing Management* 26(8): 33–4.

Rafferty, A. M., Clarke, S., Coles, J., Ball, J., James, P., Mckee, M. and Aiken, L. H. (2007) 'Outcomes of variation in hospital nurse staffing in English hospitals: cross-sectional analysis of survey data and discharge records', *International Journal of Nursing Studies* 44(2): 175–82.

RCN (Royal College of Nursing) (2007) *The Regulation of Healthcare Support Workers*, RCN Policy Unit: Policy Briefing 11/2007. Available at http://www.rcn.org.uk/__data/assets/pdf_file/0017/71045/112007_the_regulation_of_health_care_support_workers.pdf, accessed 22 September 2009.

Sullivan, E. J. and Decker, P. J. (2005) *Effective Leadership and Management in Nursing* (6th edn). New Jersey: Pearson Prentice Hall.

WIPP (Working in Partnership Programme) (2007) *Delegation to Health Care Assistants: A Guide for General Practice*. Available at www.wippp.nhs.uk, accessed 7 September 2009.

6
Financial Management in Health Care

Sharon Morrow

OBJECTIVES
- To outline the budget preparation and control responsibilities of health care providers.
- To develop an understanding of the financial planning process and budgetary tools used in health care.
- To discuss methods of attributing costs to care delivery.
- To understand ways in which value may be created in health care through effective resource utilisation.
- To acknowledge the importance of fiscal responsibility in clinical care.

INTRODUCTION

For many people financial management may seem a complex and mysterious activity which is best left to the economists, accountants and financial planners employed in the Departments of Finance and Health and Children. In recent years there has been increased awareness of and expectation of financial management skill among not only business executives but also the health care professionals working in the Irish health services. The state's estimated total gross expenditure on health care for 2009 is €14 billion (Department of Finance 2008). The scale of expenditure on health demands that financial tools are used to ensure value for money for the payer, be it the Department of Finance or the patient. The degree to which the consumer is provided value for money is seldom questioned in health care. In fact the idea of attributing costs to a service or using financial tools in the provision of health care may be regarded by some as contemptuous. Financial management is defined as a series of activities designed to allocate resources and plan for the efficient operation of the organisation. The overall goal of financial management is to meet the total financial needs of the organisation. It is important that health care providers make the best use of the financial information and resources available to them. Whatever the area of professional or management responsibility, financial management skills will enable health care providers to do so. The primary aim of this chapter is to introduce the reader to the basic principles of health care budgeting and costing. Secondary to this is an examination of how these principles are applied to the Irish setting and ways in which health care professionals may actively contribute to the monitoring of budgetary performance.

FINANCIAL RESPONSIBILITY IN HEALTH CARE

Throughout the course of their work, managers and clinical professionals are involved in and impacted on by a range of operational and strategic decisions in which financial issues play a key role. Issues such as provision and procurement of services or equipment require financial acumen to negotiate and secure best value for payers, providers and consumers within health care. Clinical staff will make clinical decisions influenced by financial decisions taken either in their immediate sphere of control or at some other juncture in the health service. A nurse making a clinical decision on wound dressing selection will be influenced by the overall purchasing decisions in relation to wound care products of the organisation in which he or she works. Surgeons will be required to evaluate the priority of patients who receive surgical procedures based on factors such as availability of critical care beds or staffing levels, which will have been influenced by the budgetary constraints of the organisation in which they work. Health care managers will be asked to evaluate, for example, 'How would a four per cent pay rise for doctors affect the operating budget?' Community managers will seek financial solutions to complex problems such as 'Are our funds sufficient to provide HPV vaccinations to all female teenagers in our catchment area?' Professionals at all levels are contributing either directly or indirectly to the financial performance of health care services at both a local and strategic level within the health system.

The understanding of financial information requires interdisciplinary knowledge of how health services operate and how management decisions are influenced by their political, economic and organisational environment. Financial information generated within health care must be accurate, timely and relevant if it is to contribute effectively to fiscal planning. The financial system is an essential subsystem of the health system. This relationship becomes clearer if you look at the elements of the basic model underlying health care, all of which have a financial dimension and which can be described in terms of input → process → outcome.

Input

Input means the resources which are used to produce health care. Examples include staff, assets, facilities, equipment and consumables. All of these inputs can be measured and valued with a common expression – money. The common basis of comparing resources is the monetary value attached to each item of input. These monetary values of the inputs are the common language which allows resource use to be analysed within a single organisation or across several organisations. The range of resources used by your organisation will encompass staff, all assets, such as land and buildings, and supplies and consumables that are needed to produce the service. Note that a distinction can be made between human and material resources. Material resources can be subdivided into capital items that have a life span of greater than one year (land, buildings, equipment) and recurrent or revenue items that are consumed in less than one year (medical supplies, consumables, energy supply).

Process

Process describes the various activities or services that use the various inputs previously described so that the desired outcomes are achieved. Examples of health care processes are the number of X-rays, surgical procedures, vaccinations, bed days or number of patients treated. Financial processes involve collecting revenue, paying staff, purchasing medication and supplies, and investing capital in buildings and equipment.

Outcome

Outcomes measure not only the financial resources consumed but also the changes to a patient's health status that can be attributed to health care. Outcome measures such as quality of life or survival rates play an important role in economic evaluation, for example assessing the inputs required to produce one additional healthy life year or a defined improvement in quality of life. Measuring outcome should take into account the benefits provided by the treatment, for example the cure rate and patient satisfaction with treatment, and will be accompanied by detailed breakdown of the financial resources consumed per case detected or patient cured.

LEADERSHIP AND MANAGEMENT FUNCTIONS

Financial planning requires vision, creativity and a thorough knowledge of the political, social and environmental forces that shape health care. Marquis and Huston (2009) differentiate the leadership and management behaviours involved in health care financial planning.

Leadership:
- is visionary in identifying or forecasting short- and long-term organisational/unit needs, and is proactive rather than reactive
- is knowledgeable about political, social and economic factors that shape financial planning and is flexible in financial goal setting
- anticipates, recognises and creatively resolves budgetary constraints and recognises when financial constraints have resulted in an inability to meet organisational or unit goals and communicates this effectively
- influences and inspires group members to become active in short- and long-range financial planning
- ensures that patient safety is not jeopardised by cost containment.

Management:
- identifies the importance of and develops short- and long-term financial plans that reflect organisational/unit needs and co-ordinates financial planning to be congruent with organisational goals and objectives
- articulates and documents organisational/unit needs effectively and ensures that documentation of patients' need for services and services provided is clear and complete to facilitate organisational reimbursement

- assesses the internal and external environment of the organisation in forecasting to identify driving forces and barriers to financial planning
- demonstrates knowledge of budgeting, uses appropriate techniques to budget effectively and co-ordinates the monitoring aspects of budget control
- provides opportunities for other team members to participate in relevant financial planning
- accurately assesses personnel needs by using predetermined standards or an established patient classification system.

PRINCIPLES OF BUDGETING

Budgeting is the planning function of financial management and translates operational plans into monetary terms. It is the process by which an organisation has the ability to plan its activities and make efforts to control costs and meet its stated goals. A budget is defined as a written financial plan that is aimed at controlling the allocation of resources and provides detailed information on both expenses and revenues incurred. Expenses are the costs of the services and revenue is the amount of money an organisation has earned by providing its services. Essentially a budget is a road map, or a tool used to monitor personnel and supply costs and thereby ensure that quality and cost-effective services are provided to patients.

Budgeting is necessary to:

1 manage the organisational programmes
2 plan for goal accomplishment
3 control costs.

Health care clinicians are closest to the patient and best placed to understand and predict what is needed to provide care and services. Clinician involvement in the budgetary process is considered essential in contemporary health care and affords health professionals a direct influence on the amount and quality of clinical care provided. Negotiating the different types of budget used in health care, in particular the operating budget (Finkler 2001a), enables clinical managers to appropriately utilise resources to maximise patient benefit.

Types of budget

Most people think of budgets as simply being a cap on expenses that tells them how much they can spend. This is a limited view of budgets and relates in fact only to the operating budget. The master budget refers to all the major budgets within a health care organisation and may include some or all of the variety of budget types described in this section.

Operating budget

The operating budget is a plan to monitor anticipated day-to-day activities, resources, personnel and supplies, typically over a one-year period (Finkler

2001a). Each clinical unit is considered a cost centre and has an operating budget. The major components of the operating budget include revenues and expenses. The largest portion of the budget expenditure is personnel budget as health care is so labour-intensive. The personnel budget includes actual worked time (productive time) and time the organisation pays the employee for not working (non-productive time). Non-productive time includes the cost of benefits, new employee orientation, employee turnover, sickness/holidays and education time. It is important to note that nursing services are included in the overall charges of room and board and nursing costs are not considered revenue producing (Graf 2001). The operating budget also includes daily expenses such as the cost of electricity, repairs/maintenance and medical/surgical supplies. If the budget shows an excess of revenues over expenses, it means the organisation expects to make a profit for its activities over the year. If the organisation is a for-profit company, some of the profits can be paid to the owners of the company in the form of dividends. Not-for-profit organisations use this excess to replace worn-out equipment and old buildings and to expand services. Public hospitals are normally classified as not-for-profit organisations.

Cash budget
Cash budgets plan for the monthly receipts and disbursement of cash from the organisation. The operating budget focuses on the revenues and expenses and if the organisation is expected to lose money, this will be reflected in the operating budget. However, it is possible for the organisation to have a cash crisis even if it is not losing money. Many of the expenses an organisation incurs are paid currently (i.e. wages), whereas revenues may take several months to collect. The survival of the organisation depends on the ability to maintain an adequate supply of cash to meet the monetary obligations of the organisation as they become due for payment.

Capital budget
A capital budget plans for the capital expenditure over a defined period. Examples of capital budgets include renovation of a department or purchasing equipment such as hospital beds. This involves budgeting for the purchase of items that will provide benefit for a number of years into the future. If capital items were only evaluated based on their benefits for the coming year, their value to the organisation would be understated. Capital items must be put into a separate budget that can evaluate their benefits over the entirety of their useful lifetime.

Performance budget
The performance budget attempts to determine how much money is being budgeted to provide direct/indirect care, to ensure quality of care, to control costs, and to provide patient and staff satisfaction.

Long-range budgets
These types of budget detail the long-range plans for a service – up to three, five

and ten years – and give the organisation a sense of commitment to the future. They allow management to focus on the cost of strategic developments and plan according to the future purpose and direction of the organisation.

Programme budgets

These are special budgeting efforts designed to analyse specific programmes or services. They are usually used for evaluating a planned new service or closely examining an existing one.

Product-line budgeting

A product line is similar to a group of patients that have some commonality that allows them to be grouped together, such as a clinical diagnosis. Traditionally, budgeting in health care organisations largely focused on departments and units, for example radiology, laboratory, catering or nursing service. It is now becoming more commonplace for budgets to be allocated to a specific type of patient across the care delivery experience. For example, the budget for a hip replacement will include the cost of diagnostics, anaesthesia and surgery time, medications, equipment, allied health/nursing care and any other related costs.

Special purpose budget

These special purpose initiatives are not considered part of the annual operating budget. They are special programmes, put together in response to a specified and current need. Screening services such as the national Cervical Check programme, which are now offered for free, are included in special purpose programmes.

Budget planning

Budgeting is a tool, and its success depends on the circumstances in which it is used. Effective budgeting requires the ability to predict, clear channels of communication, authority, responsibility and accountability, the availability of accurate, reliable and timely information and support at all levels of the organisation (Shim & Siegel 2005).

There are a number of factors which influence budget planning:

- internal and external economic environment, as well as financial means
- availability of human resources
- capacity of the organisation (e.g. opening a new unit or closing a working unit)
- service costs/market price
- organisational goals and strategic directions
- plans and objectives of one or more departments.

Alterations in one or more of the factors may require review, modification or even substantial changes to a negotiated budget. In the current recessionary environment, proper budgeting increases the chances of survival and continuation of existing services. Budgeting is a planning and control system; planning for a result and controlling to accomplish that result. Forecasting is predicting the outcome of events and it is an essential starting point for budgeting. Planning determines the activities to be accomplished so that an organisation can successfully operate its departments and units. It looks at what should be done, how it should be done, when it should be done and by whom. Planning involves determining objectives, evaluating alternative courses of action and authorisation to select programmes, and communicates to all members of the organisation what is expected of them.

Steps in budget planning

In contemporary health care, decentralised budgeting seeks to involve front-line staff at all stages of the budget process. A budget prepared and executed as a shared experience becomes an object of ownership to staff and they are more likely to put effort into working within its framework. Patient care services are labour-intensive and therefore the majority of budgetary decisions will be dominated by the provision of nursing services. This is evident in the first six budget planning steps outlined below, which highlight the personnel aspects of patient care services. The final two steps are concerned with non-labour expenses such as costs of supplies and capital expenditure.

Budget planning steps

1 Determine the productivity goal.
2 Forecast workload.
3 Budget patient care hours.
4 Budget patient care hours and staffing schedules.
5 Plan non-productive hours.
6 Chart productive and non-productive time.
7 Estimate cost of supplies and services.
8 Anticipate capital expenses.

Table 6.1: Application of budgetary steps

1 Determine the productivity goal	The clinical nurse manager, in conjunction with the relevant senior management in their organisation (e.g. diviisional nurse manager, business manager and clinical directors) determine the productivity goal for the coming fiscal year. This may be to operate a 32-bedded surgical ward with 80% occupancy for 52 weeks of the following year.
2 Forecast workload	The anticipated workload is calculated from the number of patient days expected. This is calculated by estimating the bed occupancy (80% = 25.6) and multiplying by the number of operational days (25.6 x 365= 9,344).

3	Budget patient care hours	The estimated patient care hours that may be anticipated from the expected number of forecasted patient days is calculated, preferably using data from a patient dependency system.
4	Budget patient care hours and staffing schedules	The budgeted productive patient care hours are estimated based on agreed staff and skill mix protocols per shift and per week. Productive time is time spent on the job in patient care, orientations, unit administration, and mandatory or optional educational activities.
5	Plan non-productive hours	Non-productive personnel time such as holidays, education leave, sick leave and similar hours are budgeted for the coming year.
6	Chart productive and non-productive time	To aid in the planning process, a graph is used to show nursing staff how the level of forecasted patient days, and therefore the staffing requirements, are expected to increase and decrease during the year.
7	Estimate cost of supplies and services	The estimated costs of all supplies to the unit and services to be purchased for the year are estimated (medical/surgical supplies, medications, diagnostics).
8	Anticipate capital expenses	Current and anticipated capital expenses for the coming year are included in the budgetary steps, for example a replacement ECG machine or shower replacement.

Once complete, the information generated through the eight steps results in a proposed budget for the respective unit. Depending on the organisation structure, it will be forwarded to senior administration for review and, after preliminary acceptance, sent to the accounting department, where the forecasted patient days are turned into expected revenue/costs, depending on the funding model. The budgeted productive and non-productive time is converted to euros, as are the costs of supplies, services and other operating expenses that will be allocated to a given clinical unit for the coming year.

Budgeting methods
Budgeting methods are often classified according to how frequently they occur and the basis on which budgeting takes place. There are four commonly used budgeting methods.

Incremental budgeting
The incremental or, as it is sometimes called, flat-percentage increase method is the simplest method of budgeting. This has been a traditional approach used in Irish health care and is often referred to as a 'history plus' means of determining budget needs, whereby department heads simply look at last year's budget and add a fixed percentage to the budget (Barr 2005). The budget for the coming year is projected by multiplying current year expense by a figure, usually the rate of inflation or the consumer price index. This method is quick and simple and requires little expertise on the part of the manager, but it is mostly inefficient financially as there is little

motivation for cost containment and no provision for the prioritisation of programmes or services.

Zero-based budgeting

In comparison to incremental budgeting, managers who use zero-based budgeting must rejustify the need for their service or programme every budgeting cycle (Field 2007). This method means that you cannot automatically assume that just because a programme or service has been funded in the past it will continue to be funded. This budgeting process is labour-intensive for managers as it requires some form of economic evaluation, such as a cost-effectiveness analysis, and is usually presented as a business case.

Flexible budgeting

Flexible budgets are budgets that adjust automatically over the course of the year depending on variables such as volume, labour costs and capital expenditure (Barr 2005). A flexible budget automatically calculates what expenses should be, given the volume that is occurring. Costs can be allocated on a volume basis; for example, a higher unit occupancy rate will incur greater costs. While not a new concept, flexible budgets have gained greater adoption in the past ten years (Barr 2005). This is because most health care organisations face rapidly changing census and manpower needs that are difficult to predict, despite the use of historical forecasting tools. The flexible budget can be designed to quickly identify where such variations occur and create a better picture of current finances as well as a more realistic outlook.

New performance budgeting

New performance budgeting emphasises outcomes and results instead of activities or outputs. When planning, the manager would budget as needed to achieve specific outcomes and would evaluate the success of the budget accordingly.

Where possible it is recommended that budgets should be developed without detailing each item to be purchased or each specific cost to the organisation. This is based on the idea that funds can be moved around to fit shifting needs (Osborne & Gaebler 1993). When funds are assigned in such detail to specific units, the temptation is to spend the amount budgeted, even if this exceeds the need. One such example is the development of a new cardiac rehabilitation programme which was budgeted based on this rule. Cost centre managers agreed to shift funds which would be unused at the end of the fiscal year because they could see the advantages of the programme. All unused funds were carried over to the new budget and funded the new cardiac rehabilitation programme. This policy reduces the wasteful practice of spending money to keep budgets constant or to prevent reduction.

PRINCIPLES OF COSTING

The total cost of services is determined by the resources consumed and the total cost of resources. Costing is the process of estimating the monetary value of inputs, which are necessary to deliver a particular service (Finkler 2001b). All costing exercises should start with clear identification of costing objectives in addition to detailed understanding of service delivery. There are three distinctive steps in the process of costing:

1   identification of the resources used in the delivery of service
2   measurement of the resource units used
3   attachment of a monetary value to resource use.

Direct costs

Direct costs are those costs which can be directly linked to the use of particular resources or cost objects. A cost object can be a good, a job or a service. Direct costs can be materials, labour or expenses. For example, nursing cost or medications used can be directly attributed to a particular service and are direct costs. The overall sum of direct costs, for example materials, labour and direct expenses, are referred to as prime cost. The health care equivalent of prime cost is speciality cost. Speciality cost is the total direct costs of delivering a specialist service.

Indirect costs

Indirect costs have no direct relationship with the cost object and therefore cannot easily be traced to the cost object. As with direct costs, indirect costs may also be materials, labour or expenses. For example, hospital catering, security, building maintenance, cleaning and clinical audits are all expenses classified as indirect costs of health services. Furthermore, their associated personnel are usually classified as indirect labour costs, and consumables as indirect material costs (Zimmerman 2003). Expenses such as insurance are also classified as indirect costs. Indirect costs are collectively known as overheads. The overall prime and overhead cost is known as total cost (Lucey 2002).

Cost allocation

Cost allocation is used to describe the process of assigning indirect costs to a cost object. There is consensus about the fundamental principles of cost allocation (Young 2003; Zimmerman 2003). The most widely used method is to follow the principle of full absorption cost, i.e. that all costs, direct and indirect, relating to the provision of a particular service should be included in the cost calculation. Ideally, costs should be traced directly to the patient if it is possible to do this in a reasonably cost-effective way. Indirect costs (overheads) should be allocated to service areas based on actual usage. When the correct share of indirect cost is assigned to a cost object, it is usually said that the cost object absorbs it (full cost absorption).

During the identification step, all relevant resources should be identified regardless of their impact on the total costs and of their measurability. Their relevance will be determined by the purpose of the costing exercise. The measurement of resource usage should be comprehensive, reliable, valid and representative (Swansburg 1997). In practice, there is some fundamental trade-off between information accuracy and the cost of gathering information. Managers must evaluate whether the benefits of obtaining more accurate and detailed cost information are justified by the additional costs incurred in obtaining that information. For example, if an organisation does not have a patient dependency system, it can be labour-intensive to manually capture similar data.

Cost comparison

Cost comparison seeks to estimate the resources used in different organisations for the delivery of a comparable product or service. Costing exercises must therefore assume that the services being compared will have identical outcomes (Brouwer *et al.* 2001). Comparison cost analysis can be successfully undertaken only if a detailed description of service under consideration is available, including the case mix of the target population, the organisational setting and relevant financial arrangements. Essentially, cost comparison can be meaningful only if the approach to costing is standardised and measured in the same way. Costing methods should be transparent; data should be reported in a comprehensive, well-tabulated form to promote transparency, to allow further analysis from other perspectives and to allow the application of different assumptions. Standardisation of the basic scientific principles of costing is not in itself totally sufficient to ensure comparability and sources of potential bias, such as scale, case mix or site selection, should be controlled. For example, two different organisations may have the same outcomes for patients who have had a total hip replacement. However, it costs considerably more to provide this service in one of the organisations. Cost comparison involves estimating the resources used to ascertain why one organisation is more expensive than the other. Factors including the number of total hip replacements conducted per year, the age profile of the patients, prosthetic hip suppliers and the location of the organisation should be taken into consideration to ensure a fair comparison.

Case mix

Case mix provides a means for standardising the activity and costs provided by acute hospitals so that meaningful comparisons can be made between different areas of activity and different hospitals.

Case mix has two key national programmes: hospital in-patient enquiry (HIPE); and speciality costing. HIPE is a computer-based health information system designed to collect clinical and administrative data from acute hospitals in Ireland and is the case mix classification system standardised for use in acute hospitals in the public sector. HIPE was originally established in 1971, and it is the principle source of national data on deaths and discharges from acute hospitals (Wiley and Fetter, 1990). Since 1993 the Department of Health and Children has applied a case mix adjustment in the determination of budgets for the large acute hospitals. HIPE collects information on 13 elements of in-patient care integrated into demographic data, clinical data and administrative data. The HIPE system provides the data on hospital activity which feeds into the case mix model. The cornerstone of case mix is to group cases into diagnostic-related groups (DRGs) that are clinically meaningful and resource intensive. The same procedures can appear in different DRGs. Clinicians are involved in DRG assignment and a hierarchy is developed for each DRG and procedure. For example, a patient admitted with a broken leg suffers a heart attack – are they an orthopaedic or cardiac patient?

One DRG is assigned for each in-patient stay and assignment is based upon the following considerations:

- principal and secondary diagnosis
- procedures performed
- sex
- age
- discharge status
- presence or absence of complications and comorbidities (CCs)
- birth weight (for neonates).

The DRG specifies the illness for which the person is being treated, but also provides the key to the resources being used. Each year the Department of Health and Children calculates the average cost of each DRG group for that year, taking into account the total resources consumed. DRG costs are compared across the health service as relative values (RV), an expression of the resource usage of an individual DRG relative to the average usage across all participating hospitals.

Speciality costing involves the apportioning of cost information to each speciality in the hospital after it has been broken down across 12 cost centres including theatre, nursing and laboratory. These costs are allocated to the DRGs, giving an average cost per case.

Micro-costing

Micro-costing is a detailed method of determining the direct cost of each item or resource required to provide a procedure or service. Micro-costing also attempts to account for unobserved costs, for example relations' work time lost in accompanying a patient to hospital. The approach is relatively expensive but generates very accurate cost data. Comprehensive application of micro-costing in health care would require organisations to assemble the detailed costs of all procedures. However, implementation costs are frequently prohibitively expensive, therefore most health care providers usually observe the 80/20 rule, which suggests that micro-costing should be applied to the set of procedures that represents 80 per cent of costs. In general the benefits of micro-costing outweigh the costs, especially when the data can be gathered electronically, because the precision one gains via this method allows for a more targeted health policy prescription and/or better service evaluation.

Micro-costing helps us to answer questions such as 'What is the average cost of attending a GP for the influenza vaccination?' Micro-costing includes the cost of the vaccination, estimating the time a GP will take to administer a vaccine, estimating the time a patient will spend receiving the vaccine, cost of the syringe, etc.

Activity-based costing

Traditional costing systems break costs into direct and indirect expenses. In contrast, activity-based costing (ABC) defines costs in terms of an organisation's processes or activities and determines costs associated with significant activities or events. A variety of approaches are used to cost activity to establish an ABC model. A health care organisation might begin constructing an ABC cost management system by articulating its main activities, processes or cost centres (Brimson 1991). The following three-step methodology outlined by Brimson (1991) is central to the process of activity-based costing.

1 Activity mapping: mapping activities in an illustrated sequence.
2 Activity analysis: defining and assigning a time value to activities.
3 Costing of activities: generating a cost for each main activity.

The overhead and secondary activities are also computed and included. Finally, a cost schedule is constructed to define the flow of costs throughout a health care activity. The alignment of activity to resource consumption in this way facilitates analysis of variance from the planned budget.

Clinical pathways are similar to the ABC model as they are a framework for planning, assessing, implementing and evaluating the cost-effectiveness of patient care. These instruments convey a predetermined course of progress based on specific diagnosis or procedure (Marquis & Huston 2009). Variance analysis is used to investigate any deviations from anticipated patient progress. Once the cost of a pathway has been established, analysis of the cost-effectiveness of the pathway as well as the associated cost variances is possible. By using clinical and cost variance data, decisions on changing the pathway can be made with both clinical and financial outcome projections.

Patient-level information and costing systems

Recent advancements in costing methods have seen the introduction of patient-level information and costing systems (PLICS) by the NHS (Department of Health (UK) 2009) which they define as the ability to measure the resources consumed by individual patients. Resources for in-patients are measured for each day or part day from the time of entry and admission to the hospital until the time of discharge. For outpatients and non-admitted emergency department attendances, the consumption of resources is on 'an occasion of service' basis. Resources are ascribed to patients on a clinically meaningful activity basis in accordance with the principles of activity-based costing. A minimum set of costs driven by activity should include:

- wards
- pathology
- imaging
- pharmacy services and drugs
- prostheses
- therapies
- critical care
- operating theatres
- special procedure suites
- other diagnostics
- emergency department
- outpatients.

High-cost treatments and procedures in speciality hospitals are allocated to individual patients on an activity basis. Overheads are allocated to these areas prior to the allocation of patients. Patient-level costing is the resource consequence of clinical activity and is primarily informed by the careful measurement of clinical activity data. Clinical validity is therefore underpinned by the accuracy and legitimacy of that core activity data. The involvement of clinical staff in the definition, documentation and authentication of raw data inputs into a patient-level information and costing system is crucial to its success.

Patient-level information costing systems – benefits

- Transparent financial information provides the capability to benchmark, and to evaluate overall service/patient costs and individual cost elements (e.g. nursing costs, drugs, theatre cost) against other providers.
- Promotes clinical ownership of operating information and dialogue about appropriate resource consumption.
- The process provides meaningful data to inform the optimal grouping or classification of patients and to guide negotiations with administrators/ policy makers.

Source: Department of Health (UK) (2009)

Precision in cost allocation

Media attention on the rising cost of health care is increasing and reports do highlight the scale of hospital budgets and the cost of private health insurance. There is evidence of emerging efforts to compare performance indicators such as waiting times or costs in the acute care sector. Studies of the economics of health care tend to focus on acute care hospitalisation costs. The cost of community care receives significantly less attention as it is more difficult to measure and apportion costs in primary care. Currently there are varying levels of precision in the approaches to cost allocation, which do impact on the quality of decision-making in health care as illustrated in Figure 6.1. Current national health care policy seeks to relocate services from acute or secondary to primary care settings (HSE 2007), therefore precision in the allocation of costs to resources within both acute and primary care settings will receive greater scrutiny in the coming years.

Figure 6.1: Precision in hospital costing

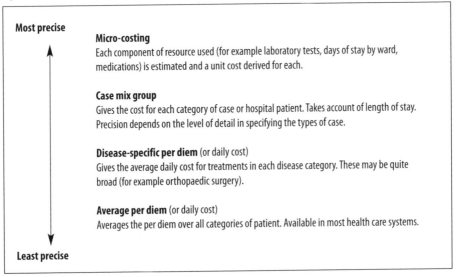

Source: Adapted from Drummond *et al.* (2005)

In health care, cost and quality do not necessarily mean the same thing and higher spending does not necessarily buy higher-quality care (O'Kane 2006). In fact, higher spending can result in unnecessary care, increased time wastage, higher risk, and may be of little real value to health consumers, but most importantly diverts resources from essential care. Unfortunately some current financial incentives within the health service are perverse and have been firmly embedded in the payment structure for generations, rewarding physicians and hospitals for providing units of care regardless of the quality of outcomes produced (O'Kane 2006). For example, reimbursement on a hundred diagnostic-related groups (DRGs) is increased when a patient contracts a hospital-acquired and preventable Staphylococcus aureus infection.

In principle, micro-costing is the best approach to determine resource measurement as it is more reliable, accurate and flexible than macro approaches.

CREATING VALUE

Value is created when customers of an organisation are willing to use the products or services of an organisation. To create value for a costumer an organisation must translate its vision into a strategy with definable objectives.

Value-creating objectives

- Acquisition or growth in the market share.
- Improvement in sales growth rate.
- Increased profit margins.
- Reduction in expenses.
- Increased asset productivity.

Source: Brimson & Antos (1999)

Each of these objectives can be applied to all health care organisations, including those that are non-profit-making. Growing business profitability over time creates value and a wide range of strategies are employed by organisations to enhance growth, such as introducing new products and services, forging alliances or acquiring competitors. Organisations can also increase their sales growth by offering new or continuously improved products or services to costumers. Increasing profit margins is an important way of growing value. One common misconception is that if you increase revenue you thereby increase profits, but this not always the case. Value creation requires companies to increase profits while increasing revenue. Volume-related increases can improve margins by decreasing unused capacity and spreading fixed costs over a greater number of products. Ill-considered volume increases can result in potentially greater costs due to inappropriate management of capacity and the creation of bottlenecks. For example, extending opening hours to maximise use of daycare facilities will result in an increased volume of patient procedures and in improved case mix figures. However, such extension can produce greater costs through overtime payments or delays in other support services, such as diagnostics, that are not operating the same extended hours. The result could be a much longer cycle time from admission to discharge for patients and an increase in the average cost per case.

Reducing expenses is an obvious approach to creating value. Expenses include cost of services provided (materials and labour), general and administrative, and research and development (R&D) expenses. Although a reduction in any of these expenses can have an immediate positive impact, greater care must be exercised to avoid damaging the organisation's long-term capability to compete. For example, dramatically reducing all R&D expenses of a pharmaceutical company will reduce costs, but it could potentially affect future revenues if the life blood of the company is rapid product production. In health care a reduction in clinical learning and development/education may impact on future innovation and the clinical skill development of staff. In health care, intellectual assets such as clinical knowledge and expertise and a trained workforce are far more valuable in many cases than fixed assets. Unfortunately, many organisations overlook effective use of assets as a way of increasing value.

CASE STUDY

The following financial and service need information is accessible to the clinical nurse manager who is involved in managing the operating budget for his/her department for the fourth quarter of the financial year. An additional member of registered nursing staff on each shift is requested due to increased acuity in recent months, which is anticipated to increase further during coming winter months. Purchase order requests for a new lifting hoist at a cost of €2,500 and a Dynamap at €4,000 are under consideration. In addition, a staff member has requested to attend a specialist conference in February at a projected cost of €1,500. The conference registration fee is €350 and is due for submission.

Operating budget report 1 October

	Annual budget (€)	Expended in September (€)	Expended year to date* (€)	Amount remaining (€)
Personnel	300,000	25,000	175,000	125,000
Overtime	50,000	3,800	50,000	0
Supplies	18,000	1,500	13,500	4,500
Travel	2,200	0	1,700	500
Equipment	5,000	0	5,000	0
Staff development	1,000	200	800	200

* Financial year begins 1 January

- How would you manage these requests, based on the budget report?
- What expenses, if any, should be declined or deferred until the new financial year?
- Consider the accuracy of and the factors that influenced projections in this budget.
- Where they controllable or predictable?

CONCLUSION

Health care providers are required to use financial planning skills, to meet budgetary responsibilities and to deliver a cost-effective, quality health care service in line with national and local health care goals. Accurate forecasting of an organisation's or unit's financial requirements is a high-level management function which demands sensitivity to the organisation's economic, social and legislative climate. Health care leaders must be flexible, creative and visionary when financially planning for future needs. Clinicians and managers are ideally placed to anticipate and articulate service need using the budgeting process to ensure adequate staffing, supplies and equipment. In a time of reducing and often inadequate financial resources, health care leaders are required to delineate budgetary needs in an assertive, professional, knowledgeable and proactive style to ensure that quality services are delivered in a fair and equitable manner.

REFLECTIVE QUESTIONS

1 Discuss why health care professionals should get involved in budgeting.
2 For the organisation or area in which you work, identify the inputs, processes and outcomes of health care delivery.
3 What types of bias can arise in the current method of cost comparison within the Irish health care service?
4 How would you increase value by effectively using the intellectual assets of your organisation?
5 Can you think of any new or continuously improved services which your organisation could sell to another organisation?

ADDITIONAL RESOURCES

For a comprehensive literature review of the main methodological issues in costing health care services go to: http://www.york.ac.uk/inst/che/pdf/rp7.pdf.

REFERENCES

Barr, P. (2005) 'Flexing your budget: experts urge hospitals, systems to trade in their traditional budgeting process for a more dynamic and versatile model', *Modern Healthcare* 35(37): 24, 26.

Brimson, J. A. (1991), *Activity Accounting: An Activity-Based Costing Approach*. New York: John Wiley.

Brimson, J. A. and Antos, J. (1999) *Driving Value using Activity-based Budgeting*. New Jersey: John Wiley & Sons, Inc.

Brouwer, W., Rutten, F. and Koopmanschap, M. (2001) 'Costing in economic evaluations' in Drummond, M. and McGuire, A. (eds), *Economic Evaluation in Health Care: Merging Theory with Practice*. Oxford University Press.

Department of Finance (2008) *Sumary of 2009 Budget Measures – Policy Changes*. Available at http://www.budget.gov.ie/2009/budgetsummary09.html, accessed 9 September 2009.

Department of Health (UK) (2009) *Definition: Patient-level Information and Costing Systems*. Available at   http://www.dh.gov.uk/en/Managingyour organisation/Financeandplanning/NHScostingmanual/DH_080055, accessed 9 September 2009.

Drummond, M. F., Sculpher, M. J., Torrance, G. W., O'Brien, B. J. and Stoddart, G. L. (2005) *Methods for the Economic Evaluation of Health Care Programmes*. Oxford: Oxford University Press.

Field, R. (2007) *Managing with Plans and Budgets in Health and Social Care*. Exeter: Learning Matters Ltd.

Finkler, S. (2001a). *The Different Types of Budgets*. Philadelphia: W. B. Saunders Company.

— (2001b). *Budgeting Concepts for Nurse Managers*. New York: WB Saunders Company.

Graf, C. (2001). *The Operating Budget*. Philadelphia: W. B. Saunders Company.

HSE (Health Service Executive) (2007) *Transformation Programme 2007–2010*. Available at http://www.hse.ie/eng/Publications/corporate/transformation.html.

Lucey, T. (2002) *Costing* (6th edn). London: Thompson Learning.

Marquis, B. L. and Huston, C. J. (2009) *Leadership Roles and Management Functions in Nursing*. Philadelphia: Lippincott Williams & Wilkins.

O'Kane, M. (2006) 'Redefining value in healthcare: a new imperative: does spending more mean better care? Not necessarily', *Healthcare Financial Management* 60 (8) 50–6.

Osborne, D. and Gaebler, T. (1993) *Reinventing Government: How the Entrepreneur Spirit is Transforming the Public Sector*. New York: Plume.

Shim, J. K. and Siegel, J. G. (2005) *Budgeting Basics and Beyond*. New Jersey: John Wiley & Sons.

Swansburg, R. C. (1997) *Budgeting and Financial Management for Nurse Managers*. London: Jones & Bartlett Publishers.

Wiley, M. and Fetter, R. (1990) *Measuring Activity and Costs in Irish Hospitals: A Study of Hospital Case Mix*. Dublin: Economic and Social Research Institute.

Young, D. W. (2003) *Management Accounting in Healthcare Organizations*. Jossey-Bass.

Zimmerman, J. L. (2003) *Accounting for Decision-making and Control* (international edn). Boston: McGraw-Hill Irwin.

7

Human Resource Management in the Health Services

Sile O'Donnell

OBJECTIVES
- To explore the context for the development of human resource management (HRM) in the Irish health care sector.
- To explore and analyse some of the main concepts of and approaches to HRM, in particular the Harvard model of HRM and its relevance to the healthcare sector (Beer *et al.* 1984).
- To analyse recent developments in the heath sector in relation to HRM and the interplay between HRM and industrial relations.
- To provide a broad overview of key HRM policy areas and their relevance to the health sector.

INTRODUCTION

Features of the [HRM] approach during the recession in the 1980s included reductions in staff numbers through the public sector embargo and a reduction of investment in training and education. We need to learn from the lessons of this experience and find new and more effective ways of reconciling hard ('headcount') and soft (employee development) approaches to HRM . . . Maintaining a partnership based approach to change and sustaining staff morale will be challenging, for example in the context of cost containment and the proposed restructuring of the health services . . . difficulties will arise in sustaining what key commentators refer to as 'the new realism', in which there is an emphasis placed on both IR [industrial relations] and HRM. It is important too that in centrally driven changes, real efforts are made to engage staff so that the change agenda does not become divorced from their day to day and increasingly pressurised working lives.

(Fleming 2003)

The effective management and development of people is a critical component in the achievement of an organisation's success, whether it is concerned with delivering products or services, cost-effectiveness or quality. Human resource management (HRM) is both important and challenging in a labour-intensive sector such as health care, in which organisations operate within a complex political, economic and legislative environment. Research by West *et al.* (2002) indicates that enhanced people management practices contribute to greater effectiveness in the health care sector, as measured by a range of variables including patient mortality levels.

In an environment of economic decline, the need to manage people effectively, through the application of HRM concepts such as flexibility, commitment and the integration of people management practices with business strategy assume even greater importance. Applying such concepts is, however, problematic in the health care sector, in which HRM policy making is influenced by a wide and diverse range of stakeholders. The reconciliation of different stakeholder interests may involve trade-offs and indeed conflicts in relation to HRM practices (Beer *et al.* 1984). Centralised policy-making in relation to areas such as pay and terms and conditions can also inhibit the individual organisation's ability to implement flexible HRM policies (Roche 1998; O'Dowd & Hastings 1997).

CONTEXT FOR THE DEVELOPMENT OF HRM IN THE HEALTH CARE SECTOR

Over 130,000 people are employed by the Health Service Executive (HSE) and the agencies and hospitals that it funds. Since the early 1980s the environment within which health care organisations operate has changed significantly. Economic, legislative, demographic and technological changes in particular have placed pressures on health care organisations to manage more effectively and efficiently in an increasingly complex environment. Labour costs comprise over 70 per cent of revenue costs for health care organisations and the multi-union, multi-professional structure that is typical within them can make the process of managing people efficiently and effectively both complex and challenging.

In 1984, with the launch of the Strategic Management Initiative (SMI), the Irish public service embarked on an ambitious programme of reform. Emphasis was placed on the need for modernisation of personnel management practices. While the need for cost-effectiveness was highlighted at the genesis of the SMI, the development of excellent customer service and contribution to national development were seen as the primary drivers for change. In other countries, such as New Zealand and the UK, the major driver for radical HRM change was the need to reduce spending. The SMI was followed by the launch of *Delivering Better Government* (Government of Ireland 1996), which set out a more detailed action plan for reform of the civil service, including its HRM policies and practices. It focused on areas such as recruitment, performance management, training and development, equality and the professionalisation of the HR function.

The implementation of reform in the Irish health sector commenced with the launch by the Department of Health and Children of the National Health Strategy, *Quality and Fairness*, in 2001 (DoHC 2001a). This strategy set out a vision of an efficient and effective patient-centred health service, at a time of considerable economic buoyancy. A key framework for change set out in the strategy was human resources. The subsequently published *Action Plan for People Management* (APPM) (DoHC 2002) set out a blueprint for the development of a strategic approach to people management in the health sector. The APPM was developed on a partnership basis between management, unions and other key stakeholders including the Department of Health and Children. It set out a range of recommendations for reform in areas such as people management and development, performance management and quality of working life (see box). The APPM was launched at a time when skilled health care workers were in short supply and labour mobility was high, and one of the biggest priorities facing health service employers was the recruitment and retention of skilled staff. The plan also focused on reform of industrial relations (IR), based on a review of the health services in 2001 by the Labour Relations Commission (LRC 2001). This review highlighted many weaknesses in the IR process, which in turn had created an escalation and disproportionate level of IR issues (for example, third party referrals) in the sector. It recommended the development of the capacity of both management and unions to manage employee relations and IR more effectively, the development of robust HRM and employee relations policies and procedures and the further development of partnership as a basis for managing change between unions and management.

The Action Plan for People Management (APPM)

The Action Plan for People Management was developed on a partnership basis by health service employers, representative bodies, the Department of Health and Children, the Health Service Employers' Agency, the Office for Health Management, the Health Services Partnership Forum and the trade unions. This was achieved through a number of mechanisms including consultative forums and working groups. Through this process, a detailed action plan was developed in seven key areas:

- Managing People Effectively
- Best Practice Policies and Procedure
- Investing in Training and Education
- Quality of Working Life
- Improving Industrial Relations
- Developing Partnership Further
- Performance Management.

Funding was provided for health boards and healthcare agencies to develop initiatives in these seven areas and progress in implementing initiatives and use of funding is monitored annually by a national partnership group. Work is ongoing in relation to the development and implementation of an HRM strategy in the HSE in order to support the achievement of the organisation's objectives and lead the development of a high-performing culture.

A full copy of the APPM can be downloaded from the website www.hseea.ie. Copies of APPM annual reports can also be obtained from this website.

More recent developments have created a very different environment and dynamic. The merging of 11 health boards and a range of other agencies into a unitary organisation took place with the establishment of the Health Service Executive (HSE) in 2005, influenced by the recommendations of a number of national reports (DoHC 2003b, 2003c). More recently, an ambitious target of 6,000 has been set by 'An Bord Snip Nua' in relation to the required reduction in workforce levels in the health services (Department of Finance 2009). In contrast to the focus almost a decade ago on the development and expansion of services and the recruitment of staff, current policies are increasingly focused on cutbacks in relation to the volume and cost of both services and staff. These changes create new challenges for the HSE and its agencies in relation to how they recruit, manage and reward employees and how they manage industrial relations and change. These challenges will be explored throughout this chapter.

WHAT IS HRM AND HOW DOES IT DIFFER FROM PERSONNEL MANAGEMENT?

The concept of personnel management has its origins in the 'welfare tradition' that emerged in the early part of the twentieth century. For example, employers such as Cadbury and Maguire and Patterson were regarded as good employers who took care of employee welfare and working conditions. Prior to this, little attention was paid to the needs of employees and poor practices prevailed, particularly in relation to health and safety. At the same time, trade unionism began to grow, with the establishment of the Irish Transport and General Workers' Union (ITGWU) in 1909, and this growth created pressure on employers to ensure better working conditions for employees.

Personnel management continued to develop as a specialism throughout the twentieth century, with an increasing focus on industrial relations (Armstrong 1997; Gunnigle et al. 2006).

However, worldwide economic decline from the late 1970s onwards forced many organisations to adopt a more strategic approach to managing their business and their employees. The 'excellence literature' of the1980s highlighted the importance of productivity through people as a critical success factor in achieving organisational success (Peters & Waterman 1982). It was against this background that the concept of HRM evolved in the early 1980s, and it was influenced by other theoretical concepts, such as motivation theories, organisation development, corporate culture and strategic management, and by environmental factors, including worldwide economic recession, increased competition, deregulation and globalisation, and legislative and social changes (Roche 1995). HRM then began to be defined as a distinct discipline through the writings of notable US and UK academics such as Michael Beer (Beer et al. 1984) and David Guest (1987).

So what is human resource management and how does it differ from personnel management? HRM has been defined by Michael Armstrong as 'a strategic approach to the management of an organisation's most valued assets – the people working there who individually and collectively contribute to the achievement of its objectives' (Armstrong 2007:6).

It has also been suggested, however, that HRM is merely 'old wine in new bottles' (Armstrong 1997) or a retitling of personnel management (Legge 1995). However, Storey (1989) identifies four features of HRM which distinguish it from traditional personnel management.

- It involves the explicit integration of people management practices with corporate strategy.
- It seeks to obtain the commitment of employees rather than their compliance.
- Employee commitment is obtained through an integrated and flexible approach to human resource policies (for example, reward, appraisal, selection, training).
- Unlike personnel management, which is primarily the domain of specialists, HRM is an integral part of the line management role.

The differences in focus between HRM and personnel management have also been categorised by Guest (1987) as summarised in Table 7.1.

Table 7.1 Differences between personnel and human resource management

	Personnel management	**Human resource management**
Timing and planning perspective	Short-term reactive ad hoc marginal	Long-term proactive strategic integrated
Psychological contract	Compliance	Commitment
Control systems	External controls	Self-control
Employee relations perspective	Pluralist collective low trust	Unitarist individual high trust
Preferred structures/systems	Bureaucratic/mechanistic centralised formal defined roles	Organic devolved flexible roles
Roles	Specialist/professional role	Largely integrated into line management
Evaluation criteria	Cost minimisation	Maximum utilisation (human asset accounting)

Some authors have argued that the difference between HRM and personnel management is purely conceptual or perhaps simply rhetoric (Legge 1995), since HRM is difficult to apply in practice. For example, the individualistic and flexible nature of HRM could create particular challenges in a unionised environment, since it may pose a threat to the approach that is typically adopted by management and unions to collective bargaining and collective agreements that benefit groups of employees. Legge (1995) also argues that commitment may often be 'compliance in disguise', whereby policies that are espoused to increase individual employee commitment may actually be designed to achieve greater compliance by employees and to 'bypass' or undermine the role of unions. The overall approach adopted in the last two decades in the health care sector represents a dualist approach (Guest 1987) or perhaps a three-strand approach (Fleming 2003), whereby there has been an emphasis on shifting from traditional personnel management to an HRM approach and on maintaining good industrial relations procedures while utilising a partnership-based approach to change. The recent development and implementation of HRM policies to reduce workforce levels and pay costs in order to reduce public sector spending has significantly tested the partnership process at both national and organisational level (see www.ictu.ie for useful reading material). This will be explored further below.

Some commentators also argue that the application of HRM to the public sector is diluted by the absence of clear business 'bottom line' strategies and by the multiplicity of stakeholders on the landscape, such as government, unions, the public, managers and employees. Beer *et al.* (1984), who are considered to be the 'founding fathers' of HRM, suggest, for example, that while HRM may be used as a symbolic action for organisational change, in introducing HRM initiatives organisations may be focusing attention away from more deep-rooted issues and ignoring the powers and interests of other key stakeholders.

APPROACHES TO HRM AND THEIR RELEVANCE TO THE HEALTH CARE SECTOR

In attempting to define and understand the concept of HRM further, four areas will be examined in this section:

- hard and soft approaches to HRM
- integration
- the Harvard model of HRM
- the role of the HR function.

Hard and soft approaches to HRM

Many authors make a distinction between hard and soft approaches to HRM (Storey 1989, 1992; Guest 1987). For example, if an organisation focuses on control of resources and achievement of strategy, it may adopt a 'hard' approach to HRM (Storey 1989) in which employees are viewed as a resource to be managed like any other factor of production. In this approach, the critical task for management is to align the HR systems of the organisation so that they drive or support the strategic objectives of the organisation. This approach is evident in the strategic model of HRM developed by Fombrun *et al.* (1984). In contrast, an organisation may place an emphasis on a 'soft' approach to HRM (Storey 1992), in which employees are viewed as a valuable asset whose commitment will assist in achieving organisational success. The objective therefore is to integrate HR policies with the strategic planning process, to gain the willing commitment of employees, to achieve flexibility and to improve quality (see Guest 1987). In practical terms, a hard approach to HRM might focus on areas such as performance management and flexible reward and employment strategies, while a soft approach to HRM might focus more on employee development and well-being.

In reality, many organisations adopt a combination of hard and soft approaches to HRM rather than having a single approach. For example, in a declining economic environment, increasing pressure is placed on health care organisations to introduce hard HRM policies, for example in relation to areas such as pay, staffing levels and performance management, and this can create pressure to reduce investment in areas such as training and development. This challenge is reflected in the current reform of the public service. A soft HRM approach is suggested in the recent conclusions of the Task Force on the Public Service:

> If reform is to go beyond compliance with technical requirements it will require public service leadership that is capable of creating a new narrative about the future role of the Public service in the context of a shared sense of civic duty. Connecting the efforts of individuals, units, teams and public servants to the achievement of societal goals will be a crucial part of this narrative.
>
> (Task Force on the Public Service 2008:27).

However, the detailed recommendations of the task force's report provide evidence of a hard approach to HRM, with a particular focus on performance measurement, performance management and flexibility.

The needs of different stakeholders also influence the adoption of hard or soft HRM approaches by organisations. For example, trade unions may accept pay containment measures in return for measures to protect wage and employment levels, and to meet employee demand for enhanced career breaks and flexible working. The influence and reconciliation of different stakeholder needs will be explored further in the final part of this section, which looks at the Harvard model of HRM.

Integration

An examination of the HRM literature highlights a recurring and distinctive theme, namely that of integration, which Guest (1987) suggests lies at the heart of HRM. He identifies integration at three levels:

- integration of HRM policies with business strategy (external fit)
- integration of a set of complementary HRM policies (internal fit)
- integration of HRM into the line management function.

This is elaborated on further by Guest and Hoque (1994:44), who, in a discussion of HRM, argue that:

. . . the key is strategic integration. What this means is that personnel strategy must fit the business strategy, the personnel policies must be fully integrated with each other and the values of line managers must be sufficiently integrated or aligned with the personnel philosophy to ensure that they will implement the personnel policy and practice . . . Where this can be achieved, there is growing evidence that a distinctive set of human resource practices results in superior performance.

Achieving integration is, however, not an easy task. For example, according to Purcell and Ahlstrand (1995), the literature provides little practical guidance in relation to linking HRM with business strategy. The hard approach to HRM posits that HRM policies should be designed to support the achievement of the organisation's objectives. This creates two challenges. First, the strategy-making process in the public sector is complicated by conflicting objectives, multiple stakeholders, short-term political pressures, and existing structures and processes (see Mintzberg 1996; Elcock 1993; Roche 1998; Lawton & Rose 1994) and therefore this compromises the potential to create clear linkages between the intended strategy of the organisation and the required HRM policies (Boyle & Fleming 2000). Second, many HRM policies in the public service are determined through central government policies or central collective agreements, which can limit the ability of the individual organisation to design HRM policies to support its objectives.

The second integrative aspect of HRM relates to internal fit, or the integration of a mutually reinforcing set of HRM policies (Guest 1987). A good illustration of this is the use of a competency-based approach, in which desired behaviours and skills are identified through the strategic management process, and recruitment, reward, development and performance management systems are designed to reflect core competencies and to complement each other (Butler & Fleming 2002). As highlighted in the previous paragraph, achieving such fit can be problematic if the organisation does not have control over key areas of HRM policy-making, and as a result, more significant HRM issues 'may actually be determined outside the plant in the higher reaches of the organisation' (Purcell & Ahlstrand 1995:3), thus limiting the ability of the line department, unit or line manager to develop flexible complementary HRM policies. The need to balance flexibility against a centralised approach to HRM policy-making is reflected in the recent Task Force Report on the Public Service: 'The challenge is to achieve flexibility across organisational, professional, sectoral and geographic boundaries while maintaining coherence' (Task Force on the Public Service 2008:27).

The decentralisation of HRM policies such as recruitment and selection and reward management from central government departments was identified as a prerequisite for the successful development of integrated HRM policies at line department level in the US civil service (Cassels, cited in Tyson & Fell 1995). Purcell and Ahlstrand (1995) suggest, however, that decentralisation of pay bargaining can lead to a 'leap-frog' dynamic, in which changes agreed in one department may create discontent in another. Similar concerns have been raised regarding the negative implications of decentralisation for areas such as equality of opportunity across line departments (OECD 1996).

The approach within the HSE is a centralised one in two respects. First, many HRM policies are determined or agreed at central level, by the Department of Health and Children and the Department of Finance and through social partnership agreements (for example in areas such as pay, grading, terms and conditions, staffing levels, performance management). Second, the objective of the HSE is to adopt a centralised approach, through standardised HRM policies and procedures, which are the responsibility of line managers to implement, while at the same time enhancing flexibility in relation to working practices and workforce resources.

The final aspect of integration relates to the line management role. Research by Bevan and Hayday (cited in McGovern *et al.* 1997) indicates that line managers may be reluctant to take on HRM responsibilities which they do not perceive to be a legitimate part of their job. Armstrong (1997) also suggests that line managers may be happy to let the personnel department deal with the people management aspects of their job, particularly in relation to disciplinary and grievance matters. He suggests that the successful devolution of HRM to line managers requires a 'delicate balance' between providing help and advice to line managers and creating a 'dependency culture' in which managers are reluctant to take responsibility for people management issues. This reluctance is not helped where there is poor organisational support for the devolution of HRM to line managers. For example, in a study of a number of UK organisations, Hope-Hailey *et al.* (1997) found that the managers' roles in HRM activities were rarely included in the objective-setting or assessment processes. This study also found that pressure to obtain results, coupled with increasing workloads, resulted in a tendency by managers to view HRM activities as less of a priority.

The structure of large bureaucratic organisations may also diminish the capacity of line managers to take on responsibilities for HRM (Armstrong 1997). A study carried out in the UK Department of Social Security (Common *et al.* 1993) highlighted that while managers were required to take full responsibility for people management, they were not given the resources required to do so, since centralised control was maintained over staff numbers and costs. This is echoed in the *Review of Industrial Relations in the Irish Health Service* (LRC 2001), which highlighted that many managers felt that insufficient authority and autonomy was devolved to them from the centre and, as a result, they were not prepared to take responsibility or initiative for fear of making a mistake or creating a precedent when dealing with industrial relations issues. This is a key challenge for the Irish health care sector, where efforts to introduce greater flexibility in work practices at organisational level are being developed within a centralised framework of HRM policy-making and cost containment.

While research indicates that the development of people management skills is a critical success factor for successful HRM (McGovern *et al.* 1997), Boyle (1995) suggests that this represents a particular challenge in the public sector, where managers may see themselves as specialists, rather than as managers of people. In addition to people management skills, managers also require practical and professional support if they are to take on responsibility for HRM (Merchant & Wilson 1994). For example, a lack of knowledge by line managers of procedures relating to disciplinary or equal opportunities matters may lead to legal or industrial relations problems.

Three factors have been identified as critical to the integration of HRM within the line management function.

- Training and development of managers to equip them with the skills and knowledge required to deal with HRM issues.
- The provision of incentives for managers to take on responsibility for HRM, for example through the incorporation of HRM objectives into the performance appraisal/performance management and business planning process.
- The creation of a culture in which HRM activities are explicitly valued by senior management. They must be prepared to reward line managers who place a priority on people management activities, and to invest the necessary resources to ensure that line managers are equipped and empowered to take on responsibility for HRM.

(Fleming 2000)

Figure 7.1: Harvard model of HRM

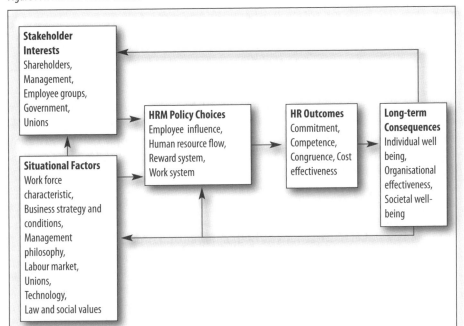

Source: Beer *et al.* (1984)

The Harvard model of HRM

The most well known 'soft' model of HRM, known as the Harvard model (Beer *et al.* 1984), has significantly influenced the theory and practice of HRM (see Figure 7.1).

This model maps out the key influences on and consequences of HRM policy choices. It proposes that a range of stakeholder interests and situational factors influence an organisation's HR policy choices and that these create consequences in terms of HR outcomes and goals. Four key HR policy areas are identified in the model:

- human resource flows (recruitment, selection, appraisal and assessment)
- reward systems (pay systems, motivation)
- employee influence (levels of authority, responsibility, power)
- work systems (design of work and alignment of people).

The model proposes that choices made in key HRM policy areas affect four HRM outcomes, which can be measured (Table 7.2).

Table 7.2 HRM outcomes and performance measures

HRM outcome	Examples of performance measures
Commitment	Turnover and absenteeism levels, employee engagement surveys.
Competence	Skills audit, performance management and development.
Congruence	Level of industrial relations activity, days lost due to strikes/work-to-rules, IR procedures.
Cost-effectiveness	Time and cost of hiring, measurement of investment in training.

The model states that these outcomes of HRM policy choices have long-term consequences at individual, organisational and societal level (see Beer *et al.* (1984) for further reading). The need for health services and the people that they employ to contribute to societal goals is a core theme of recent reports (OECD 2008; Task Force on the Public Service 2008).

It is useful to explore in more detail the situational factors and stakeholder interests that influence HRM policy choices in the health sector, given the complex environment within which health care organisations operate and the interplay between key stakeholder groups at both national and organisational level.

Situational factors include management philosophy, workforce characteristics, business strategy and conditions, and labour markets. A good illustration of the influence of situational factors is the changing labour market. At the turn of the century, one of the biggest concerns for health care organisations was how to attract and retain skilled workers in key professions such as nursing and midwifery and allied health professional grades. At this time, on foot of a number of key reports (Bacon & Associates 2001; DoHC 2001a), significant initiatives were undertaken both at home and abroad to attract and retain staff in these professions, through recruitment drives and the development of enhanced career structures and employee development initiatives. In the current environment, health service organisations are required to deliver services within a very strong cost control framework, with a focus on workforce and pay reduction, changing work practices and increased flexibility through initiatives relating to skill mix, rostering and reduced hours of work (Government of Ireland 2008; Department of Finance 2009). They must also respond to the needs of a much more diverse population, labour force and workforce.

The business environment is also changing significantly. By 2036, one in four of the population will be over 65 (currently one in ten people are over 65), and this has implications for the nature and volume of health care delivery that will be required by the population. It is projected that by 2020 there will be a 60 per cent increase in demand for public health care (HSE 2008b). Against a backdrop of increasing demand for services, recent workforce planning reports (FÁS 2005) indicate that there are still critical shortages in key health care professions, yet economic changes – and, as a consequence, central policies – require organisations to reduce staffing numbers. These changing factors will significantly increase financial and capacity pressures within the health sector, and they highlight the challenges of developing HRM policies in the health sector and the competing demands that can exist.

The Harvard model also posits that unless HRM policies meet key stakeholder needs, they can have negative short- and long-term consequences for the organisation (Beer et al. 1984). The needs of stakeholders may vary and therefore the development of HRM policies may involve trade-offs in order to reconcile different interests.

Some of the key stakeholder interests within the health sector will now be examined.

Government

The significance of this stakeholder influence is of particular relevance for the public health sector, in which the government acts as both economic regulator and employer, and this can create challenges in terms of HRM policy choices. Government may act as a key driving force for or against HRM reform. For example, radical HRM reforms implemented in the UK civil service in the early 1980s were primarily driven by the Conservative government's desire to 'roll back the frontiers of the state' and achieve greater efficiency and value for money in the public sector (OECD 1990). Conversely, a lack of political support for change was identified as a constraint on attempts to reform HRM in the Irish civil service in the 1970s and 1980s (Murray 1990).

Since the late 1980s Ireland has had a well-developed system of national pay bargaining within a partnership framework comprising government, employers, unions and the social partners. Under the 1987 social partnership agreement *The Programme for National Recovery*, in return for wage moderation, objectives were agreed to stimulate employment, to broaden the tax base and to permit lower taxation of workers' earnings (Government of Ireland 1987). From an HRM perspective, recent agreements have focused increasingly on changing work practices, performance management and flexibility, linked to pay increases, and these directly affect the HR policy choices that an individual health service organisation makes. Government reform initiatives and policy changes are increasingly focused on retrenchment in relation to pay costs and staffing levels (Department of Finance 2009) and flexibility of working practices. As a consequence, the model of social partnership that was developed with the trade unions, who are another key stakeholder within the health service, has come under threat in recent times.

Management

A second key stakeholder influence on HRM policy choices is management (Beer *et al.* 1984). In clarifying the distinction between personnel management and HRM, it has been suggested that HRM is primarily a 'discovery of personnel management by chief executives' (Fowler 1987:1), in which there is an emphasis at senior management level on the strategic use of human resources as a key factor in organisational success. Visible senior management commitment can be a powerful lever for cultural change, which shapes the behaviour, attitude and values of the organisation. In this context, the role of line managers as key stakeholders in implementing senior management's approach to HRM is equally critical, since it is argued that 'if human resources really are so critical for business managers, then HRM is too important to be left to operational personnel specialists' (Storey 1995:7).

Marchington and Wilkinson (1997), however, suggest that even when the mission statement of the organisation places an emphasis on staff development and management, line managers may pick up contrary signals from senior management about the ordering of priorities. Where there is a gap between the espoused values and behaviours and the reality of working practices, managers may decide to focus on the achievement of targets which are more measurable and valued than HRM-related activities.

Trade unions

While unions are clearly significant stakeholders in the health sector, Guest (1995) points out that most analyses consider HRM from a management perspective and fail to take account of union reaction to HRM. He suggests that the predominantly unitarist nature of HRM, which seeks to maximise employee commitment to organisational goals, may be viewed by unions as a threat to their traditional negotiating and representative roles. Many organisations have adopted a partnership approach to the development of HRM, which gives a role to unions as key stakeholders in organisational decision-making (Cradden 1992) and this is reflected in the social partnership approach adopted in Ireland over the past decade in particular. Significant efforts have also been made to develop partnership at the organisational level, and these efforts have been encouraged by the linking of partnership-based change initiatives to the pay benchmarking and pay increase process.

Some authors have argued, however, that the development of successful partnership is a slow process, particularly where there is no immediate threat to the survival of the business. In the current economic climate, unions face significant challenges in responding to government policy change, which is increasingly focused on workforce and pay reduction in the public sector. In this context, a recent comment by the National Secretary of the Irish Congress of Trade Unions is interesting:

> The reason for the Government's reluctance to abandon social partnership is not because they like us, but because they can see that a major national initiative has the greatest prospect of success. They also recognise that imposing cuts in pay and social benefits is likely to result in a stiff campaign of resistance, including strikes and civil disruption. Apart from worsening the problem, this would also jeopardise any remaining prospect of their being re-elected.
> (ICTU 2009)

The role of the HR function

Ulrich argues that 'the primary responsibility for transforming the role of HR belongs to the CEO and to every line manager who must achieve business goals' (Ulrich 1998:205). He emphasises the important role of the HR function in supporting senior and line management and he identifies four key roles for the HRM department in this regard.

1 *Strategic partner* – helping senior management and line managers to achieve business strategy through flexible, high-performing HRM practices. This has been identified as a critical success factor in research carried out in the Irish public service (Boyle & Fleming 2000; Fleming 2000).
2 *Administrative expert* – in transactional areas such as payroll, personnel administration, development of HR performance measures. Many organisations develop shared services models to achieve economies of scale in these areas, and work is currently ongoing in the HSE in this regard.
3 *Employee champion* – to ensure employee well-being and commitment. For example, the HSE has developed an employee well-being strategy which is currently being implemented.
4 *Agent of continuous transformation* – a proactive role in which HR specialists help to transform the business, its culture and 'how things are done'. The importance of HRM as a driver for change is emphasised in the HSE's Transformation Programme (HSE 2007) and its ongoing change programme.

Developing a changed role for HR, however, is challenging and is dependent on a number of factors including strong leadership, a supportive organisational culture and line management support (Fleming 2003).

DEFINING THE APPROACH TO HRM IN THE HEALTH SECTOR

Many of the challenges involved in implementing HRM were explored in the previous section. It is useful to draw these together in order to explore the overall approach that has been adopted in the health sector. HRM policies in the Irish health care system are primarily developed within centralised systems of pay, grading, terms and conditions. While this approach conflicts with the flexible, individualistic nature of HRM, there has been an increasing emphasis over the last decade on the need for flexibility and modernisation of HR and work practices and this is reflected in recent national social partnership agreements (Government of Ireland 2008). More recently, pay freezes and staff reductions within the health sector represent evidence of a harder approach to HRM, with increased pressures on managers to do 'more with less'. This approach contrasts with the 'soft approach' to HRM that predominated in the first few years of this decade, in which there was a significant focus on training and development and retention of staff.

A number of critical success factors for the implementation of HRM in the public service and more specifically the health service have been identified:

- strong, cohesive leadership of key stakeholders
- creating incentives to change and disincentives to maintaining the status quo
- effective change management, with active engagement of staff
- a greater emphasis on people management as an integral part of the line management role
- enhanced measures to professionalise and develop the HR function
- development of partnership as a real vehicle for change
- a new approach to the balancing of soft (developing staff, obtaining employee commitment, quality of working life) and hard (pressures to deliver value for money, employment control) HRM goals
- developing and sustaining commitment and engagement of all key stakeholders, including employees.

(Fleming 2003)

At a national and organisational level, it is useful to briefly explore a number of models that have been developed to describe the interrelationship between HRM and industrial relations. Drawing on models developed by Guest (1995) and Roche (1995), four categories can be identified.

1   The traditional collectivism/adversarial model – where there is a high priority on IR but no HRM.
2   The individualised HRM/non-union HRM model – where there is a high priority on HRM (in order to maximise individual employee commitment) but no priority placed on IR. This model is typically adopted within large non-unionised multinational firms.
3   The black hole/deregulation model – where there is no priority placed on either HRM or IR.
4   The new realism/partnership model – which places a high emphasis on HRM as well as IR.

Traditionally, the traditional/adversarial IR approach predominated in the public sector, although as we have seen this has changed within the past decade, with an increasing focus on HRM and partnership. The current approach is, in some respects, more akin to the new realism or partnership model in which there is an emphasis on the development of high-performing work practices, flexibility, quality and individual commitment. It could be described as an approach that embraces HRM, industrial relations and partnership, since HRM practices are developed both within the traditional industrial process and structures and in partnership with trade unions. Achieving HRM objectives on a partnership basis in a multi-union environment, in which the majority of policies are centrally determined, represents a significant challenge (Roche 1998; O'Dowd & Hastings 1997), particularly in the current economic climate.

OUTLINE OF KEY HRM ACTIVITIES

The second part of this chapter will provide an overview of the key policy areas of HRM.

Employee resourcing

The term 'employee resourcing' will be used to describe the range of activities that take place in order to ensure that the right people with the right skills are in the right jobs. The key activities include:

- workforce planning
- recruitment and selection.

Workforce planning is an important and complex component of HRM and it has been the focus of considerable attention in the Irish health sector for the past decade. The National Health Strategy (DoHC 2001a) and the Action Plan for People Management (DoHC 2002) placed a priority on the development of integrated workforce planning for the health sector and this is echoed in the HSE's recent corporate strategy (HSE 2008a).

While many detailed models and definitions have been developed, Gunnigle *et al.* provide a simple and useful definition of workforce planning: it is 'concerned with ensuring that the organization employs the right quantity of people with the necessary knowledge, skills and attitudes required for effective organizational functioning' (2006:93). (A number of useful websites that provide a detailed study of workforce planning are set out in the 'Additional resources' at the end of this chapter.)

Gunnigle *et al.* outline a useful model of workforce planning which identifies four key stages.

- Stocktaking – external and internal environment to assess business needs, trends and issues in relation to labour supply and skills and HRM needs (that are influenced by political, economic, legislative, social, demographic and technological factors).

- Forecasting – demand/supply for and of labour (through measures such as turnover analysis, absenteeism, forecasting projections).
- Planning – specific HRM action plans to address needs identified in the stocktaking and forecasting analysis (e.g. recruitment and retention plans, redundancy initiatives, training and development initiatives, equality initiatives).
- Implementing – implementing and monitoring the outcomes of HRM policies and initiatives.

(For further reading see Gunnigle *et al.* 2006.)

Work is currently under way in relation to the development of integrated workforce planning in both the Department of Health and the HSE. Workforce planning is particularly challenging in the health sector, since labour is not easily substituted, given the skills requirements of most roles, and the lead-in time to 'produce' health care workers is lengthy, given the qualifications standards for most professions. The volume and complexity of health care required is predicted to increase significantly over the next ten years (HSE 2008b). In the current economic climate, in which significant headcount reductions are to be achieved (Department of Finance 2009), workforce planning takes on a new and challenging dynamic. A number of significant strategies have been developed in relation to workforce planning for particular professions and service changes, including the Primary Care Strategy, the Hanly Report and a range of reports relating to professions such as nursing and midwifery and the allied health professional grades, for example physiotherapy, speech and language and occupational therapy (see Bacon & Associates 2001; DoHC 2001a, 2001b).

Recruitment and selection

The overall aim of recruitment is to attract a pool of suitable candidates, deter unsuitable candidates and create a suitable image of the company (Gunnigle *et al.* 2006). Recruitment and selection practices in the health sector in Ireland have been increasingly centralised in recent years, as a result of legislative requirements and the requirements of the Public Appointments Service (see www.pas.ie). Sources of recruitment may be internal or external and many existing agreements within the health services are based on internal labour markets. A detailed outline of recruitment sources is outlined in Gunnigle *et al.* (2006). Selection is the process of choosing the individual with the right requirements and skills to perform a given role and there are a range of selection techniques that can be used. The interview remains the predominant method of selection in use (Gunnigle *et al.* 2006). Efforts have been made to enhance the validity (measuring what it is supposed to measure) and reliability (ensuring objectivity in the assessment process) of the interview process in the health services, for example in competency-based interviews. Systems of recruitment and selection in the public service are very transparent, influenced very much by legislation in the areas of recruitment and freedom of information.

HSE recruitment and selection practices are carried out in the context of its commitments under both equality legislation and policies. A useful guide to equal opportunities can be obtained from www.hseea.ie.

Performance management and reward

Performance management has been defined as 'a strategic and integrated approach to delivering sustained success to organisations by improving the performance of the people who work in them and by developing the capabilities of team and individual contributors' (Armstrong & Baron 2000).

It is intrinsically linked with the line management role set out in the concept of HRM, since it provides a framework within which individuals and teams can be managed and developed.

A team-based performance management system for the heaalth sector was negotiated and developed through the national partnership agreement Sustaining Progress (Government of Ireland 2003). A recent review of the system highlighted many positive features, including greater ownership by staff or team of organisational goals and enhanced communications and teamworking. Efforts to develop an individual performance management system have, however, been slow compared with progress in the civil service (Hay Group and IPA 2004).

The recent report of the Task Force on the Public Service (2008) emphasised the need for the development of a performance management culture in the public service and it was recommended that performance management systems for individuals should be extended to all public servants, whatever their role.

The centralised nature of pay determination in the health sector has already been discussed. The linking of pay increases to organisational performance has been a feature of recent national social partnership agreements, as measured through the performance verification process.

The Programme for Prosperity and Fairness in 2000 recognised that there was a need to find a more appropriate way of determining public service pay that would benchmark public service pay by reference to pay in the labour market in Ireland generally. It was accepted that such an approach was required in the interests of fairness both to public servants and taxpayers; to assure industrial peace in the public service; and to ensure that the public service is in a position to attract and retain staff of the number and calibre needed to deliver the required quantum and quality of services that the public are entitled to expect. There was agreement that the traditional approach to pay reviews in the public service, based on analogues and relativities, had given rise to difficulties in the past. It was agreed that a pay benchmarking system which would enable a broad-based objective comparison with jobs and pay rates across the public sector and against the private sector would be introduced and that it would be linked to a continuing programme of public service modernisation. A Pay Benchmarking Body was established and it has produced two reports (for further reading see www.irlgov.ie/finance). Various initiatives have been put in place to strengthen the link between performance and reward. The link between performance and pay is the subject of much topical debate and this issue, and other elements of the reward mix, are comprehensively discussed in Armstrong and Baron (2000).

Learning and development

Significant emphasis was placed in the Action Plan for People Management (APPM) (DoHC 2002) on the need for a more strategic approach to learning and development in the health sector. A range of initiatives have been undertaken to support this, for example in the areas of management development, personal development planning and e-learning. Competency frameworks have been developed for nursing and midwifery, the allied health professional grades and for clerical, management and administrative grades, in partnership with the trade unions (see www.hseland.ie for copies of these models and related documentation). Much greater emphasis has also been placed on the measurement of investment in training and development and this has been reinforced by the setting of training and development targets in recent national partnership agreements.

A particular focus was placed on the need for a leadership development strategy for the HSE in the recent Transformation Programme (HSE 2007). There is also an emphasis in the programme on the development of clinicians in management and on the development of teams. Effective multidisciplinary teamworking, which is a key component of the Primary Care Strategy (DoHC 2001b), creates employee development needs, and increasingly the case for investment in employee development must be made against competing priorities such as service demand and cost containment policies.

The APPM also placed emphasis on the need for collaboration between the health sector and third-level education providers. This is echoed in the Transformation Programme (HSE 2007) in which the need for effective engagement with the third-level education sector is seen as a key component of engaging people in transforming health care and ensuring that the HSE can recruit and develop people with the skills required to achieve its mission and purpose.

The website www.hseland.ie contains a wealth of useful information, tools and links in relation to learning and development (to access these resources you must register as a member). It also contains all the guides and tools produced by the former Office for Health Management.

Employee relations

Employee relations is a broader concept than industrial relations. Gunnigle *et al.* (2006:263) state that 'the concept of employee relations is used as a generic term to embrace all employer, employee and state interactions on employment matters'. Given the scope and complexity of this area, this section will merely provide an outline of some of the key areas, namely industrial relations, partnership and employment law.

The practice of industrial relations between employers and workers in Ireland is conducted on a voluntary basis. Institutions such as the Labour Relations Commission are designed to support this process of voluntary collective bargaining as far as possible. Ireland has a comprehensive employment law framework in place, and individual issues are increasingly being dealt with through procedures laid down in law (see www.lrc.ie, www.equality.ie and www.irlgov/entemp.ie for further information and resources).

Changes in respect of key areas of HRM (for example pay, work practices and flexibility, performance management) in the Irish health sector have been increasingly negotiated on a partnership basis. The Programme for National Recovery (Government of Ireland 1987) represented the beginning of the social partnership model which is still in existence. This programme contained agreed mechanisms to moderate wage inflation and price inflation. Subsequent national agreements have focused on linking national pay increases to organisational performance across a range of areas including value for money and customer service.

Since 1999 a structured partnership process, supported by the Health Service National Partnership Forum (HSNPF) has been in place. Under the auspices of the forum, the Health Services Partnership Agreement (HSNPF 2006a) was developed between health service employers and trade unions. This agreement emphasises a way of working together that identifies shared interests and goals that contribute to the continuous modernisation of the health services. The agreement sets out mechanisms such as joint problem solving and interest-based bargaining whereby an agreed resolution of the issue(s) is identified that satisfies the interests of all parties. The agreement clearly states, however, that 'the partnership approach does not replace or substitute national or local industrial relations systems and procedures'.

More recently, the HSE, in consultation with the HSNPF, published a guide to managing change in the health service (HSE 2008c). This guide provides a toolkit for managers to assist them in planning, managing and implementing change and it also incorporates agreed mechanisms and protocols for managing change with trade unions (e.g. the Provision of Information and Consultation Act 2006 and the Agreed Protocol for Handling Significant Change). Further information can be obtained from www.hsnpf.ie.

Ireland has a well-developed and comprehensive employment law framework, by comparison with many other European countries. Legislation is in place to cover all areas of employment, including unfair dismissal, part-time and fixed-term working, equality, working time, redundancy and health and safety. The HSE has developed guides and resources to support employers, managers and staff in understanding their obligations and entitlements in relation to employment law. At national level there are a range of institutions in place to ensure a fair means of redress, including the Employment Appeals Tribunal, the Office of the Director of Equality Investigations, the Rights Commissioner Service, the Labour Relations Commission and the Labour Court and the proposed new National Employment Rights Authority. In addition to legal requirements, agreed discipline and grievance procedures are in place in the HSE, which individual managers and employee can invoke. Useful resources have also been developed by the HSE to assist managers to become more effective and proactive in areas such as equity and people management (see www.hseland.ie and www.hseea.ie for equality and diversity resources and the 'People Management – The Legal Framework' toolkit).

For further reading and resources in relation to employment law, a number of useful websites are recommended in the bibliography.

CASE STUDY: A HOSPITAL THAT HAS DEVELOPED AND IMPLEMENTED AN HRM STRATEGY

Hospital A is a large acute public hospital and it employs more than 3,000 staff. During the development of its corporate plan the management team identified the need for an HRM strategy as one of its core objectives. The aim of the HRM strategy would be to attract and retain the best, and to develop, manage and engage staff in order to ensure excellence in patient care and service delivery. The director of HR, who is a member of the senior management team, led and managed the formulation of the HRM strategy. A sub-group of the partnership committee was formed, and it was agreed that while senior management had a key role in championing HRM, the broad proposals of the plan would be presented to the sub-group who would design a framework to ensure effective communication and engagement in the formulation of the strategy. A comprehensive communications exercise, led jointly by the management team and the partnership committee, took place to inform people of the proposed HRM strategy, and this helped to create an environment of trust and inclusiveness. Unions were also separately briefed and consulted regarding their views. The agreed strategy focused on a number of key action areas, including:

- workforce planning, including recruitment and selection
- managing and developing the performance of the organisation, teams and individuals
- engagement and communications
- transforming HR (using the Ulrich model (1998)), which sets out four goals: employee champion; strategic partner; administrative expert; and agent of continuous transformation
- employee relations (policies and procedures, industrial relations and partnership)
- re-engineering HRM administration (payroll, employee records, pensions, HR information)
- equality, diversity and employee well-being.

The HRM strategy emphasised the role of the line manager in developing and managing performance and managing employee relations. Specific actions were set out in each of the action areas. Individual members of the partnership committee assisted in undertaking research in specific areas such as workforce planning and employee engagement. Fortnightly bulletins outlining progress were sent to staff and staff were encouraged to send feedback to the HR department via the dedicated HRM strategy hub on the organisation's intranet and to the partnership committee.

The director of HR reports to the CEO every fortnight in relation to progress in implementing the plan. A report on progress is also submitted for consideration at the monthly partnership committee meeting. The plan is also revised where required to take account of the new policy and corporate requirements, for example in relation to employment control, new legislation and regulatory issues.

Discuss how the following challenges to the formulation and ongoing implementation of the HRM strategy as identified by the HRM director may be overcome in the context of the Irish health care sector.

- The limited scope available to implement flexible HRM policies, in the light of national and corporate policy requirements, national agreements, legislation and generic terms and conditions for key areas of staffing.
- The difficulty of developing indicators to measure the achievement of HR objectives, particularly where the changes set out involve collaboration between the HR department and line managers and where many other variables can affect the outcome of an objective.

(See www.hseland.ie for HR audit resources.)

CONCLUSION

Some of the key concepts and theories of HRM were examined in this chapter. The development of HRM in the Irish health care sector was also analysed. This analysis shows that the implementation of HRM, with its emphasis on integration, flexibility, individual commitment and the role of line management, is important and challenging. Key stakeholder interests must be managed and reconciled effectively for HRM to be successful in achieving organisational and societal goals. The changing economic climate in Ireland creates additional demands, as organisations and policy makers must increasingly develop strategies which are focused on workforce and individual flexibility and cost reduction. The role of partnership, and its role in acting as a mechanism for a more integrated approach to HRM and industrial relations, was also explored in this chapter. Finally, some of the core areas of HRM, including workforce planning, performance management and development and employee relations, were outlined. A more in-depth analysis of these topics can be obtained in the textbooks and websites listed below.

REFLECTIVE EXERCISES

1 Discuss the factors that influence the desire for flexible HRM practices in the Irish health care sector and the challenges that arise in implementing such practices.

2 Using the Harvard model outlined in this chapter, identify and analyse the stakeholder interests and situational factors influencing HRM in your organisation. What opportunities and challenges do they create and how can these be addressed? What implications do these stakeholder interests and situational factors have for HRM policy choices in health care organisations?

3 A key element of HRM is the critical role of line managers in managing and developing people. Reflect on this element as it applies to your organisation and your own role in the organisation.

4 From your professional perspective, to what extent has partnership at both national and organisational level contributed to organisational change?

5 Reflect on your area of professional practice and consider the application, advantages and conflicts that may arise in the performance management/performance appraisal process.

ADDITIONAL RESOURCES

Chartered Institute of Personnel and Development (CIPD): www.cipd.co.uk

Equality Authority: www.equality.ie

Government of Ireland (1998): *Report of the Commission on Nursing: A Blueprint for the Future*. Dublin: Stationery Office.

— (2000) *Partnership 2000 for Inclusion, Employment and Competitiveness*. Dublin: Stationery Office.

— (2004) *Population and Labour Force Projections 2006 to 2036*. Dublin: Stationery Office.

Health Service Executive: www.hse.ie

HSE Learning and Development: www.hseland.ie

HSE Employers Agency: www.hseea.ie

Irish Congress of Trade Unions (ICTU): www.ictu.ie

Irish Government: www.gov.ie

Labour Relations Commission: www.lrc.ie

Lawler, E.E. III and Mohrman, S. (1987) 'Unions and the new management', *Academy of Management Executive* 1(3): 293–300.

Legge, K. (1978) *Power, Innovation and Problem Solving in Personnel Management*. New York: McGraw Hill.

— (1992) 'Human resource management: a critical analysis' in Storey, J. (ed.), *New Perspectives on Human Resource Management*. London: Routledge.

McCarthy, G., Tyrrell, M. P. and Cronin, C. (2002) *National Study of Turnover in Nursing and Midwifery*. Cork: University College Cork, National University of Ireland, Department of Nursing Studies.

OECD (1998) *Summary Record: Activity Meeting on Human Resources Management*, Public Management Committee, 25–26 June. Paris: OECD.

— (1999) *Synthesis of Reform Experiences in Nine OECD countries: Change Management*, OECD Symposium on Government of the Future, Getting From Here to There, 14–15 September. Paris: OECD (www.oecd.org/puma).

OneGov: www.bettergov.ie

Pearce, J. A. and Robinson, C. G. (1994) *Strategic Management* (5th edn). Irwin.

Schuler, R. S., and Jackson, S. E. (1987) 'Linking competitive strategies with human resource management practices', *Academy of Management Executive* 1: 3, 207–19.

Sparrow, P. and Hiltrop, J. M. (1994) 'Performance management and appraisal' in *European Human Resource Management in Transition*. UK: Prentice Hall.

Stewart, J. and Ranson, S. (1988) 'Management in the public domain', *Public Money and Management* Spring/Summer: 13–19.

Ulrich, D. (1997) *Human Resource Champions: The Next Agenda for Adding Value and Delivering Results*. Boston, MA: Harvard Business School Press.

US Department of Health and Human Services (1999) *Building Successful Organizations – Workforce Planning in HHS*. Office of Human Resources.

REFERENCES

Armstrong, M. (1997) *A Handbook of Personnel Management Practice*. London: Kogan Page.

— (2007) *A Handbook of Human Resource Management Practice* (10th edn). London: Kogan Page.

Armstrong, M. and Baron, A. (2000) *The Essence of Performance Management: The New Realities*. London: Chartered Institute of Personnel and Development.

Bacon and Associates (economic consultants) (2001) *Final Report: Current and Future Supply and Demand Conditions in the Labour Market for Certain Professional Therapists*. Dublin: Department of Health and Children.

Beer, M., Spencer, B., Laurence, P. P., Mills, D. Q. and Walton, R. E. (1984) *Managing Human Assets*. Macmillan.

Boyle, R. (1995) *Developing Management Skills: Needs and Trends in Irish Civil Service Management Practice*. Dublin: Institute of Public Administration.

Boyle, R. and Fleming, S. (2000) *The Role of Strategy Statements*. Dublin: Institute of Public Administration.

Butler, M. and Fleming, S. (2002) *The Effective Use of Competencies in the Irish Civil Service*. Dublin: Institute of Public Administration.

Common, R., Flynn, N. and Mellon, E. (1993) *Managing Public Services: Competition and Decentralisation*. Oxford: Butterworth-Heinemann.

Cradden, T. (1992), 'Trade unionism and HRM: the incompatibles?', *Irish Business and Administrative Review*.

Department of Finance (2009) *Report of the Special Group on Public Service Numbers and Expenditure Programmes, Volumes 1 and 2*. Dublin: Government Publications Office.

DoHC (Department of Health and Children) (2001a) *Quality and Fairness: A Health System for You.* Dublin: Stationery Office.

— (2001b) *Primary Care: A New Direction.* Dublin: Stationery Office.

— (2002) *Action Plan for People Management.* Dublin: Stationery Office.

— (2003a) *Report of the National Task Force on Medical Staffing* (Hanly Report). Dublin: Stationery Office.

— (2003b) *Audit of Structures and Functions in the Health Systems* (Prospectus Report). Dublin: Stationery Office.

— (2003c) *Report of the Commission on Financial Management and Control Systems in the Health Service* (Brennan Report). Dublin: Stationery Office.

Elcock, H. (1993) 'Strategic management' in Farnham, D. and Horton, S. (eds), *Managing the New Public Services* (1st edn). London: Macmillan.

FÁS (Foras Áiseanna Saothair) (2005) *Healthcare Skills: Monitoring Report*, Skills and Labour Market Research Unit. Dublin: FÁS.

Fleming, S. (2000) *From Personnel Management to Human Resource Management.* Dublin: Institute of Public Administration.

— (2003) 'Further challenges lie ahead on the route to public service modernisation', *Labour Relations Commission Review* 2(1).

Fombrun, C. J., Tichy, N. M. and Devanna, M. A. (1984) *Strategic Human Resource Management.* New York, Chichester: Wiley.

Fowler, A. (1987) 'When chief executives discover HRM', *Personnel Management* January.

Government of Ireland (1987) *Programme for National Recovery.* Dublin: Stationery Office.

— (1996) *Delivering Better Government: Second Report to Government of the Co-ordinating Group of Secretaries.* Dublin: Government Publications Office.

— (2003) *Sustaining Progress: Social Partnership Agreement 2003–2005.* Dublin: Stationery Office.

— (2006) *Towards 2016: Ten Year Framework Social Partnership Agreement 2006–2015.* Dublin: Stationery Office.

— (2008) *Towards 2016 Review and Transitional Agreement 2008–2009.* Dublin: Stationery Office.

Guest, D. E. (1987) 'Human resource management and industrial relations', *Journal of Management Studies* 24(5): 503–21.

— (1995) 'Human resource management, trade unions and industrial relations' in Storey, J. (ed.), *Human Resource Management: A Critical Text.* London: Routledge.

Guest, D. and Hoque, K. (1994) 'Yes, personnel does make a difference', *Personnel Management* November, 40–4.

Gunnigle, P., Heraty, N., Morley, M. (2006) *Human Resource Management in Ireland* (3rd edn). Dublin: Gill and Macmillan.

Hay Group (Irl) and IPA (Institute of Public Administration) (2004) *Evaluation of the Health Service Performance Management System.* Dublin: Health Service Executive Employers' Agency. Available at www.hseea.ie.

Hope-Hailey, V., Gratton, L., McGovern, P., Stiles, P. and Tuss, C. (1997), 'A chameleon function? HRM in the 90s', *Human Resource Management Journal* 7(3): 5–18.

HSE (Health Service Executive) (2007): *Transformation Programme 2007–2010*. Dublin: HSE.

— (2008a) *Corporate Plan 2008–2011*. Dublin: HSE.

— (2008b) *Towards Fully Integrated Care: Integrated Service Delivery Change Programme*, Briefing Note – Update No.1 (October), Dublin: HSE.

— (2008c) *Improving Our Services: A User's Guide to Managing Change in the Health Service*. Dublin: HSE.

HSNPF (Health Services National Partnership Forum) (2000): *The Health Service Partnership Agreement*. Dublin: HSNPF.

— (2006) *Health Services Partnership Agreement*. Dublin: Government Publications Office.

ICTU (Irish Congress of Trade Unions) (2009) *Statement on the Economy* (see www.ictu.ie).

Lawton, A. and Rose, A. (1994) *Organisation and Management in the Public Sector*. London: Pitman.

Legge, K. (1995) *Human Resource Management – Rhetorics and Realities*. London: Macmillan Press.

LRC (Labour Relations Commission) (2001) *Review of Industrial Relations in the Health Service for the Minister for Health and Children*, Advisory Development and Research Service. Dublin: LRC.

Marchington, M. and Wilkinson, A. (1997) *Core Personnel and Development*. London: Institute of Personnel and Development.

McGovern, P., Gratton, L., Stiles, P., Hope-Hailey, V. and Truss, C. (1997), 'Human resource management on the line?', *Human Resource Management Journal* 7(4): 12–29.

Merchant, G. and Wilson, D. (1994), 'Devolving HR in the civil service', *Personnel Management* January: 38–40.

Mintzberg, H. (1996) 'Managing government', *Harvard Business Review* May–June: 75–83.

Murray, C. H. (1990) *The Civil Service Observed*. Dublin: Institute of Public Administration.

O'Dowd, J. and Hastings, T. (1997) *Human Resource Management in the Public Sector*, Business Research Programme. Dublin: UCD Graduate School of Business.

OECD (Organisation for Economic Co-operation and Development) (1990), *Flexible Personnel Management in the Public Service*. Paris: Public Management Studies.

— (1992) *Public Management Development: Update*. Paris: OECD.

— (1996) *Integrating People Management into Public Service Reform*. Paris: OECD.

— (2008) *Public Management Reviews – Ireland: Towards an Integrated Public Service*. Paris: OECD.

Peters, T. J. and Waterman, R. H. (1982) *In Search of Excellence: Lessons from America's Best Run Companies*. New York: Harper Row.

Purcell, J. and Ahlstrand, B. (1995) *Human Resource Management in the Multi-Divisional Company*. Oxford: Oxford University Press.

Roche, W. K. (1995) 'The New Competitive Order and the Fragmentation of Employee Relations in Ireland', Address to the IBEC Annual Employee Relations Conference, 16 November.

— (1998) 'Public service reform and human resource management', *Administration* 46 (2), Summer: 3–24.

Storey, J. (1989) 'Human resource management in the public sector', *Public Money and Management* 9(3): 19–24.

— (1992) *Developments in the Management of HRM: An Analytical Review*. Oxford: Blackwell.

— (1995) *Human Resource Management: A Critical Text*. London: Routledge.

Task Force on the Public Service (2008) *Transforming Public Services – Citizen Centred – Performance Focused*, Department of the Taoiseach. Dublin: Stationery Office.

Tyson, S. and Fell, A. (1986) *Evaluating the Personnel Functions*. London: Hutchinson.

Ulrich, D. (1998): 'A new mandate for human resources', *Harvard Business Review* January–February.

West, M. A., Borill, C., Dawson, J., Scully, J., Carter, M., Anelay, S., Patterson, M. and Waring, J. (2002) 'The link between the management of employees and patient mortality in acute hospitals', *International Journal of Human Resource Management* 13:8, 1299–310.

Developing Professionals in the Health Service

8
Communication and Conflict Resolution

Catherine Mc Cabe

OBJECTIVES
- To outline and discuss the basic characteristics of communication.
- To discuss the types and systems of organisational communication.
- To define conflict and discuss the types and process of conflict and its management, with reference to personal and professional power.
- To outline specific personal and professional behaviours for the successful management of conflict.

INTRODUCTION

Effective communication systems are generally regarded as key components in the development, day-to-day operation and change management processes of organisations. This is because organisations comprise small, medium or large groups of people brought together on the basis of how their skills may contribute to the realisation of organisational goals. In this respect, health care organisations are no different from any other type of organisation; however, as you saw in Chapter 1, a significant number of internal and external agencies influence the structure, functioning and governance of the Irish health care system. This structure creates its own challenges for the development of effective communication systems, which are compounded by the presence, at local level, of administrators at many different levels and grades; and health care professionals who are also at many different levels and grades but, to add further potential challenges, who represent a broad range of professional health care disciplines. The ultimate aim of both hospital administrators and the various groups of health care professionals is to provide safe, efficient and high-quality patient care services. However, even with common aims and well-established communication and functional systems, conflict occurs. Although this can be viewed as inevitable and should also perhaps be regarded as normal, and, if managed well, is essential for organisational motivation and development, it is often caused by the failure of health care managers to effectively communicate the organisational strategy for the achievement of common goals.

Dealing with conflict successfully becomes difficult and challenging for health care managers because it occurs within organisational structures that are predominantly hierarchical in nature and within and between numerous groups competing for resources that are centralised. This generates perceptions of power inequality, which result in a lack of trust between the groups and often leads to fragmented communication, increased conflict and limited effective collaboration between health care professionals. In terms of health care organisations, this can obstruct or inhibit the provision of high-quality patient-centred care because the focus of health care professionals becomes the conflict, rather than the provision of a cohesive approach to planning and implementing care. Another factor that impacts on communication and is often not considered when developing and evaluating communication systems in health care organisations is the communication abilities or skills of individuals working within the system.

This chapter explores the characteristics of communication; communication systems in health care organisations; interpersonal communication; professional power issues; conflict and techniques for its resolution, for example collaboration and negotiation.

CHARACTERISTICS OF COMMUNICATION

The basic components or requirements for communication to take place are a person who sends a message and a person who receives the message (McCabe & Timmins 2006). Figure 8.1 illustrates the unidirectional nature of this approach.

Figure 8.1: Components of communication

This model is over-simplistic as it does not take into account how intrinsic and extrinsic factors influence the communication process. Intrinsic factors refer to the personal values, beliefs, goals and knowledge of those involved in the communication. Extrinsic factors include the physical environment and communication medium. These factors can create what DeVito (2002) describes as four types of noise:

- physical
- physiological (physical impairments that influence perception)
- psychological (influence of previous experience, biases, personal goals, values/beliefs)
- semantic (interpretation of meaning of words).

A more complex and comprehensive communication model that appears to incorporate intrinsic and extrinsic factors is Hargie and Dickson's (2004) skill model of interpersonal communication. It is clear from this model that in order for interpersonal communication to be effective and satisfactory to all parties, certain factors or processes need to be clear and present. These include:

- person-situation context
- goal
- mediating processes
- response
- feedback
- perception.

Person-situation context relates to how an individual's values, beliefs, culture, knowledge, skills, age, gender, self-efficacy, self-concept and personality influence how they contribute to and engage with interpersonal communication. The context in which any interaction takes place refers not only to the physical environment but also to the boundaries associated with those involved that influences people's approach and responses.

The goal/s of those involved in any communication may be similar or vary to a greater or lesser degree and the identity of these goals is not always clearly stated or evident. According to Hargie and Dickson (2004), in order for all of the goals to be achieved they need to be identified and analysed to determine compatibility and to be prioritised if necessary.

Mediating processes are influenced by the individual way in which people use their personal knowledge, beliefs and values when contemplating an issue and how this forms the basis of the attitude used in their approach and response to interaction with others. The outcome of successful mediating processes is a tentative strategy for achieving the goal/s.

Hargie and Dickson (2004) describe the 'response' component of the skill model as how communication factors (verbal and non-verbal), in conjunction with extrinsic factors such as environmental and organisational issues, affect the manner in which strategies are implemented.

Feedback is the mechanism by which those involved in communication become aware that a message has been received and also how the receiver interprets it. It is achieved through verbal and non-verbal responses and is essential in determining whether understanding and interpretation is mutual, thereby facilitating progress.

Perception is the final component of Hargie and Dickson's (2004) skill model and it relates to how individuals perceive each other. They suggest that continued self-awareness in relation to contribution and engagement in an interaction makes it possible to predict the process and outcome; however, if this is not present, negative or unsatisfactory outcomes to interactions with others may be commonplace.

This model provides quite a comprehensive and relevant framework for discussing communication issues in a health care context. It is clear that responsibility for ensuring that communication is not only effective but also positive lies first with the individuals involved and second with the communication systems in place in an organisation. It is also clear that communication is not always a straightforward matter; it needs careful consideration if conflict is to be managed well and channelled into continuous organisational development.

In order for communication to be efficient within organisations, the systems in place need to ensure that it occurs in all directions and within and between all levels of staff. Also, of equal importance, in order for it to be effective, it needs to be structured and presented and delivered in a positive manner. Organisations will have established systems for communication using mechanisms such as face-to-face meetings with individuals or specialist groups; print and electronic media; and computers. However, it is important to note that regardless of how efficient and effective communications systems are within organisations, they cannot enhance interpersonal communication. The responsibility for this lies with the individuals concerned and this is clear from Hargie and Dickson's skill model of interpersonal communication.

Example:
You receive an email from a colleague via the organisational intranet system. The message relates to the inconvenience caused to them as a result of a poor PowerPoint presentation by a member of an external agency. It goes something like this . . .

THE PRESENTATION BY MR JONES ON MONDAY WAS VERY POOR. THE FONT SIZE ON HIS SLIDES WAS ONLY 12 AND PEOPLE FOUND THEM DIFFICULT TO READ. I HAD TO PHOTOCOPY THE SLIDES FOR EVERYONE AND PASS THEM AROUND, I FOUND THIS VERY INCONVENIENT! AS YOU ARRANGED FOR THIS SPEAKER TO ATTEND, I THINK HE SHOULD HAVE BEEN INFORMED TO USE A LARGER FONT!

Regardless of the point of the email, the use of capital letters and exclamation marks portrays an aggressive tone. Even if the receiver of this email agrees that they should perhaps have provided more guidance for the speaker in relation to the most appropriate font size, it is not a collegial or positive communication. This is poor communication and creates negative feelings which, depending on the response, can escalate to unnecessary conflict. The immediate response to such an email is probably to respond in a similar manner; however, perhaps the best response should occur after some time, following contemplation, planning and the use of assertiveness skills.

In other situations, following a negative interaction, you may sometimes walk away with the awareness that you either caused or exacerbated the negative encounter. However, it is more probable that you walked away blaming the other person for being rude, unreasonable and/or aggressive. This may have been the case, but when considering the development of positive communication skills, the focus must always be on oneself and not the other person; and remember, most other people are just like you: they react to the type of communication they experience without being aware of how they contribute to the negativity.

Communication is a skill that we are born with, which develops and expands as we grow. Some people develop communication skills to a higher level than others, but perhaps what is common to most is that communication generally occurs unconsciously. We usually react and respond to our experiences in everyday life without planning or evaluating how our communication ability contributed to the encounter. This does not always result in negative communication: however, in organisations comprising many different professions and departments, which may all have a common goal but the achievement of which is subject to reaching specific and often diverse targets or objectives, it is essential that interpersonal communication is clear, focused, directional and positive.

This requires that individuals are aware of how they communicate, spend time planning how they will communicate and, most important, evaluate how they communicated. Time spent planning and practising communication may sound like time wasted, but it is necessary and prevents encounters where we walk away saying to ourselves, 'If only I had said . . .' Shea (1998) makes the excellent point that 'A few ill-chosen or ill-delivered words, a lack of tact in dealing with our employees, and how we express ourselves in front of others, can do great and lasting damage' (p.61).

The basic building blocks of communication include listening, questioning, body language and linguistics; and knowledge, understanding and skills in using these will allow an individual to develop awareness of how they communicate and also how to use these skills to communicate positively and effectively regardless of the context of the encounter. It will also allow them to develop assertive behaviours and participate in collaborative communication when necessary.

As we have seen from Hargie and Dickson's (2004) skill model of interaction, feedback is an essential component of communication that can only be delivered if the receiver truly actively listens to the message. Good listening requires conscious, active engagement with the person and message. It is not simply a matter of hearing words: other fundamental components are understanding, interpretation and feedback. In many ways it is like acting because when you are learning to be a good listener it may feel false and that you are not being yourself, but really all you are doing is focusing on another person rather than yourself and it is this behaviour that may actually be alien to you. Our ability to listen is evident to others primarily through our facial expression, body language and feedback, which can all happen without any, or with just a few, words being spoken. Active listening demonstrates respect for others and is the basis of building positive constructive relationships. Forsyth (2002) suggests that in order to listen you must:

- want to listen
- look like a good listener
- look at the other person
- react in a positive supportive manner
- stop talking
- be empathetic
- understand/seek clarity
- concentrate

- make notes of key points
- avoid personality issues.

Body language and paralinguistics are probably the most underestimated aspects of communication; according to Shea (1998), over 50 per cent of the message is transmitted via body language (including image) and 40 per cent comes from the sound, tempo and accent of the words (paralinguistics). Only 10 per cent of the message is delivered by the words used. When we think about it, we all know this – think of the 'dirty look' we have either given or received on many occasions. The result of incongruent body language and oral message is the perception that a person is not being genuine or is disinterested. An example of this is when we do not look directly at the person we are speaking to, look at our watch or use standard responses when communicating with employees. A standard response could be something like, 'Yes, that's a good point and well made, I'll be in touch with you about that.' This response should make the employee feel that the query or point was understood and that the manager would actually deal with it; however, if it is a response that is frequently used and is not followed up, the manager's reputation will be that they are just saying that to keep the employee quiet and do not mean what they say.

Questioning is also an essential communication skill and the use of pertinent questioning reflects active listening. Depending on the context and situation, questions can be used to obtain, clarify or explore different types of information. Types of question include 'open', 'closed', 'probing' and 'hypothetical'. Closed questions are used to obtain very specific information and generally require a 'yes' or 'no' answer, for example, 'Are you available to meet at three this afternoon?' Open questions are used to seek opinion or subjective accounts related to information or experiences, for example 'How do you feel about that?' Probing questions are also open but tend to seek specific information, for example, 'That sounds interesting; why do you think that happened?' Hypothetical questions are particularly useful for eliciting information about possible solutions to problems or testing an individual's decision-making skills, for example 'What would you do if an employee was continually late for work?' Questioning can be less helpful to positive communication if it is leading ('That wasn't a great idea, was it'?) or vague ('What was that all about?'). Remember, body language should also be positive and accompanied by supportive feedback, such as nodding your head in agreement, smiling and eye contact as appropriate.

A communication skill that is rarely recognised as such, is usually undervalued and often ignored is how we dress and groom ourselves. Clothes are often chosen for their convenience and comfort and in health care contexts are often dictated by the uniform associated with each profession. However, even the way in which a uniform is worn is significant. Ensuring that clothes are clean, well ironed and well fitted portrays something about the character and demeanour of the wearer and this in turn influences how they are perceived by others before any words are spoken. Shea (1998) cites Epictetus as saying 'First know who you are, then adorn yourself accordingly' (p.54). Staff expect managers to look well groomed because it gives them an air of confidence and leadership which shows that they are trustworthy and know what they are talking about, and therefore are good managers.

These basic communication skills form the basis of our communication behaviours and how we develop and use these skills influences our relationships and interactions with others. One of the key ways in which we can become aware of how we communicate with others is through self-awareness. Burnard (1997) suggests that self-awareness enhances self-understanding, self-monitoring and personal autonomy. It also allows acceptance of others and helps us deal with difficult situations. It is best described as having understanding and perception of self in terms of values, beliefs, behaviours and personal identity. The process of becoming self-aware requires introspection, reflection on feedback from others and of course a healthy degree of honesty in relation to one's strengths and weaknesses. This allows us to not just recognise and be aware of when we communicate poorly but also to change our communication behaviour. This is essential, especially for managers who are required to deal with a variety of diverse situations and people as part of their everyday work.

Exercise: How to become more self-aware

As we have said already, reflecting consciously and honestly on our own communication behaviours and actively listening to feedback from others are essential in order to develop self-awareness. One of the ways in which to do this in relation to learning more about how you communicate is to ask people to tell you what they think of your communication behaviours. It is best to do this with someone you know well and trust, perhaps someone you live with or a close friend. One word of caution with this exercise is that you need to be prepared to accept the response you get! Would you be happy if you heard that you were a good communicator about 60 per cent of the time? How do you communicate for the other 40 per cent?

Adapted from McCabe & Timmins (2006)

The communication skills presented above are needed by everyone in order to communicate effectively. The next section in this chapter looks at how these skills are particularly important for managers in communicating effectively and harnessing positive aspects of conflict to achieve organisational goals and targets.

COMMUNICATION FOR HEALTH CARE MANAGERS

Regardless of the nature of work of the organisation, managers are employed to develop, implement and evaluate strategies for the successful, efficient and economical achievement of organisational goals and targets. The achievement of these goals and targets relies entirely on the manager's ability and skill in guiding, supporting and encouraging other employees to do what is needed to be done. This requires not just the presence of effective, efficient organisational communication systems, but, perhaps more important, skilful and positive interpersonal communication. The communication skills presented in the previous section are essential for this, but other skills such as assertiveness and collaborative communication are also required. These skills help managers not only to communicate well but also to harness conflict in a positive manner that contributes towards the achievement of goals and targets.

Benefits of continuous positive communication for managers include the staff perception that they are informed, respected and valued, which results in better morale. This in turn leads to greater job satisfaction and loyalty, increased productivity, and mutual understanding of organisational goals and strategy. Job-related and organisation information needs to be passed on to employees in a consistent and reliable manner. Communication systems such as email, one-to-one meetings, group meetings, etc. will go some way towards achieving this; however, it is the interpersonal interactions and even the tone of written communication that influence the manner in which the ultimate achievement of the organisational goals and targets is reached.

Awareness of one's communication skills and behaviours is essential for successful and positive management of a workforce. Managers need always to be aware of how they communicate and how this affects others; in other words, they need to be able to manage themselves first before they can contemplate regulating or managing others successfully and positively. Goleman (1995) refers to this as emotional intelligence and suggests that there are four main types: self-awareness; self-management; relationship management; and social awareness. This is because communication is a tool for managers and must be a key factor in how they develop strategies for getting the workforce to achieve the organisation's goals and targets. In health care contexts this requires getting members within and between different professional groups to work together while respecting and valuing their individual practices and contribution to the provision of high-quality, efficient patient care services.

Assertive behaviour is another essential communication skill required to manage and regulate your behaviour and that of others. It is based on the concept of expressing individual needs and feelings but in a manner that reflects an understanding of and respect for the needs and feelings of others and does not offend or belittle others (Porritt 1990). Managers who exhibit passive communication behaviours can make employees feel frustrated; aggressive or manipulative behaviours can make them feel angry and distrustful. Assertive behaviours, on the other hand, make people feel respected and trusting. This skill is extremely useful but can be difficult to master if an individual lacks confidence or has an introvert personality; however, it is not a behaviour that needs to be used all the time. Some people find it easier than others to use assertive behaviours, therefore they will use them more frequently; those who find it more difficult can choose certain situations in which to be assertive. As already mentioned, developing new communications skills requires practice; this is particularly true in relation to assertiveness communication. Practising with friends or family might be the safest place to start!

Assertive communication behaviour requires an individual to be reflective, acknowledge criticism, seek clarification, accept compliments, be able to say 'no' and have persuasive and negotiation skills to get what they need. This behaviour also needs to be accompanied by appropriate physical appearance and dress code because of the subconscious message it sends to others: for example, a manager who has a sloppy appearance, regardless of how skilled they are, may be perceived by others as disrespectful or incompetent. Whether you are male or female, a quick check in the mirror before attending difficult or challenging committees, or even when dealing with everyday management issues, will ensure that you feel confident about how you appear to others. It will also help you to develop the ability to view yourself objectively, which is also a key factor in developing self-awareness.

Assertive communication behaviours include the following.

- Using the word 'I' to express needs or feelings.
- Accepting compliments by simply looking at whoever gave the compliment and saying 'Thanks'.
- Not blaming others for your feelings. For example, instead of saying, 'Your unprofessional behaviour is really frustrating,' try saying 'I feel frustrated by your unprofessional behaviour.'
- Not using self-deprecatory terms such as 'just', for example 'I'm just trying to explain why we need extra staff tomorrow.' Instead be direct, use a firm, slightly louder tone and say 'I need extra staff tomorrow to care for the two patients being transferred from the intensive care unit.'
- When you receive criticism, trying not to be defensive; just indicate whether you agree that all, a little, or none of it is true.
- If you are approached and asked to make a decision on something 'urgently' that you feel you are unprepared for, stating clearly that you need to think about it before responding: this is a reasonable and prudent request, so don't feel pressured.

Perhaps one of the best ways of developing assertive communication behaviours is to choose a role model and observe not only their appearance and body language but also the words they use when communicating assertively and how they say them.

It is clear that assertive communication behaviour is an essential ingredient in successfully and positively managing others in achieving organisational goals and targets. However, in complex organisational structures such as hospital and community health care settings it is important to consider the influence of professional and power issues on our ability to communicate effectively. Health care services are provided by many professional groups, including physiotherapy, nursing, occupational therapy and medicine. It is likely that each of these groups, and possibly others, will contribute to the provision of care for individual patients. However, each of these groups also regards their contribution to patient care as unique and important, and it may be that at times over the course of treatment, one type of care will take priority over another. It is important to note that regardless of which takes priority in terms of the immediate needs of a patient, there is a perceptual hierarchy among health care professions which is naturally accompanied by perceived power over others. This situation can create conflict, not just between the professional groups but also between the administrators and executive officers. In order for the different professions to contribute to policy development and compete on an equal basis for resources, communication needs to be assertive. Conflict should not be viewed as a negative aspect of health care management but rather as part of the evaluation, development and implementation of policies and services that require collaboration from many different groups.

MANAGING CONFLICT

Conflict arises when interdependent people or groups perceive others as potentially interfering with the achievement of their goals and aims (Putnam & Poole 1987), for example role conflict, competition for limited resources and interpersonal conflict among and between all grades of staff (Papa *et al.* 2008). Although conflict is regarded as an unavoidable aspect of organisational life and management, the manner in which it is managed will dictate whether it becomes a positive or negative force for the achievement of organisational goals and targets and the organisation's ongoing development. Actions related to the management of conflict should not centre on eliminating it, but should rather focus on goals such as preventing escalation; identifying and solving the problem; depersonalising the argument; building relationships; dealing with negative emotions and anxiety in a positive manner; and achieving organisational goals and targets (Barker *et al.* 2006).

Managers tend to adopt one of five basic strategies in managing conflict (Masters & Albright 2002):

- accommodation
- avoidance
- competition
- compromise
- collaboration.

Yoder-Wise (1999) highlights how the use of each of these strategies has its advantages and disadvantages: for example, in an accommodating strategy, ensuring that the needs and concerns of others are addressed is often not reciprocated, which can leave the manager feeling resentful and frustrated. The issue that should drive the use of this strategy is that it does not hinder the achievement of the ultimate goal and that positive relations are maintained.

Avoidance is regarded as an unassertive behaviour, but an advantage of it is that it gives time to 'consider the options'; it may even mean that the manager recognises that they may not be the best person to attempt to resolve the conflict or even that the source of the conflict was a trivial matter and it resolved itself. However, these issues need to be clear to the manager using this strategy and they need to question their ability to communicate assertively in difficult situations.

Competitive behaviours can be used effectively when difficult or unpopular decisions need to be made or in stimulating motivation, but consistent use of this strategy can make it difficult for a manager to work collaboratively with other groups when necessary.

Compromise can be a very effective strategy for dealing with conflict because it is based on creating or identifying a 'middle ground' where all parties get something but no party gets everything. This is important when different groups are equally committed to achieving goals that contribute to the overall organisational goal. Compromise is quite typical in health care organisations and a manager's skill in facilitating compromise between and within groups is invaluable in maintaining relations and reaching targets and goals. This will be discussed later in this chapter in relation to negotiation.

Collaboration is a strategy that requires all groups to work together, in an open and transparent manner, towards finding solutions to issues that are significant, complex and strategic. This management strategy requires the use of assertive, confident behaviour.

It is clear that conflict management is essentially an interpersonal endeavour, the aim of which should be to maintain open, effective communication. However, in order to be successful, the fundamental issues at play need to be understood.

The source of conflict is generally attributed to communication issues such as dysfunctional interpersonal interactions or interactions between groups, units or departments (Barker 2006). Smith and Eisenberg (2006) suggest that traditional conflict theory is limited in that its primary focus relates to overt goals, strategies and resources. It excludes the key, but often hidden, influence that differing world views or ideologies between groups have in causing conflict and also in its successful management. Barker (2006:214) appears to agree with Smith and Eisenberg (2006), as they define conflict as 'a disagreement between two or more people who differ in attitudes, values, beliefs or needs'. Strategies for identifying these world views enable managers to anticipate, understand and address such conflicts. As indicated earlier, although in health care systems managers and staff share the common goal of providing safe, efficient, high-quality patient care, the manner in which this is achieved is heavily influenced by professional world views or ideologies. An example of this is that clinicians need freedom to make clinical decisions and develop practice and services through the achievement of professional goals, whereas, in contrast, managers need to use organisational and defined authority structures to plan, control and allocate resources. This is evident in McCutcheon's (1998) assertion that doctors and managers have a fundamental lack of understanding of each other because of their contrasting perspectives: the former are scientists, concerned with outcomes; the latter are concerned with the structure and process of practice. Other health care professionals, for example nurses and pharmacists, may also be concerned with outcomes; however, most health care professionals also contribute to issues related to the structure and process of practice and strategic health care management issues through hospital committee membership.

In managing conflict successfully a manager will need to focus on certain issues such as preventing escalation of the problem, identifying and depersonalising the problem, and instigating and facilitating open channels of communication between the people involved with the specific aim of finding a solution that is acceptable to all parties (Barker 2006). Both managers and health care professionals need to respect each other's perspective and achieve a balance in addressing the needs of both. The desired outcome of conflict management should be fairness; otherwise it is unlikely that the solution will be effective or efficient in achieving goals and targets. It will also have the effect of reducing the sense of trust and respect that employees might have for their manager.

One of the reasons why fairness may not be achieved is if there is a perception that the views of some groups or individuals are privileged and people or groups operate with rule systems that are disempowering (Papa *et al.* 2008). This type of conflict is particularly evident in the hierarchical structures that exist not just among management staff but also among health care staff and in health care systems. The result of this hierarchical system is that conflict within groups and between groups is often related to power struggles or equality issues. In order to manage conflict in a way that is seen to be fair, managers need to be aware of these power issues and the perceptions that the various groups have in terms of their relationship, interdependence or independence within their own group and with other groups. According to Thalhofer (1993), two conditions need to be present for successful management of conflict: separateness and equal valuation. Separateness is the acknowledgement, support and promotion of the differences, in positive terms, between groups. Ensuring a sense of equality within and between groups requires managers to establish an environment in which people feel equally valued when the groups are together.

These conditions are met primarily through the use on the part of the manager of the effective and positive communication behaviours discussed in the previous sections, and the establishment of communication systems that promote the contribution of all levels of staff in a hospital to decision making and policy making. This can be achieved to some degree through electronic communication but is more effective with one-to-one or group communication. The reason for this is that it is often the non-verbal communication such as the physical presence of the manager that provides immediate feedback, both verbal and non-verbal, to staff.

Example 1

An example of this in a hospital is where the most senior nurse manager regularly visits the various units and wards. The manager may only communicate directly with the unit manager, but the perception is that they are aware of the issues that are important to the nursing staff and the conditions in which they work. His or her regular visible presence suggests that this is important to the manager, therefore the staff feel respected and valued.

Example 2

An example of where this is not so effective in a health care context is perhaps at committee level where all professional and managerial staff are represented, but one or two groups are perceived to speak louder and more often than others and this is accepted by the managers. It is in situations like this that managers need to be particularly cognisant of traditional or historical professional power issues, and to actively seek the opinion of all representatives. If this does not happen, representatives from some groups will leave the meeting feeling undervalued and not afforded equal status.

Collaboration is a management strategy that is based on recognising equality within and between groups in terms of their contribution to any issues relating to the achievement of organisational goals and targets. The often mutually exclusive needs and goals of the groups are recognised as equally important, so no one group feels undervalued. An example of how a manager can facilitate collaborative behaviour is by making the organisational goal the focus of discussions. For example, in health care contexts this would be the provision of high-quality care for patients. The manager would then ask each group around the table to outline what they perceive their role to be in reaching this goal. When facilitating such meetings, managers need to use an even tone of voice, give each group time to speak without interruption and not allow one group or voice to dominate.

Key factors in facilitating and supporting successful collaboration by a manager are preparation prior to meetings and evaluation afterwards.

Preparation includes asking the following questions.

- Is this necessary?
- What am I trying to achieve?
- What is the source of the conflict?
- Who needs to be involved?
- What information do I need?
- When is the best time for this meeting?
- Where is the most appropriate venue?
- What needs or goals do the other parties have?
- What will be the basis of any objections they raise?

Questions to consider after the meeting include:

- Did I behave in the way I wanted to?
- Did I control the room in a way that gave everyone present equal opportunity to express their views?
- Were feasible and sustainable solutions identified?
- Did the groups represented change their view or compromise in any way?

- What were relations like between the groups at the end of the meeting?

PERSUASION AND NEGOTIATION

Perhaps it is becoming clear that the ability to communicate in a clear, positive manner is the essential foundation of successful day-to-day management. As mentioned earlier in this chapter, management is basically about getting others to do what you want in order to achieve organisational goals and targets. This requires persuasion and negotiation and if a manager communicates in a poor or negative way, this will be a very difficult process for all involved.

Persuasion is the process of coming to an agreement on a decision or issue. Negotiation relates to clarifying and agreeing the relevant detail and process in implementing the decision: since different parties are involved, this can therefore be quite adversarial (Forsyth 2002). To prevent this and to ensure that all parties involved in the agreement continue to support it, assertive communication is essential. It allows the manager to protect the agreement and ensure that the process in negotiating the detail is fair and equal. A manager can become a successful negotiator with positive assertive communication and adherence to a number of basic principles. These include:

- Set clear objectives.
- Seek common ground or interests.
- Before you start negotiating know what you are prepared to compromise on.
- Demonstrate flexibility by presenting proposals rather than statements of position.
- Include direct questioning in the process.

It is essential for a manager to know what the challenges may be when negotiating details or processes and this requires that they consider the individuals or professions involved and be cognisant of the different views they hold about how to achieve overall organisational goals and targets. Learning about the people you work with and networking are important and worthwhile activities for managers in persuading and negotiating with others. Networking in particular is very valuable in that it can limit the amount of formal negotiation required if positive, courteous and informed interpersonal communication takes place during informal chance encounters in a corridor or hospital canteen.

SUMMARY

Effective and positive communication is essential for any manager in the achievement of organisational goals and targets. This requires self-awareness in terms of how they communicate both verbally and non-verbally and is a key factor in ensuring that a manager takes responsibility for how they communicate on a personal and professional basis and for their contribution to either positive or negative interactions with others.

The manner in which a person communicates is influenced primarily by their level of self-awareness. This allows them to identify what style of management they use and how this influences their communication approach. It is important for a manager to be aware of this because managers who find it difficult to delegate or devolve control to others may find collaborative communication challenging.

Developing positive and effective communication for the management of conflict requires personal reflection, awareness and the development of specific communication behaviours that need to be practised. These skills include using clear verbal communication accompanied by appropriate and congruent non-verbal communication. Awareness and understanding of the various ideologies within and between health care groups or professions will help managers to develop appropriate and inclusive communication behaviours and responses that will contribute to consistently positive and successful conflict management and support collaborative communication.

REFLECTIVE QUESTIONS

1   What type of communicator are you?
2   Have friends and family made similar comments about your communication?
3   Think of an interaction that you feel was positive and successful and consider the factors that influenced this outcome.
4   Think about an interaction that you feel was negative and consider the factors that influenced this outcome.
5   What kind of a manager are you? Do you like to always have control or are you comfortable delegating to others?
6   Are you aware of the personal and/or professional ideologies that cause conflict or influence how you manage people?
7   How do you respond to conflict? Do you listen to all sides equally or do you personally feel that one group is more powerful or important than another?

REFERENCES

Barker, A. M. (2006) 'Human resource management strategies' in Barker, A. M., Sullivan, D. T. and Emery, M. J. (eds), *Leadership Competencies for Clinical Managers: The Renaissance of Transformational Leadership*. Boston: Jones and Bartlett (pp. 213–35).

Barker, A. M., Sullivan D. T. and Emery M. J. (eds) (2006) *Leadership Competencies for Clinical Managers: The Renaissance of Transformational Leadership*. Boston: Jones and Bartlett Publishers.

Burnard, P. (1997) *Effective Communication Skills for Health Professionals* (2nd edn). Cheltenham: Nelson Thornes.

DeVito, J. A. (2002) *Human Communication – The Basic Course* (9th edn). Massachusetts: Allyn & Bacon.

Forsyth, P. (2002) *Successful Negotiating: Getting What you Want in the Best Way Possible*. Oxford: How to Books.

Goleman, D. (1995) *Emotional Intelligence*. New York: Bantam Books.

Hargie, O. and Dickson, D. (2004) *Skilled Interpersonal Communication: Research, Theory and Practice* (4th edn). London: Routledge.

Masters, M. F. and Albright, R. R. (2002) *Conflict Resolution in the Workplace*. New York: American Management Association.

McCabe, C. and Timmins, F. (2006) *Communication Skills for Nursing Practice*. London: Palgrave Macmillan.

McCutcheon, D. (1998) 'Integrating doctors and managers' in Leahy, A. L. and Wiley, M. M. (eds), *The Irish Health System in the 21st Centruy*. Dublin: Oak Tree Publications (pp. 275–81).

Papa, M. J., Daniels, T. D. and Spiker, B. K. (2008) *Organizational Communication: Perspectives and Trends*. Los Angeles: Sage.

Porritt, L. (1990) *Interaction Strateties. An Introduction for Health Professionals* (2nd edn). Melbourne: Churchill Livingstone.

Putnam, L. L. and Poole, M. S. (1987) 'Conflict and negotiation' in Jablin, F. M., Putnam, L. L., Roberts, K. H. and Porter, L. W. (eds), *Handbook of Organizational Communication: An Interdisciplinary Perspective*. Newbury Park CA: Sage (pp. 549–99).

Shea, M. (1998) *The Primacy Effect: The Ultimate Guide to Effective Personal Communication*. London: Orion Business Books.

Smith, R. C. and Eisenberg, E. M. (2006) 'Conflict at Disneyland: a root-metaphor analysis' in Putnam, L. L. and Krone, K. J. (eds), *Organizational Communication: Cultures, Globalization, and Discourse*. London: Sage (pp. 98–113).

Thalhofer, N. N. (1993) 'Intergroup differentiation and reduction of intergroup conflict', *Small Group Research* 24(1): 28–43.

Yoder-Wise, P. (1999) *Leading and Managing in Nursing*. St Louis: Mosby.

9
Working in Teams
Sandra Fleming

OBJECTIVES
- To describe the meaning of interdisciplinary work practices in health care.
- To differentiate between teams and groups.
- To identify the stages of team development.
- To explore the architecture of integrated collaborative teamwork.
- To identify frameworks for developing teamwork competencies.
- To identify the benefits and barriers of teamwork in health care.

INTRODUCTION

In the last decade in Ireland interdisciplinary work practices have been reinforced by the publication of a number of key policy documents, including *Quality and Fairness: A Health System for You* (DoHC 2001a), *Primary Care: A New Direction* (DoHC 2001b) and, more recently, *Building a Culture of Patient Safety* (DoHC 2008a). Interdisciplinary collaborative work practices are high on the policy agenda in response to recent inquiries into health system failures, the Lourdes Hospital Inquiry (DoHC 2006), the Leas Cross Review (HSE 2006) and the Doherty Report (DoHC 2008b), among others. These inquiries identified a range of issues including poor management governance and a lack of teamworking and communication between health care professionals as contributory causes to poor care, diagnosis and treatment and made recommendations for improvements in these key areas.

These developments are not unique to Ireland: indeed, interdisciplinary work practices are increasingly becoming ubiquitous in the delivery of health care services, and are seen as one of the vehicles through which health care policy and best practice can be achieved. Inter-disciplinary teams do not naturally occur: clear vision, along with considerable resources, support and time, are necessary for their development, nurturing and success. It is therefore incumbent upon health care professionals to understand the concept and context of collaborative work practice and to develop the knowledge, skills and attitudes that will enable them to embrace change and respond effectively and efficiently to collaborative work practices, and in so doing to enhance the quality of patient care and service delivery throughout the stages of the patient health care journey. The onus is not only on the professionals involved but also requires supporting organisational systems to be put into place to address and meet the changes required to develop collaborative work practices.

This chapter will give an overview of the terminology used in the literature to describe collaborative practices and in so doing will seek to explore what is meant by interdisciplinary work practices. Within the architecture of integrated collaborative teamwork practices, issues pertaining to teams, teamwork, team development and team building will be addressed and, finally, benefits and barriers to teamworking in health care will be identified.

DEFINING INTERDISCIPLINARY COLLABORATION

The context within which health care is delivered is changing. Much of the activities of health care professionals in the twenty-first century involve working with other professionals in providing safe, efficient, effective, quality patient-centred care (Fitzgerald & Davison 2008; O'Shea 2008). Whilst O'Shea (2008), in identifying the future of health services in Ireland, reports that clinicians view teamwork positively, there is acknowledgement that moving to interdisciplinary work practices requires a big change in culture. The literature abounds with terms used to describe how people work together in teams in health care settings. Interprofessional, interdisciplinary, multidisciplinary, multiprofessional, transdisciplinary are some of the terms used in this 'terminological quagmire' (Leathard 1994:5). These terms are used interchangeably and there is an assumption that not only do professionals understand these terms, but that they are cognisant of the theoretical concepts underpinning them and that as health professionals they know how to work within them. This may not, however, be the case. Despite the definitions and distinctions regarding the terms cited in the literature, there is a lack of clarity and consensus about the precise meanings of the terms, and interpretation and meaning is further obscured by the interpretation of the prefix and/or the adjective used (Leathard 1994; McCallin 2001; Mental Health Commission 2006). The terms used most frequently to describe teams are multidisciplinary, interdisciplinary and transdisciplinary.

- **Multidisciplinary team** usually refers to a group of professionals from different disciplines working independently on the same project, and then sharing the information with each other (Sorrells-Jones 1997; Faulkner Schofield & Amodeo 1999; Paul & Peterson 2001).
- **Interdisciplinary team** denotes a deeper level of collaboration between professionals of different disciplines who, through a co-ordinated process, pool and share knowledge and expertise in an interdependent manner so that solutions can be found (Sorrells-Jones 1997; Paul & Peterson 2001; Faulkner Schofield & Amodeo 1999).
- **Transdisciplinary team** refers to the practice whereby there is deliberate sharing of knowledge, skills and expertise across the professions at all levels of patient care, to the extent that professional boundaries become blurred or vanish (Paul & Peterson 2001).

There are also inconsistencies in the use of the terms 'collaboration' and 'teamwork', terms associated with multidisciplinary and interprofessional practices, and whilst these terms are also used interchangeably in the literature, they are not synonymous (Clements *et al.* 2007). The term 'collaboration' denotes working in a collegial manner towards a common goal (D'Amour *et al.* 2005) and can be described as 'a process affecting teamwork … and an outcome in and of itself'(Clements *et al* 2007:28). It can take place whether or not professionals view themselves as part of a functioning team, whereas teamwork, if it is to be effective, requires collaboration by team members in meeting identified goals. Whilst Zwarenstein and Reeves (2000) state that there is little empirical evidence to support the efficacy of interdisciplinary collaboration, it is generally recognised in the literature that collaboration is desirable (Leathard 1994: Henneman *et al.* 1995), is an important element in total quality management, provides better care and increased level of worker satisfaction (Vyt 2008), and is a satisfying, efficient and effective way to provide health services (Martin-Rodriguez *et al.* 2005). Indeed, Henneman *et al.* (1995) assert that lack of collaboration may be pivotal in fragmentation of care, poor outcome and patient dissatisfaction.

Martin-Rodriguez *et al.* (2005:145) identified that 'collaboration is essentially an interpersonal process that requires the presence of a series of elements in the relationships between the professionals in a team. These include a willingness to collaborate, trust in each other, mutual respect and communication', concepts previously identified by D'Amour *et al.* (2005). However, Martin-Rodriguez *et al.* (2005), in acknowledging the necessity of the above conditions, posit that in complex health systems professionals alone cannot generate all the necessary conditions for success and identify the crucial role the organisation needs to play, particularly in relation to human resource management and leadership.

ARCHITECTURE OF COLLABORATIVE TEAMWORK
In an effort to further expand the concept of interdisciplinary collaborative teamwork practices it is pertinent to explore the architecture of collaboration and in so doing to address what constitutes a team, the meaning of teamwork, team development and team building.

What constitutes a team?
The term 'team' has various connotations and is open to various interpretations depending on the context in which it is used and the personal experience of team involvement of the individual. For some people it will have a sporting connotation (Belbin 1993; Rabey 2003), with players being selected for the ability and skills that they bring to the team, epitomised by esprit de corps, with each team member knowing their exact role and how to combine effectively with the other members of the team to win or be the best. In work-based contexts it can be used to describe many ways of working with others to achieve a common goal and a team can be assembled by either circumstance or selection, have a permanent or temporary life cycle, or be voluntarily or involuntarily constituted. Despite the various connotations associated with the term, teams are omnipotent and have become an accepted mode of working in the workplace: in fact it is difficult to find an organisation that does not rely on teams to some extent; and, indeed, in some

instances a team approach is mandated (Opie 1997).

> A team is a small group of people with complementary skills committed to a common purpose and set of specific performance goals. Its members are committed to working with each other and jointly accountable for the team's results.
>
> (Katzenbach & Smith 1993a:45).

There are many definitions of team presented in the literature, with the following dimensions in common: members integrating and working together towards the achievement of a common goal; sharing of responsibility; and mutual accountability (Katzenbach & Smith 1993a: WHO 1984).

In some of the management and academic literature the term 'team' is seen as synonymous with a working group and the two terms are used interchangeably. Firth-Cozens (1998) claims that all teams are groups, but not all groups are teams. This is echoed by Gulliver *et al.* (2002) and Katzenbach and Smith (1993a), who assert that bringing a group of professionals together and giving them a title does not create a team. Katzenbach and Smith (1993b) differentiate between a group and a team (Table 9.1) and state that within groups, members may share information and make decisions about performance standards that enable the person to do their job better, but the focus is on the individual taking responsibility for the achievement of their own individual goals, whereas a team is epitomised by synergy and a sense of shared commitment among members in working towards a common purpose (Katzenbach & Smith 1993b). Belbin (1993) views reciprocity and dynamic engagement of players as the essence of a team. Teams require both individual and mutual accountability (Katzenbach & Smith 1993b; Castka *et al.* 2003; Bamford & Griffin 2008) and common commitment, through which they become a 'powerful unit of collective performance', and this is what distinguishes them from working groups (Katzenbach & Smith 1993b:112).

Table 9.1: Differences between a group and a team

Working group	Team
Strong, clearly focused leader	Shared leadership roles
Individual accountability	Individual and mutual accountability
The group's purpose is the same as the broader organisational mission	Specific team purpose that the team itself delivers
Individual work-products	Collective work-products
Runs efficient meetings	Encourages open-ended discussion and active problem-solving meetings
Measures its effectiveness indirectly by its influence on others (e.g. financial performance of the business)	Measures performance directly by assessing collective work-products
Discusses, decides and delegates	Discusses, decides and does real work together

Source: Katzenbach & Smith (1993b:113)

The meaning of teamwork

It is important to point out that whilst there are many benefits to working in teams, the creation of a team does not automatically guarantee success and teams can fail for various reasons. Salas *et al.* (2005) propose that the success of a team can be credited to teamwork. Teamwork is about how the team works and the values that are inherent within and support the team, that enable people to work co-operatively and effectively with each other (Katzenbach & Smith 1993a). Salas *et al.* (2005:562) identified teamwork as 'a set of interrelated thoughts, actions, and feelings of each team member that are needed to function as a team and that combine to facilitate coordinated, adaptive performance and task objectives resulting in value-added outcomes'. Teamwork processes are manifested differently in different types of team and health care teams have different meanings and interpretations depending on the contexts in which they work (e.g. hospice care, acute care, mental health, primary health care, etc.), so one cannot assume that one size fits all. Issues pertaining to status, power and authority are important issues to take into consideration when bringing a team together from different health care professional backgrounds and their significance cannot be underestimated in developing collaborative work practices.

The team input (relating to the characteristics of task, context in which it occurs and attitudes of members), team process (the interaction and co-ordination of members in working together to achieve the task) and team outcomes (results from the team) framework has traditionally being used for conceptualising teamwork and team effectiveness (Baker *et al.* 2003). Teamwork is dynamic and can be influenced by a number of variables, such as the team environment, type of task and individual differences between team members among others, and over a period of time, as members learn to work together and become more skilled and competent in their task work, teams become more effective (Salas *et al.* 2005).

Team development

Models of team development describe various stages that the team goes through in relation to team building and learning the tasks, roles and expected performance and outcome required of the team. Payne (2000) puts forward two views of how teams develop: the developmental and the situational or contingency view. The developmental view acknowledges that teams go through various developmental stages, from initiation to disbandment of the team, during which the tasks, roles, performance and outcomes expected of members and of the team are identified and developed. The four-stage linear group developmental model described by Tuckman in 1965 and amended in 1977 to include a fifth stage (Tuckman 1965; Tuckman & Jensen 1977) is the most well known and the most extensively accepted model. The model consists of five sequential stages (Figure 9.1) – forming, storming, norming, performing and adjourning – that the group passes through before effective performance is achieved. The progression and course of group development can be affected by factors such as the group setting, purpose and dynamics (Tappen 2001) as well as the group's composition, relationships, tasks and experience (Kelly 2008), and adjourning may not take place as the lifespan of the team, particularly a health care team, may be indefinite and/or part of the working of the organisation; and teams may not pass through the stages sequentially. Indeed, Porter-O'Grady and Wilson (1998) maintain that team development is not a continuous seamless process but an intermittent incremental process that alternates between periods of activity and latency, forward and backward movements, which are representative of the relationships that exist between individuals and groups.

Figure 9.1: Model of group development

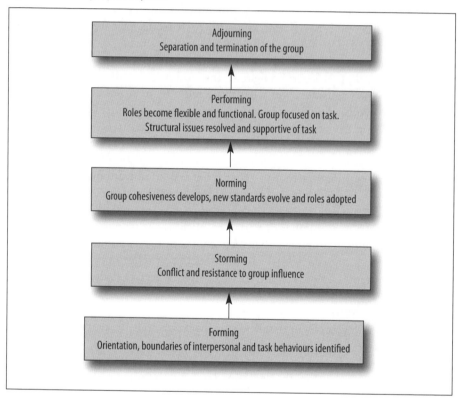

Source: Adapted from Tuckman (1965), Tuckman & Jansen (1977)

The situational or contingency view asserts that there is no 'one size fits all' approach. Within any organisation there may be a number of teams and each team will need a different approach to teamwork depending on the situations and contexts in which the teamwork takes place (Payne 2000; Salas *et al.* 2005; Lemieux-Charles and McGuire 2006). This is very pertinent to health care teams and is evident in Øvretveit's (1996) framework for describing health care multidisciplinary teams. The framework, developed from research into team organisation and developing multidisciplinary work in health services, consists of five dimensions:

- **Degree of integration** – closeness of working and integrating with others along a continuum from looseness to integrated.
- **Extent of collective responsibility** – accountability for service provision.
- **Membership** – in relation to who is a member and what that means, skill mix and number of professionals.
- **Client pathway and decision-making** – client referral process and how decisions are made about who does what and when.
- **Management structures** – the structures for managing and leading members of different professions.

The situational view will become even more significant in the future, particularly in light of the proliferation of virtual networked teams in health care, not only within organisations but also across organisations and jurisdictions.

Building an effective team

Bringing members of different professions together to work in a team does not automatically confer teamwork or collaboration (Katzenbach & Smith 1993a; Salas *et al.* 2005) and whilst the literature abounds with evidence in relation to the benefits of teams and teamwork, both for the team members and for the organisation, Klein *et al.* (2009:182) caution that the existence of a team-based organising structure is not enough to guarantee positive outcomes: 'teams must be nurtured, supported and developed'. Teamwork has its roots in the human relations movement: as a result, much of the literature on teamwork is from business corporations and may not directly translate into the more complex health care setting in which professionals from different disciplines come together to work within a team (Payne 2000), bringing with them differences emanating from their professional socialisation, theoretical perspectives, values, skills and working practices (Porter-O'Grady & Wilson 1998). Indeed, Martin-Rodriguez *et al.* (2005) assert that members of each profession know very little about professionals in other disciplines and this lack of knowledge, understanding and appreciation of these differences constitutes one of the main obstacles to collaborative practice in health care. Creating a culture for developing collaborative practices between health care professionals is challenging to both policy makers and organisational managers (Martin-Rodriguez *et al.* 2005) and it is crucial that these are aligned, for in the absence of opportunities for team training, team building, systems and structures to support collaborative practice there is a likelihood that professionals will revert to their more traditional practice of working alongside each other (Cashman *et al.* 2004). Porter-O'Grady and Wilson (1998) acknowledge that forming teams is easy; the challenge is in maintaining them. Yet, despite this, health care organisations invest substantial monies into establishing teams but little into sustaining and supporting them. Indeed, this imbalance is evident in the literature available on promoting and maintaining collaboration in health care, with less written on the latter (Freeth 2001).

Organisational structure

Effective team performance requires personal, collective and organisational commitment in working towards a common goal and depends on organisational support and resources, effective communication within the team and an acknowledgement and appreciation of the roles and abilities of team members. Traditionally, health care has been managed and delivered through vertical models of service delivery (Porter-O'Grady & Wilson 1998; Baker *et al.* 2003), an organisational system supported by autocratic hierarchical management infrastructures not conducive to an environment for the emergence of the conditions underpinning collaborative practices such as teamwork and shared decision-making (Evans 1994).

In response to the complexity of and changes in population health care and the need to deliver care and services within allocated resources, horizontal continuum-based models are emerging as the predominant framework for supporting and structuring health services (Porter-O'Grady & Wilson 1998; Government of Ireland 2008). Whilst it has been shown that a planned systematic approach incorporating a multidisciplinary collaborative and integrated system of care and service delivery is more effective than the traditional isolated approach (Government of Ireland 2008), one cannot ignore that this necessitates a significant paradigm shift at every level of the organisation in the move from a hierarchical towards a new horizontal organisational design (Henneman *et al.* 1995, Porter-O'Grady & Wilson 1998) that supports teamwork and epitomises the four national goals identified in the Department of Health and Children's health strategy: 'Better health for everyone, fair access, responsive and appropriate care delivery and high performance' (DoH&C 2001a:59). Porter-O'Grady and Wilson (1998:36) identify 'integration, linkage, continuum, teams, partnership, clinical pathways and strong service orientation' as the characteristics of these newer organisational models within health care, whilst Borrill *et al.* (2000) identify the fundamental principles underpinning the management philosophy of team-based organisations as including the following.

- Organisational goals are achieved by groups working efficiently and effectively in teams who monitor the effectiveness of their strategies and processes and share responsibility for outcomes.
- Managers listen to and encourage the views of the members.
- Emphasis on sharing and integration across and between teams, reducing the number of organisational levels and moving from a vertical to a flat organisation structure.
- Encouraging and supporting innovation and creativity and adapting to changing environments.
- Employees are clear about the objectives of the organisation and are committed to and encouraged to influence the development of the organisation.
- Through debate, employees are encouraged to be fully involved in and to

contribute to decision-making processes and to reflect upon and adapt to changes as the team develops.
- Training and education priorities of the organisation are geared towards developing and supporting team-based working.

Team role theory

When an individual is appointed to a job it is usually on the basis of the technical or professional skills and expertise that they possess and that are necessary to do the job (Belbin 1993). Belbin refers to this as the functional role and distinguishes it from the team role, which relates to the way in which a person behaves, contributes and interrelates with others in doing their job. The team role may not be as evident as the functional role and within an interdisciplinary team there may be many variations in the team roles that members have. Therefore people come to a team with functional and team roles and whilst the functional role of nurse, physiotherapist or doctor may be obvious, the team role may not be apparent. From his work with management teams Meredith Belbin developed his team role theory in 1981, with further developments in 1993, in which he identified team roles that need to be filled for optimal operationalisation to be achieved within management teams (see Table 9.2). Belbin's team role hypothesis posits that teams that have all the team roles represented or 'balanced' are self-contained and work better than those that are 'unbalanced' through overrepresentation or absence of roles. Acknowledging that an individual may have more than one natural team role that they bring to a team, Belbin (2004:73) contends that:

> The useful people to have on teams are those who possess strengths or characteristics which serve a need without duplicating those already there. Teams are a question of balance. What is needed is not well balanced individuals but individuals who balance well with one another. In that way, human frailties can be underpinned and strengths used to full advantage.

The Team Role Self-Perception Inventory (TRSPI) diagnostic tool for identifying the individual's team role has been, and continues to be, used extensively for team development and for predicting team performance. It enables the individual to understand their role in relation to how they interact with people within the team, and this knowledge can be used to manage one's strengths and weaknesses in the role and in so doing work more effectively within the team. However, Belbin's work is not without its critics and his work has been challenged, mainly in relation to its psychometric properties. Taking cognisance of the criticisms of the psychometric properties of the TRSPI reported in the literature, Swailes and McIntyre-Bhatty's (2003) study is more supportive of the instrument's reliability and structure than previously reported in the literature. This is further substantiated by Aritzeta et al.'s (2007) extensive review of 43 empirical studies on Belbin's Team Role Model, which also confirmed the validity of the definitions of the team roles. Another criticism of Belbin's work is that it is a theory for management teams as opposed to general theory for teams. Fisher et al. (2002)

asserted that, irrespective of the level of the team within an organisation, the behaviours inherent in each of the team roles is needed in making decisions and by limiting the theory role typology to management teams alone, opportunities may be missed for improving team performance in non-managerial teams within an organisation. In view of the research on the TRSPI there is evidence to support the identification of team roles within a team and this is something that could be explored within multidisciplinary teams.

Table 9.2: Belbin's team roles

Team roles		Team role contribution
Social-based roles	Co-ordinator	Recognises team's strengths and weaknesses and makes the best use of each team member's potential; clarifies goals and delegates well.
	Resource Investigator	Enthusiastic; explores and reports on ideas, developments, etc.; creates and makes useful contact for the team.
	Teamworker	Co-operative; promotes communication; diplomatic; fosters team spirit; supports members in their strengths.
Thinking/ cerebral-based roles	Plant	Imaginative and creative; advances new ideas and solves problems.
	Monitor Evaluator	Strategic; analyses problems and options so that team can make balanced decisions.
	Specialist	Dedicated; supplies knowledge and skills in rare supply.
Action-based roles	Shaper	Challenging and dynamic; sets goals and priorities; drive to overcome obstacles.
	Implementer	Disciplined and efficient; turns concepts and plans into procedures and carries out plans.
	Completer –Finisher	Conscientious; thorough; searches out omissions and errors.

Source: Adapted from Belbin (1993:23); reproduced with kind permission of Belbin Associates (www.belbin.com)

Team boundaries

Role clarity is important not only in relation to functional and team role, it is also significant when looking at professional boundaries within the team and in goal setting. Collaborative working is synergistic, with team members knowing what is distinctive and complementary about the roles of the members within the team. Sundstrom *et al.* (1990) identify that boundaries separate and link teams within the organisation, define how a team operates and are linked to team effectiveness. Rushmer and Pallis (2003) and Rushmer (2005) use connate theory to illustrate and analyse the relationships between people and to differentiate between integrated working practices and blurred boundaries in health care teams. They assert that clear boundaries, which must be specific, negotiated and open to review, are essential for integrated working. Rushmer (2005:77) defines connate theory as a 'visual metaphor which aims to make relationships between people and groups transparent and open to analysis. Complex relationships are rendered visual, so that the way the diagrams **look** says something about the way the relationship **is**'.

Figure 9.2: The individual in context

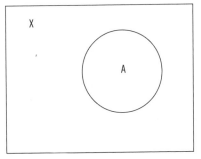

Source: Rushmer & Pallis (2003:61)

The health professional (A) is depicted in their entirety as a circle with clear boundaries (Figure 9.2), within which is contained everything that the person is, e.g. the professional's job-related and personal characteristics, knowledge, skills and attitudes, etc. X represents the context within which A works and consists of cultural norms, situational constraints, knowledge, skills and attitudes that are outside the person's control or expertise. In this diagram A's boundaries are explicit and they know what they can or cannot do within X.

In successful interdisciplinary teamworking (Figure 9.3) two professionals or two groups of professionals, A and B, have clearly differentiated boundaries. Y represents the areas that through consensus have been clearly identified as areas they have in common and share. Y has clear boundaries: this is where synergy occurs and integrated working becomes possible. The bigger this area, the more skills, expertise, etc. A and B have negotiated and share. Each person's or group's circle is still intact and members are aware of and respect each others' boundaries, so blurring of boundaries

Figure 9.3: Integrative working (successful interprofessional working: teamworking)

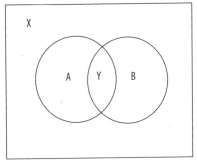

Source: Rushmer & Pallis (2003:62)

does not take place. The area not included in the overlap represents the uniqueness of skills, expertise and contribution that they bring to the team and utilise in achieving the team's goal.

When there is lack of clarity about responsibility, task allocation, expertise, etc. the boundaries between A and B disappear (Figure 9.4): there is no boundary around the area of overlap (Y in Figure 9.3), and boundaries become blurred. This can result in lack of clarity, role ambiguity and uncertainty, misunderstandings, stress and anxiety, leading eventually to the relationship becoming unsustainable.

As mentioned previously, one cannot assume that professionals will have all the

Figure 9.4: Blurred boundaries (ineffective interprofessional working: failed teamworking)

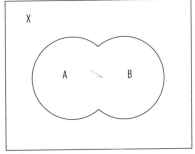

Source: Rushmer & Pallis (2003:63)

skills, competencies and prerequisites needed for working collaboratively, so they may require support in enabling them to identify and negotiate areas of integration within professional boundaries. However, gaining an understanding of and valuing the roles of the members within the team can facilitate the process of interdisciplinary collaboration (Molyneux 2001). Connate theory can be used with teams to work out, clarify and negotiate areas of responsibility that they share and have in common before the team becomes operational and in so doing this will lessen the likelihood of boundary blurring occurring. Feedback on the use of connate theory suggests that it assists and encourages professionals on their journey towards integrative working (Rushmer 2005).

DEVELOPING COLLABORATIVE TEAMWORK

Generally health care professionals come to or are invited on to an interdisciplinary team because of their expertise and professional skills in a particular clinical area or discipline. One cannot assume that they will also bring with them the attributes required to collaborate effectively within the team to enable the team to achieve its goal. Clements *et al.* (2007:31–2) identify the following factors underpinning success in implementing collaborative practices: leadership to drive the process; role clarity of team members; trust, respect and being valued; cultural readiness; and acceptance. Factors underpinning failure include: lack of time to enable people to reflect and change; lack of or insufficient interprofessional education; lack of reward for collaboration; few links between collaborative practice and individual goals; and lack of efforts to capture evidence for success and disseminate results to key stakeholders.

Numerous models and frameworks of team effectiveness are discussed in the generic literature, among which are: the ecological framework for analysing work team effectiveness (Sundstrom *et al.* 1990); themes and characteristics related to work group effectiveness (Campion *et al.* 1993); and the 'big five' in teamwork (Salas *et al.* 2005). Within health care settings, the health teams model (Mickan & Rodger 2005); the integrated (health care) team effectiveness model (Lemieux-Charles & McGuire 2006); the input, process and output model of team effectiveness (Bamford & Griffin 2008); and knowledge, skill and ability (KSA) requirements for teamwork (Stevens & Campion 1994) are among some of the team effectiveness models and frameworks that have been utilised and appraised.

In recent times there has been a shift in the literature from focusing on generic teamwork skills to specifying competencies, i.e. the qualities or attributes required by the individual team member to successfully engage within the team (Baker *et al.* 2003). Borrill *et al.* (2000) recommend that selection of team members should focus on the individuals' knowledge, skills and attitudes to teamworking as well as their professional skills. The knowledge, skills and abilities (KSAs) framework (Table 9.3) focuses on the management of individuals within the team and identifies the KSAs required of an effective team member. It consists of 14 specific KSAs categorised into two main dimensions, interpersonal KSAs and self-management KSAs. The former dimension is categorised into three KSA sub-categories that take cognisance of the interpersonal and social demands placed on employees in a team setting, with the latter dimension comprising two KSA subcategories that the team member should possess so that they can contribute to the team's success in self-managing itself. Acknowledging that the framework was developed for staffing and selection, Stevens and Campion (1999) identify that it could have potential as a framework for developing training and development activities. The generic KSAs can be imparted effectively through training (Kozlowski & Ilgen 2006) and it is within this team-building context that the framework is presented here.

Table 9.3: Knowledge, skills and ability (KSA) requirements for teamwork

I. Interpersonal Knowledge, Skills and Abilities (KSAs)	
A Conflict Resolution KSAs	1 Recognise and encourage desirable team conflict but discourage undesirable conflict.
	2 Recognise the type and source of conflict confronting the team and implement an appropriate conflict resolution strategy.
	3 To employ an integrative (win-win) negotiation strategy rather than the traditional (win-lose) strategies.
B Collaborative Problem- solving KSAs	4 Identify situations requiring participative group problem-solving and utilise the proper degree and type of participation.
	5 Recognise the obstacles to collaborative group problem solving and implement appropriate corrective actions.
C Communication KSAs	6 To understand communication network, and utilise decentralised networks to enhance communication where possible.
	7 To communicate openly and supportively, that is send messages which are: (a) behaviour or event-focused; (b) congruent; (c) validating; (d) conjunctive; and (e) owned.
	8 To listen non-evaluatively and appropriately use active listening techniques.
	9 To maximise consonance between non-verbal and verbal messages, and recognise and interpret the non-verbal messages of others.
	10 To engage in ritual greetings and small talk, and recognise their importance.
II. Self-Management KSAs	
D Goal Setting and Performance Management KSAs	11 To help establish specific, challenging and accepted team goals.
	12 To monitor, evaluate and provide feedback on both overall team performance and individual team member performance.
E Planning and Task Co-ordination KSAs	13 To co-ordinate and synchronise activities, information and task interdependencies between team members.
	14 To help establish task and role expectations of individual team members, and ensure proper balancing of workload in the team.

Source: Stevens & Campion (1994:505); reproduced with permission of Sage Publications

In their conceptual framework for describing team competencies, Cannon-Bowers *et al.* (1995) identify three types of competency or attributes that are crucial for effective teamwork: teamwork-related knowledge; skills; and attitudes. Teamwork-related knowledge competencies are required by members to function and communicate as a successful team. This means that members need to know the team's mission and goals, to have an awareness of the roles and responsibilities of team members in co-ordinating specific tasks in achieving the goals, and to know the range of skills and behaviours required and how these manifest within the team (Cannon-Bowers *et al.* 1995; Baker *et al.* 2003).

The level of interaction among team members is depicted within teamwork-related skill competencies and is classified into eight categories that have been shown to be directly related to effective performance: adaptability; shared situation awareness; leadership; performance monitoring/feedback; and interpersonal, communication, decision-making and co-ordination skills (Cannon-Bowers *et al.* 1995).

Teamwork-related attitude competencies refer to the 'internal state that influences' a team member to act in a specific way (Cannon-Bowers *et al.* 1995:352) and includes cohesion, collective orientation and efficacy. Mutual trust, positive attitudes towards the team and teamwork have been shown to be some of the essential attributes for successful team processes (Baker *et al.* 2003).

As the composition of the team changes and personnel who have been key enthusiasts and supporters in commencing and sustaining collaboration move on, new members may join the team. Joining a team can be a very formidable prospect for the newcomer. New members may or may not have experience of working in such a team, or have the same commitment to the team objectives as the rest of the members who have been privy to the clarification of roles, objectives, successes and setbacks in setting up the initiative. To ensure that team commitment, cohesiveness and effectiveness are not affected by changes to the membership of the team, it is imperative that strong links are formed with new members, through induction and team building, so that they can recognise the value and benefits of collaboration (Leathard 1994; Freeth 2001) to enable them to fit in and become part of the team.

TEAMWORK BENEFITS AND BARRIERS

Whilst the literature abounds with evidence on the benefits of teamwork in aviation, firefighting and manufacturing, it is only within the last decade or two that a growing body of empirical evidence to support the benefits of teamwork in health care has emerged (Clements *et al.* 2007). Benefits of teamwork include improved financial outcomes, reduced absenteeism and staff turnover, staff motivation, reduced conflict, higher quality of care, increased and better patient outcomes (Firth-Cozens 1998, 2001). Borrill *et al.* (2000) found that teamworking promoted effectiveness in the NHS and in their comprehensive review of the literature they highlight the research evidence that identifies among the benefits of teamwork in health care a reduction in hospitalisation rates, resulting in cost savings, improved and cost-effective service provision and increased patient and staff satisfaction.

Whilst acknowledging that teams and teamworking do not provide the panacea to every organisational need (Katzenbach & Smith 1993a), they do have many benefits. Within health care, multidisciplinary teams have been shown to contribute to efficient and effective practice and improved quality of care and service (Borrill *et al.* 2000; Carter *et al.* 2003; Moroney & Knowles 2006; Government of Ireland 2008) and a satisfying way to offer health services (Martin-Rodriguez *et al.* 2005). Developing clarity and understanding of the role of professionals from various disciplines is another benefit of teamworking (Mental Health Commission 2006). In fact Davies (2000) asserts that it is not what professionals have in common that makes collaborative work more powerful than working independently, but rather the differences between them. This is substantiated by van der Vegt and Bunderson's (2005) study of teams, which (although composed mainly of scientists, technicians and engineers) has resonance for health care teams: they found that under the right conditions expertise diversity can promote learning and innovation and overall team effectiveness.

The hierarchical culture of health care is identified as the greatest barrier to teamwork (Clements *et al.* 2007). Power, status and authority have also been recognised as barriers and from the nurse's perspective the dominance of medical power was seen as a factor affecting the interactions between members of the interdisciplinary team (Atwal & Caldwell 2006). Other barriers include the amount of time team development takes (Kelly 2008), lack of resources and opportunities for team building, professional rivalry (Mental Health Commission 2006) and role blurring and confusion (Faulkner Schofield & Amodeo 1999). The long-standing traditions of health care professions with different cultures, values, educational and socialisation processes, well-defined boundaries (Hall 2005; Fitzgerald & Davison 2008), rigidly circumcised professional jurisdictions and scope of practice (Leiba 1996; D'Amour *et al.* 2005, Clements *et al.* 2007), and lack of understanding of the unique skills of other professionals (Mental Health Commission 2006) can result in power issues and conflict between professional groups.

There are many benefits associated with teamwork; however, the greatest challenge in developing effective teamwork is to understand the barriers that impede teamwork and to capitalise on this understanding when inculcating and developing a culture that supports collaborative teamwork.

CONCLUSION

It is unlikely that in today's health care system any one group of professionals on their own will be able to address all the needs of the client. Thus it is acknowledged that, as health care continues to become more specialised, complex and technical, more health care professionals will be required to collaborate and integrate their knowledge and expertise and through cross-fertilisation of ideas and expertise work together to provide good-quality care to the patient. Teams are an attractive vehicle for bringing together professionals with the relevant areas of expertise, whereby individual and collective knowledge and expertise can be utilised in providing high-quality and seamless patient care with resulting benefits for patients, their families, health professionals and the organisation.

REFLECTIVE QUESTIONS

1 Identify the types of team in your workplace.
2 Reflect on the purpose and membership of those teams and how they may differ from teams that you may have been involved with on previous occasions.
3 What role do you have in the team?
4 What strengths do you bring to the team?
5 What impact/effect does your role have within the team and on patient care?
6 Think about the groups that you have been involved with in your work practice. What was the composition of the groups and how did they work?
7 In relation to group development, reflect on the knowledge, skills, attitudes and competencies that you brought to the group at each stage of group development.
8 How does working in an interdisciplinary team impact on your practice?

ADDITIONAL RESOURCES

Belbin, M. R.: www.belbin.com/
Borrill, C. and West, M. (2001) *How Good is Your Team? A Guide for Team Members.* Birmingham: Aston Centre of Health Service Organisation Research (ACHSOR), Aston University. Section 1 includes a team working questionnaire, scoring sheet and interpreting scores. Section 2 includes team development techniques. Available from http://www.nimhe.csip.org.uk /silo/files/how-good-is-your-teampdf.pdf
Pritchard, P. and Pritchard, J. (1992) *Developing Teamwork in Primary Health Care. A Practical Workbook.* Oxford. Oxford University Press.
HSE Learning and Development publications: http://pnd.hseland.ie/corp/ ohmpublications/ohmpublications.html
Online team effectiveness assessment: www.mindtools.com/pages/article/ newTMM_84.htm
Tim Porter-O'Grady Associates: www.tpogassociates.com/home.htm

REFERENCES

Aritzeta, A., Swailes, S. and Senior, B. (2007) 'Belbin's Team Role Model: development, validity and applications for team building', *Journal of Management Studies* 44(1): 96–118.

Atwal, A. and Caldwell, K. (2006) 'Nurses' perceptions of multidisciplinary team work in acute health-care', *International Journal of Nursing Practice* 12:359–65.

Baker, D. P., Gustafson, S., Beaubien, J., Salas, E. and Barach, P. (2003) *Medical Teamwork and Patient Safety: The Evidence-Based Relation*. Rockville: Agency for Healthcare Research and Quality.

Bamford, D. and Griffin, M. (2008) 'A case study into operational team-working within a UK hospital', *International Journal of Operations and Production Management* 28(3): 215–37.

Belbin, M. R. (1993) *Team Roles at Work*. Oxford: Butterworth Heinemann.

— (2004) *Management Teams: Why they Succeed or Fail* (2nd edn). Oxford: Elsevier Butterworth Heinemann.

Borrill, C. S., Carletta, J., Carter, A. J., Garrod, S., Rees, A., Richards, A., Shapiro, D. and West, M. A. (2000) *The Effectiveness of Health Care Teams in the National Health Service: Report*. Birmingham: Aston Centre of Health Service Organisation Research (ACHSOR), Aston University.

Campion, M. A., Medsker, G. J. and Higgs, A. C. (1993) 'Relations between work group characteristics and effectiveness: implications for designing effective groups', *Personnel Psychology* 46(4): 823–50.

Cannon-Bowers, J. A., Tannenbaum, S. I., Salas, E. and Volpe, C. E. (1995) 'Defining competencies and establishing team training requirements' in Guzzo, R. A., Salas, E. and Associates, *Team Effectiveness and Decision Making in Organisations*. San Francisco: Jossey-Bass (pp. 333–80).

Carter, S., Garside, P. and Black, A. (2003) 'Multidisciplinary team working, clinical networks, and chambers; opportunities to work differently in the NHS', *Quality and Safety in Health Care* 12: i25–8.

Cashman, S. B., Reidy, P., Cody, K. and Lemay, C. A. (2004) 'Developing and measuring progress toward collaborative, integrated, interdisciplinary health care teams', *Journal of Interprofessional Care* 18(2): 183–96.

Castka, P., Sharp, J. M. and Bamber, C. J. (2003) 'Assessing teamwork development to improve organizational performance', *Measuring Business Excellence* 7(4): 29–36.

Clements, D., Dault, M. and Priest, A. (2007) 'Effective teamwork in healthcare: research and reality', *Healthcare Papers* 7(Sp): 26–34.

D'Amour, D., Ferrada-Videla, M., Rodriguez, L. S. M. and Beaulieu, M.-D. (2005) 'The conceptual basis for interprofessional collaboration: core concepts and theoretical frameworks', *Journal of Interprofessional Care* 19(2): 116–31.

Davies, C. (2000) 'Getting health professionals to work together', *British Medical Journal* 320 (7241): 1021–2.

DoHC (Department of Health and Children) (2001a) *Quality and Fairness: A Health System for You*. Dublin: Stationery Office.

— (2001b) *Primary Care: A New Direction*, Dublin: Stationery Office.

— (2006) *The Lourdes Hospital Inquiry: An Inquiry into Peripartum Hysterectomy at Our Lady of Lourdes Hospital Drogheda*. Report of Judge Maureen Harding Clark SC. Dublin: Stationery Office.

— (2008a) *Building a Culture of Patient Safety: Report of the Commission on Patient Safety and Quality Assurance*. Dublin: Stationery Office.

— (2008b). *Report on the Circumstances that led to the Decision by the HSE in August 2007 to: Suspend Breast Radiology Services; Initiate a Clinical Review of Symptomatic Breast Radiology Services; Place Consultant Radiologist on Administrative Leave, at Midland Regional Hospital, Portlaoise* (Doherty Report). Dublin: DoHC.

Evans, J. A. (1994) 'The role of the nurse manager in creating an environment for collaborative practice', *Holistic Nurse Practice* 8(3): 22–31.

Faulkner Schofield, R. and Amodeo, M. (1999) 'Interdisciplinary teams in health care and human services settings: are they effective?', *Health and Social Work* 24(3): 210–19.

Firth-Cozens, J. (1998) 'Celebrating teamwork', *Quality in Health Care* 7 (Suppl): S2–7.

— (2001) 'Multidisciplinary teamwork: the good, bad, and everything in between', *Quality in Health Care* 10: 65–9.

Fisher, S. G., Hunter, T. A., Macrosson, W. D. K. (2002) 'Belbin's team role theory: for non-managers also?', *Journal of Managerial Psychology* 17(1): 14–20.

Fitzgerald, A. and Davison, G. (2008) 'Innovative health care delivery teams', *Journal of Health Organization and Management* 22(2): 129–46.

Freeth, D. (2001) 'Sustaining interprofessional collaboration', *Journal of Interprofessional Care* 15(1): 37–46.

Government of Ireland (2008) *Building a Culture of Patient Safety*. Report of the Commission on Patient Safety and Quality Assurance. Dublin: Stationery Office.

Gulliver, P., Peck, E. and Towell, D. (2002) 'Balancing professional and team boundaries in mental health services: pursuing the holy grail in Somerset', *Journal of Interprofessional Care* 16(4): 259–370.

Hall, P. (2005) 'Interprofessional teamwork: professional cultures as barriers', *Journal of Interprofessional Care* 19(2): 188–96.

Henneman, E. A., Lee, J. L. and Cohen, J. I. (1995) 'Collaboration: a concept analysis', *Journal of Advanced Nursing* 21(1): 103–9.

HSE (Health Service Executive) (2006) *Leas Cross Review*. Dublin: HSE.

Katzenbach, J. R. and Smith, D. K. (1993a) *The Wisdom of Teams: Creating the High-Performance Organisation*. Boston: Harvard Business School Press.

— (1993b) 'The discipline of teams', *Harvard Business Review* March–April: 71(2): 111–20.

Kelly, P. (2008) *Nursing Leadership and Management* (2nd edn). New York: Thomson Delmar Learning.

Klein, D., DiazGranados, D., Salas, E. L. H., Burke, C. S., Lyons, R. and Goodwin, G.F. (2009) 'Does team building work?', *Small Group Research* 40(2): 181–222.

Kozlowski, S. W. J. and Ilgen, D. R. (2006) 'Enhancing the effectiveness of work groups and teams', *Psychological Science in the Public Interest* 7(3): 77–124.

Leathard, A. (ed.) (1994) *Going Inter-Professional: Working Together for Health and Welfare*. London: Routledge.

Leiba, T. (1996) 'Interprofessional and multi-agency training and working', *British Journal of Community Health Nursing* 1(1): 8–12.

Lemieux-Charles, L. and McGuire, W. L. (2006) 'What do we know about health care team effectiveness? A review of the literature', *Medical Care Research and Review* 63(3): 263–300.

Martin-Rodriguez, L. S., Beaulieu, M.-D., D'Amour, D. and Ferrada-Videla, M. (2005) 'The determinants of successful collaboration: a review of theoretical and empirical studies', *Journal of Interprofessional Care* 19(2): 132–47.

McCallin, A. (2001) 'Interdisciplinary practice – a matter of teamwork: an integrated literature review', *Journal of Clinical Nursing* 10: 419–28.

Mental Health Commission (2006) *Multidisciplinary Team Working: From Theory to Practice*. Discussion Paper. Dublin: Mental Health Commission.

Mickan, S. M. and Rodger, S. A. (2005) 'Effective health care teams: a model of six characteristics developed from shared perceptions', *Journal of Interprofessional Care* 1994: 358–70.

Molyneux, J. (2001) 'Interprofessional teamworking: what makes teams work well', *Journal of Interprofessional Care* 15(1): 29–35.

Moroney, N. and Knowles, C. (2006) 'Innovation and teamwork: introducing multidisciplinary team ward rounds', *Nursing Management* 13(1): 28–31.

Opie, A. (1997) 'Effective team work in health care: a review of issues discussed in recent research literature', *Healthcare Analysis* 5(1): 62–73.

O'Shea, Y. (2008) *Nursing and Midwifery in Ireland: A Strategy for Professional Development in a Changing Health Service*. Dublin: Blackhall.

Øvretveit, J. (1996) 'Five ways to describe a multidisciplinary team', *Journal of Interprofessional Care* 10(2): 163–71.

Paul, S. and Peterson, C. Q. (2001) 'Interprofessional collaboration: issues for practice and research', *Occupational Therapy in Health Care* 15(3/4): 1–12.

Payne, M. (2000) *Teamwork in Multiprofessional Care*. Basingstoke: Macmillan.

Porter-O'Grady, T. and Wilson, C. K. (1998) *The Healthcare Teambook*. St Louis: Mosby.

Rabey, G. (2003) 'The paradox of teamwork', *Industrial and Commercial Training* 35(4): 158–62.

Rushmer, R. (2005) 'Blurred boundaries damage inter-professional working', *Nurse Researcher* 12(3): 74–85.

Rushmer, R. and Pallis, G. (2003) 'Inter-professional working: the wisdom of integrated working and the disaster of blurred boundaries', *Public Money and Management* 23(1): 59–66.

Salas, E., Sims, D. E. and Burke, C. S. (2005) 'Is there a "Big Five" in teamwork?', *Small Group Research* 36(5): 555–99.

Sorrells-Jones, J. (1997) 'The challenge of making it real: interdisciplinary practice in a "seamless" organisation', *Nursing Administration Quarterly* 21(2): 20–30.

Stevens, M. J. and Campion, M.A. (1994) 'The knowledge, skill and ability requirements for teamwork: implications for human resource management', *Journal of Management* 20(2): 503–30.

— (1999) 'Staffing work teams: development and validation of a selection test for teamwork settings', *Journal of Management* 25(2): 207–28.

Sundstrom, E., De Meuse, K. P. and Futrell, D. (1990) 'Work teams: applications and effectiveness', *American Psychologist* 45(2):120–133.

Swailes, S. and McIntyre-Bhatty, T. (2003) 'Scale structure of the team role self perception inventory', *Journal of Occupational and Organizational Psychology* 76(4): 525–9.

Tappen, R. M. (2001) *Nursing Leadership and Management Concepts and Practice* (4th edn). Philadelphia: F. A. Davis.

Tuckman, B. W. (1965) 'Developmental sequence in small groups', *Psychological Bulletin* 63(3): 384–399.

Tuckman, B. W. and Jensen, M. A. C. (1977) 'Stages of small-group development revisited', *Group and Organization Studies* 2(4): 419–27.

van der Vegt, G. S. and Bunderson, J. S. (2005) 'Learning and performance in multidisciplinary teams: the importance of collective team identification', *Academy of Management Journal* 48(3): 532–47.

Vyt, A. (2008) 'Interprofessional and transdisciplinary teamwork in healthcare', *Diabetes/Metabolism Research and Reviews* 24(Suppl. 1): S106–9.

WHO (World Health Organization) (1984) *Glossary of Terms Used in the 'Health for All' Series No. 1–8*. Geneva: WHO.

Zwarenstein, M. and Reeves, S. (2000) 'What's so great about collaboration?', *British Medical Journal* 320(7241): 1022–3.

10
Work Motivation

Elizabeth A. Curtis

> **OBJECTIVES**
>
> - To define motivation and explain the difference between content theories and process theories of motivation.
> - To identify and describe a content theory of motivation.
> - To identify and describe a process theory of motivation.
> - To acknowledge and discuss the importance of leadership in motivation.
> - To describe the relationship between motivation and performance.
> - To explain the importance of improving motivation in the workplace and discuss how you would go about doing this.

INTRODUCTION

Motivation is one of the principal topics in the social sciences and one of the first to be researched in psychology (Rainey 1993; Muchinsky 1993). Theories of motivation regarded as some of the most grand of theories were originally developed to explain why people behave the way they do. These theories, however, did not really explain motivation of workers. So another set of theories to explain the behaviour of people in the work environment was developed by psychologists. According to Muchinsky (1993), '. . . these theories are more concentrated in scope. They deal with human motivation in a refined context of which work motivation is but a subset.'

This chapter does not provide the reader with a comprehensive resource on motivation. This already exists in the form of entire books on the topic (Long 2005; Wong 2000; Brown 2000), several chapters in psychology (Spector 2006; Golembiewski 1993; Jewell 1998; Muchinsky 1993) and management (Hughes *et al.* 2006; Sullivan and Decker 2005; Daft 2000; Marquis & Huston 2000) books and many research papers (Schepers *et al.* 2005; Kanfer & Ackerman 2004; Benson & Dundis 2003; Stajkovic & Luthans 2001; Edgar 1999). Rather, the purpose of the chapter is to introduce the health care professional to the topic of motivation and draw attention to the fact that nursing managers and health service administrators must endeavour to promote motivation among staff in their units and organisations.

The chapter begins with an overview of the conceptual and theoretical literature on motivation. It then moves on to describe theories of motivation and summarises four theories. Next, it discusses the role of leadership in motivation and explores the relationship between motivation and performance. Whether or not validated theories are developed, employers and managers must think of ways to motivate employees in their organisations. Therefore, the chapter discusses some of the strategies that could be used to improve motivation in the workplace. In health care, few research studies have examined motivation, so the chapter synopsises some of the research studies that have been carried out by health care professionals. The chapter concludes with some suggestions for future research.

EXPLAINING AND MEASURING MOTIVATION

Most people think they know what motivation is, yet many researchers in the field find it difficult to define. Approximately 140 definitions have been identified (Kleinginna & Kleinginna 1981). The word 'motivation' derives from the Latin term *motus*, which means 'to move' (Steers & Porter 1987). In defining motivation, Rainey (1993:20) states, 'By motivation, we mean the degree to which a person is moved or aroused to expend effort to achieve some purpose. Work motivation on the other hand refers to how much a person tries to work hard and well – to the arousal, direction, and persistence of effort in work settings.'

Distinctions between motivation and other concepts such as job satisfaction have also been explored by motivation theorists. Job satisfaction is defined as 'an attitudinal variable that reflects how people feel about their jobs overall as well as various aspects of them. In simple terms, job satisfaction is the extent to which people like their jobs; job dissatisfaction is the extent to which they dislike them' (Spector 2006:217). Some people, however, report satisfaction without showing motivation to do well (Rainey 1993).

The different ways of measuring motivation have also been problematic for researchers. The definition of motivation given above – the enthusiasm and willingness to pursue some defined action – raises questions about what is meant by motivation. For example, is it an attitude or a type of behaviour, or both? Is it sufficient for a person to report that she or he is working hard or trying their best, or should the person be observed executing work? Motivation has been measured in different ways which suggest different answers to these questions. Some studies have explored motivation by asking people about their attitudes and behaviour, while at least one study has used peer evaluation of a person's work motivation (Guion & Landy 1972). According to Rainey (1993), very few measures of general work motivation have been identified in the literature on psychology and organisational behaviour. One measure that has been reported in the literature utilised questions about how hard a person works and how frequently they perform extra work (Patchen *et al.* 1965). While some success with this measure has been reported, another study that used it found that managers rated their work efforts very high and that most of the respondents indicted that they worked harder than their colleagues. The respondents reported such high self-ratings that it was difficult to determine differences between them (Rainey 1983).

Scales of job involvement and intrinsic or internal work motivation are also used by some researchers to explore motivation. Although these scales assess work-related attitudes, they do not really examine work effort. Instead, they imply that if an individual feels a sense of satisfaction when they do a job well, they must be motivated to perform. Likewise, some researchers use items obtained from expectancy theory of motivation to measure motivation. These items often refer to rewards such as pay and promotion and, like those used to investigate intrinsic motivation, do not directly ask respondents about the level of their work effort. Rather, this approach implies that motivation improves if employees perceive a direct relationship between performance and rewards (Rainey 1993). This discussion demonstrates the difficulty in asking individuals to report their levels of motivation and the amount of effort executed. An alternative approach to asking people to rate their own motivation is to use peer evaluations. Such an approach was used by Landy and Guion (1970), who used peers to rate managers on selected dimensions. The results, however, indicated considerable disagreement among peers, and Rainey (1993) suggested that the use of this approach requires a huge amount of time and resources, which may be one reason why other researchers have not used it to examine motivation.

THEORIES OF MOTIVATION

Authors such as Rainey (1993) and Muchinsky (1993) suggests that no single theory fully explains motivation but that each theory makes a significant contribution to its development and understanding. There are many theories of motivation and each textbook seems to group or classify them differently. According to Jewell (1998), no single method of categorisation has been accepted as the norm. Theories discussed in this chapter are categorised into content theories and process theories. Content theories suggest that people are motivated by a set of needs, wants or motives. Examples of these theories include Maslow's hierarchy of needs (1954) and Herzberg's two-factor theory (Herzberg *et al.* 1959). Process theories, on the other hand, focus on the processes that affect behaviour. Process theories include expectancy theory and goal setting theory. Rainey (1993) argues that this distinction is not exact since most of the theories contain elements of both content and process theories. In this chapter four theories will be described. For a more detailed discussion and classification of motivation theories consult Katzell and Thompson (1990) and Spector (2006).

Maslow's hierarchy of needs theory

One of the most well-known content theories was developed by Abraham Maslow (1954). In his theory Maslow suggested that people are driven by different sets of needs and that these needs are organised in a hierarchy.

1 *Physiological needs.* These are the lowest level of needs and include food, water and air. Equivalent needs in the work setting include adequate heating, air and a salary to assure survival.
2 *Safety needs.* This is the next level in the hierarchy of needs and is concerned with a desire to be protected from physical danger and to live in an orderly society. In the work environment safety needs include a safe job, job security and benefits.

3 *Belonging or social needs.* These needs include the need to be accepted by peers, to experience friendships and be loved, and to belong to groups. Similar needs in the work setting include good relationships with colleagues, participation in work groups and healthy relationships with supervisors and managers.

4 *Esteem needs* are fourth on the hierarchy of needs. These needs include the desire for a good self image and to receive respect and admiration from others. At work these needs include increased responsibility, appropriate status and due recognition for work done within the organisation.

5 *Self-actualisation needs.* These represent the pinnacle of Maslow's hierarchy of needs. They are concerned with achieving one's own potential, expanding one's knowledge and competence level and improving oneself overall. Self-actualisation needs are personal and as such will differ from person to person.

Maslow proposed that lower-level needs take priority and must be satisfied before moving on to higher-level needs. The needs are fulfilled using a sequential approach. So physiological needs are fulfilled before safety needs and belonging needs. An individual who is trying to satisfy lower-level needs will not concern themselves with esteem or self-actualisation needs. When a need has been fulfilled it no longer acts as motivator: only unfulfilled needs are considered motivators. Therefore, when a set of needs has been fulfilled the individual moves on to the next set of needs in the hierarchy.

Despite reduced acceptance of Maslow's theory as a suitable theory of motivation, his work has made a significant contribution to the field of psychology (Muchinsky 1993).

Herzberg's two-factor theory

Another well-known theory of motivation – two-factor theory – was developed by Frederick Herzberg (Herzberg *et al.* 1959). According to Muchinsky (1993:293) this theory produced a considerable amount of both 'research and controversy'. Herzberg and his colleagues Mausner and Snyderman investigated job satisfaction among engineers and accountants. These researchers asked respondents to describe when they felt good about their jobs. Feelings of satisfaction and dissatisfaction were reported. Content analysis of the interviews were carried out to determine which factors contributed to satisfaction and which resulted in dissatisfaction with jobs. Results revealed that certain factors were associated with job satisfaction and a different set of factors resulted in dissatisfaction. These findings led Herzberg to propose two different sets of factors: motivators or content factors that influence satisfaction; and hygiene factors or context factors that result in dissatisfaction. Motivators include achievement, recognition, advancement and responsibility. These became known as content factors because they related to the content of the job. Hygiene factors refer to organisational policy, supervision, salary and working conditions. These were all related to the context of the job and were therefore categorised as context factors.

Herzberg then proposed what became the most controversial feature of his theory. He suggested that when a job provides content factors – such as recognition and achievement – the individual will be satisfied with work. However, when these factors are not present in a job the individual will not be dissatisfied but rather feel indifferent or unconcerned. Conversely, when a job offers context factors – such as a good salary, or agreeable working conditions – the individual will not be satisfied but rather feel indifferent or unconcerned about the job. When these context factors are not present in the job the individual will experience dissatisfaction. Therefore, the presence of motivators or content factors will produce satisfaction while the absence of motivators will merely result in indifference. On the other hand, hygiene factors or context factors, when present in the job, will result in indifference; but absence of hygiene factors will cause dissatisfaction. So according to this theory jobs should be designed to produce high satisfaction from both content factors (so that satisfaction is ensured) and context factors (so that dissatisfaction can be avoided).

A major criticism of Herzberg's theory is that the two-factor approach has not been supported by extensive research (Spector 2006). Furthermore, both motivators and hygiene factors contribute to satisfaction and dissatisfaction rather than motivators alone resulting in satisfaction, and hygiene factors on their own producing dissatisfaction, as Herzberg suggested. Despite the deficiencies in the theory Herzberg's research has made a significant contribution to the field. It led to the reorganisation of work so that it became interesting, and it emphasised the importance of providing opportunities for employee growth and fulfilment.

Vroom's expectancy theory

Expectancy theory is based on the assumption that human beings will be motivated if they believe that their efforts or behaviour will result in rewards or outcomes that they want. If they do not think that their actions or behaviour will lead to rewards they will not be motivated to carry out those actions. If they do not want the rewards then they will not execute the actions (Spector 2006). Expectancy theory was developed in the 1930s but was not originally applied to work motivation. Researchers Georgopoulos, Mahoney and Jones (1957) were among the first to use the theory in the work environment (Muchinsky 1993), but the person credited with advancing the theory and applying it to motivation research was the psychologist Victor Vroom (1964). In summarising this theory, Weihrich and Koontz (2005:375) stated:

> Vroom's theory is that people's motivation toward doing anything will be determined by the value they place on the outcome of their effort (whether positive or negative) multiplied by the confidence they have that their effort will materially aid in achieving a goal. In his own terms, Vroom's theory may be stated as: Force = Valence x Expectancy.

Force refers to the motivation a person has for a given action or behaviour, Valence is the importance or value a person attaches to an outcome (money for example, can have different valence levels for different individuals), and Expectancy is the person's belief that the amount of effort required for a certain activity will result in a desired outcome (it is the self-confidence a person has that they can execute a given task).

Several authors (Spector 2006; Weihrich & Koontz 2005; Muchinsky 1993; Rainey 1993) have indicated that this theory offered further explanation and analysis of motivation theory. It could be applied by asking employees to articulate their views about the probable outcomes of certain actions or behaviour and to apply valuations (positive or negative) to the outcomes, and calculating a score for every employee. A number of studies tested the theory and although some claimed success, others had problems applying and validating the theory.

Locke's goal-setting theory

Goal-setting theory, developed by Edwin Locke (1968), has been recognised as one of the most successful motivation theories (Pinder 1984). The theory holds that people act or behave rationally and consciously; conscious ideas lead people to develop goals for themselves and they are motivated to work because achieving the goals is rewarding. Locke (1968) proposed two major functions of goals: they can motivate and they can direct behaviour. Goals guide the amount of effort required for work and can influence performance. Before goals can influence performance, however, two requirements are necessary. First, the employee must know about the goal; and second, he or she must accept the goal and be committed to achieving it. The theory also suggests that commitment to a goal is relative to its level of difficulty. Therefore, goals that are more difficult will require more commitment to achieving them. The theory also stresses the importance of feedback and stipulates that feedback about how performance is progressing should be given to employees since it will indicate whether they must increase their pace of work or continue with their present timetable.

Spector (2006) suggests that at the present time goal-setting theory is the most widely used theory of motivation in industrial and organisational psychology. Moreover, the theory has been subjected to extensive research and has been widely used as a mechanism for increasing job performance. Despite the successes reported, goal-setting theory is not without its limitations. Most of the research studies that used goal-setting theory involved single goals. Research involving more complex jobs and several goals demonstrated that performance was lower (Yearta et al. 1995).

This review of the theoretical literature shows that not only are there several theories of motivation but there are also several ways of classifying them. In the preceding sections theories were classified as content theories and process theories. Content theories focus on individual or intrinsic needs while process theories are concerned with the behavioural processes people use to make choices and achieve goals. Two theories from each category were presented. Muchinsky (1993) suggested that any attempt to integrate theories of motivation would be a difficult task and that it would be better to view them from different perspectives, emphasising their similarities and differences. So which theory is the most valid? This is not an easy question to answer. All the theories have been validated by research but some have received greater support than others. Also, every theory has made a contribution to understanding motivation, but the two theories that have received most success are expectancy theory and goal-setting theory. Authors such as Mitchell (1982) suggest that efforts should be made to amalgamate the current theories of motivation: new theories are not the answer. Rainey (1993) reported that suggestions for further development of motivation theory have indicated either integrating the current theories or separating them, or using aspects of both.

Literature related specifically to motivation of health care professionals, including nurses, is sparse (Dieleman *et al.* 2003; Schepers *et al.* 2005; Edgar 1999). For example, a cursory review of the literature on nursing over the last five years suggests that some studies have utilised theories of motivation. The majority, however, did not actually explore motivation but rather variables such as job satisfaction among nurses. Many of the researchers who investigated job satisfaction reported that they had used Herzberg's two-factor theory to guide their studies and that the studies were undertaken as part of doctoral research.

LEADERSHIP FOR MOTIVATION

Bass (1985), building on earlier work by Burns (1978), proposed two types of leadership that can be used to influence employees. First, transactional leadership describes an exchange between leader and employee whereby the employee exchanges some form of compliance for reward from the leader. The second leadership behaviour is transformational leadership, which has the following effects on employees: trust of the leader, respect, loyalty, commitment and motivation to perform beyond what they had expected. Bass (1985) believed that transformational leadership resulted in higher levels of employee performance than that produced under transactional leadership.

In a study examining transformational leadership effects among army personnel, Kane and Tremble (2000:157) reported that 'transformational leadership behaviours are associated with increases in motivation as well as other development of subordinates'. Data for the study was collected from 3,204 soldiers in 41 battalions at six army posts in the United States. To assess transformational leadership, respondents were asked to assess the leadership behaviour of their immediate superior officer using the 81-item multifactor leadership questionnaire (MLQ) form developed by Bass and Avolio (1991). Another study designed to gain more knowledge about the outcomes of transformational leadership reported considerable support for transformational leadership in Norway (Hetland & Sandal 2003). The results of the study, which used a sample of 100 Norwegian leaders from five companies (both private and public), indicated that transformational leadership demonstrated a strong and consistent relationship with satisfaction, effectiveness, and work motivation, irrespective of whether the ratings were made by superiors or subordinates. It is important to point out that for every leader participating in the study, ratings of her or his leadership behaviour was obtained from one superior and two subordinates using the MLQ. Another important finding of this study was the modest correlation between transformational leadership and leader personality. Personality was found to have a stronger correlation with transformational leadership than with transactional leadership and warmth was the personality variable that had the strongest correlation with transformational leadership as rated by subordinates (Hetland & Sandal 2003).

In a study to determine the impact of transformational leadership enhanced by training on follower development and performance, Dvir *et al.* (2002) reported that leaders in the experimental group (those exposed to transformational leadership training) had a more positive influence on follower development and the performance of indirect followers than leaders in the control group. This study employed an experimental design and the samples used included 54 military leaders, 90 direct followers and 724 indirect followers. Although the study utilised a large sample, given the distinctive nature of a military organisation it is difficult to generalise the findings, and the authors (Dvir *et al.* 2002) suggested replication in other non-military organisations.

Carney (2006) has suggested that health service managers need to embrace a new form of leadership for the twenty-first century. This new leadership requires that leaders are able to articulate a vision and motivate employees. They must also be able to shape the culture within the organisation and develop a climate that is healthy and conducive to change. This new leadership must shift accountability, responsibility and power from one individual to all levels of the organisation and empower employees so that they can help the leader achieve organisational goals. This new leadership appears to be consistent with the principles of transformational leadership.

MOTIVATION AND PERFORMANCE

Motivation and performance are not exactly the same. Motivation is only one of a number of variables responsible for work behaviour. A person who is very motivated may not necessarily perform well in a job. The reason for this is that performance is dependent upon a combination of motivation, ability and situational factors (Muchinsky 1993). Ability refers to a person's capacity for executing specific tasks or jobs. Although important, ability on its own does not determine performance. A person could have high motivation but lack ability or demonstrate enormous ability with little or no motivation. Motivation is when a person is enthusiastic and willing to carry out certain actions. Situational factors refer to factors within the work environment that obstruct or hamper employee performance. For example, a health care professional cannot adequately care for a patient if she or he is not given all relevant information about the patient's condition, and appropriate equipment. The health care professional will only be able to perform well if she or he has ability and the desire to carry out duties properly, and when there are no obstructions in the working environment.

Hughes *et al.* (2006) stated that motivation, satisfaction and performance are all linked. Leadership that endorses employee-centred elements such as building relationships and consideration for employees will lead to greater employee satisfaction. Employees who are satisfied are more likely to carry out their duties well and stay in their post longer. In a study to determine the job satisfaction of nurses in the Republic of Ireland, Curtis (2007) reported that professional status, interaction (opportunities for both formal and informal contact with colleagues during working hours) and autonomy contributed the most to nurses' job satisfaction. Hughes *et al.* (2006) suggested that two events have resulted in reduced job satisfaction in the United States. Several organisations have reduced the number of employees within the last decade. The intention was to reduce costs and increase profit, but these changes led to an increased workload for the remaining employees. The consequence was an increase in dissatisfaction among employees. Even though workers reported satisfaction with their choice of career, conditions such as enforced overtime, increased workload and the deterioration of trust between employers and employees led to an increase in job dissatisfaction.

Although the ability of the leader to motivate employees is crucial to morale and employee performance, it is nonetheless important to remember that performance is also dependent upon other factors. Leaders must (a) select the correct person for a task or job, (b) be credible and trustworthy, (c) be positive and enthusiastic, (d) obtain the necessary resources to perform work activities and (e) be committed to developing employee skills and advancing their continuing professional development (Hughes *et al.* 2006).

A key question for consideration in motivation research is what leads employees to continue in their efforts to execute their work in an effective and productive manner? Researchers have suggested that prosocial motivation may play an important role in answering this question. Prosocial motivation refers to a desire to perform tasks or jobs in order to benefit others (Batson 1987) and is associated with the personality trait of agreeableness, a tendency toward empathy and kindness. To test the role of prosocial motivation in persistence, performance and productivity, Grant (2008) conducted two studies using a sample of 58 firefighters and a sample of 140 fundraising callers. Grant proposed that prosocial motivation is more likely to result in persistence, performance and productivity when it is accompanied by intrinsic motivation. Intrinsic motivation, according to Gange and Deci (2005:331), 'involves people doing an activity because they find it interesting and derive spontaneous satisfaction from the activity itself'. The results indicated that intrinsic motivation strengthened the relationship between prosocial motivation and persistence, performance and productivity in both firefighters and fundraising personnel (Grant 2008). Writing about the implications of these findings, Grant reported that managers can use the findings to design work practices that promote both prosocial and intrinsic motivation among employees. For example, empowerment contributes to an increase in intrinsic motivation (Brown 2000), but because it offers additional opportunities for employees to contribute to organisational activities it may at the same time increase prosocial motivation.

In a study designed to examine the effects of leadership behaviours of nurse managers on job satisfaction, productivity and organisational commitment, Chiok

Foong Loke (2001) surveyed 100 registered nurses and 20 managers in Singapore. The results demonstrated a statistically significant relationship between managers' leadership behaviours and job satisfaction, productivity and organisational commitment. The findings also confirmed that leadership behaviours such as being considerate and caring are important to productivity. Enabling others to act is a leadership behaviour that energises employees and encourages them to make their own decisions. The results from this study found a moderately high and positive correlation between this leadership behaviour and job satisfaction, productivity and organisational commitment. In discussing the implications of the findings of this study, Chiok Foong Loke (2001:199) reported that leadership behaviours that result in job satisfaction, increased productivity and commitment to the organisation are crucial for the delivery of 'high quality care' and are necessary for the survival of health care organisations.

STRATEGIES FOR IMPROVING MOTIVATION IN THE WORKPLACE

Despite the many difficulties associated with motivation theories, it must be acknowledged that organisations need motivated employees. There is no doubt that motivation theories have provided several suggestions for improving motivation in employees, but how can this be transferred to the workplace? What strategies can managers use to create a motivating workplace? Although it is true that motivation is a multifaceted phenomenon and no single answer will suffice, several strategies have been put forward for enhancing motivation in the workplace. The following strategies are based on those suggested by Weihrich and Koontz (2005), Daft (2000), Marquis and Huston (2000), Rainey (1993) and Dixon (1991).

Work environment

Argyris (1964) believes that the work environment can affect the development and potential of employees. Organisations generally do not encourage their employees to behave in a mature way. Work activities are sometimes reduced to routine tasks and staff are not usually encouraged to be creative or invited to participate in decision-making. Organisations should, according to Argyris (1964), improve their communication processes, encourage innovation and creativity and promote job enlargement and enrichment (this will be addressed later).

Participation

Participation as a strategy for improving motivation at work has been strongly supported by motivation theory and research (Weihrich & Koontz 2005). Given that many employees possess knowledge about their jobs and can usually find solutions to problems, it seems ludicrous that they are excluded from the decision-making process. Asking the right employee to participate can result in both increasing the employee's motivation and securing knowledge that is valuable to the organisation. Participation can also be considered a method of recognition; it provides a sense of affiliation and acceptance but, more important, employees feel they have made a contribution. Managers should also consider open door policies, one-to-one discussions or exchanges, and better communication as strategies for increasing employee participation (Rainey 1993).

Gellerman (1968), a motivational theorist, argued that problems associated with motivation usually arise from the way the organisation is managed rather than from the employee's unwillingness to work efficiently. Gellerman further pointed out that managers sometimes manage too closely (over manage) and as a consequence restrict the content of an employee's job and fail to provide the employee with decision-making power. In a study to determine the satisfaction, commitment, and psychological well-being among physicians working in health maintenance organisations (HMOs), Freeborn *et al.* (2001:16) reported that 'perceived control over the practice environment' was associated with higher levels of satisfaction and organisational commitment among this professional group.

In nursing, the issue of participation in the decision-making process is an important one. It has been suggested that nurses make two types of decision concerning practice: decisions that concern patients and have a direct impact on their care; and decisions concerning work that can affect the work environment (Anthony 1999). In a study designed to explore the benefits and outcomes of staff nurses' participation in decision-making, Krairiksh (2001) reported that nurses were more interested in participating in decisions concerning patient care than in decisions regarding work environment issues. In explaining these findings, Krairiksh suggested that nurses directly involved in providing patient care encounter many opportunities during the course of their work to participate in individual decisions concerning patients and that managers should encourage this practice in order to improve care planning and patient outcomes. Krairiksh (2001) further suggested that staff nurses may be more inclined to participate in decision-making about their work environment as a group rather than on an individual basis, and that this may explain the findings of her study.

Work enhancement

Job redesign refers to changing or adjusting jobs so that they improve employee satisfaction, control and interest. Approaches used to achieve this are usually labelled job enrichment, job enlargement and job rotation.

In a paper entitled 'One more time: how do you motivate employees?' Herzberg (2003:87) stated, 'forget praise. Forget punishment. Forget cash. You need to make their jobs more interesting.' Herzberg's research identified the importance of meaningful and challenging jobs for employees. Factors such as achievement, recognition, responsibility, opportunities for growth and autonomy are regarded as motivators. Job enrichment incorporates all these factors. A job that is enriched allows the employee to take control of getting the job done, to make decisions associated with the job, to set their own work pace and to experience personal growth and fulfilment.

Job enrichment and job enlargement are different, although this is not always made clear by some authors (Weihrich & Koontz 2005; Daft 2000). Job enrichment refers to the integration of higher-level motivators into the work. Jobs can be enriched in many ways, including variety, freedom to make decisions about the job, greater participation in decision-making, more responsibility for the job, giving employees feedback on their performance, and involvement in change initiatives. Job enlargement tries to decrease the monotony associated with simple, repetitive jobs by combining a set of related tasks to create a broader job. In other words, the scope of the job is increased by including more of the same kind of tasks but with no added responsibility. For example, a student nurse can take and record a patient's temperature as well as their pulse rate and blood pressure (with supervision and guidance where appropriate) rather than taking the patient's temperature only. Similarly, a student physiotherapist can be asked to assist a qualified physiotherapist in both mobilising a patient following spinal surgery as well as assessing the patient's physical condition prior to mobilisation, rather than being asked to undertake only the first activity. Job enlargement increases the amount of variety in the job and offers greater challenges for the employee. That said, it has been criticised on the grounds that it is just a larger collection of boring tasks, given that the employee's responsibility has not been increased.

Job rotation occurs when employees are moved from one job to another. This increases the number of tasks an employee has to complete without increasing the complexity of the job. For example, nurses or physiotherapists may rotate from day duty to night duty every 12 weeks or between wards or units within a speciality (such as neurosciences). Also, nurses who participate in team nursing may change teams every two or three weeks. Job rotation can be quite efficient from a management perspective but adds variety to the job and new forms of motivation for employees (Daft 2000).

Quality of work life

Quality of working life (QWL) programmes attempt to improve the working environment of organisations by engaging in representative teams and research studies (Rainey 1993). Weihrich and Koontz (2005) believe that QWL programmes are one of the most interesting approaches to motivating employees and a useful development in the area of job enrichment. QWL draws on several disciplines including industrial and organisational psychology, sociology, organisational theory, motivation and leadership theories. It gained significance in the 1970s and there are now several QWL centres worldwide. Managers regard QWL as a useful strategy for addressing poor productivity, and employees and union officials have endorsed its use in improving working conditions and defending negotiations for pay increases. Even government agencies have found QWL programmes beneficial in increasing productivity and reducing industrial disputes (Weihrich & Koontz 2005).

In the Republic of Ireland, the Midland Health Board introduced a QWL programme in 2002. The main goal of the programme was to develop a safe, healthy work environment that valued its employees and their contributions. As part of the programme a survey of employees was carried out in 2002–2003 to determine what factors affected the quality of their working life. A five-year plan is being developed to address the priorities identified in the survey (HSE Midland Health Board).

Money

Weihrich and Koontz (2005) and Rainey (1993) have suggested money as a strategy for motivating employees. Whether it takes the form of wages, bonuses or company-paid insurance, these authors argue that money is important. Daft (2000) pointed out that organisations that have an empowerment programme (discussed below) in place often reward employees according to how well the organisation is doing. Such reward systems are usually linked to employee performance appraisals. While a case can be made for using financial rewards to motivate employees in some circumstances (Brown 2000), there are still doubts about its effectiveness as an approach for motivating employees (Franco et al. 2004; Herzberg 2003; Kerr 1999). In Ireland, money is generally not used as a strategy for motivating nurses and wages are agreed nationally with little opportunity for variation. Therefore, this strategy will not be discussed further here.

Other motivational strategies

Other motivational strategies include empowerment, performance appraisal systems, and enthusiastic role model.

One of the newer strategies for motivating employees is empowerment (Daft 2000). According to Hughes et al. (2006) there are two views of empowerment. One view is that empowerment is concerned with delegation and accountability. In a top-down approach senior managers communicate the organisation's goals, and employees are responsible for achieving them. The other view utilises a bottom-up approach, emphasises trust, ownership and change and encourages employees to ask questions, make decisions and act entrepreneurially. These two views of empowerment can have different implications for leaders and employees and can cause some empowerment programmes to fail (Hughes et al. 2006).

For empowerment to be effective employees must be given (a) information, (b) knowledge, (c) power and (d) rewards (Daft 2000).

- Information – organisations committed to employee empowerment share all information.
- Knowledge – appropriate training must be provided so that employees can acquire the knowledge and skills required to perform their jobs and contribute to organisational goals.
- Power – employees must be given the authority to contribute to decisions and influence work procedures and practices. This can be achieved through quality circles or self-managed work teams.
- Rewards – organisations that are truly committed to empowering their employees reward them for their contribution.

Rewards can take many forms but usually refer to some type of financial payment. Writers such as Peters and Waterman (1982) believe that rewards should be offered on an ad hoc basis because if they are given routinely they are likely to lose their appeal. Marquis and Huston (2000), however, disagree with this argument.

They believe that reward systems must be consistent, open and fair or they may result in conflict, tension and poor morale among employees. So managers must be careful when using rewards as a strategy to increase motivation because if it fails the consequences could mean reduced employee motivation. Reward systems are usually based on a performance appraisal system and this will be discussed later.

Many organisations are implementing empowerment programmes, but (as explained in the preceding sections) there are different conceptualisations of empowerment. The consequence of this is that some organisations view empowerment as merely encouraging employees to express their views, while managers continue to have full responsibility for decisions. Other organisations see empowerment as giving employees responsibility and authority to make decisions concerning their work and encouraging them to utilise their initiative and creativity (Daft 2000). Empowerment programmes have been used by many organisations to improve employee motivation and increase productivity. Hughes *et al.* (2006) argue that empowerment has not always been successful since there may be no difference in productivity between empowered employees and unempowered employees. One important reason for this is that some empowerment programmes are not adequately implemented. Very little training, guidance and support is given prior to and during the introduction of the programme and managers often stop the programme if employees make poor decisions. The implementation of an empowerment programme – like most management initiatives – takes time, adequate training and trust (Offerman 1997), but, regrettably, many organisations pay little heed to these factors. Daft (2000:557–8) sums up empowerment like this: 'With empowerment, workers are motivated because they are intellectually challenged, provided with opportunities to use their minds and imaginations, and given the power to make decisions that affect their work.'

Performance appraisal systems

Performance appraisal is concerned with establishing the performance of employees (Marquis & Huston 2000). It involves 'observing and assessing employee performance, recording the assessment and providing feedback to the employee' (Daft 2000:412). There are many reasons why performance appraisals are used in organisations, but the one that is relevant here concerns motivation. Employee appraisals have been in use since the 1920s but their use as a means of promoting growth and development in employees did not really begin until the 1950s. Over the years, different terms have been used to describe appraisals, including 'merit rating' and 'performance evaluation', but most health care organisations use the term 'performance appraisal'.

Employees have different views about performance appraisals and this must be taken into account if the appraisal system is to promote growth and increase motivation. Clear objectives must be set before the appraisal system begins and these must be discussed with the employee before the appraisal commences. If employees feel that their work performance rather than the nature of their relationship with the appraiser is being reviewed they are more likely to respond positively. Marquis and Huston (2000) have suggested that the following points should be considered when using performance appraisals for increasing motivation and productivity.

- The performance appraisal process and forms or documents used must be based on a standard format that is used throughout the organisation.
- The employee should participate in setting the goals for assessing performance.
- The employee must be informed in advance about the chain of events that take place if the performance objectives or goals are not met.
- The employee must be told about the nature of the information and data (and their sources) that will be used to ascertain performance.
- The appraiser must be someone who has worked with the employee and is familiar with their work.
- The appraiser must be someone whom the employee trusts and respects professionally. This is necessary for an impartial and accurate appraisal.

Performance appraisals that are used merely to fulfil organisational requirements are non-productive. If employees see appraisal as a valuable tool for assisting their professional development the potential for benefit is huge. Performance appraisals can be used not only to highlight strengths and deficiencies in performance but also to discuss improvement strategies. To further support the positive aspects of performance appraisal it is important that the appraiser is fair, objective and supportive and, above all, has experience in conducting these appraisals (Marquis and Huston 2000).

Kuvaas (2006) designed a study to examine the relationship between employee satisfaction with performance appraisal and employee outcomes. The sample consisted of 1,508 employees from 75 banks in Norway and the response rate was 593 employees from 64 banks. The key findings demonstrated a relationship between performance appraisal satisfaction and employee performance and turnover intention, and that the relationship between satisfaction with performance appraisal and work performance is affected by intrinsic motivation. Kuvaas stressed, however, that if performance appraisal is to have a positive effect on employee behaviour the employees must experience positive outcomes from appraisals. In discussing the findings, Kuvaas suggested that employees who are intrinsically motivated are self-directed and enjoy autonomy more than employees who are less intrinsically motivated. So although employees who are intrinsically motivated have positive views about performance appraisal they may have less need for control and regulation to perform their duties than employees who have low intrinsic motivation. The strong positive relationship between satisfaction with performance appraisal and motivation found in this study leads one to assume that the banks included in the study encourage autonomy and participation during the performance appraisal process. If this assumption is true, the negative correlation found between satisfaction with performance and work performance among those employees with low intrinsic motivation could be a consequence of too little control or regulation. While control and regulation may have negative implications for performance appraisal systems generally, according to Kuvaas this may not be applicable to employees with low intrinsic motivation. Rather, these employees may need high control and regulation in order to perform their tasks and jobs effectively.

Enthusiastic role model

Managers who have an optimistic and enthusiastic outlook can have a positive and motivating effect on employees and, indeed, on the work environment. Conversely, unhappy managers can have a negative effect on the morale of employees (Marquis & Huston 2000). Research on work locus of control and work excitement (Erbin-Roesemann and Simms 1997) suggests a significant correlation between control and work excitement. Those who have control in their work will experience higher levels of work excitement. Work excitement is defined as 'personal enthusiasm and interest in work as evidenced by creativity, receptivity to learning, and ability to see opportunity in everyday situations' (Erbin-Roesemann & Simms 1997:184–5). In discussing the implication of their findings Erbin-Roesemann and Simms have suggested that work should be reorganised so that employees experience greater work excitement.

Motivational language

To improve organisational outcomes effective interpersonal communication is essential. One of the ways in which this can be achieved is through the use of motivational language – 'a form of strategic verbal communication' (Mayfield 2009). According to Mayfield, motivational language has many benefits, including increased employee performance, better attendance, improved job satisfaction, reduced staff attrition and improved creativity and innovation. Motivational language theory refers to the communication processes used by managers who successfully motivate employees (Sullivan 1988). These managers not only provide information and feedback to employees but also articulate the goals of the organisation and regularly engage in informal communications with employees. Moreover, they take a real interest in communicating with employees as people rather than as employees or subordinates. This type of considerate and supportive communication will result in increased motivation among employees (Sullivan 1988).

HEALTH-RELATED RESEARCH AND MOTIVATION

Most health care organisations endeavour to improve their services through improved management initiatives such as decentralisation of responsibility (Dieleman *et al.* 2003), improved quality of care (McDonald *et al.* 2007) and evidence-based practice (Henderson *et al.* 2006). Highly motivated employees are crucial to a well-organised and effective organisation (Dieleman *et al.* 2003). Despite this, however, few research studies on the motivation of health care professionals were found in the literature reviewed for this chapter.

In a study to identify the factors for job motivation of health workers in Vietnam, Dieleman et al. (2003) reported that motivation is influenced by both financial and non-financial factors. The sample in this study consisted of 53 participants and data was collected through interviews. Participants included policy makers, health workers including medical doctors, nurses and midwives, and patients. The main factors that contributed to the motivation of these workers were: being appreciated by managers, colleagues and patients; job security; adequate income; and training. Franco et al. (2004) also explored the determinants and consequences of health worker motivation in hospitals in Jordan and Georgia. These authors suggest that although these countries differ culturally and socio-economically there were some similarities in the findings. Factors such as self-efficacy, pride, management openness and support, availability of resources and organisational citizenship behaviour had significant effects on worker motivation in both countries. An interesting point to highlight is that while workers stated that financial reward was crucial to their job satisfaction, the results indicated that non-financial variables may be more effective for improving motivation (Franco et al. 2004).

General practitioners in the United Kingdom were in 2004 given financial incentives to meet clinical targets, known as the quality and outcomes framework (Roland 2004). The framework consists of three main components: clinical care; practice organisation; and patient experience. GPs can earn a total of 1,000 points if they achieve the indicators contained in the framework document. An additional 50 points can be earned for providing rapid access to services. These points convert to pounds sterling and are claimed by the GPs annually (Roland 2004). Following the introduction of the quality and outcomes framework, high levels of achievement were reported by some practices. Financial incentives can, however, affect motivation and morale (Christianson et al. 2006). Therefore, McDonald et al. (2007) decided to explore the effect of financial incentives on general practices and the effects of internal motivation among primary care clinicians in two practices in the northwest of England. The findings demonstrated support for the quality and outcomes framework. Financial incentives did not appear to affect the internal motivation of GPs, but nurses raised some concerns. They expressed the view that collecting the information for the quality and outcomes framework did affect the quality of individual consultations and that patients were treated 'as a condition and not as the person that they really are' (McDonald et al. 2007:1377). These findings, however, should be interpreted with caution since the sample was small and convenience sampling was used to select the two practices.

During the period 1991 to 1992, Freeborn et al. (2001) conducted a study to explore satisfaction, organisational commitment and burnout among physicians working for health maintenance organisations (HMOs) in the United States of America. The results indicated that variables such as 'perceived control over one's practice environment; support from colleagues and adequate resources' were associated with greater job satisfaction, organisational commitment and psychological well-being. Interestingly, results varied depending on the speciality the physicians were working in. Physicians working in paediatrics reported higher levels of satisfaction and commitment than their colleagues working in other specialities. The study also reported that 'stress from uncertainty in patient care, job demands, and social support also affected burnout levels among physicians' (Freeborn *et al.* 2001:16). In discussing the implications of the findings the authors asked whether 'it mattered if physicians are dissatisfied, lacking in commitment, or burned out' (Freeborn *et al.* 2001:17). The authors suggest that this question is indeed important since physician dissatisfaction is associated with higher turnover rates and this could affect the overall efficiency of health care organisations.

Very few research studies have examined motivation among nurses (Schepers *et al.* 2005). This viewpoint is supported by Edgar (1999). Those studies that have examined motivation have used the job characteristics model (Hackman & Oldham 1980). To determine whether job satisfaction and work motivation is higher among nurses who use primary nursing as their preferred model of care, Kivimaki, Voutilainen and Koskinen (1995) conducted a survey of hospital nurses. The results indicated that nurses' work was more enriched when they worked on wards where primary nursing was practised compared with nurses who used functional nursing (i.e. work that is divided into specific tasks and allocated to different nurses depending on the level of skill required to execute the task) as the model of care. The results also demonstrated that motivation was higher among nurses who used primary nursing compared with those who used functional nursing as the preferred model of care. These findings are supported by Makinen *et al.* (2003), who conducted a study to examine the relationship between methods of organising nursing care and nurses' job satisfaction. Data was collected from 26 ward sisters and 568 nurses from wards using different nursing care delivery models. The findings confirmed that models of care which were patient-focused were correlated with three aspects (satisfaction with supervision, social relationships and personal growth) of job satisfaction. Primary nursing, a model of care delivery whereby a named nurse is allocated to the patient for the duration of his or her hospital sojourn, is a particular feature that distinguishes primary nursing from other care delivery models. Nurses who use primary nursing have greater autonomy and responsibility for organising care for their patients. Makinen *et al.* (2003) also reported that the most significant contributing factor to nurses' satisfaction with supervision (a facet of job satisfaction explored in this study) was being permitted to write the patient's care plan.

Janssen *et al.* (1999) conducted a study to investigate what factors contributed to intrinsic motivation, burnout and turnover intention among nurses in the Netherlands. The sample consisted of 175 nurses from one general hospital. Nine departments in the hospital agreed to participate in the study and the response rate was 156 (89 per cent). The results confirmed that intrinsic work motivation is determined mainly by those aspects of the job that are challenging, which include variety, autonomy and opportunities to learn. Higher levels of burnout occurred as a consequence of high demands from the work (strenuous work and little social support from colleagues). Turnover intentions were associated mainly with unmet career expectations. In discussing the implications of the findings, Janssen *et al.* suggested that managers must focus on the content of work if they wish to increase intrinsic motivation among nurses. Such recommendations echo those put forward by Herzberg (2003) in his paper entitled 'One more time: how do you motivate employees?' Managers could, for example, include greater variety in tasks and jobs and more autonomy and feedback. Janssen *et al.* (1999) pointed out that primary nursing is one example of job redesign in nursing. Also, several duty roster techniques can be used to bring about a more satisfactory allocation of duties and jobs in a given time period.

A study by Edgar (1999) explored the relationships between motivation, job satisfaction and the characteristics of nursing care delivery systems using the job characteristics model (Hackman & Oldham 1980). (Nursing care delivery systems refers to the method used by nurses to deliver patient or client care.) The sample for the study was over 400 nurses working in medical and surgical wards from four teaching hospitals affiliated with McGill University in Montreal, Canada. The response rate was 159 (40 per cent). The study reported that the majority of respondents were using primary nursing as the method for delivering nursing care. This study also reported support for the job characteristics model as a useful tool for measuring motivation among nurses. Findings also indicated that autonomy was important to nurses' work motivation and that effective communication was associated with nurses' job satisfaction.

FUTURE CONSIDERATIONS

Health care operates within an ever-changing environment and there is a constant need for creativity and innovation in order to improve the quality of patient care and contain expenditure (White 1998). A similar viewpoint is shared by Marquis and Huston (2000), who suggest that many organisations become involved in several projects as part of change initiatives aimed at improving quality and employee empowerment.

In addition to the many changes already taking place, health care organisations, like all other organisations, will have to face the additional challenges and burdens that have arisen as a consequence of the current economic downturn. These challenges may include fewer staff, reduced budgets, increased workload and rationalisation of services. Therefore, understanding the needs of employees and being able to motivate them during difficult times must become a priority if managers are to maintain a healthy work environment and provide quality care to patients and clients.

Benson and Dundis (2003:316) call upon health care professionals 'to revisit Abraham Maslow's Hierarchy of Needs' (1954) model as a way of understanding and motivating employees. They justify their decision on the basis that the model is useful for understanding what is important to individuals. In answering the question, 'How does one motivate employees when so many are being asked to do more with less?', Benson and Dundis (2003:319) stressed the importance of making 'the employee feel secure, needed and appreciated.' On the other hand, authors such as Schepers *et al.* (2005) have indicated that there is a paucity of research on motivation among nurses. These authors further emphasise that researchers have assumed that theories originally developed for application in for-profit organisations are also suitable for investigating motivation in not-for-profit organisations such as hospitals. This assumption is probably due to the fact that hospitals are similar in structure to for-profit organisations (Schepers *et al.* 2005). But the environment of a hospital is different from that of a for-profit organisation; therefore, the use of motivation theories developed from insights from for-profit organisations may not be entirely appropriate for investigating motivation in not-for-profit organisations and this therefore requires further empirical research.

Research on nurses' motivation suggest that they have greater motivation when their jobs are more enriched (such as in the use of primary nursing to deliver patient care) (Kivimaki *et al.* 1995) and when autonomy, skill variety and opportunities to learn are included in their jobs (Janssen *et al.* 1999). Such findings are similar to those reported from for-profit organisations, but Schepers *et al.* (2005) have suggested that further research is needed to explore issues such as what motivates nurses, the role of extrinsic factors in nurses' motivation and the characteristic differences between nurses and employees working in for-profit organisations.

Another area that warrants further research is the effect of ageing and adult development on work motivation. Authors such as Kanfer and Ackerman (2004) have reported that by 2010 almost half of the American workforce will consist of people aged 45 years and over and that a similar trend is expected for most developed countries. Factors that have contributed to an increase in an older workforce include reduced birth rates during the latter part of the twentieth century and economic conditions that discourage early retirement. Moreover, legislation against age discrimination and research evidence refuting a negative relationship between age and job performance have led some organisations to rethink their attitudes toward employing and retaining older workers. This renewed interest by organisations in motivation among the older workforce and the paucity of research on the topic led researchers Kanfer and Ackerman (2004) to explore how age can affect work motivation.

In their paper, Kanfer and Ackerman (2004:440) reported that process theories of motivation are not adequate for 'identifying the sources of age-related differences in work motivation' and proposed a framework for understanding the effects of ageing on motivation. In concluding their paper, they pointed out that their framework suggests neither theoretical nor empirical support for 'an inevitable and universal decline in work motivation with age' (Kanfer & Ackerman 2004:455) and recommend that motivation in older employees can be improved if organisational and managerial strategies and practices acknowledge the normal processes of adult development. Such research outcomes may not be relevant to the nursing profession at the present time, given that the majority of nurses (21,422) registered with An Bord Altranais (Irish Nursing Board) are between the ages of 30 and 39 (An Bord Altranais 2009). Nevertheless, we should not become complacent as the next largest group of nurses are within the 40–49 age group. Moreover, people in Ireland are living longer and in a few years' time the majority of working nurses and other health care professionals may well be over the age of 45.

There is no doubt that measuring motivation is fraught with difficulties since it cannot be observed directly and is usually inferred from accounts given by participants. Also, authors such as McDonald *et al.* (2007) and Freeborn *et al.* (2001) have called for more longitudinal studies to explore motivation and job satisfaction among physicians since the majority of studies tend to use a cross-sectional approach. Franco *et al.* (2004) suggest that health care reforms are likely to affect many of the factors that contribute to employee motivation and have urged those involved in these reforms to consider the implications of the reforms before implementing them.

CASE STUDY

You are a staff nurse in a busy surgical ward where you have been working for the past four years. You previously worked in a large medical unit in another hospital and enjoyed the four years you spent there. When you first started your current job you found it fulfilling and exciting. You were enthusiastic and wanted to make a difference to patient care. Over the past three months, you have noticed an increase in absenteeism and less commitment from staff regarding the introduction of new initiatives in the ward. The atmosphere in the ward has changed – work is not being completed on time and to the highest possible standards. Ward morale is low, and you are finding it difficult to maintain your own morale and job satisfaction levels. You have spoken to a colleague who has confided that he too is fed up and is thinking of looking for another job.

You still enjoy working in the ward and the location of the hospital is convenient for you. The ward sister is due to retire in two years and she seems to have no interest in re-establishing a happy and productive work environment.

Assignment: You must decide whether you wish to continue working in the ward. If you choose to remain, what actions will you take to try and improve staff motivation, morale and the overall quality of patient care on the ward?

CONCLUSION

This chapter addressed a number of key issues about motivation. It began by explaining what motivation is and how it can be measured. It then moved on to explain that there are several theories of motivation and that they can be classified in several ways. In this chapter, the theories were categorised as content theories and process theories; and two theories from each category were described.

Content theories suggest that individuals are motivated to satisfy a range of needs. Process theories explore the behavioural processes used by individuals to meet their needs.

Next, the chapter discussed two important issues concerning motivation: leadership and motivation; and motivation and performance. The literature suggests that transformational leadership seems to have a positive effect on the motivation of employees. Therefore, it was suggested that this leadership theory be considered as a useful framework for improving motivation among nursing personnel. It is sometimes assumed that highly motivated employees are more likely to be productive. The view taken in this chapter, however, is that performance is due not only to motivation but to a combination of other factors.

Organisations must take the responsibility for establishing and maintaining work environments that support employee motivation. Therefore, identifying and discussing strategies that managers could use for improving motivation in their departments or organisations formed a significant part of this chapter. Many strategies for motivating employees have been reported in the literature but consideration was given to those that were particularly relevant to health care professionals. The chapter also provided a summary of key health-related research studies on motivation and some considerations for future research on the topic.

In concluding, it is important to stress that the theories of motivation and the various themes discussed in this chapter cannot on their own address the issue of motivation. There is no magic formula for motivating employees. Employees' needs and problems may differ depending on the setting, the organisation, the task, or the employee's grade or level within the organisation. Therefore, it is important that health service administrators and nursing managers try to understand the needs of employees when planning and designing work systems.

REFLECTIVE QUESTIONS

1 What impact has reading this chapter had on you? Has it motivated you to explore the topic further?

2 What motivates you? How does the work environment have an impact on your motivation levels? Reflect on these questions and discuss them in the context of your current position at work.

3 How would you motivate colleagues and increase their co-operation?

4 Which of the theories discussed here would you consider suitable for nursing practice?

5 Can you think of any strategies other than those discussed here for motivating colleagues at work?

6 Think about an organisation you have worked in and explain why you think employees did not contribute to the goals of the organisation.

7 Describe in depth (a) a situation when you felt highly motivated at work and (b) a situation when you felt poorly motivated at work. Relate these to material you have read about motivation.

ADDITIONAL RESOURCES

For further information about motivating yourself, visit the following websites:
www.soulofwork.com/
www.human-resources-health.com/content/4/1/15
www.biomedcentral.com/1472-6963/8/247
www.motivation123.com
www.prenhall.com/sullivan-decker. Click on 'Chapter 19' to select activities for
the chapter (Sullivan & Decker 2005).

Further reading:
Nelson, B. (1997) *1001 Ways to Energise Employees.* New York: Workman.
Webster, D., Snowdon, S. and Shaw, B. (2008) 'Arranging staff away day events
to improve motivation', *Nursing Times* 104(41): 31–2.

REFERENCES

An Bord Altranais (2009) *Data from An Bord Altranais Active Register*
(unpublished report). An Bord Altranais.
Anthony, M. K. (1999) 'The relationship of authority to decision-making
behaviour: implications for redesign', *Research in Nursing and Health* 22(5):
388–98.
Argyris, C. (1964) *Integrating the Individual and the Organisation.* New York:
John Wiley & Sons.
Bass, B. M. (1985) *Leadership and Performance Beyond Expectations.* New York:
Free Press.
Bass, B. M. and Avolio, B. J. (1991) Multifactor Leadership Questionnaire (Form
5X). Binghamton, NY: Center for Leadership Studies.
Batson, C. D. (1987) 'Prosocial motivation: is it ever truly altruistic?' in Berkowitz,
L. (ed.), *Advances in Experimental Social Psychology* Vol. 20. New York:
Academic Press (pp. 65–122).
Benson, S. G. and Dundis, S. P. (2003) 'Understanding and motivating health care
employees: integrating Maslow's hierarchy of needs, training and technology',
Journal of Nursing Management 11 (5): 315–20.
Brown, B. (2000) *Motivating Staff for Better Performance.* Havant, Hampshire:
Rowmark.
Burns, J. M. (1978) *Leadership.* New York: Harper and Row.
Carney, M. (2006) *Health Service Management: Consensus, Culture and the
Middle Manager.* Cork: Oak Tree Press.
Chiok Foong Loke, J. (2001) 'Leadership behaviours: effects on job satisfaction,
productivity and organisational commitment', *Journal of Nursing
Management* 9(4): 191–204.
Christianson, J. B., Knutson, D. J. and Mazze, R. S. (2006) 'Physician pay-for-
performance. Implementation and research issues', *Journal of General
Internal Medicine* 21(2): S9–13.

Curtis, E. A. (2007) 'Job satisfaction: a survey of nurses in the Republic of Ireland', *International Nursing Review* 54(1): 92–9.

Daft, R. L. (2000) *Management* (5th edn). Fort Worth, TX: Dryden Press.

Dieleman, M., Cuong, P. V., Anh, L. V. and Martineau, T. (2003) 'Identifying factors for job motivation of rural health workers in North Viet Nam', *Human Resources for Health* 1(1): 10.

Dixon, R. (1991) *Management Theory and Practice*. King's Lynn: Biddles.

Dvir, T., Eden, D., Avolio, B. J. and Shamir, B. (2002) 'Impact of transformational leadership on follower development and performance: a field experiment', *Academy of Management Journal* 45(4): 735–44.

Edgar, L. (1999) 'Nurses' motivation and its relationship to the characteristics of nursing care delivery systems: A test of the job characteristics model', *Canadian Journal of Nursing Leadership* 12 (1): 14–22.

Erbin-Roesemann, M. and Simms, L. M. (1997) 'Work locus of control: the intrinsic factor behind empowerment and work excitement', *Nursing Economics* 15(4): 183–90.

Franco, L. M., Bennett, S., Kanfer, R. and Stubblebine, P. (2004) 'Determinants and consequences of health worker motivation in hospitals in Jordan and Georgia', *Social Science and Medicine* 58(2): 343–55.

Freeborn, D. K., Schmoldt, R. and Klevit, H. D. (2001) 'Satisfaction, commitment, and psychological well-being among HMO physicians', *Western Journal of Medicine* 174 (1): 13–18.

Gange, M., and Deci, E. L. (2005) 'Self-determination theory and work motivation', *Journal of Organisational Behaviour* 26(4): 331–62.

Gellerman, S. W. (1968) *Management by Motivation*. New York: American Management Association.

Georgopoulos, B. S., Mahoney, G. M. and Jones, N. W. (1957) 'A path–goal approach to productivity', *Journal of Applied Psychology* 41(6): 345–53.

Golembiewski, R. T. (1993) *Handbook of Organisational Behaviour*. New York: Marcel Dekker.

Grant, A. M. (2008) 'Does intrinsic motivation fuel the prosocial fire? Motivational synergy in predicting persistence, performance, and productivity', *Journal of Applied Psychology* 93(1): 48–58.

Guion, R. M. and Landy, F. J. (1972) 'The meaning of work and the motivation to work', *Organisational Behaviour and Human Performance* 7(2): 308–39.

Hackman, J. R. and Oldham, G. R. (1980) *Work Redesign*. Reading, MA: Addison-Wesley.

Henderson, A., Winch, S., Holzhauser, K. and De Vries, S. (2006) 'The motivation of health professionals to explore research evidence in their practice: An intervention study', *Issues in Clinical Nursing* 15(12): 1559–64.

Herzberg, F. (2003) 'One more time: how do you motivate employees?', *Harvard Business Review* 81(1): 87–96.

Herzberg, F., Mausner, B. and Snyderman, B. (1959) *The Motivation of Work*. New York: Wiley.

Hetland, H. and Sandal, G. M. (2003) 'Transformational leadership in Norway:

outcomes and personality correlates', *European Journal of Work and Organisational Psychology* 12(2): 147–70.

HSE Midland Health Board, http://www.mhb.ie/mhb/OurServices/Qualityof WorkingLife/, accessed 25 February 2009.

Hughes, R. L., Ginnet, R. C. and Curphy, G. J. (2006) *Leadership: Enhancing the Lessons of Experience* (5th edn). Boston: McGraw-Hill.

Janssen, P. P. M., de Jonge, J. and Bakker, A. B. (1999) 'Specific determinants of intrinsic motivation, burnout, and turnover intentions: a study among nurses', *Journal of Advanced Nursing* 29(6): 1360–9.

Jewell, L. N. (1998) *Contemporary Industrial/Organisational Psychology* (3rd edn). Pacific Grove, CA: Brooks/Cole Publishing.

Kane, T. D. and Tremble, T. R., Jr (2000) 'Transformational leadership effects at different levels of the army', *Military Psychology* 12(2): 137–60.

Kanfer, R. and Ackerman, P. L. (2004) 'Aging, adult development, and work motivation', *Academy of Management Review* 29 (3): 440–58.

Katzell, R. A. and Thompson, D. E. (1990) 'Work motivation: theory and practice', *American Psychologist* 45(2): 144–53.

Kerr, S. (1999) 'Practical, cost-neutral alternatives that you may know but don't practise', *Organisation Dynamics* 28(1): 61–70.

Kivimaki, M., Voutilainen, P. and Koskinen, P. (1995) 'Job enrichment, work motivation, and job satisfaction in hospital wards: testing the job characteristics model', *Journal of Nursing Management* 3(2): 87–91.

Kleinginna, P. R. and Kleinginna, A. M. (1981) 'A categorised list of motivation definitions with a suggestion for a consensual definition', *Motivation and Emotion* 5: 263–92.

Krairiksh, M. (2001) 'Benefits and outcomes of staff nurses' participation in decision making', *Journal of Nursing Administration* 31(1): 16–23.

Kuvaas, B. (2006) 'Performance appraisal satisfaction and employee outcomes: mediating and moderating roles of work motivation', *International Journal of Human Resource Management* 17(3): 504–22.

Landy, F. J. and Guion, R. M. (1970) 'Development of scales for the measurement of work motivation', *Organisational Behaviour and Human Performance* 5(1): 93–103.

Locke, E. A. (1968) 'Toward a theory of task motivation and incentives', *Organisational Behaviour and Human Performance* 3(2): 157–89.

Long, R. (2005) *Motivation*. London: David Fulton Publishers.

Makinen, A., Kivimaki, M., Elovainio, M., Virtanen, M. and Senga, B. (2003) 'Organisation of nursing care as a determinant of job satisfaction among hospital nurses', *Journal of Nursing Management* 11(5): 299–306.

Marquis, B. L. and Huston, C. J. (2000) *Leadership Roles and Management Functions in Nursing: Theory and Application* (3rd edn). Philadelphia: Lippincott Williams & Wilkins.

Maslow, A. H. (1954) *Motivation and Personality*. New York: Harper and Row.

Mayfield, J. (2009) 'Motivating language: a meaningful guide for leader communications', *Development and Learning Organisations* 23(1): 9–11.

McDonald, R., Harrison, S., Checkland, K., Campbell, S. M. and Roland, M. (2007) 'Impact of financial incentives on clinical autonomy and internal motivation in primary care: ethnographic study', *British Medical Journal* 334 (7608): 1357–69.

Mitchell, T. R. (1982) 'Motivation: new directions for theory, research and practice', *Academy of Management Review* 7(1): 80–8.

Muchinsky, P. M. (1993) *Psychology Applied to Work: An Introduction to Industrial and Organisational Psychology*. Pacific Grove, CA: Brooks/Cole Publishing.

Offermann, L. R. (1997) 'Leading and empowering diverse followers' in Hollander, E. P. and Offerman, L. R. (eds), *The Balance of Leadership and Followership*, Kellogg Leadership Studies Project. University of Maryland Press (pp. 31–46).

Patchen, M., Pelz, D. and Allen, C. (1965) *Some Questionnaire Measures of Employee Motivation and Morale*. Ann Arbor, MI: Institute for Social Research.

Peters, T. and Waterman, R. H. (1982) *In Search of Excellence*. New York: Harper & Row.

Pinder, C. C. (1984) *Work Motivation*. Glenview, IL: Scott, Foresman.

Rainey, H. G. (1983) 'Public agencies and private firms: incentive structures, goals, and individual roles', *Administration and Society* 15(2): 207–42.

— (1993) 'Work motivation' in Golembiewski, Robert T. (ed.), *Handbook of Organisational Behavior*. New York: Marcel Dekker, Inc.

Roland, M. (2004) 'Linking physicians' pay to the quality of care – a major experiment in the United Kingdom', *New England Journal of Medicine* 351(14): 1448–54.

Schepers, C., De Gieter, S., Pepermans, R., Du Bois, C., Caers, R. and Jegerrs, M. (2005) 'How are employees of the nonprofit sector motivated? A research need', *Nonprofit Management and Leadership* 16 (2): 191–208.

Spector, P. E. (2006) *Industrial and Organisational Psychology: Research and Practice* (4th edn). Hoboken, NJ: John Wiley & Sons.

Stajkovic, A. D. and Luthans, F. (2001) 'Differential effects of incentive motivators on work performance', *Academy of Management Journal* 4 (3): 580–90.

Steers, R. M. and Porter, L. M. (1987) *Motivation and Work Behaviour*. New York: McGraw-Hill.

Sullivan, E. J. and Decker, P. J. (2005) *Effective Leadership and Management in Nursing* (6th edn). New Jersey: Pearson Education International.

Sullivan, J. (1988) 'Three roles of language in motivation theory', *Academy of Management Review* 13(1): 104–15.

Vroom, V. H. (1964) *Work and Motivation*. New York: Wiley.

Weihrich, H. and Koontz, H. (2005) *Management. A Global Perspective* (11th edn). Singapore: McGraw Hill.

White, K. M. (1998) 'Planned change' in Rocchiccioli, J. T. and Tilbury, M. S. (eds) *Clinical Leadership in Nursing*. Philadelphia: W. B. Saunders (pp. 179–95).

Wong, R. (2000) *Motivation: A Behavioural Approach*. Cambridge: Cambridge University Press.

Yearta, S. K., Maitlis, S. and Briner, R. B. (1995) 'An exploratory study of goal-setting in theory and practice', *Journal of Occupational and Organisational Psychology* 68.

Developing the Health Service

11
Leading Change in the Irish Health Service

Eilísh Hardiman

OBJECTIVES
- To critically discuss the context of change in the Irish health service.
- To develop insight into individual and organisation response to change.
- To critically discuss ways of overcoming obstacles to change.
- To explore relevant theories of change in the context of health care.
- To develop an understanding of the process of planning change.

INTRODUCTION

The contemporary idea of change assumes that it involves movement between some discrete and perhaps fixed 'states', that is, a movement from an existing 'state' to another reconfigured 'state'. Change encompasses numerous variations and complexities and an experience of change can be seen as opportunistic, exciting and threatening at the same time. Therefore, any attempt to understand and manage change must take this complexity into account. Significant changes in the Irish health care service have taken place since the establishment of the Health Service Executive (HSE) in 2005, in accordance with recommendations by both the Brennan and Prospectus reports (DoHC 2003a, 2003b). Reconfiguration of Ireland's health care organisation and delivery systems has been further guided by specific reports commissioned by the HSE that have resulted in organisational change programmes, such as the Transformation Programme (2007) and the Integration Programme (2009). These organisational change programmes impact on how, where and by whom care and treatment is provided to patients/clients of the health care system by health care professionals and their support staff.

A recurring theme of this change for Ireland's health care is the shift in care and treatment delivery from a hospital-centric activity to an ambulatory or, where possible, a community/home-based activity. An innovative exemplar of this trend change in health care delivery is the drive to support early discharge from hospital of patients who no longer require acute health care intervention, with medical and nursing care, such as intravenous antibiotic treatment, delivered in the patient's home. This patient-centred approach to health care delivery challenges the traditional hospital-centric approach to care delivery. It requires stronger governance structures; communication and collaboration across acute and community services; role change and role expansion for some health care professionals; and fundamentally a visionary change in the delivery of health care in Ireland. Health care professionals are required to respond to change throughout their professional careers; and to enable a better understanding of this level of change in health care organisation and delivery, theories on change, failures of or resistance to change and models for making change happen are explored in this chapter.

ORGANISATIONAL CHANGE THEORY

There is a plethora of literature available on change and change management and one reason for this is the particular popularity of organisational change theory post-1945, when new organisations emerged whose size and complexity exceeded those of their pre-war counterparts. Fresh ideas were required to assist in the management and development of these organisations. The diversity of change theories adds to the complexity of understanding and managing change. This was demonstrated by Hal Leavitt's (1965) various approaches to address a management problem. He solicited responses to the problem from three different schools of thinking, representing organisational development (OD), operational research (OR) and the traditional general management consultancy viewpoint. Each proposal offered partially correct solutions to address the problem, that when used together provided an overall better solution. Although combining different disciplines is more complex, change is also far more likely to happen and the combined discipline approach is still in force today.

Beer and Nohria (2000) demonstrated how a shareholder-oriented, financially centred approach to change, Theory E, is effective when used in combination with its softer Theory O counterpart, which espouses values such as corporate culture, employee commitment and organisational learning. While such an approach may increase the chances of success, it is nonetheless worth remembering that around 75 per cent of change efforts fail. However, accumulating evidence in favour of a particular tool or technique is extremely difficult. Even relatively modest changes result in effects that are unexpected, hard to quantify, or only apparent months or years after the end of the programme.

TYPES OF CHANGE

The chances of choosing the right change model can be greatly increased if there is an understanding of the type of change required. Change management literature offers ample choices for defining the concept. Broadly speaking, the literature provides three types/sets of change categories (Hayes 2002). These assess change as:

- **Planned or emergent** – the extent to which change comes about through chance or through careful planned strategy analysis.
- **Episodic or continuous** – how an organisation is developing in comparison with long-term objectives.
- **Developmental, transitional or transformational** – concerned with the intensity and range of the change within an organisation.

A further review of Hayes's (2002) third change category is appropriate to Irish health care because the HSE has embarked on a transformational change management process. This category change type is further broken down and described as follows:

- **Developmental change** – this refers to the natural growth of an organisation over time, and may include staff increases, geographical relocation or expansion.
- **Transitional change** – reactive change to new environmental or market conditions. This might include investing in a new technology or refining existing processes to make them more efficient.
- **Transformational change** – alterations to an organisation's fundamental way of doing business. The changes affect the entire organisation or enterprise and are manifested in explicit changes to strategy, values and culture.

Developmental and transitional changes are known collectively as first-order change. Typically they affect processes or procedures but not the fundamental way in which organisations do business. Though important, they do not present significant challenges to leaders. Transformational change, on the other hand, is a move into the unknown, and is referred to as second-order change. In order to further explore this type of change, sentinel renowned models of change are explored.

MODELS OF CHANGE

Kurt Lewin is credited with saying that one only understands an organisation when one tries to change it. Nadler (1980) maintains that bringing about major change in large and complex organisations is a challenging task. The old way of doing tasks, jobs, procedures and structures is no longer applicable and this frequently gives rise to political behaviour. But there is nothing new in this and the process of effectively implementing organisational change has always been to the fore on leaders' and managers' agendas. Hence, the past decades have seen the evolution of a number of change models and frameworks for large systems change.

In change situations many change approaches focus on *content*, that is, what needs to change. Others focus on *process*, that is, how change is implemented. Approaching a change situation using an organisation development approach recognises the value of both, in particular the importance of paying attention to the process for implementing successful and lasting change (Coghlan & McAuliffe 2003). Kurt Lewin and John Kotter's approaches to change are two of the best-known change models.

Kurt Lewin

Lewin (1951) advanced the notion that in most situations the status quo is maintained by driving and restraining forces working in opposition. The driving forces are those things that potentially drive change while the restraining forces are those maintaining things as they are. For change to occur there must be a change in the balance of the restraining and driving forces. A force field analysis framework as illustrated in Figure 11.1 is a useful exercise in any change initiative to assist in clarification of both restraining and driving forces.

Figure 11.1: Force field analysis framework

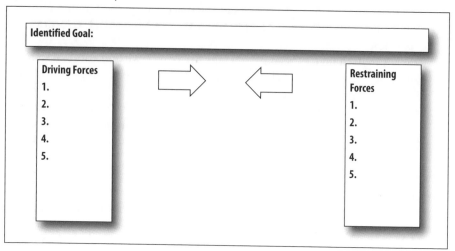

Lewin's (1951) basic model of change is a simple one involving three stages: unfreezing, changing and refreezing.

- **Unfreezing** – gaining awareness of the need for change and overcoming internal resistance.
- **Moving** – adopting the change.
- **Refreezing** – making sure the change sticks.

According to Lewin, each stage is equally important and unless all three occur, the change will not last. This linear and static conceptualisation of an organisation is a very straightforward way of planning actions by reducing a complex process into a simplistic formula. Yet organisations as complex entities are never really 'frozen', much less 'refrozen'. Virtually all models of organisation change use his approach; notwithstanding this, it is important to view organisational change as ever-present, continuous, multidirectional and multifaceted. After Lewin applied the model to more complex, real-life workplace environments, subsequent elaborations of the basic model emerged involving feedback loops between the stages so that the results of evaluation inform theory in a cyclical process of fact-finding, planning, action and evaluation.

John Kotter

John Kotter (1995), a world-renowned expert on transformational change, offers a common-sense framework grounded on simple tenets: create and communicate a vision and get the organisation onside. His eight most common errors made by organisations undertaking transformational change (see below) are used to formulate an eight-step model for successful change.

Figure 11.2: Kotter's (1995) eight-step model for successful change

```
┌─────────────────────────────────────────────────────────┐
│  ┌───────────────────────────────────────────────┐   ▲  │
│  │         Establish a sense of urgency          │   │  │
│  └───────────────────────────────────────────────┘   │  │
│                        ▼                              │  │
│  ┌───────────────────────────────────────────────┐   │  │
│  │         Form a powerful guiding coalition     │   │  │
│  └───────────────────────────────────────────────┘   │  │
│                        ▼                              │  │
│  ┌───────────────────────────────────────────────┐   │  │
│  │               Create a vision                 │   │  │
│  └───────────────────────────────────────────────┘   │  │
│                        ▼                              │  │
│  ┌───────────────────────────────────────────────┐   │  │
│  │            Communicate the vision             │   │  │
│  └───────────────────────────────────────────────┘   │  │
│                        ▼                              │  │
│  ┌───────────────────────────────────────────────┐   │  │
│  │        Empower others to act on the vision    │   │  │
│  └───────────────────────────────────────────────┘   │  │
│                        ▼                              │  │
│  ┌───────────────────────────────────────────────┐   │  │
│  │       Plan for and create short-term wins     │   │  │
│  └───────────────────────────────────────────────┘   │  │
│                        ▼                              │  │
│  ┌───────────────────────────────────────────────┐   │  │
│  │ Consolidate improvements and produce still more results │  │
│  └───────────────────────────────────────────────┘   │  │
│                        ▼                              │  │
│  ┌───────────────────────────────────────────────┐      │
│  │       Institutionalise new approaches         │      │
│  └───────────────────────────────────────────────┘      │
└─────────────────────────────────────────────────────────┘
```

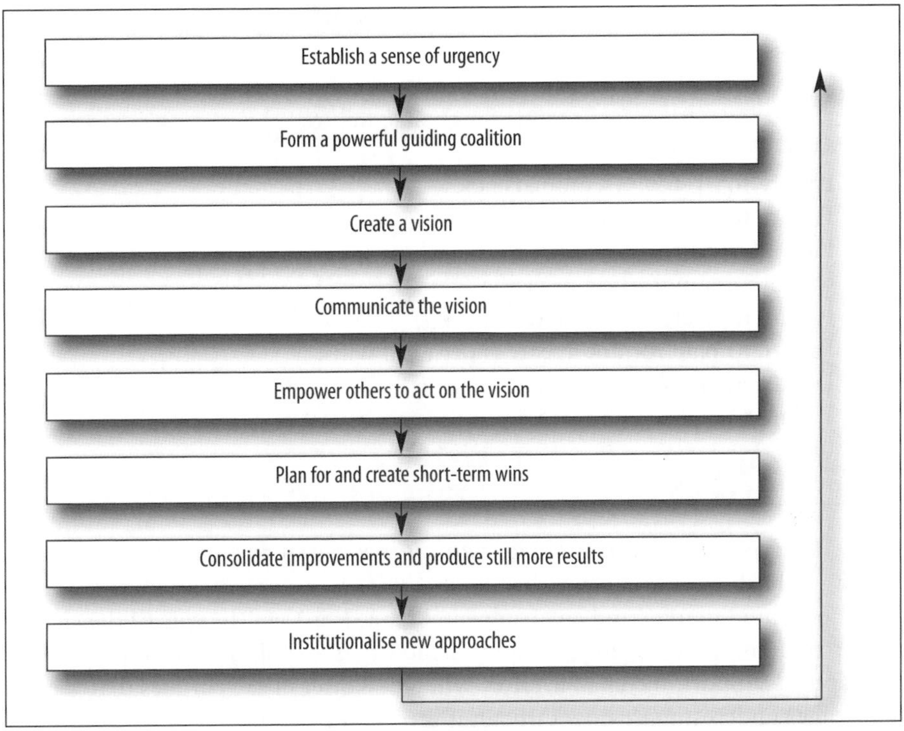

FAILURE AND RESISTANCE

Few organisational change efforts are complete failures but there is a tendency for few to be entirely successful. The process of bringing about change can be long and arduous and hence it is not surprising that most organisations encounter problems on the way. The reasons why change fails and the various causes for resistance to change are further described here.

Reasons why change fails

Over the years there have been many critiques of the failure of change initiatives to produce desired outcomes. Beer, Eisenstat and Spenser (1990) maintain that it is because change programmes are guided by a flawed theory of change. Based on their research, they deduce that change needs to begin with changing the individual's knowledge and attitudes, which in turn leads to changes in behaviour, and this ultimately has the potential to lead to organisational change. Because individual behaviour is greatly shaped by the organisational roles that people play, they believe that the most effective way to change behaviour is to put people into a new organisational context which imposes new roles, responsibilities and relationships. In reality, unexpected forces are normally encountered and it is these uncontrollable and powerful forces that pose questions about the manageability of change at all.

Kotter (1995) argues that there are eight errors commonly made by organisations undertaking transformational change. His work in this regard is among the most influential recent contributions to change management. The eight errors are as outlined below.

Reasons for change failure

- Failure to overcome complacency.
- Failure to create effective coalitions.
- Lack of or insufficient vision.
- Under-communication of vision.
- Failure to overcome obstacles.
- Failure to plan for and create short-term wins.
- Declaring victory too soon.
- Failure to embed changes within the organisation.

Adapted from Kotter (1995).

Error 1 – Not establishing a great enough sense of urgency

When establishing the case for change, it is vital to outline a clear business case based on sound market and environmental data. It is then the role of the change leader to communicate this strongly to the organisation as a whole. Without widespread support, the change effort will fail. Kotter (1995) argues that leaders sometimes underestimate how difficult it is to shake people out of their 'comfort zones'. In addition, staff can be put off by the unpleasant realities of change. He recommends a full and frank discussion between the change leader (either at the CEO or divisional level) outlining the problems with the existing situation and the need for change. Particular attention should be paid to making sure that staff understand change and feel part of the process.

Error 2 – Not creating a powerful enough coalition

It is not possible to convince everyone in the organisation that the change programme proposed is the correct one. However, it is vital to establish a coalition of the most influential people (a dominant coalition) to get behind the idea. Without visible management buy-in, staff will not be convinced. The coalition should grow in size over time, as a convincing business case is made.

Error 3 – Lacking a vision

It is the explicit task of the coalition to establish a compelling and pragmatic vision for the change programme. The vision must appeal to the organisation as a whole. Kotter says that if the vision cannot be communicated in five minutes or less, it is likely to be too inaccessible.

Error 4 – Under-communicating the vision by a factor of ten
Successful change leaders use every possible medium of broadcast to communicate their vision. Open and transparent communication is particularly important if downsizing, reorganisation or reconfiguration is likely to be an element of the change programme. Executives should incorporate discussion of the vision into their day-to-day dealings with all relevant stakeholders.

Error 5 – Not removing obstacles to the new vision
Any potential obstacles to the vision must be removed. These might include the organisational structure, compensation or appraisal systems or unwilling individuals in management positions. Obstacles should first be identified and then addressed.

Error 6 – Not systematically planning for and creating short-term wins
It will be extremely difficult to keep the entire organisation onside if there is not visible evidence of success within the first 12 months of the change programme. It is the job of the coalition and change leaders to make sure that short-term goals are incorporated into the longer-term vision.

Error 7 – Declaring victory too soon
Kotter argues that the change process can take up to ten years before it sinks in fully. If the change team is impatient, or a great enough sense of urgency is not generated, victory might be declared too early. A premature celebration will breed complacency.

Error 8 – Not anchoring changes in the organisation's culture
New behaviours have to be rooted in the culture, values and daily practices of the organisation. If they are not, it will be all too easy to slip back into old habits. In order for this to happen, staff have to be shown the benefits of the new organisation. In addition, new management have to understand and personify the new approach.

Overall, it could be argued that successful change programmes are founded on the principle of organisational learning. The term 'learning organisation' is primarily attributed to Peter Senge (1990), who defined it as an ideal organisation that can cope with continued change and transformation. Senge (1990) believes that organisations learn through individuals who learn. Individual learning does not guarantee organisational learning, but without it no organisational learning will take place. The five essential components of a learning organisation, according to Senge (1990), are as follows:

1   **Systems thinking** – the way in which we consider and solve problems and interpret solutions.
2   **Personal mastery** – defining what you want to achieve and how you are going to get it.

3   **Mental models** – deeply held beliefs about the way the world works.
4   **Shared vision** – sharing common values, beliefs and goals as an organisation.
5   **Team learning** – learning as a group, sharing experience and expertise.

Of these essential components, systems thinking poses the greatest problem in implementing a learning organisation. It is only by addressing outdated systems thinking that there can be success in building a learning organisation, which is a prerequisite for effective transformational change. Therefore, in *The Dance of Change*, Senge *et al.* (1999) refined his earlier theory, based on the experience of business people who took his initial advice. Their experience was that the learning and change paradigm that Senge (1990) espoused in *The Fifth Discipline* was much more difficult to implement than initially thought. Senge (1990) observed that traditional change models (with change being led by senior management) have a poorer record of success. This is not due to lack of resources or intelligence, but rather because organisations are viewed as machines rather than 'embodiments of nature'. Rigid hierarchical structures contribute to this idea of the company as a machine. However, the low rate of success in change programmes indicates that this view is flawed and with this in mind Senge recommends a slow, organic attitude to change, rather than a formalised programme. He also claims that having one change leader is likely to be ineffective. It is vital to have leaders at all levels of the organisation because innovation and effective change grow out of middle managers and line managers taking action. This exploration leads him to a new definition of a leader as someone who has the ability to produce change. Senge also recommends starting the change process on a small scale, with a group of informed stakeholders who make up a pilot team. The team should conduct a force field analysis identifying current processes that will aid the change programme, and root out those that will hinder it. He believes that the effectiveness of the pilot team as a change agent is enhanced because the individuals involved develop a personal stake in the change initiative.

Resistance to change

Change has always been a constant in human and organisational life and, just as change is inevitable, so too is resistance to change. Zaltman and Duncan (1977:63) define resistance as 'any conduct that serves to maintain that status quo in the face of pressure to alter the status quo'.

They consider that resistance may even be justifiable in cases where the change may be harmful to individuals or to a group. Lawrence (1954) contends that resistance to change should not be entirely eliminated because it may serve to alert the organisation to investigate and re-examine the change. Overall, resistance to change is the term given to perceived behaviour of organisational members who seem unwilling to accept or implement an organisational change. Consequently, it is often seen as a negative force that needs to be overcome in order to move forward. Resistance can come at an institutional level (the organisation as a whole, its culture and values), at the individual level (staff reluctance to change, fear of the unknown) or both, and it can also be demonstrated at the group or team level. In general, a change process frequently involves inter-team conflict in situations where a management group promotes change: those affected by change feel apart from that group and they oppose the change.

MAKING CHANGE HAPPEN

Several frameworks exist to guide the planning, implementation and benefits realisation of change initiatives. All of these have common themes around the following five areas.

Determining the need for change

Nadler (1998) describes this as 'recognising the change imperative' or, more simply, determining 'what's wrong here'. Establishing that change is required, as well as the reasons why change is needed, is an important first step that should not be taken for granted. Coghlan and McAuliffe (2003) state that external forces, brought about through economic or political shifts, regulation, consumer demand or calls for greater transparency or efficiency, may initiate change. Alternatively, the key change drivers may be internal, resulting from factors such as: budget shortfalls; customer preferences; low staff morale; a workforce with changing requirements and expectations; inter-departmental animosity; or a need to replace ineffective hierarchical management styles with a more collaborative approach involving devolved decision-making. Either way, analysis of the factors driving change is an essential first step to bring about successful change. Once the factors driving change are evaluated, it is necessary to consider the multiplicity of options that a change initiative brings.

A third stage in understanding the imperative for change is that of deciding the scale of change required. Coghlan and McAuliffe (2003) define the scale of change as either first- or second-order change:

- **first-order change** – improving what an organisation does and how
- **second-order change** – a system-wide change in the operation of, and attitudes within, an organisation.

Finally, it is important to understand the processes underlying how one individual's perception of the need for change is communicated throughout the organisation. Rashford and Coghlan (1994) point out that the move from individual to team to cross-departmental group is an iterative process. That is, as each group adopts the previous group's position, the latter's position is strengthened in a snowball effect which places the original idea on an increasingly solid base. The following steps help to make change happen.

Defining the desired future

Nadler (1980) believes that the next step in overseeing the change process is 'developing a shared direction' where an organisation's appearance post-change is defined. This provides the necessary focus and allows organisation-wide input into what people want to see as a result of the change. It also counters the inevitable preoccupation with all those negative factors that necessitated the change in the first place.

Assessing the present in terms of the desired future

This is the assessment of what needs to be changed, and what does not, in reference to the defined desired future. At this stage the change may be broken down into subgroups and prioritised logically so that not only are the most important changes tackled first, but they are also tackled in the most efficient order. For example, if A is changed, will it impact on B or C next? This is also the stage to identify which parts of the organisation need to be involved in which parts of the change. Beckhard and Harris (1987) state that two factors should be assessed: readiness (the willingness to change); and capability (the ability, psychologically or otherwise, to change). This particularly applies within and between teams and involves factors ranging from the inevitable political tensions to knowledge-based factors, such as information management or IT literacy.

Implementing the change and managing the transition

This is the process of change itself, where the present moves towards – and hopefully becomes – the projected desired future. Between these two states is the difficult transition period, which Coghlan and McAuliffe (2003) believe requires two things. First, a strategic and operational plan, which sets out goals, activities, structures and projects, needed to reach the end of the process. Such a plan also serves as a helpful reminder that the transition period is just that, and should not be taken for the culmination of the change. Second, commitment of all those involved should be sought during the transition, if it is not already in place.

Consolidating and sustaining the change

Relaxing too soon is the downfall of many a change intervention, whilst consolidation is often the key to its success. The change requires monitoring, refinement and assessment if it is to become fully accepted as 'normal' or to make it 'stick'. HR plays a key role here by encouraging people to align 'the informal organisation with the formal', accepting the change by no longer regarding it as a threat. This process of 'normalisation' of course has potential to pose problems in the future, as future change occurs and is resisted by those accustomed to the new normal changed organisation.

CHANGE AND LEADERSHIP

There are two essential conditions for any change effort to be effectively managed. First, the organisation leadership must be aware of the need for change and its consequences in terms of their actions. Second, the organisation leadership must have a relatively clear idea of the desired outcome (Beckhard & Harris 1987). Early definitions of leadership concentrated on personality characteristics and traits, values and beliefs, but it is not possible to predict characteristics or traits that would work in all situations. The emphasis then moved to leadership styles and behaviours required for successful change management. During the 1980s the importance of vision, a participatory rather than autocratic leadership style and a democratic approach to change began to emerge in the writings of Peters and Waterman (1982) and Moss Kanter (1983). Rosbeth Moss Kanter argues that organisations that cope well with change share three common features, all of which are associated with particular leadership behaviours:

- **The imagination to innovate** – leaders must be able to encourage innovation.
- **The professionalism to perform** – leaders lead by example, setting out impeccable behaviour and competencies for the rest of the organisation to follow.
- **The openness to collaborate** – leaders network, forming relationships with other stakeholders.

These attributes reflect behaviours as opposed to processes and this means that they are more difficult to learn. Moss Kanter (1983) argues that in their absence, change will prove awkward, particularly if people feel that it is compelled by crisis. Since the 1980s, the notion of one best leadership style has been criticised. Dunphy and Stace (1990) believe a contingency approach to leadership, where a particular style of leadership is adopted depending on the organisational conditions, works best.

Burns's (1978) seminal work on leadership looked at the distinction between transactional and transformational leaders. Transactional leadership focuses on the transaction that takes place between the leader and the follower. It occurs when a leader takes the initiative and some form of return, such as pay, promotion and/or recognition, is given to the follower for performance. Transformational leadership is where charisma is used to transform a vision into shared objectives. Because it represents a process for engaging staff to a shared vision and values, it is particularly important in leading change. The five key tasks of moving change through a system, such as an organisation, a team or a unit, have already been explained as:

- determining the need for change
- defining the desired future state
- assessing the present in terms of the desired future to determine the changes to be made
- implementing the change and managing the transition
- consolidating and sustaining the change.

The role of leadership in this model is to steer and guide the system through the demands of each of the five tasks (Beckhard & Pritchard 1992). In their edited work on *The Leader of the Future*, Hesselbein *et al.* (1996) consider leadership in terms of what skills, actions and strategies are needed for the organisation of the future. The need for leaders to envision, empower, coach, serve, lead diversity and shape culture, to be learners themselves and manage their own self-learning were recurrent messages for the leader of the future. All of these are essential for the successful implementation of any change programme.

MANAGING THE TRANSITION

Implementing a change involves moving an organisation to some desired future state (Nadler 1980). Changes can be considered in terms of transitions (Beckhard & Harris 1987), as depicted in Figure 11.3.

Figure 11.3: Transition in organisational change

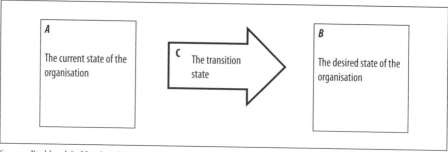

Source: Beckhard & Harris (1987)

According to Nadler (1980), at any point in time the organisation exists in its current state (A), which is how the organisation functions prior to the change. The future state (B) described how the organisation should be functioning in the future, and the period between A and B can be considered as the transition state (C). Effective management of change involves understanding the current state, and moving the organisation from A through the transition period to B, that is, the future desired state.

CASE STUDY

The Community Intervention Team (CIT) was introduced in 2006 as part of the reform agenda in the HSE as an initiative between the acute services (hospitals) and the community-based services (nurse-based service) to reorientate health services towards the community. The 'hospital-in-the-home' concept is a well-developed construct in international health care delivery systems. Models to implement this concept were explored by the HSE in 2007/8. It concluded that it is feasible, safe, patient-focused and, by utilising existing resources, it is also more economical to deliver specific treatments in the community/home that were previously solely delivered in the hospital setting. This shift in service delivery resulted in change for health care professionals across the acute hospitals and community services. The principal role of this nurse-led service is to provide a rapid response from community services to patients so that unnecessary referrals to emergency departments and/or hospital admissions can be avoided and patients can be cared for at home in their community where most prefer to stay. The advantages of this type of service are numerous and include the following.

- **Reduction in hospital admissions.** This service can avoid patients being admitted from the emergency department by enabling follow-up care or supervision in their home or in a nursing home on discharge from the department. (A good example is a dehydrated patient from a nursing home who needs 12–24 hours of intravenous hydration.) The CIT can prevent patients having to go to the hospital for simple interventions such as urinary catheter changes or peripheral intravenous central line (PIC line) flushing to maintain line patency.
- **Reduction in length of stay.** Patients can be discharged earlier, for example on intravenous antibiotics (given in the home by the CIT nurse).
- **Efficient use of services.** Out-of-hours services can enable the discharge of a patient late in the day (after 5 p.m.) with the facility to have the nurse call into them before 10 p.m. that night to monitor their progress. Acute hospital beds are freed up for those who need them.
- **Enhanced patient outcomes.** Patients can be nursed in their own homes with the support of family, thereby increasing patient satisfaction and reducing the risk of hospital-acquired complications.

This type of initiative involves close collaboration between the hospital and community-based service managers and front-line staff and required a number of changes to the traditional approaches used in community care in the Irish Republic. Critical to the initiative was the development of strong clinical governance structures which steered hospital consultants into 'shared care' programmes around specific chronic diseases (chronic obstructive pulmonary disease, heart failure) with their GP colleagues in the community. Each hospital had to identify a single consultant as the point of contact for the CIT to liaise with if there was an issue with a patient in the community. Drugs normally not administered in the community had to be prepared, dispensed and made available for use out of hours. Public health nurses had to agree to take on the services initiated by the CIT if these services were required longer than a week.

1   Identify who the key stakeholders would be in the above scenario.
2   Use a force field analysis framework to identify the driving and restraining forces in implementing such a service in your locality.
3   Discuss how potential barriers to this proposed change could be overcome.
4   Using a model of change, outline how this type of service might be implemented in your area.

CONCLUSION

All organisations need to continuously review their structures to ensure contemporary 'fit' with changes in their environment. This strategic renewal imperative involves redesigning organisation structure and therefore managing organisational change. This chapter focused on change management theory, with the main types of change and its characteristics outlined. Why change initiatives fail and resistance to change were explored, using Kotter's (1995) eight errors that organisations commonly make in undertaking change. The concept of Senge's 'learning organisation' was explained to demonstrate how an ideal organisation can cope with continued change and transformation, thereby minimising the chances of change failing. Models for change from Lewin and Kotter briefly highlighted that choosing the right model and understanding the type of change and the context in which it operates is imperative in approaching any change situation. The final sections addressed key issues in relation to leadership in change situations and managing the transition. It has been highlighted that organisation structure design and, in particular, change management are bewilderingly complex. While choosing the right model and understanding the required type of organisation structure design change and its context is important, of equal concern to organisations are the practical aspects of implementing an organisational structural change programme.

In summary, there are a number of markers from the literature that can assist in successfully managing and leading change in Ireland's health care system. Some knowledge of the history of change management provides the necessary context for managers and organisation leaders to construct a change initiative. While many of the best change management frameworks and models are decades old, they are still highly relevant. One key to successful change management is to understand the choices available and to select change techniques or models that suit the speed and scope of change required. During a change strategy it is important to remain alert to what is going on, both internal and external to the organisation. The ever-changing environment requires continuous renewal of an organisation's strategy if organisations, including health care organisations, wish to remain sustainable in meeting their core objectives.

REFLECTIVE EXERCISES

1 In your capacity as a health care professional, consider a change at work that you resisted. Reflect on the stages you experienced before you reached acceptance.

2 Discuss the concept of resistance to change in health care work environments and approaches to overcoming resistance.

3 For the organisation or area in which you work, identify a change that would benefit patient/client care and identify the driving and restraining forces.

4 Using a selected strategy for change, design a plan that would enable you to implement this change.

ADDITIONAL RESOURCES

Health Service Executive: *The Change Hub*. Available at www.hseland.ie/tohm/default.asp

REFERENCES

Beckhard, R. and Harris, R. (1987) *Organisational Transitions: Creating and Leading Fundamental Change in Organisations*. Reading, MA: Addison-Wesley.

Beckhard, R. and Pritchard, W. (1992) *Changing the Essence: The Art of Creating and Leading Fundamental Change in Organisations*. San Francisco: Jossey-Bass.

Beer, M., Eisenstat, R. and Spenser B. (1990): 'Why change programs don't produce change', *Harvard Business Review* November–December, 158–66.

Beer, M. and Nohria, N. (2000): 'Resolving the tension between Theories E and O of change' in Beer, M. and Nohria, N. (eds) *Breaking the Code of Change*. Boston: Harvard Business School Press.

Burns, J. M. (1978) *Leadership*. New York: Harper & Row.

Coghlan, D. and McAuliffe, E. (2003) *Changing Healthcare Organisations*. Dublin: Blackhall.

DoHC (Department of Health and Children) (2003a) *Report of the Commission on Financial Management and Control Systems in the Health Service* (Brennan Report). Dublin: Stationery Office.

— (2003b) *Audit of Structures and Functions in the Health Systems* (Prospectus Report). Dublin: Stationery Office.

Dunphy, D. and Stace, D. (1990) 'Transformational and coercive strategies for planned organisational change: beyond the OD model' in Massarik, F. (ed.), *Advances in Organisation Development* 1: 85–104.

Goodman, P. S. and Penning, J. M. (1980) 'Critical issues in assessing organizational effectiveness' in Lawler, E. E., Nadler, D. A. and Cammann, C. (eds), *Organizational Assessment*. New York: Wiley.

Hayes, J. (2002) *The Theory and Practice of Change Management*. London: Palgrave.

Hesselbein, F., Goldsmith, M. and Beckhard, R. (1996) *The Leader of the Future*. San Francisco: Jossey-Bass.

Kotter, J. P. (1995) 'Leading change: why transformation efforts fail', *Harvard Business Review* March–April, 59–67.

Lawrence, P. (1954) 'How to deal with resistance to change', *Harvard Business Review* May–June; and in Dalton, G. W., Lawrence, P. R. and Greiner, L. E. (eds), *Organisational Change and Development*. Homewood, IL: Irwin.

Leavitt, H. (1965), 'Applied organizational change in industry: structural, technological and humanistic approaches' in March, J. G. (ed.), *Handbook of Organizations*. Chicago: Rand McNally.

Lewin, K. (1951) *Field Theory in Social Science*. New York: Harper & Row.

Moss Kanter, R. M. (1983) *The Change Masters*. New York: Simon & Schuster.

Nadler, D. A. (1980) 'Concepts for the management of organisation change' in Tushman, M. L., O'Reilly, C. and Nadler, D. A. (eds), *The Management of Organizations* (1989). New York: Harper & Row (pp. 490–504).

— (1998) *Champions of Change*. San Francisco: Jossey-Bass.

Nadler, D. A. and Tushman, M. L. (1988) *Strategic Organization Design: Concepts, Tools, and Processes*. Glenview, IL: Scott, Foresman and Co.

Peters, T. J. and Waterman, R. H. (1982) *In Search of Excellence*. New York: Harper & Row.

Rashford, N. S. and Coghlan, D. (1994) *The Dynamics of Organisational Levels: A Change Framework for Managers and Consultants*. Reading, MA: Addison-Wesley.

Senge, P. (1990) *The Fifth Discipline: The Art and Practice of the Learning Organisation*. London: Century Business.

Senge, P., Kleiner, A., Roberts, C., Ross, R., Roth, G. and Smyth, B. (1999) *The Dance of Change*. London: Nicholas Brealey.

Zaltman, G. and Duncan, R. (1977) *Strategies for Planned Change*. New York: Wiley.

12
Quality Improvement in Health Care Services

Anne-Marie Brady, Breda Doyle & Anne Carrigy

OBJECTIVES

- To define quality in health care.
- To review the history of quality improvement in health care.
- To develop understanding of some models of quality improvement.
- To increase awareness of significant developments in the areas of quality improvement and safety in Irish health care.
- To analyse the relationship of patient safety, risk management and organisational culture to quality improvement.
- To develop understanding of concepts of quality improvement, including clinical governance, clinical audit, accreditation and business continuity.
- To introduce quality improvement tools.

INTRODUCTION

Excellence in health care is defined by the quality of care delivery and the clinical outcomes achieved. Increased accountability and consumer expectations in health care have resulted in growing attention to the systems and procedures aimed at enhancing patient safety within the health care system. In the past, the issues of quality in health care were determined and monitored within the professions and were for the most part a private affair (Kimberly & Minvielle 2000). The concept of quality in health care was originally an American phenomenon, but it has become an increasingly global concern and indeed a very public issue with increased requirement for transparency within the health care industry. Internationally, professional associations dealing with quality are becoming commonplace, and in Ireland the Health Information Quality Authority (HIQA) and the Irish Society for Quality and Safety in Healthcare (ISQSH) have been established. Quality improvement strategies are integral to the health strategy reform agenda (DoHC 2008; HSE 2007) and operate not only at institutional care sites but also through primary, community and continuing care (PCCC), involving all individuals who work in health care.

This chapter will seek to illuminate the importance of service quality across the organisation and consider the different perspectives on quality in the health service, including those of the patient/client. It will consider a variety of initiatives within health care that are associated with quality improvement, including continuous quality improvements frameworks, patient safety, risk management, accreditation and business continuity management, in addition to some of the tools that may be used to measure quality.

QUALITY

Quality in health care is complex, multi-faceted, and influenced by an array of factors including the competence of health care professionals and the policies and procedures operative in the settings in which they practise. The concept of quality has evolved considerably in recent times with an emphasis on the contribution of individuals to their own health status adding further complexity to the interpretation of quality in health care (Kinsella 2003). Quality improvement in health is concerned with both the process of care and clinical outcomes. Quality of care is defined as the 'degree to which health services for individuals and populations increase the likelihood of desired health outcomes and are consistent with current professional knowledge' (IOM 1999). Achieving a high level of safety is an essential first step in improving the quality of care overall (IOM 2001). Quality may also be interpreted from an outcome perspective, through measures of morbidity, mortality and consumer satisfaction. Other definitions of quality do emphasise the continuous improvement of health care outcomes but also include fiscal responsibility and decreasing expenditure on health care as being cornerstones of the same process. This desire for value for money in health care is reflected in the definition of quality in health care as 'fully meeting the needs of those who need the service most, at the lowest cost to the organisation, within limits and directives set by higher authorities and purchasers' (Ovretveit 1992). Steffen (1988) emphasises that any definition of quality must include an assessment of the patients' goals and values.

Quality is an all-encompassing concern, but different aspects will receive more prominent attention from some contributors to the health care industry than others. Health care professionals are largely concerned with clinical outcomes, safety and the quality of health care delivery. Policy makers and service providers may have particular interest in more population-based measures of health care, such as equality of access and cost-effectiveness of the care provided. Patients and consumers will no doubt be very concerned with efficacy of clinical outcomes but will also value aspects of care such as the provision of information, communication with their health care providers, ease of access to services and the surroundings in which the health care is delivered.

In summary, health care quality may be defined as doing the right thing consistently and safely to ensure the best possible clinical and patient satisfaction outcomes and as being reliant on appropriately skilled staff operating within financially responsible institutions. It is a multi-faceted concept that encompasses safety; clinical effectiveness/health outcomes; service configuration/best practice; equity/access; efficiency; processes/risk management; records management; and customer service.

HISTORICAL DEVELOPMENT OF QUALITY IN HEALTH CARE

The notion of quality in health care was documented over two thousand years ago by Hippocrates, who vowed 'Primum non cocere' ('First do no harm'). The work of Florence Nightingale in the 1850s first demonstrated the positive impact of quality measures in health care in saving the lives of British soldiers in the Crimean War. Florence Nightingale, in her hospital notes, argued, 'often it was bad sanitary, bad architectural and bad administrative arrangements' (Nightingale 1860:68) that contributed to negative outcomes of health care. Ernest Codman, a US surgeon, championed a system of auditing surgical care and published the results in his personally published book *A Study of Hospital Efficiency* (Codman 1916). He is thought to have been the founder of outcomes-based patient care and was a pioneer of transparency in health care, believing that information should be made public to guide patient choice of hospital and physician. The influence of the original work on total quality management (TQM) by W. Edward Deming in the 1950s, which was concerned with production in a manufacturing context, and which contributed to the successful rise of Toyota in the Japanese car industry, is still evident in contemporary health care. It has been suggested that translating quality improvements used in manufacturing does not give sufficient and explicit attention to the service aspects of health care quality (Walshe and Boaden 2006). A systems perspective of quality in health care was advocated in the 1960s and 1970s by Donabedian, who proposed specific structure, processes, and outcomes criteria for quality improvement that could be defined, assessed and measured. He proposed that these criteria should include all attributes in health care provision including human, material and financial resources, the organisation of those resources, and should include both the practitioners and the patient contribution in achieving and sustaining health and well-being. This interpretation of quality in health care was broadened in the 1980s by Don Berwick (1989) to a more patient/client-focused view, promoting many of the quality initiatives we are now familiar with in contemporary work environments, such as teamwork, process analysis and guideline development.

QUALITY AND SAFETY IMPROVEMENT INITIATIVES

National strategy planning documents have created specific targets on quality and safety (DoHC 2001, 2008) and have resulted in a huge impetus in the quality agenda through all hospital and health care settings, underpinned by recent legislation and regulations (the Health Acts 2004 and 2007; the Medical Practitioners Bill 2007). The Irish Society for Quality and Safety in Healthcare (ISQSH), a non-profit, non-governmental agency, was founded in 1994. In Ireland, the Clinical Indemnity Scheme (CIS) was established in 2002 in order to rationalise pre-existing medical indemnity arrangements by transferring to the state, via the Health Service Executive (HSE), hospital and other health agencies, responsibility for managing clinical negligence claims and associated risk in Ireland (CIS 2009). The National Clinical Incident Reporting System, an electronic database, was rolled out in 2003 by the State Claims Agency and requires each hospital to report adverse events and near misses. The Health Information and

Quality Authority (HIQA) was established as a result of the Health Act 2007 and is an independent authority reporting to the Minister of Health that aims to advance the quality safety, accountability and optimum use of resources in the Irish health and social care services (Government of Ireland 2007). The Social Services Inspectorate (SSI) and Irish Health Services Accreditation Board (IHSAB) have been integrated into the new authority. HIQA's responsibilities include:

- setting standards in health and social services
- monitoring health care quality
- Social Services Inspectorate
- health technology assessment
- health information initiatives.

Accreditation standards, hygiene standards, decontamination standards and medical record audits have all been undertaken by the HSE or HIQA in recent times. Recent public inquiries into patients' safety in the Irish Republic, including the Lourdes Hospital Inquiry (DoHC 2006), the Leas Cross Inquiry (DoHC 2009) and the Rebecca O'Malley Inquiry (HIQA 2008b), resulted in the establishment of the Commission for Patient Safety. The Commission Report made 134 recommendations for driving safety and quality across the Irish health service (DoHC 2008). The Health Statistics database was rolled out in 2009 and provides benchmarking information on the performance of health care facilities in relation to access, integration and use of resources.

Key recommendations: Commission of Patient Safety and Quality Assurance

Mandatory licensing system
A system will be enacted following appropriate legislation to license all acute care hospitals and other health care facilitates such as those that deliver cosmetic surgery, and medical/dental treatment with general anaesthesia or sedation.

Governance of health care organisations
All health care facilities to implement a framework of governance so that responsibilities, reporting relationships and accountability are clearly established. Specific guidance for minimum governance in licensed health care facilitates to include legal accountability for patient safety at CEO and board level.

Professional regulation
Reform of the disciplinary procedures is recommended to ensure greater public representation, consistency and consensus across professions and is inherent in this aspect of the regulatory function. Guidance is given in relation to the implementation of a credentialing system to review qualifications, competence

assurance and track records of all health care professionals. All curricula to incorporate technical and human factors related to safety and quality.

Clinical audit
All licensed practitioners and clinical staff will be required to actively engage in clinical audit and seek to ensure compliance with national standards and priorities of care.

Adverse event reporting
Recommendations include the introduction of a mandatory reporting system for adverse events to be complemented by a voluntary system of reporting close calls or near misses to advance organisational learning.

The European Charter of Patients' Rights provides 14 rights of patients, which are the right to: preventive measures; access; information; consent; free choice; privacy and confidentiality; respect of time; observance of quality standards; safety; innovation; avoidance of unnecessary suffering; personalised treatment; compensation; and, finally, the right to complain (O'Mathúna *et al.* 2005). These rights are summarised under four themes in Table 12.1.

Table 12.1: Themes in the European Charter of Patients' Rights

Theme	EU Patient Charter rights
Access to health care	Right to preventive measures
	Right of access
	Right of free choice
	Right to respect of patient's time
	Right to innovation
	Right to personalised treatment
Informed consent	Right to information
	Right to consent
Safety and quality assurance	Right to observance of Quality Standards
	Right to safety
	Right to avoid unnecessary suffering and pain
	Right to privacy and confidentiality
Redress	Right to complain
	Right to compensation

Source: O'Mathúna *et al.* (2005)

Quality and safety, terms often used interchangeably in the literature, are interlinked priorities in health care provision and it is argued that safety is a prerequisite for quality. Reports prepared by the Institute of Medicine, such as *To Err is Human: Building a Safer Health System* (IOM 1999) served as a vehicle to increase awareness among policy makers and the general public of issues around quality in health care and represented the first effort to approach the field of patient safety through the eyes of evidence-based medicine (Stelfox *et al.* 2006). There are a number of terms used interchangeably to document patient safety occurrences, including 'adverse events', 'clinical errors', 'medical error', 'near misses', making comparison of studies somewhat problematic. It is has been estimated that around ten per cent of patients admitted to NHS hospitals are subject to patient safety incidents and that up to half of these incidents are preventable (NPSA 2004). These incidents also generate a significant burden that includes avoidable prolonged care, additional treatment and litigation costs (Milligan 2007). Studies of a similar nature conducted in the USA, Australia, the United Kingdom, Denmark, New Zealand and Canada have documented rates of adverse events in health care ranging from 3.5 per cent to 21 per cent (Brady *et al.* 2008). There are no specific statistics on the rate of adverse events in the Irish context.

The National Clinical Incident Reporting System recorded 83,661 adverse events in the 12 months between 1 January and 31 December 2008 (CIS 2009). Of those documented, the top five were as follows: 31,170 (37 per cent) attributed to slips, trips and falls by patients; 8,650 (10 per cent) to violence/harassment/aggression; 6,785 (8 per cent) to medication incidents; 5,373 (6 per cent) to treatment incidents; 5,070 (6 per cent) to records/documentation.

The 'other' category (26,613 events, 33 per cent) included issues relating to records and documentation, unplanned events, diagnosis, infection control, events before and after birth, equipment/devices, peri-operative/procedure, self harm, discharge, blood transfusion and confidentiality incidents.

Figure 12.1: The Swiss cheese model: how defences, barriers and safeguards may be penetrated by accidental trajectory

Source: Reason (2000:767). Reproduced with permission.

Health care risk management is the process by which potential for errors is identified, minimised or eliminated. The issue of error in health care may be viewed in two ways: from the perspective of the individuals, centring on the actions of service providers; and the system thinking view, which advocates concentrating on complex organisational issues that contribute to reduced defence against errors in health care. Reason (2000) explains that 'holes in defences' occur because of underlying causes described as 'active failures or 'latent conditions'. The active failures are those associated with human behaviour, including deviations from procedures, while the latent conditions are those not always readily visible as the cause, but that can predispose to errors, such as staffing conditions, work design and equipment difficulties.

ORGANISATIONAL CULTURE

Health care delivery is dependent on a broad range of interlinked administrative and clinical functions and if any one part of the health system is inadequate for purpose the whole service is impacted on. In system-thinking organisations there is a shared vision among staff and users of what constitutes quality (Senge 2006), with efforts to objectify the work so that the system can be viewed from the user perspective. 'The key is to understand the chains of causality, the sequence and mutual interactions of the numerous individual cause and effect relationships that underlie the system of interest' (Sherwood 2002:70). Culture represents the personality of an organisation, and it has a major influence on both employee satisfaction and organisational success. Organisational culture can be described as a complex framework of national and professional attitudes and values within which groups and individuals function (Wachter 2008) and comprises shared beliefs and assumptions that underlie how people within the organisation go about their tasks (Claridge & Sandars 2007). Safety culture is a subset of an organisational culture relating specifically to the beliefs and values concerning health and safety in an organisation. Safety culture can be described as the ability of organisations to deal with risks and hazards so as to avoid damage and yet achieve their goals (Reason 2000).

There has being a growing recognition in the health care community of the importance of transforming organisational culture in order to improve patient safety (Nieva & Sorra 2003). Effective systems are reliant on a partnership between stakeholders with a constant flow of information and transparency about work practices and outcomes at all levels of the organisation. Creating a safety culture is dependent upon making patient safety a top priority within the organisation and upon commitment from all stakeholders to address patient safety issues. An effective system for reporting errors, without attaching blame, is necessary in a learning organisation (Leape 1999). Rather than adopting the standard approach of naming, blaming and shaming an individual when an error or adverse incident occurs, a safety culture encourages the reporting of such incidents in a non-punitive manner. A blame-free, non-punitive culture encourages clinicians to report errors and thereby learn from their mistakes (Handler *et al.* 2000; Leape & Berwick 2005; Ursprung *et al.* 2005). Creating a safety culture has become one of the main strategies for promoting patient safety so that staff and processes are focused on improving the reliability and safety of care for patients.

There are barriers to reporting errors, often due to uncertainty about criteria for reporting, resource pressures, team loyalty and fear of repercussions. Errors are more likely to be reported when clinicians 'feel safe to do so and it becomes a culturally accepted activity' (Cohen 2000:729). Major health care policy documents have acknowledged that there is a need to move away from the blame response culture that has been quite prevalent in health care, as it contributes to issues with acknowledgment of error and therefore obstructs or limits learning possibilities (HIQA 2008a). The biggest challenge in moving towards a safer health system is changing the culture from one of blame to one in which errors are treated as opportunities to improve the system and prevent harm (IOM 2001). However, Walton (2004) does caution that 'no blame' does not absolve health care providers from their professional responsibilities and does not mean that they will not be held to account for their actions. Walshe and Boaden (2006) identified that there are many challenges ahead in relation to incident reporting, including reducing the under-reporting of incidents; ensuring the involvement of patients and their carers in reporting incidents; and the need to place incident reporting in a broader context by having a multi-faceted approach to measurement, surveillance and risk management.

The most common method of self-reporting of errors is usually referred to as incident reporting. Incident reporting systems are emerging as a major tool to help identify patient safety issues and provide information for organisational system learning. In most organisations the reporting system is used as part of the overall safety and quality improvement strategy, but there is a risk that it may be dominated by managing claims and complaints (Vincent *et al.* 2004). An effective reporting system must be confidential, and must promote and encourage open discussion of adverse incidents. Much of the design of error reporting systems is based on approaches that have being successful in other high-risk industries for years (Walshe & Boaden 2006).

In a study of a quality cost and electronic adverse incident recording reporting system, Walsh and Jiju (2007) found that the key to electronic adverse incident recording and reporting is to use the linkages of quality cost to improve patient care and patient safety by integrating the information from the adverse incidents into international quality improvement plans. By focusing on change, rather than blame, they can also help to increase the level of trust within an organisation (Kohn *et al.* 2000). The IOM (1999) report identified mandatory and voluntary reporting systems as important components of patient safety improvement. Avoidance of a blame culture will maximise the opportunity for organisational learning and Irish health care strategy documents do outline a commitment to developing a culture for supporting patients, families and clinicians when things go wrong (HIQA 2008a). As mentioned earlier in the chapter, the National Clinical Incident Reporting System requires each hospital to report adverse events and near misses.

CLINICAL GOVERNANCE

'Clinical Governance is a framework through which organisations are accountable for continuously improving the quality of services and safe-guarding high standards of care by creating an environment in which excellence in clinical care will flourish' (DoH 1998:2). It requires a cultural shift within health care from the traditional patterns and structures of health care delivery to patient-centred care delivery. Competing interests of funders, policy makers, administrators, health professionals and patients are put aside in a culture of openness and honesty in mutual pursuit of excellence in care and a high-quality service. Wright and Hill (2003) argue that clinical governance is not a separate or bureaucratic activity but is a central function of the business of health care and should be naturally manifested in the work of all professionals working in this industry. Wright and Hill (2003) described the aspects (audit, research and development, lifelong learning, clinical guidelines, teamwork and collaboration, risk management, evidence, patient views and implementation) that contribute to clinical governance as parts of a puzzle, which when joined together will provide coherence to quality improvement work. The multiple fragments of clinical governance that contribute to quality improvement in clinical care, including clinical effectiveness and audit, risk management and patient safety, learning and use of information, staff management, service improvement, and patient and public involvement, are evidenced in the framework for integrated quality, safety and risk management being advanced across the HSE (see Figure 12.2), including the establishment of a National Directorate for Quality and Clinical Care, and the appointment of a national clinical director.

Figure 12.2: *Towards Excellence in Clinical Governance: A Framework for Integrated Quality, Safety and Risk Management across HSE Providers.* (Reproduced with permission.)

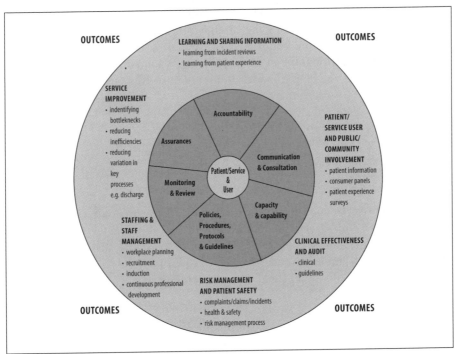

The standard of any aspect of health care service is defined by the structure, process and outcome criteria that are associated with it (Donabedian 1990, 2003). The achievement of best practice standards of care is contingent on reaching the right balance between the structure, process and outcome criteria, and these should be measurable.

- **Structure:** human, physical and financial resources that contribute to the standards. Examples include building, staff and equipment.
- **Process:** activities that contribute to process. Examples of discrete steps may be staff training, care pathways, guidelines or procedures.
- **Outcome:** the outcomes or results of the service. Examples include length of stay, mortality and morbidity rates, and patient satisfaction (Donabedian 2003).

Quality improvement model

The quality cycle is a basic framework suitable for health care and it is designed to promote the principles of the continuous quality improvement process. This universal improvement methodology is commonly known as the 'plan–do–check–act (PDCA) cycle'. It is a continuous quality improvement model based on four repetitive stages, which ensure a structured approach to the improvement of quality. There are many variations of the cycle; Deming modelled his on the original PDCA, the 'Schewart Cycle', named after his mentor and the father of statistical quality control; however, it has since become known as the Deming cycle, Deming wheel or the continuous improvement cycle (Bicheno & Catherwood 2005). It refers to the cycle of activities advocated for achieving process or system improvement. The cycle emphasises the continuous nature of quality improvement, illustrating the careful planning and implementation steps involved, in addition to the importance of measuring the impact and results of these activities as an ongoing systems process (Wachter 2008). Langley *et al.* (1996) explain that the PDCA model of quality improvement is guided by three questions:

- What are we trying to accomplish?
- How will we know that a change is an improvement?
- What changes can we make that will result in improvement? (Langley *et al.* 1996:4)

This represents a trial and learning methodology and the use of the work study in the third phase emphasises the acquisition of new knowledge to continually develop services (Langley *et al.* 1996); see Figure 12.3. The PDCA cycle can be used for all quality initiatives to ensure that the best possible results are achieved, and the process should be repeated on an ongoing basis.

Figure 12.3: The quality improvement cycle (PDCA)

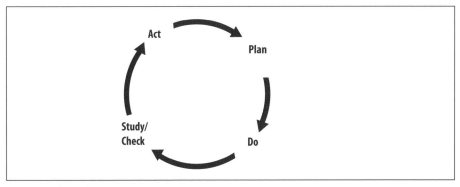

Source: Langley *et al.* (1996)

Table 12.2: The plan–do–check–act quality improvement cycle

Plan the change	• Identify the concern or problem.
	• Set clear objectives.
	• Collect data /identify potential root causes.
	• Educate as necessary.
Do the change	• Implement the improvement.
Check and monitor	• Evaluate success of objectives.
	• Review root cause of problem.
	• After-action review.
	• What can be done better next time?
	• Is the problem completely solved?
Act – revise and plan new change	• Identify further improvements.
	• Communicate the outcomes.
	• Prepare plan to . . .
	• Ongoing monitoring.
	• Celebrate.

Accreditation

Accreditation is a self-assessment and external peer review process used in health care organisations to accurately assess level of performance against established standards. It 'provides a framework to identify, prioritise and implement ways to continuously improve their services' (IHSAB 2005:1). The award of accreditation status communicates that a health care facility has implemented an organisation-wide risk management system. Essentially, accreditation is about patient safety, staff safety and providing a quality patient service. The process of accreditation originated in the United States with the initiation of a programme of standards by the American College of Surgeons in 1917. The Independent Joint Commission on

Hospital Accreditation was established in 1951, and is now known as the Joint Commission on Accreditation of Healthcare Organisations (JCAHO). The emphasis of accreditation has changed over the years: originally it had a voluntary focus that assessed structural elements of hospital care, but it has evolved into multidisciplinary assessment of health care processes, functions, organisations and networks (DoHC 2008).

The development of accreditation in Ireland commenced in 1999, when the Major Academic Teaching Hospitals of Ireland (MATHs) identified the need for a national accreditation programme. A steering committee, which consisted of quality experts and representatives from the Department of Health and Children, consumers and senior health care professionals, was set up to explore international experiences in accreditation. The Canadian Council on Health Services Association (CCHSA) framework for accreditation was adapted for use in the Irish health care system and implemented by the MATHs as a pilot initiative in 2000. The Irish Health Services Accreditation Board (IHSAB) was established as an independent body in May 2002. The standards were then reviewed and re-launched as the Acute Care Accreditation Scheme (ACAS), a voluntary scheme, in February 2004, which was in keeping with the quality cycle and the focus on continuous quality improvement. By 2006, over 95 per cent of the acute care sector had applied to participate in the ACAS.

Acute Care Accreditation Scheme (ACAS)

The ACAS was a framework for quality and safety that was implemented over a three-year cycle. It helped guide health care organisations to identify their strengths and also their opportunities for improvement and to better understand the objectives and complexities of their operations. With this knowledge, organisations were able to address short- and longer-term plans to improve their performance and use their resources to most effectively meet their needs. The overall purpose of the accreditation scheme was to provide an environment which assured safety for patients/clients, staff and the public, within a framework of continuously improving quality of care. Accreditation sought to ensure that organisations not only provided a sufficient level of care to their patients/clients but could also be recognised as centres of excellence (IHSAB 2005).

The ACAS process consisted of four phases:

- preparation and self-assessment by the organisation
- peer review/accreditation survey to validate the self-assessment
- provision of outcome report and award of accreditation
- continuous assessment – quality improvement report and review visit.

Standards of excellence

The ACAS standards identified the desired care or outcome of service and outlined the specific criteria that guide the attainment of those standards (see Table 12.3).

Table 12.3: ACAS standard groupings

Leadership and Partnership Standards: includes aspects of governance, management and collaborative performance.
Information Management Standards: includes all aspects of information and data management across the organisation (not exclusively IT).
Human Resources Management Standards: human capital concerns such as recruitment, performance management, work environment, staff and training.
Environmental and Facilities Management Standards: includes all aspects of performance that relate to equipment and physical environment.
Care Services Standards: the patient's journey is assessed with particular emphasis on a population health approach to care delivery coupled with the provision of integrated care across the continuum.

Source: IHSAB (2005)

Self-assessment

Each organisation set up self-assessment care teams to facilitate analysis of the quality and safety functions of the organisation, and the number of these reflected the type or activity of the organisation rather than its size. The teams were multidisciplinary and reflected the journey of the patient through the organisation. The rating system was designed to assist self-assessment teams and the organisation in general, to prioritise areas for development, and to rate its level of compliance against a set of criteria by examining the structures, processes and outcomes that would have to exist for full compliance.

Peer review

The selected peer review survey team were specifically trained in accreditation; members were drawn from management, medical, nursing and service users and included some international surveyors. The peer review survey aimed to validate the self-assessment, determine the level of compliance with agreed standards, and included provision for documentation review, tours of the relevant facilities as well as interviews with the self-assessment teams, patients/clients and staff.

Accreditation award

The accreditation report provided a general summary of performance, team-specific summary, risk rating and recommendations, quality dimensions analysis and accreditation award decision. A health care organisation which achieved accreditation status was to be acknowledged as a centre of excellence in the specific areas of patient/client care that it provided. Accreditation status did not mean, however, that the organisation did not have the potential to fall short of the desired level of service, but it did provide a system by which it could identify, address and prevent recurrences (IHSAB 2005).

Accreditation award meant an organisation status had demonstrated:

- 'An extensive organisation-wide risk management process to ensure maximum patient safety.'

- 'A comprehensive quality system which actively seeks to identify problems within the provision of care and rectify them.'
- 'That it is predominately compliant with all of the key aspects of health provision.' (IHSAB 2005:60)

Benefits of accreditation

- Earns public trust that an organisation is committed to safety and quality care.
- Contributes to safe work environment and worker satisfaction.
- Provides a quality of care to enable negotiation with payers and policy makers.
- Provides a vehicle for patient and family involvement in health care.
- Creates a learning culture where adverse events and concerns are reported.
- Establishes a leadership agenda to prioritise quality and patient safety (Joint Commission International 2008).

Continuous review

Accreditation focuses on continuous quality improvement, quality patient care and the safety of all patients, staff and visitors (IHSAB 2005). The benefits of accreditation highlight the quality agenda in the participating organisations, it uses the quality cycle of plan–do–check–act (PDCA) and it reinforces the quality improvements that are ongoing, but also focuses on the opportunities for improvement. It provides organisations with an opportunity to review their services, it demonstrates commitment to quality, and it can provide a vision of excellence for the organisation that is in keeping with the organisation's mission statement. It allows an opportunity for service users to be part of the quality agenda in the organisation. Health care accreditation has been expanding globally, and accreditation organisations now exist in over 70 countries. The merits of accreditation in terms of demonstrable improvement in health care have not yet been independently validated through research, and further study is warranted on the impact of accreditation by health organisations globally.

The previous section described the system of accreditation that was advanced nationally until mid-2009. IHSAB has since been subsumed into HIQA and at the time of writing it is understood that the accreditation system developed by IHSAB is not to be continued through HIQA. Instead it is to be replaced with National Standards, which will provide a framework for licensing both private and public health care organisations. HIQA is currently working on the development of national standards on quality and safety that will be applied across all health care settings and will encompass some of the principles of accreditation as previously described (personal communication with HIQA, 2009). However, accreditation processes of the nature described above are continuing in many organisations throughout the health service. Private hospitals are often required by insurers to provide evidence of accreditation to meet contract conditions and some of them are using the Joint Commission (USA) International Branch.

HEALTHSTAT

HealthStat is a database of performance information that provides detailed monthly benchmarking results against national and international targets for Irish health care facilities. This database, which will be extended to all acute hospitals and all health and social care services, measures access, integration and appropriate use of resources in the public health care system.

Table 12.4: HealthStat performance indicators (HSE 2009)

Access	Waiting times for outpatient clinics, diagnostics services, treatment procedures and emergency surgery.
Integration	Information on length of stay, appropriate use of in-patient, outpatient or day care.
Use of resources	Data pertaining to staffing, absenteeism, budget compliance and target activity.

Source: HSE (2009)

The database operates a traffic light system to identify performance: green = good performance; amber = average performance with room for improvement; red = unsatisfactory performance requiring attention (HSE 2009).

Clinical audit

In order to ensure that the quality of care meets defined standards, a comprehensive system of clinical audit will be required to support clinicians. Clinical audit can be defined as 'a quality improvement process that seeks to improve patient care and outcomes through a systematic review of care against explicit measures and the implementation of changes in practice if needed' (Dixon 2006:3). This is a relatively new concept in Irish health care and a nationally co-ordinated approach to integrate clinical audit into quality improvement is only beginning to emerge. The implementation of an annual clinical audit forward plan in health care organisations is anticipated within a safety and quality governance framework and it should be part of the education and training process within the organisation. Clinical audit comes under the umbrella of clinical governance, it forms part of the system for improving the standard of patient care and it is one of the principal methods used to monitor and evaluate clinical quality.

Aspects of the structure, process and outcomes of care are selected and systematically evaluated against explicit criteria. Clinical audit objectives should ideally be linked to service plans and to local and national practice guidelines. There are challenges to clinical audit: disclosure, lack of incentive and resources, and lack of education and training. Clinical audit recognises all participants in the process as partners and peers and requires agreement between professionals on the priorities for clinical audit. Regular audit activity helps to create a culture of quality improvement in the clinical setting and offers a way to assess and improve care, to uphold professional standards and to do the right thing. Clinical

Figure 12.4: The audit cycle

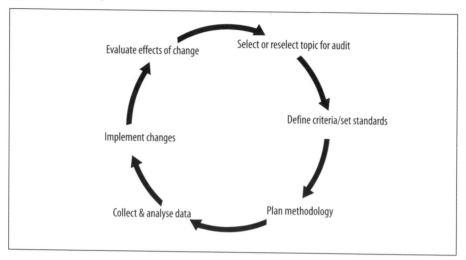

audit is educational for participants and it involves being up to date with evidence-based practice. It offers an opportunity for increased job satisfaction and is increasingly seen as an essential component of professional practice.

Changes are currently being made to the strategy for clinical audit: detailed guidance on this topic can be found on the HSE's website, www.hseland.ie.

QUALITY IMPROVEMENT TOOLS

There are a number of quality improvement instruments that can be used by health professionals to analyse the care delivery processes and to facilitate decision-making in relation to quality improvement. Statistical analysis will assist health professionals to analyse complex relationships between variables and therefore garner meaningful information to help identify optimal solutions to improving service.

Flow charts

These enable analysis of the steps in a process and allow people to closely examine and understand the elements that contribute to any health care process. They can be time-consuming to prepare but will afford a detailed understanding of the multiplicity of factors that can influence a service. A

Figure 12.5: Flow chart

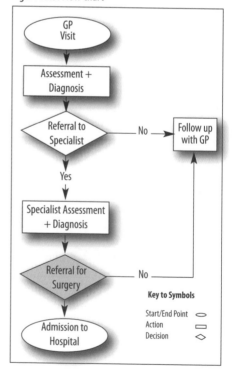

visual layout on the interconnected elements in any health care service will enable providers to identify areas for improvement.

Cause and effect diagrams

Sometimes known as a fishbone/ishiwaka diagram, this is used for analysing process dispersion. It is particularly useful for root cause analysis as it is a method that can facilitate brainstorming and analysis of the causal factors in a particular problem. The head of the fishbone is used to illustrate the main problem and all the related minor and contributing factors are placed on the arms.

Figure 12.6: Cause and effect diagram

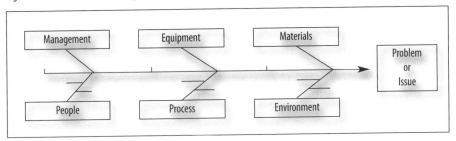

Pareto charts

These are based on the Pareto principle, which stipulates that 80 per cent of problems can be attributed to 20 per cent of causes. A Pareto chart organises and displays information to demonstrate the relative importance of variables. It enables an organisation to analyse the frequency of a problem and determine the risk of occurrence in order to determine how to prioritise their quality improvement endeavours.

Figure 12.7: Pareto chart

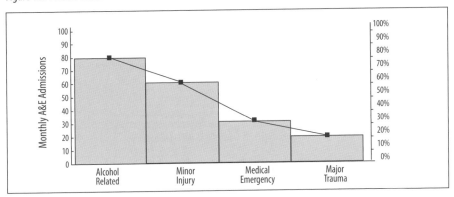

Histograms

Histograms are used to demonstrate statistical frequencies and variations around the central statistics such as the mean medial and the normal distribution. This type of graphical presentation can make it easier to interpret statistical information.

Figure 12.8: Histogram

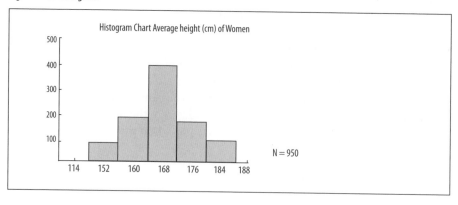

Time series charts

Time series charts show change over time and demonstrate trends and characteristics. The horizontal axis is always time, and these charts are particular useful for examining relationships or changes over time.

Figure 12.9: Time series chart

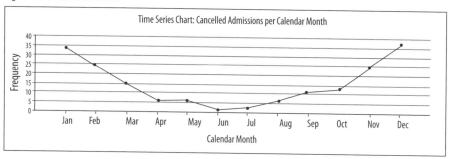

Control charts

A control chart is used to monitor a process to determine whether it is within the anticipated range. The range or control limits represent the tolerance for variation (the upper and lower boundaries).

Figure 12.10: Control chart

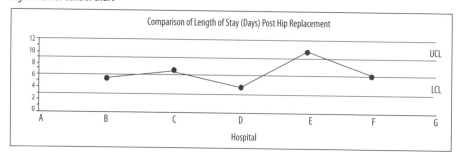

Scatter diagrams

A scatter diagram is a graphical illustration of the relationship or correlation between two variables.

Figure 12.11: Scatter diagram

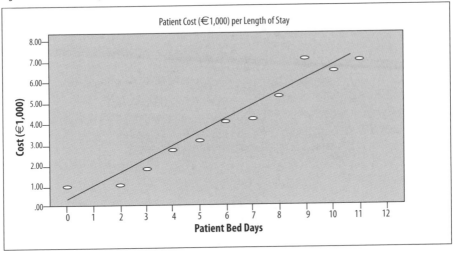

BUSINESS CONTINUITY MANAGEMENT (BCM)

Business continuity management (BCM) is a relatively new concept in health care in Ireland and has evolved as a result of development in emergency planning, security, health and safety, and crisis management. BCM can be defined as 'a holistic management process that identifies potential impacts that threaten an organisation and provides a framework for building resilience and the capacity for an effective response that safeguards the interest of its key stakeholders, reputations, brand and value creating activities' (BCI 2007:6).

Although each industry has a unique set of challenges when responding to business disruptions, continuity of operation in health care goes far beyond maintaining or recovering basic business operations and IT systems – it is a matter of life and death. For hospital organisations, BCM is about identifying those parts of the organisation that you cannot afford to jeopardise, such as patients, staff, medical records, information, stocks and premises, and planning to recover and maintain these if an incident occurs. BCM interlinks risk management, health and safety, quality management and emergency management and aims to improve an organisation's resilience by identifying, in advance, the potential impacts of a wide variety of sudden disruptions to the organisation's ability to succeed. The BCM lifecycle is a step-by-step guide to business continuity, is directly linked to corporate governance and seeks to plan in detail how organisations can quickly recover from disruptions (see Figure 12.12). A documented and well-tested business continuity plan involves the participation of various managerial, operational, administrative and technical disciplines and allows health care organisations to react to almost any situation in an efficient, timely manner, and to recover critical business processes within established timeframes (Barnes 2004).

Figure 12.12: Business continuity management

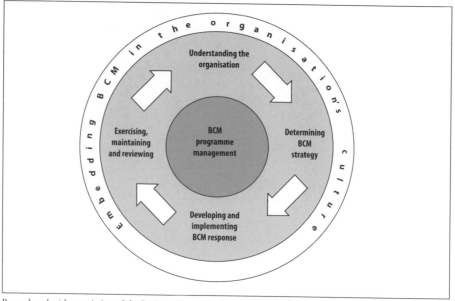

Reproduced with permission of the Business Continuity Institute (BCI 2007)

CASE STUDY

You have recently been appointed clinical director of a cardiothoracic surgical unit in a large teaching hospital. The business manager has brought to your attention that length of stay for the coronary artery bypass graft diagnostics related group (DRG) has increased by an average of two to three days over the last year. Recently the microbiologist has contacted you to report that he is seeing an increase in the number of post-operative wound infections in the cardiothoracic surgical wards. At a directorate meeting you undertake to organise a team to improve the safety and clinical outcomes for this area.

- Who would you ask to participate in this group?
- What sources of information would you utilise to advance your objectives?
- What outcome measures would be useful?
- How might this problem be solved?

CONCLUSION

The health care industry has become quality-driven, with a greater emphasis on transparency and accountability. The growing demand for improved quality and safety in health care from patients, providers, insurers, regulators and purchasers is evident in all health care environments. Payees and consumers are more informed as to what constitutes quality in health care. The search for value by purchasers and consumers of the service will continue, and as it does, more refined ways to measure and manage quality will be developed. The ability to monitor performance, though challenging in health care, is essential to improving quality of care. The HSE's Transformation Programme seeks to deliver an accessible health service with high-quality care for all, where staff have confidence and pride in the service they deliver (HSE 2007). Such reform necessitates fundamental changes to health care delivery and patient-centred care processes and services.

REFLECTIVE EXERCISES

1   What is your definition of quality in health care?
2   Who are your customers in health care?
3   How might you apply the PDCA model to your area of work?
4   Discuss how clinical governance is evidenced in your place of work.
5   Discuss some topics that pertain to your work area that may benefit from audit.

OTHER RESOURCES

Health Service Executive Learning Programmes: Clinical Audit: www.hseland.ie
World Health Organisation World Alliance on Patient Safety: www.who.int/patientsafety/en/World

REFERENCES:

Barnes, J. C. (2004) 'Business continuity planning and HIPAA' in Barnes, D. and Rothstein, J. (eds), *Business Continuity Management in the Health Care Environment*. Brookfield CT: Rothstein Associates.

BCI (Business Continuity Institute) (2007) 'Business continuity management: good practice guidelines' in *A Management Guide to Implementing Global Good Practice in Business Continuity Management*. BCI.

Berwick, D. M. (1989) 'Continuous improvement as an ideal in healthcare', *New England Journal of Medicine* 320(1): 53–6.

Bicheno, J. and Catherwood, P. (2005) *Six Sigma and the Quality Toolbox: For Service and Manufacturing*. Moreton Press.

Brady, A.-M., Redmond, R., Curtis, E., Fleming, S., Keenan, P., Malone, A. M. and Sheerin, F. (2008) 'Adverse events in health care', *Journal of Nursing Management* 17(2): 155–64.

CIS (Clinical Indemnity Scheme) (2009) *STARSWeb Statistics 2008: Top 5 Clinical Events Reported in 2008*. Available at: http://www.stateclaims.ie/ClinicalIndemnityScheme/starswebStats.html, accessed 17 November 2009.

Claridge, T. and Sandars, J. (2007) 'Patient safety culture' in *ABC of Patient Safety*. Oxford: Blackwell.

Codman, E. A. (1916) *A Study of Hospital Efficiency: The First Five Years*. Boston: Thomas Todd.

Cohen, M. (2000) 'Why error reporting systems should be voluntary', *British Medical Journal* 320: 728–9.

DoH (Department of Health (UK)) (1998) 'Delivering quality standards' in *A First Class Service: Quality in the New NHS*. Available at http://www.dh.gov.uk/prod_consum_dh/groups/dh_digitalassets/@dh/@en/documents/digitalasset/dh_4045152.pdf, accessed 19 November 2009.

DoHC (Department of Health and Children) (2001) *Quality and Fairness: A Health System for You*. Dublin: Stationery Office.

— (2006) *The Lourdes Hospital Inquiry: An Inquiry into Peripartum Hysterectomy at Our Lady of Lourdes Hospital Drogheda*. Report of Judge Maureen Harding Clark SC. Dublin: Stationery Office.

— (2008) *Building a Culture of Patient Safety: Report of the Commission on Patient Safety and Quality Assurance*. Dublin: Stationery Office.

— (2009) *Final Report of the Commission of Investigation (Leas Cross Nursing Home)*. Dublin: Stationery Office.

Dixon, N. (2006) *Getting Clinical Audit Right to Benefit Patients*. Romsey, Hampshire: Health Care Quality Quest.

Donabedian, A. (1990) 'The seven pillars of quality', *Archive of Pathology Laboratory Medicine* 114: 1115–18.

— (2003) *An Introduction to Quality Assurance in Healthcare*. Oxford: Oxford University Press.

Government of Ireland (2007) *The Health Act* Number 23. Dublin: Stationery Office.

Handler, S. M., Castle, N. G., Studenski, S. A., Perera, S., Fridsma, D. B., Nace, D. A. and Hanlon, J. T. (2000) 'Patient safety culture assessment in the nursing home', *Quality and Safety in Health Care* 15: 400–4.

HIQA (Health Information and Quality Authority) (2008a) *Patient Safety*. Available at http://www.hiqa.ie/patient_safety_WHOProject.asp, accessed 19 November 2009.

— (2008b) *Report of the Investigation into the Circumstances Surrounding the Provision of Care to Rebecca O'Malley in Relation to her Symptomatic Breast Disease, the Pathology Services at Cork University Hospital and Symptomatic Breast Disease Services at the Mid Western Regional Hospital, Limerick*.

HSE (Health Service Executive) (2007) *Transformation Programme 2007–2010*. Available at: www.hse.ie/eng/FactFile/HSE_Approach/Transformation_Programme_2007-2010, accessed 1 October 2009.

— (2009) *HealthStat*. Available at: http://www.hse.ie/eng/Healthstat/, accessed 1 April 2009.

IHSAB (Irish Health Services Accreditation Board) (2005) *Acute Care Accreditation Scheme. A Framework for Quality and Safety* (2nd edn). Dublin: Irish Health Services Accreditation Board.

IOM (Institute of Medicine) (1999) *To Err is Human: Building a Safer Health System*. Washington, DC: National Academy Press. Available at http://www.nap.edu/openbook.php, accessed 27 October 2008.

— (2001) *Crossing the Quality Chasm: A New Health System for the 21st Century*. Report of the Committee on Quality of Health Care in America. Institute of Medicine and National Academy Press (Washington, DC). Available at: http://www4.nas.edu/onpi/webextra.nsf/web/chasm?Open Document, accessed 28 August 2009.

Joint Commission International (2008) *Joint Commission International Accreditation Standards for Hospitals* (3rd edn). Illinois: Joint Commission International.

Kaissi, A., Johnson. T. and Kirschbaum, M. S. (2003) 'Measuring teamwork and patient safety attitudes of high-risk areas', *Nursing Economics* 21: 211–18.

Kimberly, J. R. and Minvielle, E. (2000) *The Quality Imperative: Measurement and Management of Quality in Healthcare*. London: Imperial College Press.

Kinsella, R. (2003) *Acute Healthcare in Transition in Ireland: Change, Cutbacks and Challenges*. Cork: Oak Tree Press.

Kohn, L. T., Corrigan, J. M. and Donaldson, M. S. (2000) *To Err is Human: Building a Safer System* (2nd edn). Washington, DC: National Academy Press.

Langley, G. J., Nolan, K.M., Nolan, T.W., Morman,C.L. and Provost, L.P. (1996) *The Improvement Guide: A Practical Approach to Enhancing Organisational Performance*. San Francisco: Jossey-Bass.

Leape, L. (1999) 'Error in medicine' in Rosenthal, M. M., Mulcahy, L. and Lloyd-Bostock, S. (Eds) *Medical Mishaps*. Buckingham: Open University Press.

Leape, L. L. and Berwick, D. M. (2005) 'Five years after *To Err is Human*: what have we learned?', *American Medical Association* 293: 2384–90.

Milligan, F. J. (2007). 'Establishing a culture for patient safety – the role of education', *Nurse Education Today* 27(2): 95–102.

— (2008) 'Scope of problem and history of patient safety', *Obstetrics and Gynecology Clinics of North America* (35): 1–10.

Nieva, V. F. and Sorra, J. (2003) 'Safety culture assessment: a tool for improving patient safety in healthcare organizations', *Quality and Safety in Health Care* 12: ii–17.

Nightingale, F. (1860) *Notes on Nursing*. Available at http://digital.library.upenn.edu/women/nightingale/nursing/nursing.html, accessed 20 April 2009.

NPSA (National Patient Safety Agency) (2004). *Seven Steps to Patient Safety; An Overview Guide for Staff* (2nd edn). London: NPSA.

O'Mathúna, D., Scott, A., McAuley, A., Walsh-Daneshmandi, A. and Daly, B. (2005) *Healthcare Rights and Responsibilities: A Review of the European Charter of Patients' Rights*. Dublin: Irish Patients Association.

Ovretveit, J. (1992) *Health Service Quality*. Oxford: Blackwell Science.

Pronovost P., Nolan, T., Zeger, S. Miller, M. and Rubin, H. 'How can clinicians measure safety and quality in acute care?', *Lancet* 363 (9414): 1061–7.

Reason, J. (2000) 'Human error: models and management', *British Medical Journal* 320: 768–70.

Senge, P. M. (2006) *The Fifth Discipline: The Art and Practice of the Learning Organisation*. London: Random House Business.

Sherwood, D. (2002) *Seeing the Forest for the Trees: A Manager's Guide to Applying Systems Thinking*. Finland: WS Bookwell.

Steffen, G. E. (1988) 'Quality medical care', *Journal of the American Medical Association* 260(1): 56–61.

Stelfox, H., Palmisani, S., Scurlock, C., Orav, E. J. and Bates, D. W. (2006) 'The *To Err is Human* report and the patient safety literature', *Quality and Safety in Health Care* 15: 174–8.

Ursprung, R., Gray, J. E., Edwards, W. H., Horbar, J. D., Nickerson, J., Plsek, P., Shiono, P. H., Suresh, G. K. and Goldmann, G. K. (2005) 'Real time patient safety audits: improving safety every day', *Quality and Safety in Health Care* 14: 284–9.

Vincent, C., Ennis, M. and Audley, R. J. (2004) 'Analysis of clinical incidents: a window on the system not a search for root causes', *Quality and Safety in Healthcare* 13(4): 263– 79.

Wachter, R. M. (2008) *Understanding Patient Safety*. USA: McGraw-Hill.

Walsh, K. and Jiju, A. (2007) 'Quality costs and electronic adverse incident recording and reporting systems: is there a missing link?', *International Journal of Health Care Quality Assurance* 20(4): 307–19.

Walshe, K. and Boaden, R. (2006) *Patient Safety: Research into Practice*. Buckingham: Open University Press.

Walton, M. (2004) 'Creating a "no blame culture": have we got the balance right?', *Quality and Safety in Healthcare* 13: 163–4.

Wright, J. and Hill, P. (2003) *Clinical Governance*. London: Churchill Livingstone.

13
Integrated Care Pathways (ICPs)

Marie Kehoe

OBJECTIVES

- To define integrated care pathways (ICPs).
- To outline the history of ICPs.
- To understand the process of developing, implementing and evaluating an ICP.
- To understand how ICPs drive quality improvement, risk management and health care governance.
- To understand the critical success factors for developing, implementing and sustaining ICPs.
- To identify the key strengths and weakness of ICPs.

INTRODUCTION

The concept of integrated care, where all staff involved in health care work together as an effective team around the patients' care, is one that is gathering momentum in today's health care environment. There is considerable variation across the health care services in the interpretation of integrated care. Multidisciplinary teamwork is not a new concept in the Irish Republic. There are good examples where integrated approaches have been successfully applied, where consultants, nurses, allied professions and support staff have developed a team approach to facilitate the patient journey. However, less transparent work practices in some areas have resulted in a lack of uniformity in standards of care throughout the health service. The Health Care Strategy (DoHC 2001b) and other strategic reports (DoHC 2003a, 2003b, 2003c) highlighted the contribution of inadequate teamwork to fragmented and underdeveloped health care services with poor integration between community and acute sectors in particular. One of the main challenges facing health care professionals, managers and administrators today is trying to make the best use of resources, whilst providing high-quality, timely, evidence-based care, centred on the needs of the patient and their family/carers. As a result there is new emphasis on the provision of a model of integrated care. Integrated care pathways (ICPs) are a means by which standards of best practice can be determined and care processes streamlined with the consensus of the health care team. There is some scepticism as to the usefulness of ICPs and for some health care professionals they represent a threat to clinical autonomy. The successful redesign of an integrated approach to health care will be dependent on successful teamwork. In the current climate of health care reform, an opportunity exists to take a considered approach to the redesign of health care services. Audit, research, risk management and quality/accreditation can no longer be interpreted as separate management concerns but can be actively integrated through the use of ICPs in the everyday process of planning and care delivery by all staff.

This chapter will discuss the use of ICPs and their contribution to multidisciplinary teamwork, service user involvement, quality improvement, risk management and clinical governance. It will discuss the benefits of analysing the patient journey and the practical issues of designing, implementing and evaluating integrated care pathways in practice.

INTEGRATED CARE PATHWAYS – WHAT ARE THEY?

In 1994, the National Pathway User Group (NPUG), later the National Pathways Association (NPA) for England, Wales and Northern Ireland, was established to increase the level of interest and involvement in the formulation, implementation and use of integrated care pathways. The NPA (1998) composed the following definition:

> An integrated care pathway determines locally agreed, multidisciplinary practice based on guidelines and evidence where available, for a specific patient/client group. It forms all or part of the clinical record, documents the care given and facilitates the evaluation of outcomes for continuous quality improvement.
>
> (NPA 1998:1)

A narrower definition, offered by Ellis and Johnson (1999:61), that focuses on the actual content of the ICP is 'all the anticipated care, treatments, assessments, tasks and activities and tests of all members of the multidisciplinary team are mapped out for the achievement of agreed goals and outcomes, based on evidence where available'. More recently, an ICP has been described as 'a methodology/complex intervention for the mutual decision making and organisation of predictable care for a well-defined group of patients during a well-defined period' (EPA 2008:1).

Essentially, an ICP provides a blueprint for planning, implementing and evaluating care delivery based on empirical evidence. Consensus among the multidisciplinary team is a prerequisite for the development of these detailed maps to guide and predict the patient journey over a specified period. There are a variety of terms used internationally to describe these types of integrated approach to care, for example Care Map©, clinical protocols, care plans, clinical pathways, to name a few.

HISTORY OF INTEGRATED CARE PATHWAYS

Since the 1980s governments in many countries, including Ireland, have sought to reform their health care services. This has been due to a number of factors including ageing populations, advances in technology and the rising costs of health care. The concept of ICPs originated in America at the New England Medical Centre, Boston, Massachusetts and arose as a way of formalising known patterns of care in order to capture predictability and provide for the transfer of knowledge. They began as case management plans, evolved into critical paths and eventually into a Care Map© medical record between 1985 and 1986. In the United States other hospitals piloted this concept between 1986 and 1988, especially those who had a high volume of Medicare patients (older populations), such as Arizona, Rhode Island and Florida. Initially Care Maps© were used for cases in high-volume and predictable surgical populations such as orthopaedics and coronary artery bypass grafts. From 1989 the concept was introduced to Australia and the United Kingdom.

While ICPs were originally developed as a tool for project management, pathways are now being promoted internationally in response to the demand for increased standardisation in care delivery, enhanced patient safety and the need for fiscal responsibility in health care (Bragato & Jacobs 2003). In the mid-1990s other countries, such as Spain, New Zealand, South Africa and Saudi Arabia, began to use this idea of a patient pathway or map, followed closely by Belgium, Japan, Singapore, Germany, South Korea and Ecuador. Integrated care pathways are now seen as an example of clinician- rather than management-led reform, with focus firmly placed on the process of care rather than the hierarchical and rigid structures traditionally associated with the delivery of health care (Bragato & Jacobs 2003). Care pathways have been used extensively in the acute hospital sector, and are becoming an increasingly popular development in primary and community settings (Campbell *et al.* 1988).

AIMS AND BENEFITS

The aim of an ICP is 'to enhance the quality of care by improving patient outcomes, promoting patient safety, increasing patient satisfaction and optimising the use of resources' (EPA 2008:1). The purpose of ICPs has remained steady throughout the last two decades: to support quality care and patient satisfaction while managing resource utilisation. An ICP aims to have:

- the right people
- in the right order
- in the right place
- doing the right thing
- at the right time
- with the right outcomes (NLIAH 2005:7).

A model of ICPs developed by multidisciplinary health care teams, with the active involvement of patients, offers a practical means of embedding best practice, role clarity and efficiency into the complex processes of care. Integrated care pathways offer a means to 'facilitate and coordinate quality on a systematic and intentional basis in healthcare' (Grubnic 2003:286), supporting the delivery of a quality service and quality improvement by enabling health care professionals and administration in the following ways.

Incorporate evidence-based guidelines into everyday practice

The methodology for developing ICPs does not accept simply bringing a multidisciplinary team together and developing a pathway based on the team members' professional experience or anecdotal evidence but rather recommends extensive research into evidence-based practice in the area for which the ICP is being developed. This prevents individual preferences which have no research base and improves the quality of care for all patients.

Continually inform evidence-based practice

An integral part of a fully operational ICP is concurrent auditing of variances in the care pathway. Variance tracking, as it is known, will be discussed in more detail later in this chapter. By concurrently auditing the variances in practice, the body of knowledge around a particular path of care is continually increasing, for example if certain pain medications are being utilised as part of the ICP and it is found during variance analysis that the medications are having little effect in reducing pain, this can be modified and the findings published in peer review journals. This also promotes continuous and transformational improvements in practice by completing the audit cycle – *checking* that the medication is effective and *acting* to ensure that an alternative is found.

Manage clinical risk by increasing transparency and eliminating duplication

A criticism of the Irish health care system is the lack of accountability at times for the actions of members of the multidisciplinary team and the lack of transparency following an adverse event. Due to the fact that the ICP is developed as a team, all members of that team have ownership of the process. Each member then has authority to complete the actions required by that professional discipline and the accountability for using his/her professional judgment. For example, the ICP for a patient presenting to A&E for chest pain states that at 12 hours following the episode of chest pain a Troponin T Level is checked and if that test is negative and the patient is symptom-free, with no contraindications for exercise stress testing (EST), they will be ready for EST. As this has been agreed by the multidisciplinary team when developing the ICP, the nurse can make the decision to send the patient for EST *without contacting the consultant or other doctor* as long as that nurse has used his/her clinical judgment to meet the criteria. This is a much more efficient use of time and resources as the patient can be scheduled for the test without waiting for a doctor to give the order. The nurse is clearly accountable for that decision and is legally covered as long as the criteria were met.

Provide an opportunity for health care professionals to work in partnership with patients

As is clearly outlined throughout this chapter, an integrated care pathway is the *patient's* pathway – in other words, it is the journey that the patient will take from the time they receive a diagnosis to the time they are transferred back into the community. If it is a community/hospital care pathway or a care pathway for chronic illness, such as diabetes or asthma, the patient is on that care pathway right up until their death. It is critical during the development phase to involve that patient so that health care professionals can see the journey through the patient's eyes. This also provides the patient with an opportunity to be an active partner in their care and provides health care professionals an opportunity to discuss expectations with patients and their families.

'The implementation of ICPs could unleash an explosion of human potential' (Professor Brendan Drumm at the Irish Society for Quality and Safety in Healthcare (ISQSH) National Conference, Kilkenny 2005). Concrete examples of the quality improvements enabled through the use of ICPs in Ireland were discussed at the 2005 ISQSH conference in Kilkenny. A properly structured department of elderly medicine using an integrated care approach had contributed to improved efficiency in the hospital and continuing care utilisation by 20 per cent (Dr Declan Lyons, geriatrician, Limerick). Dignity and respect could be afforded to people in their last days and hours of life through a planned, thoughtful and considered approach to their care through the use of ICPs, according to Mervyn Taylor, Director for Hospice Friendly Hospitals, an initiative of the Irish Hospice Foundation. Integrated care pathways across the continuum of care can provide a meaningful bridge by which acute and community services can be successfully integrated, as in the Neurology Department in Beaumont Hospital, thereby improving the experience and clinical outcomes for patients with chronic long-term conditions. Each of these is an example of clinically led and team-based approaches to care. However, the care pathway of a patient following a brain injury or a person living with a debilitating disease such as motor neuron disease does not stop following discharge after an acute episode. These experiences should be the norm and not the exception.

BARRIERS TO SUCCESS

ICPs are not an easy project to begin in a care setting. There are many reasons why it can be difficult and very time-consuming to develop care pathways. Hierarchical approaches to work design in health, the absence of integrated approaches to care and resistance to change are just some of the obstacles that must be tackled as part of the planning phase. Sale (2005:118) identified that 'many professional staff do not have the skills necessary to conduct the essential research on international best practice, and even when they do identify the research they may not have the skills to critically appraise and analyse it'. As stated above, when professional disciplines have worked in silos it is often very difficult for them to let go of their 'own documentation' whether it be nursing care plans, social workers' or doctors' notes, and the professionals may feel very insecure about using one set of notes for all professionals. In worst-case scenarios, some professionals will continue to resist the ICP by 'forgetting' to write in them, adding their own discipline notes to the 'comment' section of the ICP or sometimes even going so far as to add in pages for their own notes. If the ICP is not located in a central, convenient place, there will also be resistance to completing the documentation.

The reasons for this resistance are varied – sometimes clinicians view ICPs as 'cookbook' medicine and fear that they are losing their clinical autonomy and that the ICP does not allow them to give individualised care to their patients. These concerns are all very valid but they are also concerns that can be dealt with by a good ICP facilitator who must use excellent negotiation skills and strong research to back their belief that the ICP is a positive way forward.

ICPs aim to improve the standardisation of care and embed evidence-based practice. If the ICP is not developed properly, the opposite will happen. The ICP methodology is not only time-consuming in the initial development phase; it also requires constant monitoring to ensure that it is always up to date with evidence-based practice. Due to the constant turnover of staff in facilities, as a result of teaching programmes or use of agency staff, it is critical that all new staff are given clear induction which includes the ICPs in use and their locations.

Integrated care pathway development is about 'making a positive difference for patients receiving healthcare' (NCPDNM 2006:3). They enable the health service to harness the professional capacity of its employees to contribute to enhanced patient outcomes and service delivery (NCPDNM 2006).

Figure 13.1: Effects of ICPs

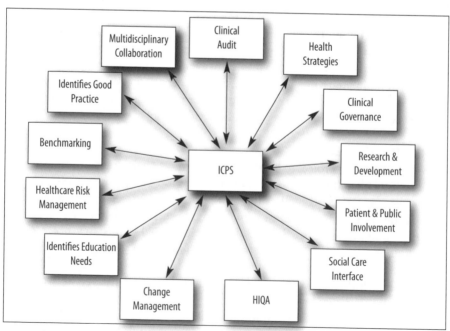

DEVELOPING AND IMPLEMENTING THE INTEGRATED CARE PATHWAY
Change management

There are a variety of change management and quality improvement frameworks at one's disposal to assist during the initial phase of ICP development, for example plan–do–check–act (PDCA), process mapping, SWOT analysis, fishbone (ishiwaka) diagrams and balanced scorecards (Institute for Healthcare Improvement website).

The plan–do–check–act (PDCA) quality improvement model is recommended by the Institute for Healthcare Improvement (IHI). Improvement is the result of a continuous series of cycles building on previous results. Each PDCA is short, making small improvements in process over time.

Figure 13.2: PDCA model (IHI website)

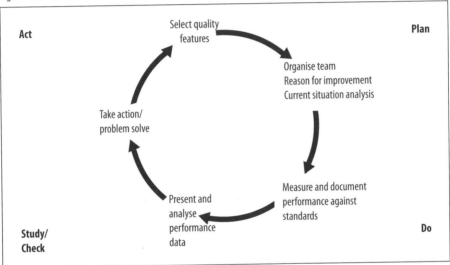

What are we trying to accomplish?

The start of the improvement process should be a statement of the aims of the project. It is impossible to reach a goal without knowing what it is. The goal statement should be clear, specific, aspirational and measurable. In the case of ICP development the goal statement should be the patient's and multidisciplinary team's goals for the care that will be given to the patient during the episode of care.

How will we know that a change is an improvement?

The key to an effective improvement process is measurement. Without effective measurement there is no way of knowing whether any change is improving the process, and a range of measurements of improvement is central to any improvement process. Variance tracking is the method by which improvement is measured in the integrated care model.

What changes can we make that will result in improvement?

The PDCA cycle is a way of testing suggested improvements in a controlled environment. Changes can come from staff suggestions, from other sites that have looked at the same problems or from the literature. These changes are then tested, using the PDCA cycle. The process of variance analysis in the ICP model identifies any components that are not contributing to improved patient outcomes, which can then be modified.

ICP development is essentially about promoting change and this cannot be achieved without the support of all the key stakeholders: frontline staff, patients, carers, clinicians, management, allied health professionals, etc. Most people are frightened by change because it forces them to step outside their comfort zone and learn something new. Implementing change often means challenging people to work differently when they would prefer things to stay as they are. Unless managed effectively, this can lead to resistance to the project. One of the most effective ways of bringing people on board is helping them to identify 'what is in it for me?' Everyone has some motivation for either adopting or resisting change – the key is in finding the individual's motivation for adopting. Facilitators must help stakeholders to identify what they do not like about the current process. In order to manage change successfully, these drivers must be identified and used by the team facilitator. If he/she is able to ensure that solutions meet the needs of the staff, the solutions will be much easier to implement (NLIAH 2005).

Successful development of ICPs is dependent upon synergy between management and lead clinicians. The time commitment involved during the development phase of the ICP is not to be underestimated. Change can either be developed from below – driven by frontline staff (bottom up) – or imposed by senior management (top down). If driven by management, with a clear strong mandate, it will usually have a clear plan with objectives outlined, support and possibly leadership. However, this is not a complete recipe for success as staff can view the proposed change as an imposition from above and they may not feel as though they are party to the process. This has the potential to lead to increased resistance from frontline staff. However, if frontline staff are actively the drivers of change, initiatives such as ICPS are more likely to succeed. Enabling frontline staff to take control and ownership of the process will make a significant contribution to overcoming resistance to change. Changes driven by frontline staff with the co-operation of management are more likely to be continuous than episodic (NLIAH 2005). However, success is contingent on clear commitment from senior management to enhance the provision of appropriate leadership, resources and support. The National Leadership and Innovation Agency for Healthcare (NLIAH) (2005) identified four essential factors that are needed in order for staff to embrace change – dissatisfaction, vision, capacity and understanding of first steps – and these provide a framework for advancing the initial stages of ICP development.

When applying these factors to decisions to develop ICPs in an area, it is not only staff who may be unhappy with the process of care as it currently is. Quite often it is patients or families who complain, as they are the only people who truly see the journey through the eyes of the service user. Frequently these complaints are brought to the attention of staff who then become unhappy themselves with the process of care. The vision is then identified *with* the patients and families – by seeing the vision through the patient's eyes, staff will be more willing to give up what they are currently doing.

The capacity issue is a difficult one when it comes to ICPs because the development and maintenance of ICPs are labour-intensive and it will take a person with a dedicated post to lead, facilitate and maintain the momentum. ICPs have been around for a long time now (over 20 years) so there are good examples of ICPs that can be shared with staff to provide them with a model of what it is they are going to be working towards.

Table 13.1: Essential factors in embracing change

Dissatisfaction	Staff must be unhappy with the process of care as it currently is.
Vision	There must be a view that things could be better and an agreed vision of how the ICP will be. We do not give up what we have without a clear idea of what we will have in its place.
Capacity	There must be capacity to change – this will include having the resources to initiate, develop, implement, evaluate and sustain the change. There must be commitment from senior management to the change in order to provide the resources that will be necessary. In the case of ICPs this most often means a dedicated post of ICP facilitator (this role will be discussed later in the chapter).
First steps	There must be clear understanding by all of what will happen first. Participants will want to see a defined plan with manageable first steps.

Source: NLIAH (2005)

STAGES IN DEVELOPING, IMPLEMENTING AND EVALUATING ICPS

There are variations in the literature as to the exact number of stages in developing an ICP (NLIAH 2005; Sale 2005; NCPDNM 2006). The Irish National Council for the Professional Development of Nursing and Midwifery's 2006 publication, *Improving the Patient Journey*, identified five key steps to developing and introducing care pathways. While there are differences in the number of steps, the key components in each stage remain the same in the literature – below is an eight-step method designed by the NCPDNM that brings together the key essential elements needed to develop, implement and evaluate ICPs.

1   Setting the stage.
2   Putting together the team.
3   Baseline assessment.
4   Clarifying the current situation.
5   Designing the ICP.
6   Piloting the ICP.

7   Implementing the ICP.

8   Evaluating the ICP.

1 Setting the stage

As with any change management strategy, careful preparation must take place and a sense of urgency must be felt among key stakeholders that the way things are being done is not working, so a new model of integrated care is necessary. There can be many drivers for this sense of urgency.

- An increase in patient dissatisfaction, either at local or national level, and a recognition of the need to involve service users in the planning of their care.
- Frustration among staff that outcomes for patients should and could be better if a new system of care were introduced.
- The introduction and implementation of national standards, for example standards on quality and risk management (HSE 2007a), residential care (HIQA 2009), decontamination (HSE 2007b) and hygiene (HIQA 2008), that must be implemented.

This sense of urgency will enable the staff to identify the priority areas and decide on the most appropriate ICP (topic) to develop.

2 Putting together the team

The Primary Care Strategy (2001) specifically highlighted the need to improve integration of services so as to create a seamless, people-centred service. Many of the recent strategy documents have emphasised the people, tools, skills, structures or frameworks that are necessary for effective quality improvement initiatives at ground level (DoHC 2001a, 2001b, 2003a, 2003b, 2003c). One significant early benefit to any health care service during the development of a local ICP is that it optimises communication and collaboration among interdisciplinary team members as well as with the patient/family, in addition to making transparent the process of care. A critical step associated with the successful development and implementation of ICPs is to identify and include the key stakeholders to inform and steer the project. This step is critical to the success of the ICP as it is essential that all persons who will be asked to utilise the ICP will be represented on the working group. This will include all the key health care professionals – doctors, nurses, pharmacists, physiotherapists – as well as ancillary staff – health care assistants, caterers, maintenance staff, porters, laundry workers and administrators – as appropriate. It also needs to make provision for stakeholders who may not be directly accessible in the location where the pathway is to be implemented, such as admissions staff or pharmacy staff. In their research on the evolving role of pharmacists, Al-Shaqha and Zairi (2001) highlighted an example of potential professional isolation that can impact on this process. A significant finding of the research found professionals' (such as pharmacists') inter-professional relationships may be limited because of the physical location of practice: physicians and nurses are traditionally in the patient care areas and the pharmacists are often in the central hospital pharmacy. In some instances health care professionals and support staff may not have traditionally worked outside their own professions or work areas, so this may be the first opportunity for many to meet and work with their colleagues.

At this stage, it is important to discuss the role of the ICP facilitator. Debate persists as to the most suitable professional to drive the successful development and implementation of ICPs. What is clear is that this process requires not only multidisciplinary commitment but also support from senior management. The experiences of those who lead the way in developing ICPs have shown that in order to successfully drive, implement, evaluate and sustain ICPs, a person dedicated to the role should ideally be in place (Bragato & Jacobs 2003; Kent & Chalmers 2006). This individual will be responsible for identifying the key stakeholders, forming the team, facilitating the working group meetings, offering support to staff during the implementation phase, auditing the variances, compiling reports and driving the overall process. Depending on the size of the project and local resources, the facilitator may also act as the administrator – convening the meetings, typing and distributing minutes, typing the ICP drafts and managing all related documentation. This is a demanding role requiring patience, tenacity and persistence, in addition to a significant time commitment. It is therefore recommended that a dedicated person take on the job – it is very difficult for someone to take on this role as an 'add-on' to an existing job.

When putting together the team, it is also critical to remember the role of the service user. Patients' views are commonly elicited during their hospital stay or at the end of their treatment (Smith & Ross 2007), but there is limited evidence to demonstrate that ICPs are being developed in active partnership with patients and/or carers. Understanding patients' experiences and their reactions to the health services is an important step in building quality ICPs. Involving patients in their care and taking on board their views is a specific ICP aim and ICPs can improve communication between professionals and patients and their carers because they inform patients about their expected care. Therefore active user membership within the working group and/or liaison with relevant patient groups is essential for the development of ICPs that truly reflect the user perspective.

3 Baseline assessment

Analysis of current service performance through the collection of relevant baseline data will assist the project team to identify opportunities for improvements through the use of ICPs. The target population for the ICP is initially identified and existing baseline outcomes established. Data can be derived from a variety of sources and include demographics, co-morbidities, patient journey, length of stay, clinical interventions, and acute and community care delivery services. When evaluating both internal and external processes that contribute to and represent the existing treatment parameters, the critical questions should be considered.

Baseline assessment questions

Identifying problems in care delivery:

- What is done and why?
- What is the value of the process?
- How could the care delivery be modified, redefined or administered more efficiently or effectively?
- What are the barriers (for example access, availability, resources, etc.) to effective treatment?

---

4 Clarifying the current situation

Clarifying the current situation is essential in order to accurately identify the actions to plan and implement change. In order to develop an ICP, the team must gather all the evidence needed to underpin the ICP. This will entail process mapping and developing a flow chart of the patient journey as it currently is, then conducting a literature review to identify any national or international guidelines that pertain to the topic of the ICP. A baseline audit of current practice will contribute to increasing the accuracy of the 'as is' situation and will also enable comparative evaluation of the ICP's success. Other tools that can be used to brainstorm current practice and invite suggestions for the ICP are patient/staff questionnaires, focus groups with either staff or patients and patient shadowing.

Process mapping

Understanding the processes and systems issues that can affect the patient journey are key to the successful development of ICPs. Unique criteria that define the stages and outcomes of the patient's journey can be illustrated through the use of process maps to capture those aspects of services that may impinge on the timely and safe progression of the patient through any health service interaction. 'A process is a series of connected steps or actions to achieve an outcome' (NHS National Modernisation Agency and NICE 2005:11). The production of valid and reliable ICPs is made possible by initial work on developing detailed process maps that reflect all the junctures in, and the personnel and procedures that affect, a defined patient journey. Illustrating the patient journey enables the multidisciplinary team to fully grasp the direct and indirect elements that influence the patient's journey.

5 Designing the ICP
Identify the optimum outcomes

It is essential that the ICP is underpinned by best practice evidence for the relevant area. Evidence can be derived from a variety of sources, such as published evidence of good practice and the expert opinion of stakeholders, and can include care protocols, research studies, evidence-based practice guidelines, accounts of other organisations' experiences, expert opinion and views of patients and families. A detailed literature review is usually required to identify and critically evaluate existing national and international evidence in relation to the proposed area for ICP development. All relevant evidence should be analysed by the team and a synthesis of the findings will take place based on relevance, applicability, quality and other criteria emerging from the materials.

Figure 13.3: Sample process map of patient journey – surgical procedure

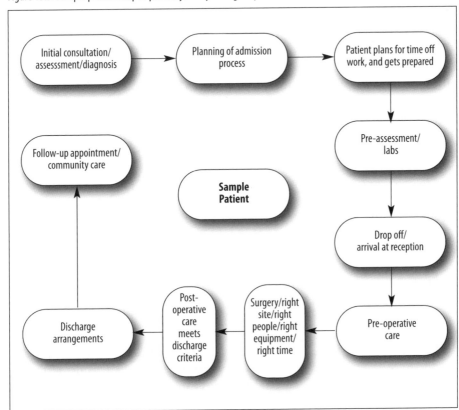

Agreement on clinical guidelines

Following the process mapping exercise and the development of an agreed optimal patient journey, clinical guidelines/protocols and standards to support and guide the care delivered need to be developed or reviewed and adapted if already established. Clinical guidelines/protocols are systematically developed statements to assist practitioner decisions about appropriate health care for specific clinical circumstances. Clinical guidelines/protocols must be:

- underpinned by robust methods for evaluating research evidence to support practice
- based upon evidence linked to practice

- developed by inter-/multidisciplinary teams with patient consultation
- flexible enough to adapt to local conditions
- evaluated and updated regularly.

6 Piloting the ICP

Once consensus is achieved among stakeholders and the draft pathway has undergone any formal authorisation process required before implementation, the pilot process can be undertaken. The ICP will then be printed and distributed to the pilot sites – it is critical that training and support is given to staff on site throughout the pilot. During the pilot phase, there will be duplication of effort, as most professionals will want to retain the 'old system' until they know that the new system is clearly working, is better, and all the 'kinks' have been worked out. All aspects of using the ICP are given consideration in the pilot, including staff effort, time commitment and variance analysis. The pilot affords the opportunity to evaluate compliance with the organisational philosophy and objectives and evaluate the fitness for purpose of the ICP. Suitable educational support materials and resources must be available to support all those involved in the pilot process, such as training on documenting on the one record, how to record variances, etc. At the end of the pilot phase, the ICP will need to be evaluated for ease of use, effectiveness, and impact on patients and service users, all involved in providing the health care service, the supporting departments, health care governance, and health care audit and overall quality improvement and risk management.

Once the pilot phase is completed and the ICP amended it should be submitted for external review and comment by other relevant practitioners and stakeholders. Finally, it must be submitted for approval and signed off by the inter-/multidisciplinary team for official endorsement and adoption by the organisation (Graham & Harrison 2005). It is important from a risk management perspective that at the point before final sign-off the organisation's legal team also review the document. After final sign-off, it is reprinted and distributed to all areas.

Some hospitals in the UK and the USA are now using electronic care pathways, but these are at an early stage and there is not sufficient research available to date to show their effectiveness. The National Electronic Library for Health (NeLH) Pathways Database was launched in 2002 to facilitate sharing of ICPs and ICP projects across the UK (http://libraries.nelh.nhs.uk/pathways/aboutICPs.asp). The 'Protocols and Care Pathways' section provides a database of available ICPs in use throughout the UK as well as a 'knowledge zone' which provides information about the ICP tools and how they are developed and evaluated.

7 Implementing the ICP

The next step is the introduction and implementation of the newly developed ICP into a clinical environment. This requires careful planning so that patient care is not disrupted and staff enthusiasm is both engendered and maintained throughout.

At the beginning of the implementation process it is imperative to meet with the staff and agree specific measurable goals to be achieved by the introduction of the ICP. These goals must be aligned with the individual organisational culture, systems and goals. As this may be a new and unfamiliar process it is critical that educational support and training is provided for staff. Staff release for education and training is one of the biggest challenges in the current health care environment, so it must be planned with both staff and management in an innovative manner. This frequently means education sessions at ward level (or health care setting if a community ICP); the training may be held during staff meetings and, as the ICP is a model which covers care around the clock, it is also important that education sessions are offered for staff working on all shifts. A convenient time to offer an education session on ICPs is often the hours that cover a change of shift (8–9 a.m. or 5–6 p.m., for example) so that both staff coming on and staff going off their shift can attend. Ongoing support will also be required for at least the initial six months of implementation – this may vary from ongoing meetings with staff to address any questions or concerns to providing a contact number for the co-ordinator, who will be available to answer questions at any time.

As with any change in practice, it is critical to seek feedback from staff and to give feedback to staff. With ICPs it is very important that results and analyses of the variances are given to inter-/multidisciplinary team members. This will lead to staff ownership, buy-in and less resistance if staff believe that their feedback is being valued and that it is not simply a 'paper exercise'. It is critical to review the ICP with the staff on an ongoing basis (even weekly during the initial months) and modify to continue improvement or maintain outcomes. In order to maintain the ICP and enthusiasm for the process, the cyclical process (PDCA, as described previously) of introducing, analysing, modifying and re-introducing should be continued on a regular basis (Interhospital and Agency Clinical Pathway Group 2002; NHS National Modernisation Agency and NICE 2005).

A detailed time line can be illustrated with a Gantt chart and this will assist greatly in establishing a realistic picture of the work to be done and the expected timeframe in which tasks need to be achieved. The following is an example of a Gantt chart used in a community care centre in Ireland when implementing an ICP for falls prevention with older clients. This provides a clear visualisation of the process to be undertaken.

Table 13.2: Gantt chart: ICT for falls prevention (Dublin Community Care)

TASK	Responsibility	Sept. 2006	Oct. 2006	Dec. 2006	May 2007	June 2007	Aug. (end) 2007	Sept. 2007
Set up Primary Care Falls Team	Ground up initiative	▲						
Set up Local Health Office, Dublin North Central steering group (multidisciplinary)	Ground up initiative		▲					
Conduct SWOT analysis				▲				
Set up partnership group	Merging of SG & PCFT					▲		
Organise working group (multi-agency /multidisciplinary)	Set up by SG & PCFT				▲			
Map current situation	Wk Gp 1				▲		❑	
Develop screening tool	Wk Gp 2				▲		❑	
Pilot screening tool	Wk Gp 2							❑ (early)
Develop shared folders ICT	Wk Gps 2, 3, 4, 5					▲	❑	
Agree components of DOAS (do once and share) tool that are feasible	Wk Gp2				▲		❑	
Agree protocol for focused medical assessment	Wk Gp 2				▲		❑	
Agree documentation for focused medical assessment	Wk Gp 2				▲		❑	
Develop interventions, e.g. physical activity programme, vision, arts programme, outline of health & well-being, advice, etc.	Wk Gp 3					▲	❑	
Implement interventions	To be determined							
Develop training programme components to include information giving, training on usage of tools & DOAS pathway, standardisation of health education messages, etc.	Wk Gp 4				▲			❑

TASK	Responsibility	Sept. 2006	Oct. 2006	Dec. 2006	May 2007	June 2007	Aug. (end) 2007	Sept. 2007
Consultation with older people								▲
Implement training programme, awareness-raising sessions, calibration sessions, IT training	To be determined							
Setting criteria for evaluation	Wk Gp 5				▲			❑
Collection of evaluation data	To be determined							▽
Finalise programme proposal and submit funding bid	Wk Gp 5		▲					
Initiate pilot programme								
Process evaluation	All		▲					
Draft report including recommendations	To be determined							
Dissemination of report	To be determined							

▲ = has been initiated   ❑ = date due for completion   ▽ = has not yet been initiated

8 Evaluating the ICP

The evaluation of ICPs is an ongoing process and there are a variety of ways in which they can be evaluated. Variance tracking enables demonstration of the consistency of clinical outcomes, in addition to uncovering any risk management or quality improvement opportunities. The Integrated Care Pathway Appraisal Tool (ICPAT) was originally developed as an instrument to evaluate the quality of developed ICPs (Whittle *et al.* 2004). However, it can also be used very effectively during the development process as a 'how-to step-by-step' guide for teams who are at the initial or early stages of ICP development. It is essential to clearly isolate whether the process, and subsequent document, being used is indeed an ICP as per the ICPAT guidelines (see Appendix 1). This process of review can be done as a self-audit by the working group or facilitated through a peer review exercise, as is the case with the Irish Care Pathway Network (ICPN). It is important to carry out evaluations not only on the effectiveness of the ICP in improving clinical outcomes but also on such factors as multidisciplinary teamwork – effectiveness of communication, patient involvement/satisfaction, improvement in streamlining and making more efficient use of resources, benchmarking against international standards and value for money.

Clinical effectiveness

Patient outcomes may be evaluated through the use of ICPs. In a literature review of the effectiveness of ICPs in the UK, Whittle and Hewson (2007) found numerous studies that demonstrated the effectiveness of ICPs in terms of patient outcomes (falls prevention, diabetic ketoacidosis in children, hip and knee arthroplasty, colorectal cancer and stroke). One of the findings in this review of the literature showed that patients undergoing total knee arthroplasty between September 1997 and December 1998 had a shorter stay if their care was organised as part of an ICP (Lane *et al.* 2001). These patients also experienced less pain and better function and did not have an associated increase in post-operative infection. Davis (2004) showed that patients are more satisfied if their care is organised as part of an ICP because they feel more in control of their care.

Concurrent evaluation

The variances in the ICP must also be tracked and analysed to promote quality improvement, risk management and clinical governance. Nyatanga and Holliman (2005) define a variance as 'any deviation from the expected outcome in the ICP that can be either avoidable or unavoidable as exemplified through the patient's physiological problem, an omission or delay in completing an intervention by the care giver or as a result of the system through institutional practice patterns, policies or procedures' (Nyatanga & Holliman 2005). Auditing processes have typically been retrospective in nature; concurrent variance tracking offers an opportunity to monitor the quality of care, compliance with standards and patient involvement on a continuous basis, thereby improving the overall patient experience and quality of care. Most ICPs allow space to the side of each page of the ICP document to note the variances from the planned care on the pathway and this area also allows the professional to identify reasons for the variance. As stated before, it is critical, in order to improve the quality of care, that the tracking, analysis and modifications to the ICP are discussed and reviewed with the staff on an ongoing basis.

Integrated Care Pathway Appraisal Tool

This evaluation instrument is divided into six sections (outlined below) and provides a comprehensive framework to fully evaluate an ICP. This tool is used by the members of the Irish Care Pathway Network (ICPN) to peer review ICPs as they are being developed and after they are developed. The tool is accompanied by a user guide and includes a glossary of terms. (See Appendix 1 for ICPAT and User Guide.)

Integrated Care Pathway Appraisal Tool

The instrument evaluates the following:

1   Is it an integrated care pathway?

---

2   The integrated care pathway documentation.
3   The development process.
4   The implementation process.
5   Maintenance of the integrated care pathway.
6   The role of the organisation.

Source: West Midlands NHS (2006)

CASE STUDY

You are the ICP facilitator in a major teaching hospital which contains an orthopaedic unit. Below is a scenario of a typical patient who enters your hospital for orthopaedic surgery.

A 42-year-old man injures his knee while out jogging. He goes to his primary care physician, a GP, who issues a referral to a physiotherapist authorising a series of visits for physiotherapy. Because the public waiting list is too long, the patient attends a private physiotherapist who treats the man, but his outcomes are only marginal so he returns to visit his GP. This time the GP issues a referral for the man to see an orthopaedic surgeon. The patient is put on a waiting list for the orthopaedic surgeon. After four months he is given an appointment with the surgeon. He has been in severe pain during this time and has been receiving pain relief from his GP. The surgeon orders diagnostic tests, including an X-ray, and sends the man to the radiology department. After reviewing the X-ray, the surgeon sends the man back to the radiology department for a scan. After reviewing the knee scans, the surgeon recommends surgery. A month later the surgeon performs surgery to repair damaged knee cartilage. The patient is sent home with a referral for the physiotherapist but no appointment or directions on how to contact the public physiotherapy department. He is also advised to attend the outpatient department for a follow-up visit with the orthopaedic surgeon six weeks post-discharge.

Case questions

1   Who are the key stakeholders who need to be on this team?
2   What steps will you take to prepare for your initial team meeting?
3   Develop a flow chart for the 'as is' situation.
4   Where will you pilot this ICP?

ICPs – QUALITY IMPROVEMENT

Continuous quality improvement (CQI) is growing in importance for health care organisations, nationally and internationally. CQI is defined as 'an integrated, corporately led programme of organisational change, designed to engender and sustain a culture . . . based on customer oriented definitions of quality' (Kogan *et al.*1994:10). Consumer demand for patient centredness and clinical effectiveness in health care is growing. Health care consumers are more informed in relation to best practice and empowered to engage as active participants in their own health care. The increase in advocacy groups has provided greater opportunity for the patient voice to be heard, with the result that all health care consumers anticipate the highest quality of care.

The use of ICPs does promote a culture of continuous review. It is anticipated that following the introduction and implementation of ICPs their applicability and usage will be sustained through adherence to the process of continuous improvement cycles. This provides a mechanism to overcome outdated and established patterns of care as there is requirement for a constant revisiting of standards. ICPs are utilised as a quality improvement tool because of their emphasis on multidisciplinary involvement, in contrast to the traditional unidisciplinary and professional or departmental isolation approaches in health care. The development phase and implementation of the ICP unite occupations involved in the care of patient groups.

Increased survival rates for people with chronic disease and older persons means there is an ever-growing health care demand for strategies both to assist independent living and to reduce demand on acute hospital beds. Thomas *et al.* (2007) examined alternative clinical management options such as early intervention via ICPs for chronic disease management. This study of older patients concluded that an integrated primary and secondary approach to care, such as an ICP, that crossed between hospital and community enhanced the care of patients with chronic disease who need acute care and in the acute management of elderly patients (Thomas *et al.* 2007). In order to improve quality of patient care, there is a need to develop a more integrated health care system to provide a more co-ordinated approach to acute medical patient needs and keep people in their own homes as much as possible.

ICPs are developed through multidisciplinary consensus in relation to best or 'gold standard' rather than average standards of care, therefore they have the capacity to raise expectations of care delivery and promote acceptance of consistency in quality (Schmid & Conen 2000). The development of ICPs in the UK arose primarily to improve the quality of patient care and the standards of associated documentation by systematically managing the processes of clinical care (Currie & Harvey 2000).

As a method for improving the quality of patient care, ICPs can:

- promote multidisciplinary, patient-focused care
- facilitate the implementation of evidence-based care
- improve the quality of documentation
- improve communication between health care professionals (Whittle & Hewson 2007:301).

The change management involved in introducing ICPs is not as difficult as other initiatives because ICPs provide a means for 'managers to better plan and evaluate the care processes, whilst the central focus on the patient at the heart of the process is valued by professionals as an appropriate model for practice' (Whittle & Hewson 2007:304).

A review of the literature by Joosten, Bongers and Meijboom (2007) demonstrated the improvements in quality of care that were achieved when ICPs were used in conjunction with care programmes for patients with mental illness. Mental health care is more person-centred and not as predictable as other areas of health care. The authors concluded that if ICPs can improve both processes of care and overall service quality, the increased usage of ICPs for well-defined groups of patients could contribute to enhanced outcomes with many more mental health illnesses and services (Joosten *et al.* 2007).

ICPs – RISK MANAGEMENT

In addition to acting as a very effective quality assurance tool, ICPs have also been identified as critical to proactive risk management. Clinical risks have led to spiralling costs to international governments for negligence claims. In 1990, litigation cost the NHS £53 million; in 1996/1997 it cost £300 million. The projected cost for 2001 was over £500 million (Department of Health (UK) 1996).

Nyatanga and Holliman (2005) posited that as a clinical risk, health care-acquired infections (HAI) could be reduced through ICP development and implementation by anticipating potential risks when drafting the ICP, so that preventative action and risk assessment tools are included in the ICP. Compliance with these particular action guidelines would then be monitored during the variance tracking process (Nyatanga & Holliman 2005).

This could be said for all identified clinical risks – falls, skin breakdown, medication errors, misdiagnosis, environmental risks, etc. One care pathway initiated in Ireland at St Vincent's University Hospital for outpatient management of deep vein thrombosis (DVT) decided to develop a care pathway because they realised that a number of major medical conditions were not being uncovered until the patients were being discharged at the 'exit clinic', three to six months following initial diagnosis and treatment for a DVT. Lack of identification and management of health care risks can lead to financial costs to the institution as a result of inefficient use of resources (both human and technological), increased length of stay (bed days) in acute care and, in the worst case scenario, poor outcomes for patients resulting in litigation and adverse media attention. During a six-month audit following implementation of the care pathway for outpatient management of deep vein thrombosis, the authors identified that 102 Doppler ultrasounds were avoided, a significant number of previously undiagnosed illness were picked up at the initial assessment, and due to 81 per cent of patients being discharged during the study period, the hospital had saved 288 bed days and €181,300 in resource costs over the six months. By reducing the number of Doppler studies, the hospital saved a further €18,360 (Kidney & Hosny 2008:3).

Care pathways are often referred to as the patient journey and the goal of the ICP is that the patient follows a 'planned' journey that is evidence-based. Bragato and Jacobs (2003) point out that the planned and documented journey, represented by the ICP, will carry less risk that the unplanned journey and the 'knowledge of the pathway by the traveller (patient) will allow him/her to feel safe and reassured about outcomes of the entire journey' (Bragato & Jacobs 2003).

Variance tracking

The ICP is also a standard or universal plan for how a patient with a particular condition will be treated. Variance tracking makes it possible to identify when the progress of the patient does not match this standard plan. By auditing the ICPs frequently it is possible to track the variances and to identify the root cause of these variances. The reasons for variances are varied; examples include environmental factors, staff training, staff resources, patient group, availability of technology and geographic location. By analysing the variances, actions can be put in place to reduce the risk to patients due to variations in care – deviations from the recognised and agreed standard of care. Variances from the planned path of care are recorded on the pathway documentation, which becomes a vehicle for the documentation of quality control and risk management issues. The variations from the standards are open to subsequent inspection and challenge.

Cowan (2003) sought to understand if ICPs work as an effective risk management tool for all care groups when she examined risk management in the National Service Framework for Older People, following concern that the information about clinical incidence of errors leading to harm is still rudimentary for this age group. All aspects of clinical services have risks attached and without attention to detail, systems can be put in place or not reviewed, leading to the potential for generating repeated errors due to systems problems (Cowan 2003). Where ICPs are utilised, with variance tracking, the analysis of care pathways does not take a great deal of time for the well-trained risk manager and may add some invaluable and objective insight to identifying areas of potential risk or harm.

The simplest interaction of patient and health care provider often needs the input and knowledge of, and effective communication between, several individuals (Kavanagh & Cowan 2004). Work teams have not traditionally arisen in health care as a result of patient need but are instead the result of historical accident or professional associations (Kavanagh & Cowan 2004). The challenge for clinical teams is to select members, organise their processes and interactions and choose their leadership in such a way as to give themselves the best chance of effective performance. Simply leaving teams to evolve in a haphazard fashion without examination of tasks, organisation and outcome delivery is a poor approach to risk management. ICPs provide a useful route to define team objectives and identify protocols and procedures which need to be followed (Kavanagh & Cowan 2005).

ICPs – HEALTH CARE GOVERNANCE

Health care governance is a framework through which health services and organisations are accountable for continuously improving the quality of services and upholding high standards of clinical care to ensure patient safety. In order to achieve this, health care governance defines the values, culture, behaviours, processes and procedures that are essential for the provision of safe, sustainable quality services (Scottish Executive 2005). A care pathway is a method for delivering evidence-based practice as part of everyday care. The fact that the ICPs are developed by the multidisciplinary team who will be utilising them and not taken 'off the shelf' leads to less resistance and increased involvement and ownership of the ICP (Sale 2005:111).

According to Sale (2005), ICPs are a vehicle by which clinical governance may be realised. ICPs do this by involving staff in concurrent and retrospective clinical audit (through variance tracking) and promoting evidence-based practice (EBP) and national standards in everyday care. As it is a single multidisciplinary document, the ICP promotes communication between disciplines (Sale 2005:121). As each member of the team signs off on the actions as they are completed, there are more clearly defined roles, responsibilities and lines of accountability.

There has been much discussion regarding the transparency of health care decisions. The idea is now being developed around patient-held records – this is already being utilised in maternity services where the expectant mother carries her ICP with her to all her appointments. Hill *et al.* (2000) found that the communication advantages that such a process provides are particularly apparent in the management of long-term or chronic conditions such as coronary heart disease. The ICP can also be used as a very effective teaching tool for patients and allows them to take responsibility for their role in their own health care.

The pathway itself is also a very useful tool for clinical governance when it is used as a guide for new staff, or staff who are moved from one ward to another, as it provides a guide that the health care professional can follow, thereby ensuring best practice and standardisation of care. It also clearly outlines the roles and responsibilities of each member of the team and holds them accountable for their own practice by ensuring that they 'sign off' on their specific actions as soon as they are completed.

STRENGTHS AND WEAKNESSES OF ICPs

The main strengths and weakness of ICPs can be summarised as follows.

Strengths

ICPs:
- promote evidence-based care and the use of clinical guidelines in practice
- drive optimal quality of care and provide a means of continuous quality improvement
- improve inter-/multidisciplinary communication, teamwork and care planning
- sustain continuity and co-ordination of care across different clinical disciplines and sectors

- provide explicit and well-defined standards of care
- reduce variations in patient care (by promoting standardisation)
- improve clinical outcomes
- streamline, reduce and improve patient documentation
- support education and training
- optimise the management of resources
- reduce costs by shortening hospital stays
- provide support for clinical judgment
- assist in the management and reduction of clinical risk
- support clinical audit and clinical effectiveness
- provide a consistent guide for staff who are new to clinical area (locums, students, agency staff, etc.).

Weaknesses

- Some staff lack the skills to critically appraise the evidence/research.
- Considerable time and skill is required to develop and maintain the ICP.
- Documentation may not be completed or professionals may continue to use their own discipline's notes.
- There can be a lack of knowledge of ICP among locums, agency and bank staff as they may not have been involved in development and may not have received training in the use of ICPs.
- The location of an ICP is not convenient to all.
- There can be medico-legal problems if an ICP is out of date with evidence-based practice.
- It needs commitment from the whole team.
- A dedicated post (ICP co-ordinator) is needed to drive, sustain, audit variances, train and modify.

CONCLUSION

These are challenging times for all who work in the Irish health system and, indeed, internationally in health care. Health ministries are required to provide high-quality health care systems with increasingly stringent budgetary constraints and changing demographics. The frustration levels of both patients and clinicians have probably never been higher. Outmoded systems of work present considerable risk and raise quality issues in health care. Poor health care designs set up the workforce to fail. Higher levels of quality cannot be achieved by further stressing current systems of care. Trying harder will not work; changing systems of care will. In the main, people present themselves to the health service with a common range of problems that are entirely predictable – chronic lung disease, asthma, heart disease, diabetes, etc. As a first step, we must understand how these are diagnosed and treated and ensure that they are managed consistently in line with best practice. We must also work with patients, learn from them, and educate them to manage their health in a more proactive way. Where an admission is necessary, we must work on the patient journey through the system and design our systems to make the patient experience an effective and efficient journey, doing the right thing at the right time in the right place.

Properly developed ICPs can help us reduce complexity, work in effective teams and improve the patient experience. In order to support the development of ICPs in Ireland, critical success factors will need to be put in place. The HSE must demonstrate commitment (by providing resources) at senior management level and clinical levels. Staff must be given dedicated time to become involved as a multidisciplinary team during planning and development. Patients must receive training on the ICP process and on the role of patient advocate or 'expert patient'. ICPs must be included as part of an organisational quality improvement programme. Service funding must revolve around the patient journey. ICPs must be 'owned' by the clinical staff and patients. There must be local and national champions for the concept. ICPs must be based on available evidence and best practice, including milestones and expected outcomes. Variations must be collated, analysed and fed back to staff – then shared with other hospitals or community sectors throughout the country. There must be a programme of education for all members of the multidisciplinary teams on quality improvement tools, team-building, etc. Health Research Board (HRB) grants and other research grants need to promote the concept of ICPs by offering funding to research the use and effectiveness of ICPs here in Ireland and to promote the work in this country internationally.

A lot of energy has been focused on capacity issues in our health system. ICPs are not the solution to all these problems; but they may, however, be a very valuable tool in focusing attention on variable practice and waste, on improving effectiveness and efficiency in a systemised way, and in involving patients as partners in their care. Once they are implemented we may then be better able to articulate where the real gaps in capacity lie so that we can invest in and build the health service that patients deserve.

Is there support for interested parties who wish to know more about or become involved in this process? The Irish Society for Quality and Safety in Healthcare has extensive experience with ICPs and has developed a training programme for ICP facilitators and a national organisation called the Irish Care Pathway Network (ICPN) for any individuals who have experience in the area or who are interested in developing ICPs in Ireland. The network offers support to those working in this area and works closely with international groups such as the International Society for Quality (ISQua), the European Pathway Association (EPA), and the USA's Institute for Healthcare Improvement (IHI) and National Association for Healthcare Quality (NAHQ). The network also utilises many of the resources referred to in this chapter, such as the National Electronic Library for Health (NeLH), where many of the do once and share (DOAS) care pathways can be accessed. The websites of all these organisations are provided in the 'Additional Resources' section below.

REFLECTIVE QUESTIONS

1 How does an ICP differ from other structured care methodologies?
2 How do you define the patient journey?
3 What are the critical success factors in developing ICPs?
4 How can one evaluate ICPs?
5 How do you see ICPs benefiting the area in which you work?
6 How do you see the concept of ICPs developing in the Irish health care context?

ADDITIONAL RESOURCES

Aetna clinical policy guidelines: www.aetna.com/about/cov_det_policies.html
Agency for Health Care Research and Quality (AHRQ): www.ahrq.gov/clinic/index.html#online
Agree: www.agreecollaboration.org/
American Society of Anaesthesiologists: www.asahq.org
Australian Government National Health and Medical Research Council: www.nhmrc.gov.au
Belgian Dutch Clinical Pathway Network: www.nkp.be
Canadian Council on Health Services Accreditation: www.cchsa.ca
Canadian Medical Association: www.cma.ca
Care Quality Commission: www.cqc.org.uk
Clinical Governance Support Team: www.cgsupport.nhs.uk
Cochrane Collaboration: www.cochranelibrary.com/clibhome/clib.htm
E-guidelines: www.eguidelines.co.uk
European Pathway Association: www.e-p-a.org
European Society for Quality in Healthcare: www.esqh.net
Evidence-based Medicine Resource Center: www.ebmny.org/cpg.html
Health Web: www.healthweb.org
Institute for Healthcare Improvement: www.ihi.org
International Journal of Integrated Care: www.ijic.org/index.html
International Society for Quality in Health Care: www.isqua.org
Irish Care Pathway Network (ICPN): www.isqsh.ie
Irish Health Services Accreditation Board: www.ihsab.ie
Irish Society for Quality and Safety in Healthcare (ISQSH): www.isqsh.ie
Joanna Briggs Institute: www.joannabriggs.edu.au/
Journal of Integrated Care Pathways: www.rsmpress.co.uk/jicp.htm
Medical Journal of Australia: www.mja.com.au/public/guides/guides.html
National Guideline Clearinghouse: www.guideline.gov
National Institute for Clinical Excellence (NICE): www.nice.org.uk
New Zealand Guidelines Group: www.nzgg.org.nz
NHS Health Information Resources (formerly National Library for Health): www.library.nhs.uk
NHS Integrated Care Pathway Users Scotland, *Introducing Integrated Care Pathways: Benefits of ICPs*: www.icpus.org.uk/

Nurse Web: http://nurseweb.ucsf.edu/www/arwwebpg.htm

Ottowa General Hospital – Clinical Pathways: www.ottawahospital.on.ca/
   hp/dept/nursing/pathways/index-e.asp

Resource Library (Medical Clinical Guidelines): www.rmlibrary.com/sites/
   medclini.htm

Royal College of Nursing (UK): www.rcn.org.uk

Royal Society of Medicine Press Limited: www.rsmpress.co.uk

Scottish Intercollegiate Guidelines Network: www.show.scot.nhs.uk/

Therapeutic Guidelines Ltd: www.tg.com.au/home/index.html

APPENDIX 1: INTEGRATED CARE PATHWAYS APPRAISAL TOOL (ICPAT)

West Midlands **NHS**

INTEGRATED CARE PATHWAYS APPRAISAL TOOL

(I.C.PAT)

REVIEWING

> THE INTEGRATED CARE PATHWAY DOCUMENT

> THE DEVELOPMENT, IMPLEMENTATION AND
   MAINTENANCE OF THE INTEGRATED CARE PATHWAY

> THE ROLE OF THE ORGANISATION

CONTENTS

Section 1

Is it an Integrated Care Pathway? (What are you appraising?)

There is much confusion around the term Integrated Care Pathway (*de Luc 1999*). This section is designed to highlight whether the tool being appraised is an Integrated Care Pathway. There is no single definition of an Integrated Care Pathway so this list of questions has been compiled by examining a number of well-known definitions for an Integrated Care Pathway within the UK (*Riley 1998, Johnson 1997, Wilson 1997, Middleton & Roberts 2000*). It also builds on some work undertaken by the National Pathways Association Mental Health sub-group (unpublished). All items marked * in the text are listed in the glossary.

Question	Yes	No	NOTES/ACTIONS
1.1 Does the Integrated Care Pathway have an identified start point?			
1.2 Does the Integrated Care Pathway have an identified finish point?			
1.3 Does the Integrated Care Pathway reflect a service user's journey* i.e. moving along a continuum of days/weeks/months/stages/objectives/programmes etc?			
1.4 Does the Integrated Care Pathway reflect 24-hour continuous care/treatment (where appropriate)?			
1.5 Does the Integrated Care Pathway form the record of care for an individual service user*?			
1.6 Can the Integrated Care Pathway documentation be individualised to meet the service user's* needs?			
1.7 Does the Integrated Care Pathway outline the anticipated process of care/treatment?			
1.8 Does the Integrated Care Pathway act as a prompt/ reminder for staff <u>at the point of care?</u> (It should not contain reference only material).			
1.9 Does the Integrated Care Pathway act as a decision support tool, prompting consideration of various factors like – additional problems/co-morbidity, risk factors etc?			
1.10 Is there space on the Integrated Care Pathway document to record individual service user* exceptions or variations from the Integrated Care Pathway?			

Please indicate the degree to which you agree (or disagree) regarding the Integrated Care Pathway.

1.11 The Integrated Care Pathway is a cohesive document with all of it used in the delivery of care/treatment?

Strongly Agree [ ][ ][ ][ ] Strongly Disagree

1.12 The Integrated Care Pathway reflects the input of all those who contribute in the care/treatment e.g. is it multi-professional and/or multi-agency (where appropriate)?

Strongly Agree [ ][ ][ ][ ] Strongly Disagree

Section 2

The Integrated Care Pathway Documentation

Integrated Care Pathways form the actual documentation where care/treatment is recorded for individual service users*. This documentation may be used in cases of complaint or negligence. The same standards of documentation apply to Integrated Care Pathways as they do to other health and social service records.

To date, most Integrated Care Pathways developed in the UK are paper-based. This section of the appraisal instrument has been developed with this in mind. However, it is believed that many of the principles identified in this section are transferable to an electronic medium and would apply to e-ICPs*. All items marked * in the text are listed in the glossary.

	Question	Yes	No	NOTES/ACTIONS
2.1	Are the relevant service user's* clearly identified in the title of the Integrated Care Pathway? i.e. Integrated Care Pathway for Laparoscopic Cholecystectomy.			
2.2	Does the documentation indicate the circumstances when a service user* should come off or should not be put on (exclusion criteria)?			
2.3	Does the documentation meet local and national minimum standards for documentation? (e.g. Royal Colleges guidelines or the Integrated Care Programme & Care Management approach) e.g. signatures, dates & times etc.			
2.4	Is there a reminder that says professional judgement must be applied whilst taking into account the Service User's wishes & needs? i.e. the Integrated Care Pathway is not a tramline and can be varied.			
2.5	Is the evidence on which the content is based, referenced?			
2.6	Is the date of development of the document marked on the Integrated Care Pathway?			
2.7	Is there space for the identification of the individual service user* on each page?			
2.8	Is there a version number on the documentation?			
2.9	Are there individual page numbers on all the pages?			
2.10	Do the page numbers relate to the total number of pages in the Integrated Care Pathway? i.e. page 1 of 10.			
2.11	Are all abbreviations explained in the document?			
2.12	Does the variation/exception reporting system* collect the following: - date - time - description of variance - action taken - signature Answers to all of these must be 'yes.'			
2.13	Are there instructions on how to use the documentation?			

	Question	Yes	No	NOTES/ACTIONS
2.14	Is the date of planned review of the document clearly marked?			
2.15	Does the service user* have unrestricted access to their Integrated Care Pathway?			
2.16	Is there provision for the service user* to complete some parts of the Integrated Care Pathway?			
2.17	Is it clear where the Integrated Care Pathway is to be stored whilst in use?			
2.18	Are there prompts to identify whether the service user* is on another Integrated Care Pathway? (where appropriate).			
2.19	Does the Integrated Care Pathway ask for sample signatures of those completing the document?			
2.20	Does the Integrated Care Pathway include service users* consent to treatment/care (where appropriate).			
2.21	Are there are instructions where to store additional documentation to the Integrated Care Pathway documentation e.g. test results?			
2.22	Are there instructions on how to record the variation/exception reporting* system within the Integrated Care Pathway?			
2.23	Is there a prompt of the importance of completing the variation/exception system (for legal reasons)?			

Please indicate the degree to which you agree (or disagree) regarding the Integrated Care Pathway.

2.24	The instructions for using the Integrated Care Pathway are clear.

Strongly Agree [ ][ ][ ][ ][ ] Strongly Disagree

2.25	The outcomes/goals for the service user* are clearly identified.

Strongly Agree [ ][ ][ ][ ][ ] Strongly Disagree

2.26	There are prompts within the documentation for service user* participation in the Integrated Care Pathway.

Strongly Agree [ ][ ][ ][ ][ ] Strongly Disagree

2.27	The variations (recorded on the Integrated Care Pathway) are discussed with the service user*.

Strongly Agree [ ][ ][ ][ ][ ] Strongly Disagree

Section 3

The Development Process

The process of development of the Integrated Care Pathway is as important as the finished product (*de Luc 2000*). This is because the Integrated Care Pathway is a tool to be used to critically review the care/treatment provided and for improvements to that process to be identified. This will involve changes in practice (*Andolina 1995, Dykes 1997, Overill 1998*).

In this section the appraiser is looking for evidence that the staff* have ownership of the Integrated Care Pathway. This might be indicated by their involvement in the decision to develop the Pathway, a clear stipulation of the reasons for developing the Integrated Care Pathway or in their attendance and participation at meetings to develop the Integrated Care Pathways. The development phase is defined as from the first Multi Disciplinary Team* meeting to completion of the piloting /testing phase. All items marked * in the text are listed in the glossary.

	Question	Yes	No	NOTES/ACTIONS
3.1	Is there a record of the decisions made concerning the content of the Integrated Care Pathway?			
3.2	In the notes or minutes of meetings is there a description/list of the staff* who were involved in the development of the Integrated Care Pathway?			
3.3	Was a literature search carried out to gather the evidence base for the clinical content of the Integrated Care Pathway?			
3.4	Do the notes of the development meetings record the rationale for including pieces of evidence/guidelines?			
3.5	Do the notes of the development meetings record the rationale for not including pieces of evidence/guidelines?			
3.6	Has the Integrated Care Pathway been piloted/tested?			
3.7	Was the completion of the Integrated Care Pathway documentation audited after the pilot?			
3.8	Were the variation/exceptions* audited after the pilot?			
3.9	Were the outcomes/goals audited after the pilot?			
3.10	In the pilot were the results of the audit of Integrated Care Pathway fed back to those who completed the documentation?			
3.11	Has the person with responsibility for the Data Protection Act reviewed the Integrated Care Pathway?			
3.12	Has the 'Caldicott Guardian'* reviewed the Integrated Care Pathway?			
3.13	Was pre-existing practice reviewed prior to development of the Integrated Care Pathway i.e. a baseline review was completed?			

Please indicate the degree to which you agree (or disagree) regarding the Integrated Care Pathway.

3.14	Clinical risk was considered as part of the content of the Integrated Care Pathway.?

Strongly Agree ☐☐☐☐☐ Strongly Disagree

3.15	The training, education and competency of staff* was considered as part of the content of the Integrated Care Pathway.

Strongly Agree ☐☐☐☐☐ Strongly Disagree

3.16	The service users* have been involved in the development of the Integrated Care Pathway. (This might be using a variety of methods e.g. focus group, questionnaires, complaints, development group representation, patient diaries etc).

Strongly Agree ☐☐☐☐☐ Strongly Disagree

3.17	The service users* multicultural needs have been taken into account.

Strongly Agree ☐☐☐☐☐ Strongly Disagree

3.18	All representatives of the staff* using the Integrated Care Pathway been involved in its development (including appropriate agencies, all levels of staff – junior/senior staff, day/night staff etc.).

Strongly Agree ☐☐☐☐☐ Strongly Disagree

3.19	The discussion concerning the content of the Integrated Care Pathway was comprehensive.

Strongly Agree ☐☐☐☐☐ Strongly Disagree

3.20	Is any evidence/guideline/protocol referred to in the Integrated Care Pathway readily available for the staff* to refer to.

Strongly Agree ☐☐☐☐☐ Strongly Disagree

3.21	There was a significant sample size of service users* put onto the Integrated Care Pathway to test it.

Strongly Agree ☐☐☐☐☐ Strongly Disagree

3.22	The Integrated Care Pathway pilot results/findings have been discussed with the service users*.

Strongly Agree ☐☐☐☐☐ Strongly Disagree

| 3.23 | In the pilot the audit indicated that a satisfactory level of documentation was completed for legal requirements. |

Strongly Agree ☐☐☐☐☐ Strongly Disagree

| 3.24 | In the pilot any areas of non-compliance present an acceptable risk to the organisation(s) using the Integrated Care Pathway. |

Strongly Agree ☐☐☐☐☐ Strongly Disagree

| 3.25 | In the pilot any areas of non-use present an acceptable risk to the organisation(s) using the Integrated Care Pathway. |

Strongly Agree ☐☐☐☐☐ Strongly Disagree

| 3.26 | All staff and service users* involved in the pilot are required to complete the Integrated Care Pathway, did so. |

Strongly Agree ☐☐☐☐☐ Strongly Disagree

| 3.27 | The standard of pre-existing documentation was audited prior to development of the Integrated Care Pathway (completeness, readability etc). |

Strongly Agree ☐☐☐☐☐ Strongly Disagree

| 3.28 | The appraisal of the clinical evidence/research literature was comprehensive. |

Strongly Agree ☐☐☐☐☐ Strongly Disagree

3.29	Which of the following formed the basis of your evidence:	Please tick
-	Systematic review	
-	Meta-analysis	
-	Qualitative study	
-	Randomised control trial	
-	Case control	

Other evidence (please specify):

| 3.30 | The service user* opinions about the Integrated Care Pathway were collected as part of the pilot/testing procedure. |

Strongly Agree | | | | | | Strongly Disagree

| 3.31 | The staff* opinion's about the Integrated Care Pathway were collected as part of the pilot/testing procedure. |

Strongly Agree | | | | | | Strongly Disagree

Section 4

The Implementation Process

For the purpose of this document the implementation phase of the Integrated Care Pathway has been defined as follows, 'when the development process (including the testing or piloting phase) is complete and the group who developed the Integrated Care Pathway are ready to put it into practice'. The questions are aimed at ensuring effective implementation and use of the Integrated Care Pathway. All items marked * in the text are listed in the glossary.

	Question	Yes	No	NOTES/ACTIONS
4.1	Has an on-going training programme for the staff* been established?			
4.2	Have resources (individuals/time etc) been identified to undertake the training on how to use the Integrated Care Pathway?			
4.3	Is there a system in place to feedback the variations of the Integrated Care Pathway to the staff*?			
4.4	Is there a system in place to feedback the variations of the Integrated Care Pathway to the service users*?			
4.5	Has an agreement been reached as to where the Integrated Care Pathway documentation will be stored once finished?			
4.6	Is there evidence that the organisation carried out an assessment of the risks involved in an Integrated Care Pathway development before commencement?			

Please indicate the degree to which you agree (or disagree) regarding the Integrated Care Pathway

4.7	The assessment carried out in 4.6 above was adequate.

Strongly Agree | | | | | Strongly Disagree

Section 5

Maintenance of the Integrated Care Pathway

One of the critical success factors cited in the successful use of Integrated Care Pathways is the on-going maintenance of the Integrated Care Pathway. This is required to make the Integrated Care Pathway a dynamic tool which evolves in response to the demands of the service user's* and the changes which occur in the care/treatment required (introduction of new evidence etc). Consequently, the content and design of the Integrated Care Pathway needs to be continually reviewed (*Dykes 1998, de Luc 2000*). All items marked * in the text are listed in the glossary.

	Question	Yes	No	NOTES/ACTIONS
5.1	Is there a named individual responsible for maintaining the Integrated Care Pathway?			
5.2	Is training provided to staff* when a change to the Integrated Care Pathway content is made?			
5.3	Is the review date one year or less?			
5.4	Is regular training provided for new staff that will be using the Integrated Care Pathway?			

Please indicate the degree to which you agree (or disagree) regarding the Integrated Care Pathway

5.5	The Integrated Care Pathway content and documentation is regularly reviewed (minimum annually) in terms of new clinical evidence.

Strongly Agree | | | | | Strongly Disagree

5.6	The Integrated Care Pathway content and documentation is regularly reviewed (minimum annually) in terms of use/completion of documentation.

Strongly Agree | | | | | Strongly Disagree

5.7	The Integrated Care Pathway content and documentation is regularly reviewed (minimum annually) in terms of variations.

Strongly Agree | | | | | Strongly Disagree

5.8	The Integrated Care Pathway content and documentation is regularly reviewed (minimum annually) in terms of achievement of outcomes/goals/ objectives.

Strongly Agree | | | | | Strongly Disagree

5.9	The Integrated Care Pathway content and documentation is regularly reviewed (minimum annually) in terms of service user* comments.

Strongly Agree | | | | | Strongly Disagree

5.10 The Integrated Care Pathway content and documentation is regularly reviewed (minimum annually) in terms of staff* comments.

Strongly Agree □ □ □ □ □ Strongly Disagree

5.11 The variations* and achievements of goals/outcomes/objectives have been fed-back to the staff*.

Strongly Agree □ □ □ □ □ Strongly Disagree

5.12 There is evidence that staff* feedback has changed practice.

Strongly Agree □ □ □ □ □ Strongly Disagree

5.13 The variations* and achievements of the goals/outcomes/objectives from using the Integrated Care Pathway have been fed-back to the service user's* of the Integrated Care Pathway.

Strongly Agree □ □ □ □ □ Strongly Disagree

5.14 There is evidence that service user* feedback has changed practice (when required).

Strongly Agree □ □ □ □ □ Strongly Disagree

5.15 Service users* have been involved in the review of the Integrated Care Pathway content.

Strongly Agree □ □ □ □ □ Strongly Disagree

5.16 The variation codes* used have been reviewed and checked for use, consistency etc.

Strongly Agree □ □ □ □ □ Strongly Disagree

5.17 The variation codes* have been updated in line with organisational/local requirements.

Strongly Agree □ □ □ □ □ Strongly Disagree

Section 6

The Role of the Organisation

All items marked * in the text are listed in the glossary.

Question	Yes	No	NOTES/ACTIONS
6.1 Is the Integrated Care Pathway development programme endorsed by the Trust Board/Clinical Governance Committee?			
6.2 Within the organisation is there a plan specifically for Integrated Care Pathway development?			
6.3 Are Integrated Care Pathways evident in the organisation's Clinical Governance Strategy?			

Please indicate the degree to which you agree (or disagree) regarding the Integrated Care Pathway

6.4   Within the organisation, targets for Integrated Care Pathway development are achievable.

Strongly Agree   ☐☐☐☐☐   Strongly Disagree

6.5   The individual Integrated Care Pathway development is clinically led?

Strongly Agree   ☐☐☐☐☐   Strongly Disagree

6.6   The organisation recognises that Integrated Care Pathways involve long-term programme commitment to organisational change.

Strongly Agree   ☐☐☐☐☐   Strongly Disagree

6.7   There is a comprehensive training package for staff in the use and development of Integrated Care Pathways.

Strongly Agree   ☐☐☐☐☐   Strongly Disagree

6.8   There is a strategic group reviewing all the Integrated Care Pathway developments within the organisation.

Strongly Agree   ☐☐☐☐☐   Strongly Disagree

6.9   The Integrated Care Pathway development programme is managed.

Strongly Agree   ☐☐☐☐☐   Strongly Disagree

6.10 There is evidence that the Integrated Care Pathway has been integrated into other organisational initiatives (CPD*, audit).

Strongly Agree ☐☐☐☐☐ Strongly Disagree

6.11 There are organisation-wide template/proforma style guidelines for the Integrated Care Pathway documentation.

Strongly Agree ☐☐☐☐☐ Strongly Disagree

6.12 The variation reporting system* reflects the organisation template/style of variation reporting.

Strongly Agree ☐☐☐☐☐ Strongly Disagree

6.13 Organisational risk management issues are addressed in the Integrated Care Pathway development.

Strongly Agree ☐☐☐☐☐ Strongly Disagree

6.14 The Integrated Care Pathway documentation reflects any organisation-wide developments with clinical documentation including medical records standards and EPR/ICRS*.

Strongly Agree ☐☐☐☐☐ Strongly Disagree

6.15 Dedicated (protected) facilitation time is identified for development of individual Integrated Care Pathways.

Strongly Agree ☐☐☐☐☐ Strongly Disagree

Summary sheet for Notes/Action Points.

REFERENCES

Al-Shaqha, W. and Zairi, M. (2001) 'Pharmaceutical care management: a modern approach to providing seamless and integrated health care', *International Journal of Health Care Quality Assurance* 14 (7): 282–301.

Bragato, L. and Jacobs, K. (2003) 'Care pathways: the road to better health services?' *Journal of Health Organisation and Management* 17(1): 164–80.

Campbell, H., Hotchkiss, R., Bradshaw, N. and Porteous, M. (1988) 'Integrated care pathways', *British Medical Journal* 316: 133–7.

Cowan, J. (2003) 'Risk management and the NSF for older people', *Clinical Governance: An International Journal* 8(1): 92–5.

Currie, L. and Harvey, G. (2000) 'The use of care pathways as tools to support the implementation of evidence-based practice', *Journal of Interpersonal Care* 14(4): 311–24.

Davis, M. (2004) 'Way to go', *Health Service Journal*, 13 May, 24–5.

De Luc, K. (2000) 'Are different models of care pathways being developed?' *International Journal of Health Care Quality Assurance* 13 (2): 80–6.

Department of Health (UK) (1996) *On the State of the Public Health: The Annual Report of the Chief Medical Officer.* London: Stationery Office.

DoHC (Department of Health and Children) (2001a) *Quality and Fairness: A Health System for You.* Dublin: Government Publications.

— (2001b) *Primary Care: A New Direction.* Dublin: Government Publications.

— (2003a) *Audit of Structures and Functions in the Health System.* Dublin: Government Publications.

— (2003b) *Report of the Commission on Financial Management and Control Systems in the Health Service.* Dublin: Government Publications.

— (2003c) *Report of the National Task Force on Medical Staffing.* Dublin: Government Publications.

Ellis, B. W. and Johnson, S. (1999) 'The care pathway: a tool to enhance clinical governance', *British Journal of Clinical Governance* 4(2): 61–71.

EPA (European Pathway Association) (2008) *Newsletter*, 5 October (online). Available at www.e-p-a.org, accessed 25 October 2008.

Graham, I. and Harrison, M. (2005) 'Evaluation and adaptation of clinical practice guidelines', *Evidence-Based Nursing* 8(3): 68–72.

Grubnic, S. (2003) 'Care pathways: conceptualising and developing a multi-skilling initiative', *International Journal of Health Care Quality Assurance* 16(6): 286–92.

Hill, P., O'Grady, A., Millar, M. and Boswell, K. (2000) 'The patient care development programme: organisational development through user and staff involvement', *International Journal of Health Care Quality Assurance* 13(4): 153–61.

HIQA (Health Information and Quality Authority) (2008) *National Hygiene Services Quality Review 2008.* Available at www.hiqa.ie/media/pdfs/hygiene/HIQA_hygiene_Service_review_for_web_080827.pdf, accessed 23 November 2009.

— (2009) *National Quality Standards for Residential Care Settings for Older People in Ireland*. HIQA.

HSE (Health Service Executive) (2007a) *Quality and Risk Management Standard*, http://hsenet/HSE_Central/Office/Office_of_the_CEO/Quality_and_Risk/Documents/OQR009_Quality_Risk_Management_Standard.pdf.

— (2007b) *Code of Practice for Decontamination of Reusable Invasive Medical Devices*. Available at http://www.hse.ie/eng/Publications/services/Hospitals/HSE_Publications/Code_of_Practice_for_Decontamination_of_Reusable_Invasive_Medical_Devices_1.pdf

Institute for Healthcare Improvement *Methods – How to Improve* http://www.ihi.org/IHI/Topics/Improvement/ImprovementMethods/HowToImprove.

Interhospital and Agency Clinical Pathway Group (2002). *Clinical Pathways Educational Package – Putting the Pieces Together*. Perth, Western Australia: Department of Health.

Joosten, T., Bongers. I. and Meijboom, I. (2007) 'Care programmes and integrated care pathways', *International Journal of Health Care Quality Assurance* 21(5): 472–86.

Kavanagh, S. and Cowan, J. (2004) 'Reducing risk in health-care teams: an overview', *Clinical Governance: An International Journal* 9(3): 200–4.

Kent, P. and Chalmers, Y. (2006) 'A decade on: has the use of integrated care pathways made a difference in Lanarkshire?', *Journal of Nursing Management* 14: 508–20.

Kidney R. and Hosny, G. (2008) 'A care pathway for outpatient management of deep vein thrombosis', *Clinical Indemnity Scheme Newsletter*, March.

Kogan, M., Henkel, M. and Joss, R. (1994) 'An evaluation of total quality management in the NHS', *Centre for the Evaluation of Public Policy and Practice*. Bristol: Brunel University.

Lane, J. V., Lingard, E. A. and Howie, C. R. (2001) *Integrated Care Pathways and Outcome in Total Knee Arthroplasty*. British Orthopaedic Research Society, Belfast, April 22–24. Available at http:libraries.nelh.nhs.uk/pathways/aboutICPs, accessed 23 April 2009.

NCPDNM (National Council for the Professional Development of Nursing and Midwifery) (2006) *Improving the Patient Journey: Understanding Integrated Care Pathways*. Dublin: NCPDNM.

NHS Integrated Care Pathway Users Scotland. *Introducing Integrated Care Pathways: Benefits of ICPs*. Available at http://www.icpus.ukprofessionals.com/leaflet2.html, accessed 1 November 2008.

NHS National Modernisation Agency and NICE (National Institute for Clinical Excellence) (2005). *A Step-by-step Guide to Developing Protocols*. Available at http://www.modern.nhs.uk/protocolbasedcare, accessed 18 November 2008.

NLIAH (National Leadership and Innovation Agency for Healthcare) (2005) *Integrated Care Pathways: A Guide to Good Practice*. Wales: Crown.

NPA (National Pathways Association) (1998) 'A definition of a care pathway', *Association Newsletter*, Spring.

Nyatanga, T. and Holliman, R. (2005) 'Integrated care pathways and infection control', *Clinical Governance: An International Journal* 10(2): 106–17.

Sale, D. (2005) *Understanding Clinical Governance and Quality Assurance*. New York: Palgrave Macmillan.

Schmid, K. and Conen, D. (2000) 'Integrated patient pathways: "mipp" – a tool for quality improvement and cost management in health care – pilot study on the pathway "acute myocardial infarction"', *International Journal of Health Care Quality Assurance* 13(2): 27–92.

Scottish Executive (2005) *Framework for Developing Nursing Roles*. Edinburgh: Scottish Executive.

Smith, E. and Ross. F. (2007) 'Service user involvement and integrated care pathways', *International Journal of Health Care Quality Assurance* 20(3): 195–214.

Thomas, P., Makinde, K., Watkins, A. and Gupta, A. (2007) 'Acute medical assessment/admission units: clinical performance indicators', *Clinical Governance: An International Journal* 12(4): 222–32.

West Midlands NHS (2006) *Integrated Care Pathways Appraisal Tool (ICPAT)*. West Midlands NHS.

Whittle, C. and Hewson, A. (2007) 'Integrated care pathways: pathways to change in health care?', *Journal of Health Organisation and Management* 21(3): 297–306.

Whittle C., McDonald, P., Dunn, L., and De Luc, K. (2004) 'Developing the integrated care pathway appraisal tool (ICPAT): a pilot study', *Journal of Integrated Care Pathways* 8: 77–81.

14
An Introduction to Health Informatics
Paula Hicks

OBJECTIVES

- To provide a broad understanding of the principles underlying the field of health informatics (HI).
- To provide an overview of health information technology (HIT), including electronic health records (EHR).
- To provide an overview of the challenges of information and communications technology (ICT) in healthcare.

INTRODUCTION

This chapter aims to provide an insight into the field of health informatics. Some of the many aspects and complexities challenging the use of information and communications technology (ICT) in the health care setting are also presented. In recognising the role that ICT can play in health care it is also important to have an understanding of the fundamental foundations of health informatics, such as modelling in the health care domain and the importance and variances of data, information and knowledge. A number of hospital information systems (HIS) are introduced, along with the 'holy grail' of health informatics in the form of the electronic health record (EHR), and a brief look at the role of the Internet and e-health and how they shape and influence health care delivery.

1 INTRODUCTION TO HEALTH INFORMATICS

Health care is one of the largest consumers of public funds, and plays a vital role in economic policy throughout the world. The core objectives in the health sector today are twofold – improving efficiency and effectiveness, whilst containing costs and improving quality.

The 'citizen-/person-centred care' that is the focus of health sectors today encourages patient empowerment and involvement in their health care. The focus on improving quality of care while containing costs is a challenge that is reflected in health sectors worldwide. Health care generates volumes of data daily from hospitals, laboratories, GPs' surgeries and speciality clinics. Other information-intensive industries such as banking have successfully applied ICT to improve efficiencies. The health care industry has been slow to embrace this technology. Although Knapp *et al.* (1987) and Whiting-O'Keefe *et al.* (1985) conclude that computer implementation enhances medical care, there has been a history of non-use and resistance to computers by health care professionals. According to Shekelle *et al.* (2006), health information technology (HIT) has the potential to transform health care delivery, making it safer, more effective and more efficient. These sentiments are echoed throughout the literature, where it is clear that health care experts, policy makers and consumers believe that health information technologies are central to transforming the way in which health care is delivered (Bates *et al.* 1999; Bates 2000; Institute of Medicine 2000; Weir *et al.* 2006; Chaudhry *et al.* 2006). There is considerable evidence to support the potential for improvements to patient safety through access to electronic health records, which provide structured, legible details supported by decision support and knowledge bases offering up-to-date medical knowledge to the clinician (Weir *et al.* 2006). A systematic review of the impact of HIT by Chaudhry *et al.* (2006) highlighted improvements in quality, through adherence to guidelines, and a decrease in medical errors.

Conversely there is some negativity to any ICT implementation. Some of the causes of this negativity stem from organisational aspects, including lack of consultation in the change process, leading to poorly designed systems, and individual psychological factors such as attitudes. Technical barriers to implementing information technology in health care include: lack of standards in relation to medical information; inadequate electronic data exchange between existing systems, leading to fragmentation; interoperability of systems; and the challenge of protection of privacy and confidentiality (Grimson & Grimson 2000; Hersch 2002).

Modern health care systems find it increasingly difficult to provide the level of care expected by health consumers. Health care is a continuously evolving industry driven by:

- exponential growth of knowledge in the biomedical and clinical sciences, and the need to process this knowledge as an accessible and coherent electronic resource
- rapid pace of innovation in ICT, and their increasingly pervasive deployment in biomedicine and health care
- rapid change in social, professional, legal and organisational contexts of health care, associated with greater emphasis on cost-effective delivery of quality services. (Zieliński *et al.* 2006)

Whetton (2005) describes how the traditional hierarchical health systems are today challenged by changing demographics and medical problems, an emphasis on consumer-centred service delivery, continuity of care across all services, evidence-based practice and the shift of resources beyond hospital to community care and preventative programmes. As health informatics is introduced it challenges many of the assumptions and structures underpinning traditional health care delivery. Whetton also suggests that health informatics 'can be a catalyst for reinventing health care'. Information and communications systems are in their essence designed for collaboration and information sharing and involve interactions among professionals that offer new dimensions to work routines, workflow and work relationships. In order for health information systems to be successful they must take into consideration the complexity of the modern health care environment and its key players.

Health informatics (also referred to as medical informatics, computer-based medicine) is 'the science that studies the use and processing of data, information, and knowledge applied to medicine, health care and public health' (van Bemmel & Musen 1997). Health informatics involves the services of data collection, processing, transformation and presentation, and uses ICT to enable the sharing of data and knowledge-based systems including decision support systems. The predominant technologies that health informatics employs are computers and networks.

Aspects of health informatics include:

- architectures and developments of electronic health records and other health information systems
- decision support systems in health care, including clinical decision support systems
- standards (e.g. DICOM, HL7) to facilitate the exchange of information between health care information systems – these specifically define the *means* of exchanging data, not the content
- coding and classification of medical terminology, such as the Systematized Nomenclature of Medicine – Clinical Terms (SNOMED CT), Logical Observation Identifiers Names and Codes (LOINC), OpenGALEN Common Reference Model or the highly complex UMLS, which are used to allow a standard, accurate exchange of data content between systems and providers
- imaging systems
- increasingly, software embedded in medical devices

1.1 Health informatics in practice

In the latter part of the twentieth century, the proliferation and accessibility of ICT in all walks of life, from industry to education, led to an optimism and expectation that it could have a similar impact on health services. Some early successes in the health care domain included an expert system (Garvan-ESI) designed and developed in Australia in 1984 to assist with the interpretation of thyroid levels, which had a very high level of accuracy. There are comparative examples of what would be considered failures, such as the London Ambulance Service Computer Aided Despatch (LASCAD) system, which was designed in 1992 to automate the deployment of London ambulances with minimum waiting time. After two days of operation the system response time began to slow down until it failed altogether two weeks later. The subsequent investigation blamed a wide range of factors, including technical, managerial, human and environmental issues. Some blame was placed upon incomplete software and inadequate testing; the human factors aspects included the fact that staff had little or no confidence in the system and had not been trained in its operation. Historically, there are many and varied reasons for the slow uptake of ICT in the health care domain, including lack of appropriate investment, challenges that the diverse and varied nature of health data imposes, and a lack of people with the relevant skills (Grimson & Grimson 2000).

The bureaucratic structures of large, complex organisations with managerial personnel on one hand and medical personnel on the other led to a more complex system of management and power structure. The emergence of departments of information management, and the role of chief information officer (although not yet in Ireland) at senior management level reinforces the strategic importance of information in today's health care environment. Other related roles include informatics nurse and clinical manager, which have evolved in an effort to 'bridge the gap' in order to involve clinicians more directly in the management process and gain their support and co-operation.

1.2 Health informatics definitions

The term 'informatics' has been defined as 'the study of the application of computer and statistical techniques to the management of information' (CancerWeb 2008). It has been applied to various disciplines, including the health care domain, where it is referred to as health informatics, and has emerged as an area of specialisation which is now recognised as one of the fastest growing career fields in health care (Hebda *et al.* 2005).

Table 14.1: Informatics definitions

Informatics	The science that studies the use and processing of data, information and knowledge applied to medicine, health care and public health. (van Bemmel & Musen 1997)
Health informatics	Multi-disciplinary and multi-dimensional field that seeks to facilitate the effective collection, management and use of information in the health care environment. (Whetton 2005)
Nursing informatics	Speciality 'that integrates nursing science, computer science, and information science to manage and communicate data, information, and knowledge in nursing practice . . . accomplished through the use of information structures, information processes, and information technology'. (American Nurses Association 2001)
Bioinformatics	'[C]ollection, organization, and analysis of complex biological structures, specifically the genome sciences.' (Hebda *et al.* 2005)
Public health informatics	The application of health information systems and strategies to public health research, education and practice. (Whetton 2005)

Health informatics is a 'multi-disciplinary and multi-dimensional field that seeks to facilitate the effective collection, management and use of information in the health care environment' (Whetton 2005). It brings together the fields of medicine, computer science, management science, statistics and engineering, among others. These different disciplines bring their own priorities, issues and solutions to the field of health informatics, making it more complex. The use of ICT in health care offers many possibilities for providing information in the right format and at the right time and is no longer viewed as a peripheral issue but rather as a central means of improving the overall efficiency and effectiveness of health care delivery.

2. FOUNDATIONS FOR HEALTH INFORMATICS
2.1 Modelling the health care environment
The complex and diverse use of data and understanding the processes involved in a particular health care domain can be difficult to emulate with computerisation. The use of modelling to support this process has become an increasingly invaluable tool. A model will take the form of a diagram with supporting explanatory and formal text. It will describe processes and entities in a particular area, the flow of information both externally and internally and the processes involved within the organisation. Models offer an understanding to the project team of a particular domain and can act as a common reference for discussions and development of systems. It is important to know 'what is to be computerised' and 'why is it needed'. Information systems should support policy, management, decision making and evaluation (van Bemmel & Musen 1997). Information systems are about developing a model of the real world: an example would be the routine way in which a clinician records patient details in a notebook, or the way a triage nurse assesses patients on arrival in A&E. A model forms the basis of the way we learn about and interact with the physical world, the processes and external influences that impact on our daily routine. Models that copy these processes are abstractions of the real world scenario and are hence less detailed. In this way they impose a point of view upon the observed world. This view can depend upon the use to which the model will be put: each health care professional will have their own area of interest within an information system and all detail may not be relevant to their particular speciality. In this way there is no such thing as the most correct model; models are simply better or worse suited to accomplishing a particular task (van Bemmel & Musen 1997; Coiera 2005: Whetton 2005).

An analogy using a map as a model or representation of the physical world is presented by Grimson (2008b). In this model the map has many different uses depending on the individual who is using it; for example, a motorist will look for roads, a hill-walker will look at pathways: both are looking at the same map but each requires different pieces of information from it.

2.2 Data, information and knowledge
In the course of a patient's encounter with the health care environment, information is collected, stored, manipulated and analysed in order to support diagnosis and treatment. This **data** is a collection of facts, measurements or observations. Examples of such facts are vital signs, laboratory results, X-ray images, patient history or a response to treatment. A single piece of data has little meaning. Interpretation of data which has been collected becomes **information** (Saba & McCormick 2006). The combination of data and its subsequent interpretation help form the basis of a diagnosis. An example of this would be the recording of vital signs: on their own they are not of much significance, but over time, when plotted

on a graph and compared to normal values, they become meaningful information. A health care professional brings understanding to this information and produces **knowledge**. In medicine human reasoning is crucial, and this reasoning involves the interpretation of real-world observations. These real-world observations in the context of information systems can be data and their interpretation by domain experts becomes knowledge. Similar to models (mentioned above), which are abstractions of the real world and impose a view of a domain, the level of knowledge of individual clinicians can vary. Hence variations in diagnoses and treatment based on similar data may reflect differences in clinical knowledge or experience. In medicine clinicians need to base decisions on incomplete knowledge and data (Coiera 2005). Computers can support the decision-making process, but it is essential to understand their potential and limitations in the health care environment. Understanding the difference between data, information and knowledge is therefore important in thoroughly comprehending the potential that computers can offer (van Bemmel & Musen 1997).

3 ENABLING TECHNOLOGIES

Information management is at the core of health informatics and the tool used for managing this information is ICT. The terms ICT and IT are used interchangeably, since communication is now regarded as an integral part of technology. It is essential to have an understanding of the capabilities, limitations and implications of ICT as it relates to the health care environment. IT refers to computer hardware, software and communications technology used for the input, storage, processing and communication of information. Whetton (2005) makes the distinction that IT does not include 'processes or people, which distinguishes information technology from information systems. Information systems incorporate people, processes, and information technology'. The conclusion can be drawn, then, that ICT is an enabling tool and not the pure focus of health informatics. A basic level of knowledge of computer hardware, software and networks is assumed (for further reading please see Additional Resources, below).

3.1 Databases

A database is a *persistent* collection of related data supporting several different applications within an organisation. A database may also be manual, as in files stored in a filing cabinet, but characteristically the data is organised in a systematic manner, enabling easy retrieval. Data that is stored in a database is related in some way. A database supports data for several different applications, for example a patient administration system (PAS) contains information that is stored once but used across multiple departments in a hospital. Databases are the core tool in health information management. Database technology underpins virtually all health information systems today, e.g. PAS and laboratory information systems (LIS). They have applications in clinical areas, research, education and management of health information. They are also pivotal to the provision of knowledge bases to support evidence-based practice (e.g. MEDLINE, CINAHL).

Data is input manually (e.g. keyboard) or automatically through the use of bar-code readers, laboratory analysers, monitors, etc. Given the strategic importance of data within an organisation and the large increase in the volume of patient data, storing this information electronically is much more efficient and cost effective and provides fast and reliable access to the data.

3.1.1 Database management systems (DBMS)

Database management system (DBMS) software controls the organisation, storage, retrieval, security and integrity of data in a database or databases. It accepts requests from the application and instructs the operating system to transfer the appropriate data.

DBMS software is the set of software which manages a database or set of databases. A DBMS is not application-specific, i.e. the same software may be used in a bank or a university. A DBMS takes care of storing and accessing data, leaving the application-specific tasks to the application programs. Data is stored in linked tables and can be easily updated and accessed by multiple users. Many organisations (including health organisations) are critically dependent on their computer-based information systems.

DBMS provides the technology for managing the information resource efficiently, reliably and securely. The database approach to information management eliminates data duplication (redundancy); data from all applications is integrated and stored only once. Key people involved in database development include a database designer, database administrator (responsible for policies and access) and a data administrator, who is responsible for managing the data resource of an organisation (Hederman 2008).

4. HOSPITAL INFORMATION SYSTEMS (HIS)

Complex organisations such as hospitals depend heavily on the availability of data. This data can also support a wide range of organisations for policy, strategic planning, research and education purposes. Early hospital information systems (HIS) focused largely on supporting the management and administrative functions of health care organisations. This situation changed in the 1980s, with increasing functionality being added to these systems to support direct patient care: these additions included order entry systems, pharmacy systems and much more advanced imaging systems (van Bemmel & Musen 1997). This trend is reflected in the literature with the distinction of HIS as administrative information systems (hospital-centred, supporting the budgeting, management and co-ordination of services in the hospital) and as clinical information systems (patient-centred, reflecting the quality of care and treatment of a patient) (Hebda *et al.* 2005). The nature and complexity of health information makes the integration and sharing of information across systems more challenging. Whetton (2005) describes some of the critical factors important in the development of health information systems:

- *Organisation approach* – organisational approach to identifying the information requirements and relating them to the overall strategic directions of the organisation.

- *Senior management support* – confirms strategic-level acceptance and helps facilitate acceptance at lower levels in an organisation.
- *Project champion* – a key individual who drives the project at all levels and influences opinion.
- *Project management* – formally plans, develops and implements the project.
- *Project team membership* – people with a mix of backgrounds in IT and health, who will commit to support the project plan.
- *End-user input and participation* – participation by end users is essential in ensuring the system will meet the end-user needs.
- *Change management* – with the introduction of any system there is a process of change: effectively managing this change as part of the project planning will support the process.
- *Communication* – informing and seeking feedback at all stages of the project will ensure that expectations are realistic.
- *End-user skill development* – quality training should be provided for those end users in order to enhance user acceptance.

Examples of hospital information systems include the following.

4.1 Computerised physician order entry (CPOE) systems

CPOE systems allow for clinicians to order tests, investigations and medications on a computer system. These are directly transmitted to the appropriate laboratory, pharmacy or department. In more elaborate systems the orders can be supported by a decision support system ensuring adherence with best practice guidelines (Bates *et al.* 1994). Eslami *et al.* (2008) undertook a systematic review of computerised physician medication order entry in hospital settings, and their overall findings indicated that CPOE can improve patient safety, through reducing adverse drug events, and improve adherence to guidelines. At a fundamental level CPOE changes the ordering process, and it can have an impact on cost, length of stay and improve compliance with guidelines (Kuperman 2003). The use of CPOE has the potential to improve the work flow processes, eliminating illegible handwriting and the subsequent ambiguity that it causes, automatically generating related orders, checking for duplicate orders and reducing the time spent on filling out orders. CPOE can also improve quality through standardising processes and providing guidance to clinicians as they care for patients (Clarke 2008).

4.2 Picture archiving and communication systems (PACS)

PACS have been designed to store digitally represented medical images in many modalities (e.g. standard X-rays, CT, MRI, ultrasound) and allow these images to be distributed electronically and interpreted on computer workstations. There is no longer a need to store large volumes of film images, and instant simultaneous access to digitally stored data is possible immediately after processing (Czekierda *et al.* 2006).

Imaging has been one of the pioneering areas in which computers have impacted on health care and which is now virtually impossible without technology. Computers are used to construct an image from measurements; obtain an image reconstructed for optimal extraction of a particular feature from that image; present images; improve image quality by image processing; and store and retrieve images.

Potential benefits of PACS identified by Clarke (2008) include reduction in repeat tests, improved work flows and availability of images for simultaneous users. In a case study undertaken by Nitrosi *et al.* (2007), key indicators such as radiology examination turnaround time, number of radiology procedures performed and in-patients' length of stay were analysed before and after the introduction of PACS to a 900-bed public acute hospital. The study found that radiology department productivity increased by 12 per cent, turnaround time improved by 60 per cent with the further benefit of a decrease in length of hospital stay.

4.3 Decision support systems (DSS)

Decision making forms a large part of the activities in health care. From the first patient encounter the data that is collected forms the basis for the decisions made about a patient's treatment and diagnosis. Early DSS can be traced back to the late 1950s, when they were based on methods using decision trees; later systems were based on statistical methods; more recently, expert systems provide a knowledge base to assist the decision-making process. The latter provides the clinician with support based on a knowledge database and requires intensive input from domain experts (van Bemmel & Musen 1997). Influential developments in DSS have come from the field of artificial intelligence and information systems. DSS has been defined by Gorry and Scott-Morton (1971) as 'a decision support system [which] couples the intellectual resources of individuals with the capabilities of the computer to improve quality of decisions. It is a computer-based support system for management decision makers who deal with semi-structured problems.' The potential for DSS to reduce medical errors is a major influencing factor in their development. DSS can assist health professionals at the point of care, where, it is reported, medical errors most commonly take place (Trowbridge & Weingarten 2002).

DSS have a wide-ranging application in health care and can support clinical decisions, reminders and alerts, and prescribing systems.

4.3.1 Clinical decision support (CSS)

Clinical decision support is defined by Shortliffe and Cimino (2006) as 'any computer program designed to help health professionals make clinical decisions'. One of the first examples of clinical decision support was a system called MYCIN, an expert system for diagnosing and recommending treatment for bacterial infections of the blood. CSS can be used in many domains of health care and can support prognostic decision-making, interpretation of laboratory results, therapy planning and clinical management. Designing such 'intelligent' systems imposes the challenge of modelling intelligent human behaviour and decision making. Zvárová (2006) and Whetton (2005) make the distinction between explicit and tacit knowledge. Explicit knowledge is knowledge that is descriptive (situations, people, places) and practical (knowing how to). Tacit or inferential knowledge involves reasoning and it is this form of knowledge that forms the basis of clinical decision support systems. Important aspects of data, information and knowledge modelling play a key role in this type of system development. Representing this inferential knowledge drawn from evidence or reasoning is a significant challenge for system developers. Another issue is the rapid pace at which this knowledge is changing. A comparative study by Tang and Gorden (1999) of physicians using an EHR system and traditional paper records found that more appropriate clinical decisions were made as a result of the EHR supporting clinical decision support.

Clinical guidelines are useful for standardising and improving health care outcomes: they have the potential to benefit clinicians, through improving quality of clinical decisions, and as a result can improve patient outcomes. Clinical guidelines are the basic directions or principles that assist a clinician with patient care decisions on appropriate diagnostic, therapeutic or other clinical procedures. The intent of clinical guidelines is 'to ensure consistent high quality clinical practice' (Isern & Moreno 2008). In the context of CSS, clinical guidelines can be embedded into the system to form the basis for clinical decisions.

4.3.2 Reminders and alerts

Reminders and alerts can have an impact at all levels of the health care environment, from primary care to acute clinical settings. This type of decision support offers the professionals timely alerts and reminders that are patient-specific during consultations. An example in a primary care setting may be immunisations that need to be carried out. In an acute clinical setting the alerts from patient monitoring devices can warn of changes in a patient's condition.

4.3.3 Prescribing systems (e-prescribing)

Prescribing systems automatically offer the clinician suggestions for appropriate dosages and check for drug allergies, drug–drug interactions and other contraindications.

There are many examples of decision support systems in health care at varying levels of impact in the decision-making process. DSS have historically been confined to research laboratories and few have made it into routine clinical practice. The primary reasons for this are the complexity of differing work practices, the difficulties of integrating systems and a basic suspicion that exists among clinicians as to the reliability of such systems.

5 ELECTRONIC HEALTH RECORDS (EHR)

Berg (1998) describes the medical record as 'a tool . . . it does not represent the work, but feeds into it, it structures and transforms it in complex ways: it structures the communication between healthcare personnel, shapes medical decision making, and frames relations between personnel and patients.'

The evolution and challenges of health care discussed earlier in this chapter have resulted in increasing volumes of information for which paper-based systems are simply not adequate. The paper record has many shortcomings (noted by van Bemmel and Musen (1997) and Hebda *et al.* (2005)).

- Availability and accessibility: is the paper record available to all those who need to access it? It can only be used by one person at any one time.
- Security and confidentiality: how secure are paper records? Often they are left on trolleys waiting to be transferred to speciality clinics, or can be incorrectly filed or mislaid.
- Format of the data: reading records can be difficult; locating information relevant to the task at hand is not always easy.
- Missing data: records are not always up to date, results may be pending or some key information may be missing.
- Availability and access for secondary use: collecting and retrieving data for secondary uses such as research or policy planning can be difficult and time-consuming.

The medical record is an essential tool in supporting quality care; it has many potential uses and users, including, to name but a few, patients, clinicians, hospital managers, primary carers, legal advisers, clinical researchers and health economists. Each requires access to information related to their specific domain.

Clinicians require access to patient information that may be distributed across multiple sites. This fragmentation of information can lead to key sources of information not being available when required. The information is also held in varying formats, from paper to electronic, including narrative, structured, coded and multimedia elements. The promise of the EHR is a much-anticipated solution to improving access to this distributed record, but it does not come without many challenges. The goal to provide different health care professionals across primary, secondary and tertiary care with an integrated view of the complete health care history of each patient has so far not been met in totality. Although much research and progress has continued over 40 years to achieve this goal, the EHR is now recognised as an essential requirement for the delivery of health services (Kalra & Ingram 2006).

EHRs ensure that data is captured only once at the point of care and it may be used many times to support delivery of services to the patient. This data can then be re-used to monitor the quality of care the patient has received, or for clinical audit; a further important role is the use of such data for population health trends and research.

The EHR has been defined as follows.

The Electronic Health Record (EHR) is a secure, real-time, point-of-care, patientcentric information resource for clinicians. The EHR aids clinicians' decision making by providing access to patient health record information where and when they need it and by incorporating evidence-based decision support. The EHR automates and streamlines the clinician's workflow, closing loops in communication and response that result in delays or gaps in care. The EHR also supports the collection of data for uses other than direct clinical care, such as billing, quality management, outcomes reporting, resource planning, and public health disease surveillance and reporting.

(HIMSS)

Research into EHRs has been ongoing for some 40 years with the last decade seeing a significant upsurge in activity. Some of the stumbling blocks in implementing EHRs include: lack of standards to facilitate the sharing of EHRs between care providers and organisations; lack of an understanding of the organisational impact of EHRs; lack of political and organisational will; concerns about privacy; and confidential and innate conservatism and suspicion of technology (Grimson & Grimson 2000). Trying to convince busy health professionals to embrace technology and investigate its potential in their speciality is proving to be a significant stumbling block. There are many challenges to address before the EHR can become a reality. An integrated strategic approach with backing at government level is required.

Many industrial nations worldwide are looking at modernising and improving health care delivery and for many it has become a key political issue. A key driver for EHRs is the potential it offers to improve patient safety and manage care. The use of EHRs has the potential to impact on both patients and a variety of health professionals including clinicians, administrators and national agencies. Hebda *et al.* (2005) detail some of the general benefits of the EHR:

- improved data integrity: information is more readable, better organised and more accurate and complete
- increased productivity: care providers are able to access client information when required at multiple locations, resulting in more timely decisions based on appropriate data
- improved quality of care: the EHR supports clinical decision-making processes
- increased satisfaction for care providers: care providers are able to access relevant important data and be supported by decision support and knowledge bases.

The foundations for the delivery of EHRs are being put in place in a number of nations with the help of national information strategies. These strategies are key to enabling within a legal framework the collection, sharing and exchange of health-related data across a variety of services.

The National Health Service (NHS) in the UK is in the process of implementing two separate EPR systems: a national summary care record (SCR), which is currently being piloted; and a detailed care record (DCR), which will contain more detailed clinical information, although this is still in the planning stages. The NHS Care Records Service will enable each person's detailed records to be securely shared between different parts of the local NHS, such as the GP's surgery and hospital (NHS *Connecting for Health* website).

In the USA a proposed interoperable EHR, the Nationwide Health Information Network (NHIN), is expected to be in operation by 2014 (DHHS 2009).

Canada Health Infoway is Canada's catalyst for collaborative change to accelerate the use of electronic health information systems and electronic health records across the country. It will bring together existing information systems and develop other essential systems to form a complete electronic health record (Canada Health Infoway).

In Ireland, there are hopes that the Health Information Bill (HIB) will lay the legal framework for all aspects of collection, storage and sharing of health-related information. The objectives of this bill are 'to establish a legislative framework to enable information in whatever form to be used to best effect to enhance medical care and patient safety; to facilitate the greater use of information technologies for the delivery of patient services and to underpin an effective information governance structure for the health system generally' (DoHC website). In parallel with the HIB, one of the six key priorities of the Health Service Executive's Transformation Programme 2007–2010 is 'to develop integrated services across all stages of the care journey'. It is anticipated that this will pave the way for enabling the development of EHRs. Key projects identified in order to facilitate this development are the establishment of a Unique Health Identifier (discussed later in this chapter) and a National Imaging Information System (NIMIS) (HSE website).

The OpenEHR Foundation is an independent, not-for-profit organisation and community that facilitates the creation and sharing of health records by consumers and clinicians via open-source, standards-based implementation. This creation and sharing is reflected in their mission statement:

> To improve the clinical care process by fostering the development and implementation of open source, interoperable EHR components. These components should be based on internationally agreed requirements and address the need for privacy and security, while supporting the development of interoperable and evolving clinical applications.
>
> (OpenEHR website)

Developments towards implementing EHRs are gathering momentum. As existing hospital information systems, national disease registers (e.g. the National Cancer Registry) and new, innovative technologies for e-health develop and integrate, so do the possibilities for a complete and comprehensive electronic health record.

6 HEALTH AND THE INTERNET

The Internet is the largest and best known wide area network in the world. Some of the services and resources it offers include access to the World Wide Web, electronic mail, file transfer, database searches, remote log-on, discussion/news groups and instant messaging (Hebda *et al.* 2005). There are a vast number of health-related resources available on the Internet. The Internet offers huge advantages over traditional communications systems in terms of speed, cost, flexibility and range of access. From an organisational and management perspective it is important to have policies in place against misuse of the Internet. Many institutions will have created their own private intranet. An intranet uses Internet protocols and technologies, including web browsers, servers and languages, to facilitate collaborative data sharing. Intranets can be used for the dissemination of documents within organisations and offer varying degrees of services to employees. Their origins were based in fears about the security of the Internet.

Originating in the 1990s, the term e-health was originally used in relation to medical services offered through the Internet. Today it encompasses other areas, beyond the use of the Internet alone, including other communications technologies. E-health has been defined by Duplaga and Zieliński (2006) as 'the use of modern information and communication technologies, specifically the Internet, for maintaining health and improvement of healthcare'. The use of alternative technologies (such as telephone) expands the range of e-health where Internet penetration is low. According to Duplaga and Zieliński (2006), e-health development results from the 'increasing prevalence of chronic disease, aging of the population, and growing costs of healthcare'.

One of the most important uses of the Internet for health professionals is the access to medical literature databases. The US National Library of Medicine provides a collection of 40 computerised databases called MEDLARS (Medical Literature Analysis and Retrieval) containing 18 million references, and is available free via the Internet. MEDLINE is another example of a comprehensive online database of current medical research, including over 3,700 journals published since 1996.

Patients and citizens demand better access to reliable health-related information. A US study indicated that at least 50 per cent of all adults accessing the Internet searched for information related to health and medicine (Duplaga and Zieliński 2006). The Internet has fuelled an insatiable demand for health care services from increasingly knowledgeable consumers. This also has implications for health services delivery and developments in influencing, for example, changes in forms of communication. Consumers look to the Internet for information on medication and diseases, suggested cures and support groups. The growing popularity of the Internet has made it easier and faster to find health information. Much of this information is valuable; however, the Internet also allows rapid and widespread distribution of false and misleading information. The US National Cancer Institute is one of many organisations that provide advice and guidance for citizens using web resources. Key information that should be easy to access on a website is: who is responsible for the site (organisation or individual); the original source of the information; and their credentials (for providing health-related information) (National Cancer Institute website).

Email is one of the most frequently used Internet applications among organisations, universities, corporations and private individuals' homes. It is a powerful connectivity tool that encourages networking among peers and facilitates the sharing of resources. Borowitz and Wyatt (1998) report on a three-year study by a paediatric practice which offered free email as an option for communication with patients and their families. A total of 1,239 emails were received from parents (81 per cent) and health care providers (19 per cent), and the overall result was that it proved an effective means for communication. Despite initial concerns of clinicians with regard to liability, confidentiality and privacy issues, and response times, clinicians were able to respond to emails in less than four minutes.

7 CHALLENGES TO IMPLEMENTING TECHNOLOGY IN HEALTH CARE

Throughout this chapter the motivation, potential and actual benefits of HIT have been discussed. The many challenges that exist to implementing technology in health care have also been the topic of much research and debate for the past four decades. Bates (2003) states that despite the many opportunities for improvement in patient safety, adoption of information technology remains limited. He identified numerous barriers that exist but also believes that many approaches to overcome these are under way. The challenges exist in parallel for all HIT, including the electronic health record. Some of these challenges and barriers are discussed below.

7.1 Standards

Standards in relation to health informatics are crucial to the facilitation of the sharing and exchange of information between departments in hospitals and health care professionals and also external health agencies. A standard is defined as 'a document, established by consensus and approved by a recognized body, which provides rules, guidelines, or characteristics for activities' (van Bemmel & Musen 1997).

In order to facilitate the sharing and exchange of information there is a requirement for agreement on standards, from both a technical interoperability and a data interoperability aspect. Standards bodies exist at international, European and national level and work very closely together to ensure full consensus.

Standards exist at various levels in relation to health care and they include the following.

- Structure and content standards – architectures (for interoperability) and development of electronic health records and other health information systems.
- Messaging standards (e.g. HL7, DICOM) to facilitate the exchange of information between health care information systems – these specifically define the *means* of exchanging data, not the content.
- Clinical vocabularies – coding and classification of medical terminology, such as the Systematised Nomenclature of Medicine – Clinical Terms (SNOMED CT), MEDCIN, Logical Observation Identifiers Names and Codes (LOINC), OpenGALEN Common Reference Model and the highly complex UMLS, that are used to allow a standard, accurate exchange of data content between systems and providers.

- Security standards.

In relation to health care, the standards bodies include:

- International Organization for Standardization (ISO) – the ISO Technical Committee 215 (Health Informatics) supports the compatibility and interoperability of ICT systems in health care. The ISO forum brings together the health service and other stakeholders in an effort to define standards for the EHR (ISO website).
- HL7 – Health Level Seven is an organisation established in the United Sates. The HL7 protocol is a collection of standard formats that specify the interfaces for electronic data exchange. HL7 is also the standard adopted for the Healthlink project to facilitate the exchange of messages between GPs and hospitals throughout Ireland (Health Level Seven website).
- CEN/TC251 (Comité Européen de Normalisation) is a European standards organisation whose activities include standards for communications; information models, messaging and smart cards; health care terminology, semantics and knowledge bases; medical imaging and multimedia; health care security, privacy, quality and safety; technology for interoperability (CEN website).

7.1.1 Standard vocabularies

To derive the utmost benefits from data it must have a consistent or standard meaning across a health care organisation both regionally and nationally. Many efforts to develop uniform languages are under way and cross a large array of specialties. Some examples of these are: Systematised Nomenclature of Medicine (SNOMED), which contains over 300,000 coded medical terms; Logical Observation Identifier Names and Codes (LOINC), which provides a standardised set of terms for laboratory tests and observations; and the International Classification of Disease (ICD), which provides a classification for surgical, diagnostic and therapeutic procedures (Hebda *et al.* 2005). There are also standards in relation to clinical concepts, such as discharge summaries or referral letters, and standards for data definitions to ensure a common understanding of terms.

7.2 Unique identifiers

The adoption of unique identifiers (UI) potentially has many benefits in providing a common identity across a variety of services for patients. UIs are also essential to the development of EHRs. Currently, multiple identifiers exist across a variety of services in Ireland, and linking this information together to form a longitudinal record is important in order to provide a comprehensive view of patient information. Issues opposing the introduction of unique identifiers include privacy and confidentiality of often sensitive health data. There are potential benefits to having a UI in a health context: to patients it offers the potential for their related health information to be available across multiple sites; for health care professionals a UI provides a way to identify an individual accurately and improves patient safety and quality; and for policy and decision makers a UI allows data to be linked to monitor the health status of the population and to plan the necessary services and resources. When used in an electronic context, UIs are also required for health professionals in order to track and audit their interactions with electronic records.

7.3 Security, privacy and confidentiality

The sensitive nature of health information requires that its privacy and confidentiality be rigorously protected. In parallel to this ideal there is a need to have information more widely available across departments and organisations. There are many theories as to who should have access to what information, and these provide many challenges for ensuring the security, privacy and confidentiality of this information. There are many organisations providing guidance for the securing of data, at organisational, national and international levels.

Privacy refers to the right of an individual to limit access to personal information, and confidentiality refers to the purpose for which the information was gathered. The purpose of use of the information is a fundamental aspect of information held electronically. The primary use should be to support the delivery of care to the individual patient; a secondary use might be, for example, to support audit or to research population health. The Data Protection Acts of 1988 and 2003 protect an individual's right to privacy. These Acts also influence the methods by which information is stored by organisations and their role in ensuring its safety and security.

7.4 Organisational barriers

Some of the barriers mentioned earlier in the text include attitudes of health professionals to change and acceptance of information technology. Their concerns relate to the impact it may have on work flow and work routines. There are implications for change management, and ensuring that end users are involved in the process has been shown to improve user acceptance. For health administrators and managers, issues of security and confidentially, compatibility of systems, ownership and maintenance are of primary importance (Whetton 2005).

Bates (2003) concludes that there is general consensus that IT is essential to the provision of quality, safe and best practice patient care. He further states that health care professionals, health care providers and governments need to recognise that investment in and adoption of new forms of information technology must be considered as being as vital to good patient care as the adoption of new technological tools for diagnosis and treatment.

8 HEALTH INFORMATICS IN IRELAND

The ICT Directorate of the Health Service Executive (HSE) is responsible for the provision of ICT services across the HSE, which currently has 100,000 employees. At the time of writing, a new ICT director has been appointed. A new ICT strategy is currently in the development stages and will reflect priorities from the HSE's transformation programme, one of which is 'to develop integrated services across all stages of the care journey' (HSE website). It will provide a single strategy for health care and a framework for the procurement of health information systems. Many of the challenges that exist for health informatics globally pertain to the Irish situation, and there remains a lack of acceptance by management and government of the important role that ICT can play in the delivery of health services. Ireland has also suffered from a lack of investment in ICT and trying to convince government of the effectiveness and efficiency that ICT can provide is something that will continue to be a priority in order to progress health informatics nationally. Ireland has experienced its own difficulties in implementing complex systems in the health care setting, one being the recent example of PPARS (Personnel, Payroll and Related Systems), which had the ambitious aim not simply to computerise personnel records or to replace existing payroll systems for over 110,000 health service workers, but to enable the transformation of human resource management in the health service. HSE called a halt to its national rollout in 2005 as costs ballooned from an initial estimate of €9 million to in excess of €220 million, and it was able to do just a fraction of the work intended. In contrast there are a number of successful examples of health informatics in health care settings across Ireland.

8.1 National Haemophilia Electronic Patient Record (NHEPR)

The NHEPR is a comprehensive information management system that aggregates patient data into a single, organised, haemophilia-specific electronic medical chart. Developed for the National Centre for Hereditary Coagulation Disorders, the EPR maintains accurate electronic medical records, accessible at any designated treatment centre throughout Ireland. The system also incorporates the ability to track and trace haemophilia products using global barcode standards (GS1) which enables growing clinics to adopt advanced techniques including an electronic real-time medication recall, protecting investments while improving the quality of care and safety. The valuable information presented by the Clintech solution helps the haemophilia comprehensive care centres plan for expansion and refinement of clinical practices to continuously improve patient outcomes and forward population-based haemophilia research (McGroarty 2008).

8.2 TELESYNERGY® to support multidisciplinary team meetings (MDTs)

Teleconferencing capabilities have given rise to many potential opportunities in facilitating working partnerships across institutions. In a health care setting this technology can support the multidisciplinary team meetings that form an essential part of health care delivery but also the triple assessment process in cancer care. TELESYNERGY® is a video conferencing system that provides medical professionals with all the components necessary to collaborate with one another on cancer research and treatment, regardless of geographical location. The system's multi-imaging capabilities integrate peripheral images (e.g. radiology, pathology) into one system to be used together during a video conference where they can be viewed at near-diagnostic quality. Currently being piloted at a major acute hospital in Dublin, the TELESYNERGY® teleconferencing system is the result of a collaborative telemedicine initiative with the National Cancer Institute in the USA (Kane *et al.*, 2005).

8.3 Hospital In-patient Enquiry scheme (HIPE)

HIPE is a computer-based system designed to collect demographic, clinical and administrative data on discharges and deaths from acute hospitals nationally. All acute public hospitals in Ireland participate in HIPE, reporting on over 1.3 million records annually. This national database is currently managed by the Economic and Social Research Institute (ESRI) in association with the Department of Health and Children and the HSE. Since 1 January 2009, all HIPE discharges are coded using ICD-10-AM/ACHI/ACS (sixth edition), which is the International Statistical Classification of Diseases and Related Health Problems (tenth revision, Australian modification) in conjunction with the Australian Classification of Health Interventions (ACHI) (sixth edition). HIPE data is used by the Department of Health and Children and the HSE in the planning, provision and measurement of acute hospital services. Other uses for HIPE data include:

- epidemiological studies – hospital activity statistics related to diseases/procedures
- input to population health profiles at the health board/health region level
- quality assurance studies
- market research
- drugs trials, etc.

Data can be filtered to define a subset of HIPE data: the selection criteria fall into the broad categories of patient, geographical location, clinical and case mix. Case mix relates to a method of quantifying hospital workload which takes account of the complexity and resource intensity of the services provided. For the purposes of national planning and budgeting, a case mix budget model is derived using data from the HIPE system, along with data related to particular case mix parameters such as diagnosis related group (DRG) or major diagnostic category (MDC). Data accuracy, quality and integrity are hugely important to the HIPE system as it plays such an important role in determining budgets and programme planning by the HSE (ESRI website).

8.4 Healthcare Informatics Society of Ireland (HISI)

From 1978 to 1996, the Healthcare Specialist Group of the Irish Computer Society represented health care informatics interests in Ireland. In May 1996 the members of the Healthcare Specialist Group formed a new society, the Healthcare Informatics Society of Ireland (HISI), in order to broaden the base of membership and increase the range of services offered. HISI is affiliated nationally with the Irish Computer Society, the Royal Academy of Medicine in Ireland and the Irish Forum for Health Informatics. At European level HISI represents the interests of

Ireland with the European Federation for Medical Informatics, and ProRec Ireland is the Irish national body within the EuroRec Institute. Its mission is to promote the adoption and extended use of high-quality standardised electronic health records and the required infrastructure. It contributes to supporting national health care initiatives and its priorities for promoting EHRs are informed by national objectives. One of the first initiatives of ProRec Ireland, in collaboration with the Centre for Health Informatics, Trinity College Dublin, was the development of an e-learning module on the EHR (www.cs.tcd.ie/chi). The annual conference presents some of the successful projects around the country (HISI website).

8.5 Irish Council for Health Informatics Professions (I-CHIP)

HISI, in collaboration with the British Computer Society and the NHS, have set up a framework to reflect the specific skills that health informatics requires. The culmination of this work has resulted in I-CHIP, a new professional body which will promote professionalism in health informatics. It operates a voluntary register of health informatics professionals who work to standards that are clearly defined, providing individuals and employers with a recognised framework for professional recognition and development.

- **For individuals,** registration with I-CHIP validates expertise by benchmarking their profiles against the ICT industry standard Skills Framework for the Information Age (SFIA). It provides independent evidence of professionalism, clarifying progression pathways and facilitating career planning in a structured manner.
- **For employers,** I-CHIP can be used as a recruitment tool to streamline selection procedures, with independent assessment of applicants' professional levels, even in specialised areas. It enables an employer to set goals appropriate to the needs of the organisation and of the individual.
- **For health care,** I-CHIP aims to advance the application of informatics in the promotion of health and well-being, and to uphold and improve the standards of qualifications and competence in the field (I-CHIP website).

8.6 Health Information and Quality Authority (HIQA)

The Health Information and Quality Authority was established on a statutory basis in May 2007, following the signing into law of the Health Act 2007. It holds responsibility for driving quality and safety in Ireland's health and social care services through:

- setting standards in health and social services
- monitoring health care quality
- social services inspectorate
- health technology assessment
- health information.

HIQA is an independent authority and reports to the Minister for Health and Children. HIQA will play a key role in driving quality, safety, accountability and the best use of resources in our health and social care services (HIQA website).

CASE STUDY

Healthlink – an electronic health care messaging service

Healthlink is an electronic communications project initiated by the Mater Hospital, Dublin in 1995, which evolved into a national project, Healthlink Online, in 2003. The main objective of the Healthlink project is to implement a prototype health care communications network with specific reference to primary care practitioners and acute hospital and agency relationships and data exchange.

Live messages are currently being delivered every hour via Healthlink to over 1,200 primary care participants dispersed throughout Ireland. The GPs, nurses and practice staff involved can receive information from more than one hospital if their patients attend more than one. Healthlink currently represents the delivery mechanism for over half of all electronic messaging between primary and secondary care in Ireland. Currently over 1,200 GPs are linking to 19 hospitals around the country.

At a technical level, Healthlink is a standards-based scalable messaging system that delivers in excess of 280,000 messages per month. Up to 11 different types of information can be exchanged with the GP, including laboratory and radiology results, discharge summaries, A&E attendance notifications, death notifications, laboratory orders and neurology referrals. This information is downloaded to the GP's local machine and can be integrated into their practice management system. All the major practice management systems in Ireland have worked in conjunction with Healthlink to enable Healthlink messages to be integrated directly into GPs' systems using the HL7 Messaging Standard (National Healthlink Project website).

(HL7 provides a framework (and related standards) for the exchange, integration, sharing and retrieval of electronic health information. The standards, which support clinical practice and the management, delivery and evaluation of health services, are the most commonly used in the world (Health Level Seven website).)

Discussion points:
- Is there any other information that you feel would be useful to provide to GP clinics which would promote more efficiency for the patient?
- Can you identify some of the concerns that a GP considering linking with the Healthlink project might have?

CONCLUSION

This chapter has attempted to give an overview of the field of health informatics. In appreciating the need for the discipline of health informatics an understanding must also exist of the health care environment which contributed to its existence. The key message is to encourage participation in and ownership of IT projects in order to reap the potential benefits and improve user acceptance. The rapid pace of the development of new technologies, including new Internet technologies, will also play its part in the evolution of technology in health care.

REFLECTIVE QUESTIONS

1   What are the key drivers for the use of information technology in the health care setting?
2   What are the advantages and disadvantages of a distributed electronic health care record?
3   Discuss the main barriers to the implementation of ICT in the health care environment.

ACKNOWLEDGMENTS

I would like to thank Professor Jane Grimson (Director, Centre for Health Informatics, TCD) for her support in writing this chapter.

ADDITIONAL RESOURCES

HSE Transformation Programme 2007–2010: http://www.hse.ie/eng/services/Publications/corporate/transformation.pdf
Tanenbaum, A. (1996) *Computer Networks*. New Jersey: Prentice Hall.

Health informatics organisations

American Society for Testing and Materials – a consortium of scientists and engineers that recommends international standards.
ANSI (American National Standards Institute) – accredits standards in the United States and co-ordinates US standards with international standards.
Canada Health Infoway – a federally funded, not-for-profit organisation that promotes the development and adoption of EHRs in Canada.
CCHIT (Certification Commission for Healthcare Information Technology) – a federally funded, not-for-profit organisation that evaluates and develops the certification for EHRs and interoperable EHR networks (USA).
CDISC (Clinical Data Interchange Standards Consortium) – a non-profit organisation that develops platform-independent health care data standards.
CHI (Consolidated Health Informatics Initiative) – recommends nationwide federal adoption of EHR standards in the United States.
ELINCS (EHR-Lab Interoperability and Connectivity Standards) – run by the HL7 group to help provide lab data and other EHR interoperability.
HIMSS (Healthcare Information and Management Systems Society) – an international trade organisation of health informatics technology providers.

IHE (Integrating the Healthcare Enterprise) – a consortium, sponsored by the HIMSS, that recommends integration of EHR data communicated using the HL7 and DICOM protocols.

OpenEHR – provides open specifications and tools for the 'shared' EHR.

W3C (World Wide Web Consortium) – promotes Internet-wide communications standards to prevent market fragmentation.

Health informatics standards organisations

ANSI X12 (EDI) – transaction protocols used for transmitting patient data. Popular in the United States for transmission of billing data.

CEN's TC/251 – provides EHR standards in Europe, including:
  EN 13606 – communication standards for EHR information
  CONTSYS (EN 13940) – supports continuity of care record standardisation
  HISA (EN 12967) – a services standard for inter-system communication in a clinical information environment.

Continuity of Care Record – ASTM International Continuity of Care Record standard.

DICOM – an international communications protocol standard for representing and transmitting radiology and other image-based data, sponsored by NEMA (National Electrical Manufacturers Association).

HL7 – a standardised messaging and text communications protocol between hospital and physician record systems, and between practice management systems.

ISO
  ISO TC 215 – provides international technical specifications for EHRs
  ISO 18308 – describes EHR architectures.

APPENDIX 1 GLOSSARY OF TERMS

Aetiology: The causes of a disease or malcondition.

Application: synonym for a computer program that carries out a specific task.

Artificial intelligence (in medicine): the application of artificial intelligence methods to solve problems in medicine, e.g. developing expert systems to assist with diagnosis. See also Expert system.

Audit trail: means for documenting actions on data.

Bandwidth: the amount of data that can be transmitted across a communication channel over a given period of time.

Case-based reasoning: an approach to computer reasoning that uses knowledge from a library of similar cases, rather than by accessing a knowledge base containing more generalised knowledge, such as a set of rules. See also Artificial intelligence, Expert system.

Clinical guideline/pathway/protocol: an agreed set of steps to be taken in the management of a clinical condition.

Code: in medical terminology systems, the unique numerical identifier associated with a medical concept, which may be associated with a variety of terms, all with the same meaning.

Computerised protocol: clinical guideline or protocol stored on a computer system, so that it may be easily accessed or manipulated to support the delivery of care.

CPR: computer-based patient record.

Data: representation of observations or concepts suitable for communication, interpretations and processing by humans or machines. Interpreted data form information.

Data acquisition: identification, selection and sampling of data for further computer processing.

Database: a structured repository for data, usually stored on a computer system. The existence of a regular and form indexing structure permits rapid retrieval of individual elements of the database.

Data collection: the gathering of source data.

Data communication: the movement of digitally encoded data by means of electrical or electromagnetic transmission systems.

Data dictionary: a description of files, fields and variables in a database, mostly maintained in a computer.

Data entry: the process of entering data into a computer, most often by human action.

Data security: encompasses confidentiality, integrity and availability of data.

Data validation: the examination of data for correctness.

Decision support system: general term for any computer application that enhances a human's ability to make decisions.

Distributed computing: term for computer systems in which data and programs are distributed across different computers on a network, and shared.

EDI: electrical data exchange, a form of email for sending and receiving standard electronic messages, in which the syntax and the semantics are described.

EDIFACT: Electronic Data Interchange for Administration, Commerce and Transport: an EDI standard especially in use in commercial environments, EDIFACT is widely adopted in Europe.

Encryption: the process of encoding data such that a specific key is needed to decode the data, mostly by means of methods that are based on the use of prime numbers.

Epidemiology: a health science that (1) deals with the distribution and incidence of diseases in human populations; (2) identifies aetiologic factors in the pathogenesis of diseases; and (3) prepares data for planning, implementation and assessment of measures for the prevention, suppression and treatment of diseases.

Evidence-based medicine: a movement advocating the practice of medicine according to clinical guidelines, developed to reflect best practice as captured from a meta-analysis of the clinical literature.

Expert system: a computer program that contains expert knowledge about a particular problem, often in the form of a set of if-then rules, that is able to solve problems at a level equivalent to or greater than human experts. See also Artificial intelligence.

GALEN: reference model for medical concepts.

Graphical user interface (GUI): that part of a computer application seen and interacted with by its user.

Handheld computer: a small computer that can be held in one's hand so that it can be used at the point of care.

Hardware: the physical components of a computer system, e.g. monitor, keyboard.

HIS: Hospital Information System – typically describes the hospital computer system with functions such as patient administration and discharge, order entry for laboratory tests or medications, and billing information.

HL7: Health Level 7 – a healthcare-specific communication standard for data exchange between computer applications.

ICD-10: International Classification of Diseases (tenth edition), published by the World Health Organisation.

Internet: a worldwide network of computer networks.

LAN: local area network, a network of computers within a restricted area.

Log in: procedure to obtain access to a computer, usually consisting of identification by a user identification and authentication by a password.

Middleware: a software shell between the operating system and the applications or the user.

Multimedia: computer systems or applications that are able to manipulate data in multiple forms, including still and video images, sound and text.

Multimedia patient record: medical record with text, images, signals and sound.

Network: set of connected elements. For computers, any collection of computers connected together so that they are able to communicate, permitting the sharing of data or programmes.

NLP: natural language processing – accessing data in narrative or free text form and creating machine-understandable interpretations of those data.

Open system: computer industry term for computer hardware and software that is built to common public standards, allowing purchasers to select components from a variety of vendors and use them together.

Order entry system: part of a hospital information system (HIS) that handles the orders of physicians and nurses to laboratories, pharmacy departments, etc.

PACS: picture archiving and communication system, a system for digital acquisition, storage and retrieval of images.

Prototype: a preliminary system that has part of the required properties of the intended system, such as the user interface.

Semantics: the meaning associated with a set of symbols in a given language, which is determined by the syntactic structure of symbols.

SNOMED: Systematised Nomenclature of Medicine. A commercially available general medical terminology for coding several aspects of diagnosis.

Software: computer program or application.

Standard: a document, established by consensus and approved by a recognised body, which provides rules, guidelines, or characteristics for activities.

Standardisation: activity of establishing a standard.

Syntax: the rules of grammar that define the formal structure of a language.

TCP/IP: transmission control protocol/Internet protocol. Widely used protocol for communicating data over networks.

Telematics: contraction of telecommunications and automatic information processing: the use of information technology over wide-area networks.

Telemedicine: the delivery of health care services between geographically separated individuals using telecommunication systems, e.g. video conferencing.

Terminology: a set of standard terms used to describe clinical activities.

Unique patient identifier: a unique code that identifies the patient and that can be used as a key to his or her data records.

Validity check: a check on the correctness of data by using their semantics.

WAN: wide area network. A communications network that may span a large geographical area.

REFERENCES

American Nurses Association (2001) *Scope and Standards of Nursing Informatics Practice.* Washington DC: American Nurses Publishing.

Anthony, Denis (1996) *Health on the Internet.* Oxford: Blackwell Science.

Bates, D. W. (2000) 'Using information technology to reduce rates of medication errors and adverse drug events', *British Medical Journal* 320(7237): 788–91.

— (2003) 'Improving safety with information technology', *New England Journal of Medicine* 348(25): 2526–34.

Bates, D. W., Kuperman, G. and Teich, J. M. (1994) 'Computerized physician order entry and quality of care', *Quality Management in Health Care* 2(4): 18–27.

Bates, D. W., Teich, J. L., Deger, D., Kuperman, N., Ma'Luf, N., Boyle, D. and Leape, L. (1999) 'The impact of computerized physician order entry on medication error prevention', *Journal of American Medical Informatics Association* 6(4): 313–21.

Berg, M. (1998) 'Medical work and the computer-based patient record: a sociological perspective', *Methods of Information in Medicine* 37(3): 294–301.

— (2001) 'Implementing information systems in health care organisations: myths and challenges', *International Journal of Medical Informatics* 64: 143–56.

Borowitz, S. M. and Wyatt, J. C. (1998) 'The origin, content, and workload of e-mail consultations', *Journal of the American Medical Association* 280(15): 1321–4.

Cala, J., Czekierda, L. and Zieliński, K, (2006) 'Internet technologies in medical systems' in Zieliński, K., Duplaga, M., Ingram, D. (eds) *Information Technology Solutions for Healthcare.* London, Springer-Verlag.

Canada Health Infoway, Toronto [website], http://www.infowayinforoute.ca/lang-en/, accessed 29 September 2009.

CancerWeb (2008) *Online Medical Dictionary* [Internet, US]. Available at http://cancerweb.ncl.ac.uk/cgi-bin/omd?informatics, accessed 29 September 2009.

CEN (Comité Européen de Normalisation (European Committee for Standardisation)), Brussels [website], www.cen.org, accessed 29 September 2009.

Chaudhry, B., Wang, J., Wu, S., Maglione, M., Mojica, W., Roth, E., Morton, S. and Shekelle, P. (2006) 'Systematic review: impact of health information technology on quality, efficiency, and costs of medical care', *Annals of Internal Medicine* 144(10): 742–52.

CHIME (Centre for Health Informatics and Multiprofessional Education) (1995) *Good Electronic Health Record*, London [Internet]. Available at http://www.chime.ucl.ac.uk/work-areas/ehrs/GEHR/, accessed 29 September 2009.

Clarke, C. (2008) *An Analysis of how Information Technology can Contribute to Reducing Acute Hospital Admissions and Length of Stay* (unpublished master's thesis). Trinity College Dublin.

Coiera, E. (2005) *Guide to Health Informatics* (2nd edn). London: Hodder Arnold.

Czekierda, L., Dańda, J., Loziak, K., Sikora, M., Zieliński, K. and Zieliński, S. (2006) 'Wireless systems in e-health', in Zieliński, K., Duplaga, M. and Ingram, D. (eds) *Information Technology Solutions for Healthcare*. London: Springer-Verlag.

DoHC (Department of Health and Children) [website], http://www.doh.ie, accessed 28 November 2008.

DHHS (Department of Health and Human Services) (USA) (2009) *Health Information Exchanges*, Washington [website], http://www.hhs.gov/fedhealtharch/tools/exchange/, accessed 29 September 2009.

Duplaga, M. and Zieliński, K. (2006) 'Evolution of IT-enhanced healthcare: from telemedicine to e-health', in Zieliński, K., Duplaga, M. and Ingram, D. (eds) *Information Technology Solutions for Healthcare*. London: Springer-Verlag.

Eslami, S., de Keizer, N. and Abu-Hanna, A. (2008) 'The impact of computerized physician medication order entry in hospitalized patients – a systematic review', *International Journal of Medical Informatics* 77: 365–76.

ESRI (Economic and Social Research Institute), Dublin [website] www.esri.org, accessed 29 September 2009.

Gorry, G. A. and Scott-Morton, M. S. (1971) 'A framework for management information systems', *Sloan Management Review* 13(1): 55–71.

Grimson, J. (2008a) MSc in Health Informatics lecture notes. Trinity College Dublin.

— (2008b) personal communication.

Grimson, J. and Grimson, W. (2000) 'Personal electronic healthcare records' in Abbott, W., Bryant, J and Bullan, S. (eds), *Current Perspectives in Health Informatics*. Guildford: British Computer Society.

Health Level Seven (HL7), Ann Arbor [website], http://www.hl7.org/index.cfm, accessed 28 November 2008.

Hebda, T., Czar, P. and Mascara, C. (2005) *Handbook of Informatics for Nurses and Health Care Professionals*. New Jersey: Pearson Prentice Hall.

Hederman, L. (2008) MSc in Health Informatics lecuture notes. Trinity College Dublin.

Hersch, W. R. (2002) 'Medical informatics: improving health care through information', *Journal of American Medical Informatics Association* 288(16): 1955–8.

HIMSS (Healthcare Information and Management Systems Society), Brussels [website], www. himss.org, accessed 29 September 2009.

HIQA (Health Information Quality Authority), Dublin [website], www.hiqa.ie, accessed 29 September 2009.

HISI (Health Informatics Society of Ireland), Dublin [website], www.hisi.ie, accessed 29 September 2009.

HSE (Health Service Executive) [website], www.hse.ie, accessed 28 September 2009.

I-CHIP (Irish Council for Health Informatics Professions), Dublin [website], http://www.ics.ie/ichip/, accessed 29 September 2009.

Institute of Medicine (2000) *To Err is Human: Building a Safer Health System.* Washington: Institute of Medicine/National Academy Press.

Isern, D. and Moreno, A. (2008) 'Computer-based execution of clinical guidelines: A review', *International Journal of Medical Informatics* 77: 787–808.

ISO (International Organisation for Standardisation), Geneva [website], www.iso.org, accessed 29 September 2009.

Jha, A, Doolan, D., Grandt, D. Scott, D. and Bates, D. W. (2008) 'The use of health information technology in seven nations', *International Journal of Medical Informatics*, 77(12): 848–54.

Kalra, D. and Ingram, D. (2006) 'Electronic health records' in Zieliński, K., Duplaga, M. and Ingram, D. (eds) (2006) *Information Technology Solutions for Healthcare.* London: Springer-Verlag.

Kane, B., Luz, S., Menezes, G. and Hollywood, D. (2005) 'Enabling change in healthcare structures through teleconferencing', *Proceedings of the 18th IEEE Symposium on Computer-Based Medical Systems.*

Knapp, R., Miller, M. and Levine, J. (1987) 'Experience and attitudes towards computers in medicine of students and clinical faculty members at one school', *Journal of Medical Education* 62: 344–6.

Kuperman, G. J. (2003) 'Computer physcian order entry: benefits, costs and issues', *Annals of Internal Medicine* 139(1): 31–9.

McGroarty, F. (2008) 'Using GS1 standards for tracking blood derivatives', *Proceedings of GS1 Healthcare Conference*, Washington DC. Available at http://www.gs1.org/docs/healthcare/members/160609/W13_McGroarty_St%20James%20Ireland_Traceability.pdf, accessed 29 September 2009.

National Cancer Institute (USA) [website], http://www.cancer.gov/cancertopics/factsheet/information/internet#1, accessed 29 September 2009.

National Healthlink Project, Dublin [website], http://www.healthlink.ie/, accessed 29 September 2009.

NHO (National Hospitals Office), Dublin [website], www.hse.ie, accessed 28 November 2008.

NHS (National Health Service) (UK) *Connecting for Health*, London [website], www.connecting for health.nhs.uk, accessed 29 September 2009.

Nitrosi, A, Borasi, G., Nicoli, F. and Modigliani, G. (2007) 'A filmless radiology department in a full digital regional hospital: quantitative evaluation of the increased quality and efficiency', *Journal of Digital Imaging* 20(2): 140–9.

OpenEHR [website], http://www.openehr.org/home.html, accessed 29 September 2009.

Saba, V. and McCormick, K. (2006) *Essentials of Nursing Informatics*. New York: McGraw Hill.

Shekelle, P. G., Morton, S. C. and Keeler, E. B. (2006) *Costs and Benefits of Health Information Technology*. Evidence Report – Technology Assessment (Full Rep.) (132) 1–71.

Shortliffe, E. H. and Cimino, J. J. (eds) (2006) *Biomedical Informatics: Computer Applications in Health Care and Biomedicine* (3rd edn). New York: Springer.

Tang, P. and Gorden S. M. (1999) 'Use of computer-based records, completeness of documentation and appropriateness of documentated clinical decisions', *Journal of American Medical Informatics Association* 6(2): 115–21.

Teich, J. M. (2002) 'Inpatient order management' in Lewis, R. (ed.) *The Impact of Information Technology on Patient Safety*. Chicago: Healthcare Information and Management Systems Society.

Trowbridge, R. and Weingarten, S. (2002) 'Clinical decision support systems', in *Health Services/Technology Assessment Text* (Chapter 53). National Library of Medicine. Available at http://www.ncbi.nlm.nih.gov/books/bv.fcgi? highlight=support,decision,clinical&rid=hstat1.section.62572, accessed 2 November 2008.

van Bemmel, J. H. and Musen, M. A. (eds) (1997) *Handbook of Medical Informatics*. Heidelberg: Springer-Verlag.

Weir, C., Hicken, B., Rappaport, H. and Nebeker, J. (2006) 'Crossing the quality chasm: the role of information technology departments', *American Journal of Medical Quality* 21: 382–93.

Whetton, S. (2005) *Health Informatics: A Socio-technical Perspective*. Oxford: Oxford University Press.

Whiting-O'Keefe, Q. E., Simborg, D., Epstein W. and Warger, A. (1985) 'A computerised summary medical record system can provide more information than the standard medical record', *Journal of American Medical Informatics Association* 254: 1185–92.

Zieliński, K., Duplaga, M. and Ingram, D. (eds) (2006) *Information Technology Solutions for Healthcare*. London: Springer-Verlag.

Zvárová, J. (2006) 'Decision support systems in medicine' in Zieliński, K., Duplaga, M. and Ingram, D. (eds) (2006) *Information Technology Solutions for Healthcare*. London: Springer-Verlag.

Index